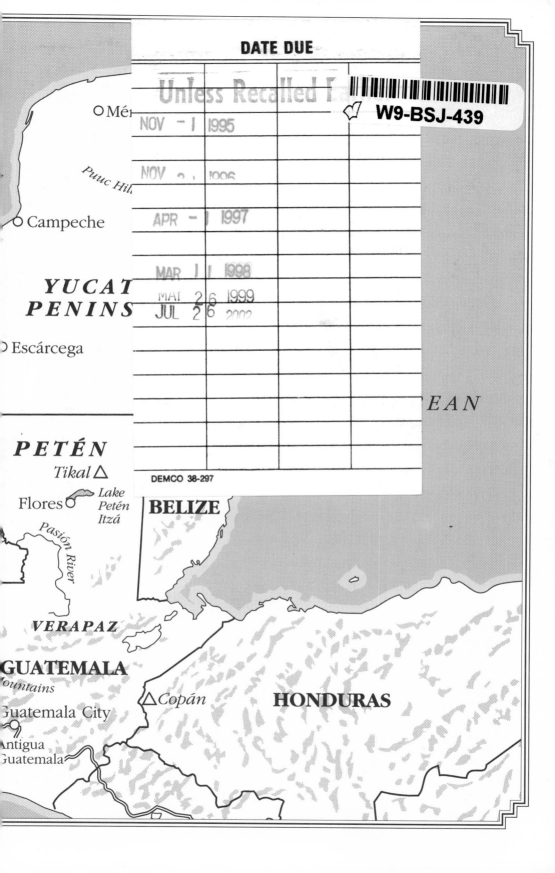

DATE DUE

W9-BSJ-439

O Mé

Puuc Hills

O Campeche

YUCAT
PENINS

O Escárcega

PETÉN

Tikal △

Flores O ⌒ *Lake*
            Petén
            Itzá

Pasión River

BELIZE

EAN

VERAPAZ

GUATEMALA
ountains

uatemala City
⌒
Antigua
Guatemala

△ *Copán*   **HONDURAS**

THE
HEART
OF
THE SKY

THE HEART OF THE SKY

Travels Among the Maya

PETER CANBY

HarperCollins*Publishers*

Lyrics from "Zion Train" written by Bob Marley, © 1980 Bob Marley Music Ltd. Used by permission. All rights reserved.

HarperCollins books may be purchased for educational, business, or sales promotional use. For information, please call or write: Special Markets Department, HarperCollins Publishers, Inc., 10 East 53rd Street, New York, NY 10022. Telephone: (212) 207-7528; Fax: (212) 207-7222.

FIRST EDITION

Designed by Alma Hochhauser Orenstein

Endpaper map by Paul J. Pugliese; text maps redrawn by Paul J. Pugliese after originals by Peter Canby/Anne Putnam

Library of Congress Cataloging-in-Publication Data

Canby, Peter.
    The heart of the sky : travels among the Maya / Peter Canby.—
1st ed.
        p.   cm.
    Includes bibliographical references and index.
    ISBN 0-06-016705-X
    1. Mayas. 2. Mexico—Description and travel—1981– 3. Guatemala—
Description and travel—1981– 4. Canby, Peter. I. Title.
F1435.C3155   1992   91-50474
972—dc20

92 93 94 95 96 ❖/HC 10 9 8 7 6 5 4 3 2 1

To Annie

Keje k'ut xax k'o wi ri kaj nay puch, u K'ux Kaj.
Are ub'i ri k'ab'awil, chuch'axik.

And of course there is the sky, and there is also the Heart of Sky. This is the name of the god, as it is spoken.

POPUL VUH,
Quiché Maya Creation Story

Contents

Acknowledgments

There are certain logistical problems implicit in writing any experiential book on the modern-day Maya. The Maya speak thirty distinct, mutually unintelligible languages. Although these languages are descended from a common linguistic stock and to a certain degree Spanish is a lingua franca, the most interesting aspects of Maya culture can only be viewed through a linguistic kaleidoscope. Early on, I decided that the way to overcome this obstacle was to try to approach different Maya groups through people familiar with specific languages and customs. I hoped thus to understand what otherwise would have been inaccessible. Finding the right person often proved impossible, though, and frequently I wound up exploring a region by whatever means were available. As a result, many different kinds of people appear in this book, from those I met on buses to world-renowned experts in various fields. I owe a debt to all of them, and thank them for their willingness to share.

I wish especially to thank Linda Schele. As soon as I contacted Linda, she invited me to her annual Maya hieroglyph seminar at the University of Texas. Although in theory I learned how to read Maya hieroglyphs (and as a final assignment managed to render the famous Palenque tablet of the ninety-six glyphs into English), in fact I mostly came to appreciate how other people read them, which ultimately proved just as useful. Even after the seminar was over, Linda took an interest in my progress. The work she and her colleagues have done on the Maya is truly revolutionary and I am grateful for her support and insights.

The people mentioned in the book are only a part of a much larger group who helped the project succeed. For much of the time while I was conducting research my wife and I lived in the Mexican city of San Cristóbal de las Casas, where our neighbors Bob and Mimi Laughlin were among those who were particularly helpful. Mimi is an excellent writer and a good friend. Bob, someone explained to me, "*is* Zinacantec" (referring to a nearby Maya group that Bob has studied extensively). He has a profound understanding of the Maya and although he does not appear in the book per se, it is pervaded with his spirit. In San Cristóbal our lives were also enriched immeasurably by a number of other people, but especially by Susanna Ekholm, Joan and Barry Norris and their sons Chan K'in and Chan K'ayum, Jane Taylor, and Percy and Nancy Wood. It is hard to imagine spending such an enjoyable eighteen months in San Cristóbal without them. I wish also to thank Ignacio March, Deborah Colvin, Pablo and Patricia Farías, Rosa María Vidal, Mica McGuirk, Francesco Pellizi, Jill Brodie and Doug Bryant, Bob and Ginny Guess, Jan de Vos, Merielle Flood, Nancy Modiano, and our neighbor Fernando Trujillo Pilcastro and his family. Alfred Bush generously rented us his house, providing us not only with an island of tranquillity but also with access to his inspiring library.

I am especially thankful to my parents, Courtlandt and Natalie Canby, who only months after lecturing me on my alleged fiscal irresponsibility, told me that money wasn't everything and urged me to leave my job and write the book. Thanks also to my brother Henry for his confidence, which was deeply appreciated. At *The New Yorker,* where I formerly worked, I wish to thank Bob Gottlieb, Pat Crow, Hal Espen, Nancy Franklin, Mark Singer, John Bennet, Anne Mortimer-Maddox, Liz Macklin, Martin Baron, and Dan Menaker.

Among the personal friends who encouraged me were Susan Allport, Katherine Bouton, Meredith Davis, David and Connie Green, David Howell, Gary Jacobson, Lex Kaplen, Anne Nelson, Nicholas Peck, Strat Sherman, and Bridget Thorne. While my wife and I were in Mexico, Kit White, Andrea Barnet, Linda Olle, and Susan Angevin took wonderful care of different aspects of our absented lives. Although my mother-in-law, Frances Tilt, was convinced that her daughter and I were going off to our shared doom, once we actually left, she provided invaluable logistical help. In terms of personal support, I wish finally to acknowledge my friend Harvey Oxenhorn, at the time completing his own first book. Harvey was always willing to ask big questions about life and, like my parents, helped me put this undertaking in perspective. Unfortunately, Harvey was killed in an automobile accident a few weeks after the publication of his book and long before my own project was complete. I wish he were here to read the results.

One of the pleasures of writing this book was the openness of so many Mayanists. Chip Morris was generous with his knowledge and his contacts and helped me get started. No matter how often I called Mary Ellen Miller in the middle of dinner, she always found time to talk. I spent several days traveling to a Chamulan Maya rain forest colony with Duncan Earle; although I was not able to use the chapter that resulted, Duncan, an initiated Quiché shaman, was an entertaining, perceptive, and enthusiastic guide. Sisters Bernice Kita and Peggy Janicki shared their experience with Guatemalan refugees and gave me a sense of how exciting the possibilities were for that country before the army began its campaign of repression. Dennis Tedlock generously translated the Popul Vuh quotation from which I took the book's title back into its original Quiché. In Antigua, Guatemala, Nora England not only introduced me to the Academia de Lenguas Mayas, but also gave me the opportunity to talk with the class of young Maya linguists with whom she is working.

Over the length of my research, I spent many months on the road. Among those whose hospitality lightened my traveler's hours were, in Mexico City, Juan and Mary Enriquez; in Guatemala City, Peter and Eugenia Fairhurst; and in Antigua, Victor Perera, Paul Goepfert, Jim and Mary Nations, Mary Jo McConahay and her husband Robert, and the staff of the Centro de Investigaciones Regionales de Mesoamerica (CIRMA). I spent several delightful days in Cobán with Kirk and Leslie Fairhurst and a fascinating afternoon with Padre Ricardo Terga. In Mérida, Joanne Andrews generously permitted me to use her library, and Chris, Caroline, Toby, and Charles Fallon not only cut down the time I otherwise would have spent examining my hotel room walls but also introduced me to the delights of their adopted city.

In Mérida I'd like also to thank the Yucatec archaeologists Luis Millet, Fernando Robles Castellanos, Peter Schmidt, and Augustín Peña, and in the United States Edward Kurjack, William Ringle, Wyllys Andrews V, and David Freidel. I am especially grateful to Tomás Gallareta Negrón, who took time off from a pressing schedule to show me around Chichén Itzá for another chapter that I ultimately could not include.

I want to thank my agent Jed Mattes for helping me arrive at the subject of this book and for his enthusiastic support while I wrote it. At HarperCollins, Larry Ashmead not only helped frame the subject properly, but sent idiosyncratic care packages to Mexico. Jon Ewing and Keonaona Peterson were excellent editors, and Katherine Scott was an excellent copy editor. I would especially like to thank Katherine for the improvements she made in the manuscript's logic and flow. Wayne Furman of the New York Public Library gave me access to the library's writers' room, which became a Midtown refuge and a source of sympathetic companionship, and vastly facilitated research during the final phases of the book. Jeannie Hutchins and Kati Sokoloff helped with the Spanish, and Andrea Barnet, Jeannie Hutchins, Strat Sherman, Barbara Wright, and my parents, Court and Natalie Canby, read all or parts of the manuscript and gave invaluable critiques. I owe a debt of gratitude to each of them.

Finally, I wish to thank my wife, Anne Eliot Putnam. Annie not only thoroughly edited the manuscript, improving its clarity beyond what I dreamed possible, but also left friends and a promising new job to accompany me to a remote and challenging place. I could never have completed this book without her and my gratitude knows no bounds.

PETER CANBY
New York, 1992

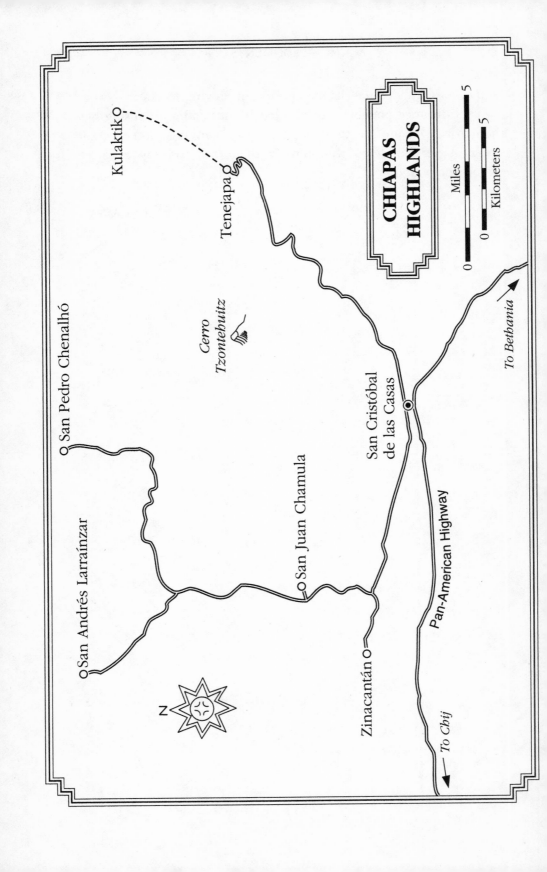

CHIPAS HIGHLANDS

Miles

Kilometers

Kulaktik

Tenejapa

San Pedro Chenalhó

Cerro
Tzontehuitz

San Andrés Larraínzar

San Juan Chamula

San Cristóbal
de las Casas

Zinacantán

Pan-American Highway

To Betbania

To Cbij

N

CHAPTER 1

San Andrés Larraínzar

SAN ANDRÉS LARRAÍNZAR is a Maya village that sits high on a ridge in the mountains of southern Mexico, a hundred miles or so from the Guatemalan border in Chiapas state. The *andresanos,* as the residents are called, speak Tzotzil, a Maya language meaning "people of the bat." Before the arrival of the Spanish, San Andrés was known as Sac'om Ch'en, or "white cave," because of the proximity of a cave in a nearby limestone escarpment. Caves are important to the Maya because they are believed both to be the source of rain and to lead into the realm of the Earthlord, a powerful, morally ambiguous figure who not only rules the world of the dead, but is also the source of the earth's fertility. In his dual role, the Earthlord is strikingly similar to ancient Maya underworld gods whom modern-day students of Maya hieroglyphs describe, for lack of their original names, with such labels as God L and God N. The Earthlord, however, is just one way in which the residents of San Andrés maintain the world of their ancestors. Within the privacy of secretive religious fraternities, for example, the *andresanos* note the daily passage of the sun—Htotik, "our father"—a god who, like Christ, dies and is resurrected but, unlike Christ, dies and is resurrected every day.

Htotik's progress across the heavens, moreover, is carefully noted on a calendar that consists of eighteen twenty-day months plus five end-of-the-year *ch'aik'in* ("lost," "bitter," "evil," "unholy") days and is the same calendar that was in use among the ancient Maya.

In all this, the *andresanos* are not alone, for San Andrés is only one small Maya village on the edge of a hundred-thousand-square-mile region that the Maya have inhabited for close to five thousand years. This region stretches from Yucatán in the north through Guatemala to contiguous Honduras in the south, and from Belize and the Caribbean in the east through to the Chiapas highlands in the west. It is a land of wonderful diversity, encompassing everything from dry scrub to dense tropical rain forest to near-alpine highlands, and within its varied confines today there are seven million Maya who speak thirty distinct yet closely related languages.

All these Maya are heirs to the civilization of the ancient Maya, perhaps the most accomplished of the pre-Columbian New World civilizations. Maya civilization reached its florescence in the eighth century A.D., half a millennium earlier than that of either the Aztecs or the Incas. Although the Maya never achieved the political or organizational complexity of these two huge empires—indeed never developed beyond the level of competing city states—they were supreme in what the archaeologist Norman Hammond calls "the realms of the mind." The Maya developed the only true writing system in the Americas, a beautiful hieroglyphic script that, as the epigrapher Linda Schele puts it, "was capable of recording every nuance of sound, meaning, and grammatical structure in the writers' language." They invented the mathematical concept of zero, made precise astronomical calculations, and developed a highly accurate calendar with which they projected dates as far as 142 nonillion (10^{30}) years into the future.

Yet despite the continued existence of villages such as San Andrés, most people have the impression that the Maya vanished long ago, leaving only their abandoned cities as mute testimony to their considerable accomplishments. There are reasons for this impression. Maya civilization reached its height during the "Classic" period, from approximately A.D. 200 to 800, when the Maya built huge cities in the lowland rain forests of what is now southern Mexico, northern Guatemala, and Belize. During the ninth century, however, Classic Maya civilization came to a precipitous end. The population of the rain forest heartland dropped drastically. For reasons that are still unclear, cities with magnificent two-hundred-foot-tall temples and twenty, thirty, forty thousand residents were abandoned to strangling lianas and the buttressing roots of jungle trees. Yet even as the rain forest core collapsed, powerful Maya states arose on the periphery, especially in Yucatán and in the Guatemalan highlands. When, in 1517 and 1518, the Spanish first arrived on the shores of Yucatán, they noted with awe that the Maya cities "were so large that the city of Seville might not seem larger or better." They were impressed by the cleanliness, the variety of the food, the height of the temples, and also by the fierceness of Maya resistance.

The Conquest-era Maya were, in fact, far more unyielding than the Aztecs were. This can be attributed in part to their political decentralization but it can also be partly credited to a Spaniard named Gonzalo Guerrero, a fisherman from the Spanish town of Palos who had been shipwrecked and washed up on the eastern shore of Yucatán in 1511 and had defected to the Maya—tattooing his face, piercing his ears, and marrying the daughter of a Maya nobleman. Cortés' chronicler, Bernal Díaz del Castillo, relates that when Cortés landed on the island of Cozumel in 1519 and heard of Guerrero's situation, he sent an emissary with some green beads offering to ransom him. Guerrero refused the offer, explaining to Cortés' emissary that he was married and had three children and "the Indians look on me as a cacique [a lord] and a captain in wartime.... Look how handsome these boys of mine are, for God's sake, give me those green beads you have brought, and I will give the beads to them and say that my brothers have sent them from my own country."

When Cortés heard Guerrero's response, he exclaimed, "I wish

I had him in my hands, for it will never do to leave him here."

Cortés was right. Guerrero became an implacable foe of the Spaniards, organizing and leading the Maya resistance until he was killed by a shot from a Spanish arquebus seventeen years later in the Ulúa River valley in Honduras.

It took the Spanish well over twenty years to subdue the major Maya groups and another hundred and fifty to conquer the last independent kingdoms. Devastating as was the Maya's eventual military defeat, however, it was nothing compared to what followed. By the second half of the sixteenth century, when the major military campaigns were out of the way, the Spanish unveiled a second phase of their plans for the New World. What they had in mind was, in the words of historian John Armstrong Crow, "imperialistic conquest in the Roman sense: to impose their language, their culture and their way of life on millions of colonial subjects." They burned books. They smashed idols. They hung or sold into slavery those who persisted in rebellion. This was all part of a campaign to transform the Maya into a compliant, Hispanicized peasantry. In the end, however, despite years of effort, the Spanish were unable to remake the Maya. The best they could do was to drive what had once been a sophisticated urban culture into villages such as San Andrés, where the descendants of the ancient Maya live today.

I slept badly the night before I left for San Andrés. I was staying in a hotel in San Cristóbal de las Casas, the colonial capital of the Mexican state of Chiapas. San Cristóbal is a city of cobblestone streets and crumbling Baroque churches. The Spanish placed the town in its remote, seven-thousand-foot valley in order to subdue the Tzotzils and their Maya neighbors, the Tzeltals. Once pure Spanish, San Cristóbal is now a Ladino town, which is to say that its residents are now Spanish speakers of mixed racial heritage. Mixture, however, does not imply acceptance. As is the case throughout the region, the Ladino population of San Cristóbal harbors considerable racial contempt for its Indian neighbors. Despite this, San Cristóbal makes its living off the Indians. Every day the Maya from the surrounding countryside flood into the city to sell or buy produce. At night the flood is reversed and the Maya return to their villages, but the ethnic exchange seldom goes the other way. A Maya village is another world—remote, stark, beautiful, and, for a *hrinko* (a gringo) or a *coleto* (a Ladino resident of San Cristóbal), difficult to reach and sometimes dangerous.

I had been to San Andrés once, with Chip Morris, a Tzotzil-speaking American textile expert who had lived there fifteen years earlier. I'd been to other Maya villages too, but never on my own. My Spanish was workable, but not many people in San Andrés would, or could, speak Spanish, and my Tzotzil consisted of a few weeks' accumulation of pleasantries. Nevertheless, I had a plan—to visit a weaver to whom Chip had introduced me. She was a gentle, dignified woman whose father had been a shaman. She worked for months at a time making extraordinarily beautiful *huipiles,* or blouses, which were like maps of a Maya woman's cosmos. They showed the sun's passage through the thirteen layers of the heavens. They showed toads, the servants of the Earthlord, dancing rain clouds out of the mouths of caves. They showed the four sacred directions, and in the end, when the wearer pulled the *huipil* over her head, they served by design to make her the fifth direction, the center, the source of life. I was attracted to the spirituality of this woman, but beyond the awe I felt for her weavings and my interest in connecting with the inaccessible world of the Maya in some way, I wasn't really sure why I was going to see her, or what I was going to do when I got there. She spoke only rudimentary Spanish, and since there are no telephones in San Andrés, she had no way of knowing that I was coming. Still, I told myself, if I was interested in the Maya I had to start somewhere.

Despite sleeping badly, I managed to miss the six-thirty A.M. bus to San Andrés. It was just as well. I had decided that I needed a house present. I wandered into the market and found an Indian woman sitting cross-legged beside a mound of pineapples on a straw mat. I picked out a large one and bought it. Pineapple, traditional symbol of hospitality.

I went back outside and asked around for a ride. Someone pointed to a man loading boxes of cooking oil and bags of onions onto the back of a truck. I asked if he was going to San Andrés.

"Yes," he said.

"When?" I asked.

"Now," he told me.

I joined several other passengers in the back, and soon we were climbing out of the San Cristóbal valley and up into the highlands. Technically the Chiapas highlands are a plateau, but they are not flat. Rather, the plateau consists of a fantastically eroded landscape of sheer cliffs, deep valleys, and frequent caves—all broken by occasional volcanic intrusions. The reason for this distinctive topography is that Chiapas, like most of the Maya region, is underlain by porous limestone. Over the millennia, water has worked down into the bedrock, widening valleys and digging caves in such a way that good-sized rivers plunge suddenly into the ground, only to reemerge elsewhere in a manner to create a healthy legacy of human respect for the earth gods. As we jostled our way along one of the rutted, potholed roads that in the 1970's the Mexican government, flush with oil revenues and anxious to further integrate the Indians into the economy, had pushed into the Maya area, I stood up and watched the unfolding landscape.

We skirted lurid-green valleys dotted with corn fields and crisscrossed with footpaths. We passed clusters of adobe huts with high, Oriental-looking thatched roofs. In the distance they looked like doll houses. Feathery pines lined the ridges, while lower down, sheltered from the wind, were groves of fantastically coppiced Arthur Rackham oaks. I watched an Indian woman tending a flock of sheep; Chip had told me that sheep were a Spanish import and that their Tzotzil name meant "cotton deer."

After an hour of driving we rounded a bend and saw, along the top of a distant ridge, a town of white walls and red roofs clustered around a large church. It was San Andrés. It looked like an Italian hill town. I laughed to myself at this impression. After this first visit to San Andrés I mentioned the image to a Mexican friend in San Cristóbal.

"Italian hill town!" she'd exclaimed. "For all the trouble there's been in that town!"

Half an hour later we arrived. I paid the driver two thousand pesos—a little less than a dollar—and jumped down from the truck bed. We had come to a stop at the foot of the town plaza, a wide, treeless expanse surrounding a bandstand. At one end stood San Andrés's monstrous Roman Catholic church; at the other, its arcaded town offices. Although I knew that on festival or market days the plaza would be filled with *andresanos* in colorful *traje,* or traditional costume, now it was empty except for a few vendors selling sodas and *palomitas,* "little doves," as popcorn is called.

San Andrés is the municipal center for a population of several thousand *andresanos* who live scattered in *parajes,* rural hamlets, throughout the surrounding mountains, and its basic plaza-church–municipal building layout is one repeated throughout the Maya region. People assume that this design has something to do with the traditional layout of towns in Spain, but in fact it has more to do with the political ambitions of the Spanish court at the time of the Conquest. Many of the post-Conquest administrators of the Spanish colonies were idealistic friars who hoped both to convert the Indians to Christianity and to protect them from what they considered to be rapacious conquistadors. To accomplish their goals, the friars set out to congregate the Indians in standardized towns with central plazas that were Renaissance versions of the ancient Greek stoa and marketplace and reflected the friars' orderly and humanistic designs for the New World. No one asked the Indians if they wanted to live in the model towns. If they didn't leave their own lands voluntarily, they were forcibly removed, "although in the removal," the friars instructions cautioned, "violence should not be used, but much gentleness." Just in case, however, the friars burned the Indians' houses behind them—"so that they would lose the longing to return."

The problem was that the Indians refused to stay in the friars' towns. The Maya had always lived in their *parajes,* and no matter how often the friars tried to herd them into the municipal centers, they persisted in returning to their hamlets. Eventually a compromise evolved. Towns such as San Andrés became what anthropologists call vacant centers—administrative and ceremonial centers that consisted of the church, the plaza, the town offices, and little more. The Maya gathered there for religious festivals and on market days, but lived in the *parajes* the rest of the time.

Like many other Maya towns, however, San Andrés had undergone a further evolution during the late nineteenth century. Beyond its plaza lay a neighborhood of Ladino-style brick-and-tile houses. It was these houses that gave San Andrés its hill-town appearance. After my first visit, I asked Chip about them.

"It's simple," he told me. "Until fifteen years ago there were a thousand Ladinos living in San Andrés."

Chip explained that until Mexico became independent from Spain, in 1821, San Andrés, and other Maya towns like it, had been exclusively Maya, protected from non-Indians by Catholic church administrators and royal decree. During the war of independence, however, both the church's and the crown's authority had been broken and by the end of the nineteenth century Ladinos began gradually moving into the Indian towns. In San Andrés, the first Ladino to actually take up residence was a labor contractor who arrived just before the year 1900. The Indians called him *el enganchador,* "the hooker," because of his loan-sharking. During the period of rampant corruption that led up to the Mexican Revolution of 1910, he lent money at eighteen percent interest a month, signed illiterate Indians to unfulfillable labor contracts, and wound up owning a good part of San Andrés' land. His success prompted other Ladinos to follow his example. By the mid-1970's the *andresanos,* who by this time knew something more about the ways of the outside world, decided they'd had enough. Armed with machetes, they went door-to-door telling the Ladinos that they had a week to leave San Andrés or they'd be killed. As they did this, other *andresanos* began systematically cutting down the fence posts around Ladino fields.

"The funny thing," Chip told me, "is that this happened while I was living in San Andrés. But it went on so discreetly that I was able to remain friends with both sides. I'd go down and have lunch with the municipal president, who was Indian, and he'd act as if nothing was going on. Then I'd go up and have a beer with the *enganchador*'s son, who was a friend of mine. He'd tell me, 'They tried this in the thirties, but we got our rifles, hid around the top of a hill and ambushed them. That put an end to it.'"

From the Indian point of view, the eviction of the Ladinos proceeded flawlessly until a group of Ladinos resisted having their fences cut down, and a shootout ensued. Three Ladinos were killed and seven Indians were wounded. After that the Mexican army was called in. The wounded Indians were taken to a lowland hospital. There, someone dragged them out of their beds and beat them up. Still, "The Ladinos got the message. Now only a few families remain."

The weaver whom I was going to visit was one of the beneficiaries of the mass Ladino eviction—she'd gotten a bargain-price town house. After fortifying myself with some popcorn, I put my pineapple under my arm and strode off toward her house.

I knocked on the gate. No answer. Neighbors stepped out of their houses and peered curiously.

I knocked again. Still no answer. Neighbors craned their necks around doors, out windows, over walls. Their curiosity was such that they stared at me openly, without even a pretense of modesty.

A small boy leapt out into the street, scaled monkeylike up the weaver's wall, peered over the top, and pronounced triumphantly, "*No está!* She's not there!"

Did anybody know when she'd be back, I asked.

"Later," one of the neighbors said noncommittally.

I decided to walk. I walked all around the town. I climbed to a chapel dedicated to the Virgin of Guadalupe on a knoll outside town, admired the view, and then, when an Indian man asked me pointedly what I was doing, came back down and walked all over town again. There aren't many streets in San Andrés, however, and no matter where I went, I always seemed to wind up back in the central plaza. Eventually I just sat down in the bandstand. That's when Maya time set in.

It started with lethargy born of hopelessness. It had gotten hot. Stray dogs sat on piles of superheated dirt, eyes closed, heads resting on crossed paws. They looked like emaciated sphinxes. They couldn't even muster the energy to snap and growl. In emulation of the dogs, I closed my eyes. I listened to roosters crowing, turkeys gobbling, little chicks peeping. Tinny strains of hopelessly Okie *ranchero* music floated over the valley. From inside the church came the low droning of an Indian ritual. I had tried to go in and see what was happening but a hatchet-faced man wearing a straw hat hung with multicolored ribbons frowned and turned me back—or maybe I just imagined it. A fly landed on my head. I swatted and missed. Maya time.

I decided to try the weaver's house again and trudged back up the hill to her house.

"*No está!*" her neighbors responded in the singsong tone that Maya women use when they are playing the role of the complete innocent.

I returned to the plaza and began thinking about taking the bus back to San Cristóbal. Unfortunately, there wasn't one until three-thirty. Chip, too, had had a difficult time when he'd first arrived in San Andrés. Having dropped out of Columbia during one of the student strikes of the early seventies, he'd moved to San Cristóbal, become interested in Maya textiles, and decided that he would learn Tzotzil by living with a Maya family. When no Maya family would take him in, Chip armed himself with some evangelical texts written in phonetic Tzotzil and sat in the San Andrés plaza for a month reading Bible passages out loud that he did not understand. Finally, a local family adopted him for his humor value. The family had a three-year-old son with a round head, nicknamed "Melon." Melon learned Tzotzil more quickly than Chip and used Chip as the butt of all his jokes.

Chip's reading of evangelical texts was not entirely coincidental, for among other things, the new roads have brought evangelical religions into the Indian villages. Many Maya, confronted with a rapidly changing world, have abandoned their traditional religion, which is a hybrid of Catholicism and Maya, and become evangelicals. This has led to conflict within the villages. An optimistic friend in San Cristóbal told me that the Maya were "grasping at other religions because they were unsure of their own, but that eventually they would take what they needed of other religions and make something new."

The second stage of Maya time turned out to be the evangelical. It was part of the experience. No question. Two squat Ladina girls had been circling the plaza, making eyes at me. They were, no doubt, the belle monde of San Andrés. They had shiny satiny dresses and high heels that looked as if they'd been carved from blocks of wood. After much giggling, they sat down and introduced themselves. Let's say their names were Lupe and Dolor de Maria.

There was not a lot of small talk: What was my name? Where did I come from? Was I married? Did I have any children? What was my religion? Did I believe in God? Did I think that the end of the world was coming?

Lupe was quite forward. She was an *evangelica*. She lived in San Cristóbal and was in San Andrés on a visit. Dolor was Catholic, more reserved, apparently one of the Ladinas who'd remained behind in San Andrés.

With much batting of eyelashes, Lupe raised again what seemed to be her central question: "Do you think the end of the world is coming?"

I laughed to myself. This had to be the only place in the world where women picked you up to ask you about the Apocalypse. I shrugged. "Perhaps if there were an atomic war."

Lupe's eyes suddenly acquired a glow. She assured me there'd be famine. There'd be plague. Perhaps, as I had correctly noted, there'd be war! God would come and all those who were *enraptos de Dios* would be saved.

Dolor looked at me plaintively, as if to say, "We've argued this over and over again. Will you tell me if she's right?"

I pointed out that people were *enraptos de Dios* in their own ways. God was no doubt broad-minded enough to grant that. But Lupe only nodded vaguely. She seemed to have been transported by her vision. She had friends in Texas, she interjected, who were *evangelicos.* They'd assured her that everything she'd told me was not only true, but imminent.

Finally, my weaver was at home—or, rather, someone was at home. I knew this because although I'd been knocking on the door and no one had answered, the monkey had scaled the wall again and had reported that someone, indeed, was there. Found out, the someone reluctantly came to the door. It was the weaver's son, a schoolteacher. He greeted me with a notable lack of enthusiasm. Perhaps he hadn't been there the previous six times I'd knocked. I don't know. But where else would he have been?

The weaver's son told me that his mother had gone to San Cristóbal for the day. She'd be back on the afternoon bus. I sat down and tried to make conversation, but he was not receptive. I no longer really cared. My hours in the plaza had left me with a severe sense of dislocation, or sunstroke, or both. I handed the pineapple to the weaver's son, asked him to give it to his mother, and, told him that I had to go wait for the bus for San Cristóbal, even though it wasn't due for another hour.

Back in the plaza, I reached a third level of Maya time. This was the *borracho,* drunken, level. A tall, broad-chested *andresano* stumbled toward me. His eyes were bloodshot and out of focus. I took one look at him, grabbed a book out of my bag and put my nose into it. Undeterred, the man demanded in a loud voice to know where I was from. I told him that I was from the United States. It didn't seem to register. With a look of intense annoyance he asked me the same question over again. This time I continued staring at my book, hoping he'd go away. It didn't work. He raised the level of his voice and began to shout. People began staring. I no longer had any idea what he wanted. Nor did he, it seemed. I got up and walked away. He followed, becoming increasingly truculent.

We were running in circles around the bandstand when the bus from San Cristóbal arrived. I used the distraction to give the man the slip and walked over to the bus. It was packed. People flowed off in a steady stream, including, eventually, the weaver. I'd somehow known this would happen. I greeted her, told her that I'd come to call on her but now had to take the bus back to San Cristóbal. I told her that I'd left a pineapple with her schoolteacher son. She looked embarrassed. We mumbled apologies and I watched her trudge up the hill toward home.

To my surprise, however, when I tried to board the bus, I was told it was not going back to San Cristóbal, but farther out into the mountains. It would return to San Cristóbal the next morning at five-thirty. I waited for another forty-five minutes until the bus that was supposed to return to San Cristóbal that afternoon was long overdue. Even though everyone assured me that it was coming, no one else seemed to be waiting. I began to make inquiries.

"That bus didn't come up this morning," a reliable-looking storekeeper told me, "therefore it won't be going back tonight."

At first I choose to dismiss this observation. It wasn't what I wanted to hear. But after further questioning, I was forced to conclude that it was probably correct, since it was now four-thirty in the afternoon. It was also at a point in the rainy season when the rain started in the late afternoon and was likely to continue all night. Storm clouds were gathering around the mountain tops. Occasional trucks were still coming into town from the direction of San Cristóbal, but for several hours, not a single one had headed back. I knew, because I'd asked each one. I conferred with the storekeeper. "That's it for the night," he told me, "although six or seven kilometers away there's the junction with the road to Chenalhó and you might catch something there."

I could hear thunder in the distance. It was about to pour. It would soon be dark. I didn't have a sleeping bag. I had no evidence that the road from Chenalhó, an even more remote Indian village, would produce any more traffic than the San Andrés road. It was twenty-two miles through the mountains to San Cristóbal. Logically, I should have swallowed my pride and walked the hundred yards up the hill to the weaver's house, but I couldn't bring myself to. I set off walking.

At first I had the illusion I was outrunning the storm. While I followed the high road along the ridge, it seemed to slide along the valley below me. I was going at a good clip. The mountain air filled my lungs and I began to perspire lightly. But two kilometers and two steep climbs later—too late, in my opinion, to turn back to San Andrés—I saw that the storm had outrun me. It had circled around in front of me and was waiting in ambush. I kept walking anyway. Over the third ridge, the rain began. I pulled out my bottom-of-the-line rain jacket. It was a curious jacket. Although it gave the illusion of keeping out the rain, the jacket's interior was always lined with moisture, whether through condensation or leaks I could never decide. I trudged on. No traffic had passed me in either direction and darkness was beginning to fall quickly.

Between San Andrés and San Cristóbal lies Chamula, the land of the Chamulas, the largest, poorest, and most belligerent of the Tzotzil groups. As I crossed the line into Chamula, I found four or five hopelessly drunk Chamulas lying outside a house in the rain. One of them held out his hand and asked me for a thousand pesos. Welcome to Chamula.

I had come into an Indian hamlet, a *paraje,* strung out along both sides of the road. I began to notice kids peering at me from behind rocks and bushes. I smiled and waved as if nothing were wrong. "Just another tourist out for a rainy night-time stroll!"

Instead of waving back, they ran—without smiling. A woman herding a flock of sheep in front of me quickened her pace and brandished her machete in the air as if fighting off invisible spirits. As I passed a school, two boys taunted me from a distance.

I began to realize that although it was easy enough to pass through this territory on a bus, it was another thing to be a stranger, walking in the rain, with night approaching. It didn't have so much to do with the imminent possibility of my getting lost, or freezing, or catching pneumonia. It had to do with the Maya conception of what kind of person would be out walking by himself in the mountains at night.

The Tzotzils believe that they live in the center of the world.

They also believe that the edges of the world, near where Htotik, the sun, plunges daily into the underworld, is a dangerous place. It is filled with demons, wild animals, and strange human beings who are related to the Earthlord. Among such people are the foreigners, the *kashlan. Hrinkos,* gringos, are *kashlan.* Like the Earthlord himself, the *kashlan* can be a source of great wealth, but they're very powerful and extremely dangerous. Count one against me. I am *kashlan.*

Second, the Tzotzils divide the earth into the *naetik,* the parts of the world in which the gods have been placated and human activities are safe, and the *te'tik,* the wild, wooded areas that, like the edges of the world, are filled with dangerous animals and people. Only shamans or witches, who are capable of transforming themselves into other shapes, would walk alone in the *te'tik* at night. More witches than Indian communities care to talk about have been chopped up by machetes when they were caught wandering alone at night.

I may look like a *kashlan,* but perhaps I'm really a witch masquerading as one.

These things were on my mind when, after an hour or so of hard walking, my feet and trousers soaked, my upper body bathed in sweat, I finally saw the Chenalhó road in the distance. I also saw a man in the road ahead of me. I soon overtook him and stopped him to explain my plight. His name was Marcelino. He was a Chamula and a *chofer,* a driver, although he had apparently misplaced his vehicle. He pulled out his *chofer* card to show me. It had his picture on it. Marcelino, too, seemed to have been drinking, but at least he was cheerful. He told me he'd driven all over Mexico, from California to Quintana Roo. "California, Quintana Roo," he repeated, laughing hysterically as if it were some comic mantra.

I was tremendously relieved to encounter Marcelino. He didn't know it, but his fate was now linked to mine. He was my guide, my interpreter, my friend my ("Mexico, Quintana Roo! Ha, ha, ha!") Virgil.

I asked Marcelino where he was planning to spend the night. In Chamula, he told me—San Juan Chamula. This was reassuring, because San Juan Chamula, the Chamulas' municipal center, was only a few miles from San Cristóbal.

"But how will you get there?"

Marcelino didn't answer. He just laughed as we wandered off into the gloom.

A little way beyond the road junction, we came upon a house by the side of the road. I followed Marcelino into a dirt-floored, dimly lit room with bags of corn in one corner. Some young Indian men entered behind us. Everyone seemed to know Marcelino. Marcelino asked if I'd like a *refresco,* a soda. I accepted and reached for some bills to pay for it. He waved my gesture aside and said something in Tzotzil. One of the Indian men reached into the corner, picked up a rusted enamel coffee pot, filled a dirty glass with clear liquid, and presented it to me. It was moonshine, or *pox* ("posh"). Pretty hard to refuse in my situation. I downed the glass in two gulps. My stomach rebelled. My eyes misted over. The top of my head felt as if it were lifting off.

The man was pouring me a second glass, when suddenly, in the distance, I heard the grinding of a motor. It was the Chenalhó bus. We leapt out of the house and flagged it down. I got on first. Behind, Marcelino—forgetting all about me—picked up the bucket that the driver used to fill his leaky radiator (every bus in the region has a leaky radiator and every bus carries a bucket with which to refill it at roadside pools and streams), inverted it, sat down next to the driver, and began making loud jokes. I eased into a regular seat farther back. My seatmate was a tiny Indian man with a crew cut. The bus was an old schoolbus, as most of them are. It was warm and moist inside, and pitch black by now outside. The windows were fogged up. The motor made a comforting roar. We shifted into gear and headed for San Cristóbal. It was like heaven. The impression was furthered by a Virgin Mary surrounded with twinkling lights, mounted over the windshield. Below this little shrine, along the top of the windshield itself, was a fringe of braided material that looked like a Shetland pony's bangs. It was absurdly beautiful. I had an overwhelming sense of well-being.

I suddenly noticed that my seatmate was fingering my leaky rain jacket. How much did it cost, he wanted to know. I told him. He leaned back into what I assumed was a stunned silence. The sum I'd named was probably close to the gross national product of his hamlet. A few minutes later he nudged me. How much did I want for it? I thought for a moment, peeled it off, and handed it to him. Somehow he didn't seem surprised.

"*Dios te paga.* God will pay you," he said.

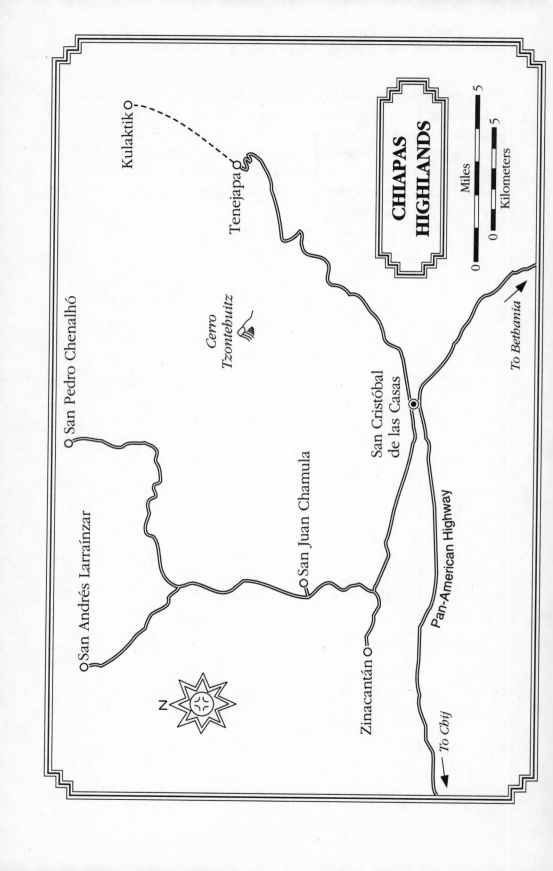

CHIAPAS
HIGHLANDS

Miles

Kilometers

Kulaktik

Tenejapa

San Pedro Chenalhó

Cerro
Tzontehuitz

San Cristóbal
de las Casas

To Bethania

San Juan Chamula

San Andrés Larraínzar

Pan-American Highway

Zinacantán

To Chij

N

CHAPTER 2

Tenejapa

I WAS WITH AN AMERICAN anthropologist friend on a bus leaving San Cristóbal and heading for the northern highlands when I met Antonio Mendez. We noticed a young Indian man across the aisle from us writing rapidly in a diary notebook. This was curious enough in an area where few Maya have more than an elementary-school education, but as we peered indiscreetly, words began to leap off the page—English words. Overcome with curiosity, my friend leaned over and asked. The man looked up, smiled, and introduced himself in American English as Tony Mendez. Next to him was a handsome, lean Indian of about fifty, whom Tony introduced as his father, Alonso Mendez Girón, former *presidente* of the Indian municipality of Tenejapa. They were going to Pantelhó, another Indian municipality, to visit Tony's mother, Alonso's former wife.

"I haven't seen either of my parents in years," Tony said, his English still bizarrely incongruous. "I live in New York now, and seeing my parents is what this trip is about for me."

I arranged to meet Tony in San Cristóbal a few days later, and when I did he invited me to accompany his father and himself on an overnight trip to Kulaktik, the *paraje* within the larger municipality of Tenejapa in which Tony had been born. I left my rented house in San Cristóbal at six one morning and made my way to Colonia Revolución, a new barrio on the northern edge of the city. Colonia Revolución was a neighborhood of low cinder-block houses painted in bright pastels, its rutted dirt streets bearing the long, florid names of Mexico's postrevolution presidents. Inside his house, Alonso was sitting at a kitchen table just off a small concrete courtyard. His young wife, Antonia, a stout, barefoot Tenejapan probably thirty years his junior, was stirring a soup made from vegetables and the dried, heavily salted shrimp that are a delicacy to the highland Maya. She ladled out bowls for Alonso, Tony, and me, put a pile of tortillas and a plateful of chilis in the middle of the table, and went off to get the oldest of their five young children ready for school.

Alonso wanted to take a seventy-pound tank of propane to Kulaktik. The truck from Tenejapa to Kulaktik didn't leave until late in the day. Since Tony wanted to walk, we helped Alonso carry the tank of propane to the bus terminal, and set out for Tenejapa on our own.

The ride to Tenejapa isn't a long one. From San Cristóbal the bus climbs out of the valley, turns north across the eastern edge of the municipality of Chamula, skirts Tzontehuitz, an extinct volcano that at close to ten thousand feet is the highest mountain in the region, and then, forty-five minutes later, plunges downward toward the town. Somewhere along the route you cross the invisible line that separates Tzotzil speakers from the speakers of the other major Chiapas Maya language—Tzeltal, the language of Tenejapa. Dennis Breedlove, a botanist whose life work has consisted of compiling a sixteen-volume flora of Chiapas, explained to me the difference between these two closely related languages: Tzotzil contains words for the dry-country plants to the west of the Chiapas highlands; Tzeltal has words for the jungle plants of the rain forests to the east. A combination of time and geographical isolation have produced the differences between the two languages.

Tenejapa is located in the bottom of a deep valley with nearly vertical walls. As our bus ground its way down one side of the valley wall, the whole town lay spread out beneath us. At its center, facing the plaza, was a massive, austere church with a low-pitched tile roof. Its thick walls were supported by crude buttresses. The municipal offices were located across the plaza, and were surrounded by clusters of one-story dwellings that Tony said belonged to Ladinos who, like those of San Andrés, had moved into Tenejapa within the last century. The terra-cotta roof tiles of the Ladino houses were so densely packed that they almost looked like bare, clay-colored earth.

Tony and I got off the bus on the edge of the plaza. He had not been back to Tenejapa in a number of years and looked apprehensive, as if he were stepping back into his childhood. He stood for a moment and, when it became apparent that no one was paying any notice, began to walk nervously around the plaza. When we reached the front of the church, we entered. The interior was dark and cavernous, ten degrees colder than the outside, and filled with incense. We could hear a strange chanting coming from a side altar, which Tony said was a shaman conducting a curing ritual. When I asked what the priests felt about Maya shamans using the church, he told me that because there was no longer a resident priest in Tenejapa, the Maya had usurped the church for their own purposes. He pointed out a notice from the San Cristóbal archdiocese posted on the church door. It warned the Tenejapans to beware of a con man in the area claiming to be a priest, performing priestly functions and soliciting contributions.

Across the plaza, on a bench under the arcade of the municipal offices, were the members of the Indian municipal government. They wore ceremonial Tenejapan clothing: heavily embroidered white shorts, a knee-length brown woolen tunic tied with a woven sash, and palm hats hung with colored ribbons. Almost shyly, Tony approached one of the office holders and struck up a conversation, in Tzeltal. The man was a *regidor*, a ceremonial policeman. In addition to the rest of his formal costume, he was carrying the badges of his office: a *bastón,* (Maya billy club) and, around his neck, a cross suspended from a necklace of antique coins. Tony told the *regidor* that he was the son of Alonso Mendez Girón, the former president. Did the man remember him?

"Ahh," the *regidor* responded uncertainly, "you must be Antun [Tzeltal for Antonio], right?"

Tony looked pleased. As we walked away he said, "People say that with my knowledge of the outside world, I could come back to Tenejapa and be *presidente* some day."

As we followed a street lined with low, tile-roofed houses, I asked Tony how it was that he'd first gone to the United States.

He explained that shortly after his birth, in 1958, his father, Alonso, had become a *regidor* in Tenejapa. While there, he'd met Dennis Breedlove and another American botanist who were then compiling a flora of the Tzeltal area. Alonso had begun collecting plants for them. The work had required him to go into San Cristóbal for a week at a time. But Tony's mother didn't like San Cristóbal and became increasingly unhappy with her husband's frequent absences. Eventually she left his house and moved back in with her parents. Afterward, in San Cristóbal, Alonso met an American woman named Frances. They were married, and eventually Frances took them all to the United States. Tony went to kindergarten in Carbondale, Illinois, and then to first grade in Denver. But Alonso never really liked the United States. For one thing, he didn't learn English. Eventually he came back to Chiapas on his own.

Tony told me that he'd shuttled between Tenejapa, San Cristóbal, and the United States for a few years. Eventually he'd wound up living with his father and going to school in San Cristóbal. When he flunked some courses—"civics, protocol, things like that"—Alonso told him that he'd embarrassed him and threw him out of the house. Tony stayed in San Cristóbal doing odd jobs for a year and went to Mexico City when he was thirteen.

"My father and I actually traveled there together," Tony told me, "because at the same time he'd been given a job with the Indian lands agency. But once we got to Mexico City, we split up."

Tony moved in with some students from Chiapas and found a job selling records door-to-door. By the time he was fifteen he was traveling by bus selling records all over the country. He went from Chihuahua to Durango to Mérida. He even traveled down into South America, going to Peru, and from there to Rio de Janeiro. When he was seventeen or eighteen, he wound up back in San Cristóbal.

"I'd learned to play the guitar," Tony told me. "Some guys I knew had a rock band and when their guitarist quit, I took his place. I played with that band for two years. We played salsa—dancing music. I made the band because I could sing in English. People loved that."

"What happened to your father during all this time," I asked.

"I don't know yet," he said. "I really haven't seen much of him since we split up in Mexico City in 1971. I'm interviewing him about his life now, and we haven't gotten that far."

"Do you resent your father for throwing you out of the house?"

"I'm glad he did. I'm glad for everything that's happened."

At the edge of town the path to Kulaktik rose steeply up the valley wall. Tony paused just before beginning the ascent. "When I was a kid I used to hate this walk," he said. "It seemed endless. That was before the road went in. We always had to carry something."

We began to climb. The trail was steep and slippery—a slick red clay over polished knobs of limestone. Along the sides of the trail you could see that even in the flat spots there was only an inch or two of topsoil over the clay. Nevertheless, halfway up the valley wall we came upon a milpa—one of the tiny fields in which from time immemorial, Maya farmers have grown the trinity of squash, beans, and corn.

For the Maya, milpas are more than simply their place of work. Among the Tzotzils milpa land is referred to as *hamalaltik* and represents a third category of space after *naetik* and *te'tik*. Milpa land is land reclaimed from nature, after the gods have been appeased and represents the collaboration between man and the gods that is the basis of life for the Maya. Milpas are scrupulously tended, kept clean. Even Maya who, for whatever reason, don't need corn, still make a milpa. It's considered an act of piety, something to honor the ancestors, something close to the Maya conception of self.

I sat down on a rock to rest. Tony was standing, looking at a ridge across the valley. He told me that once, with a Canadian caver friend who'd taught him how to use ropes and lamps, he'd followed a river into a cave on the other side of the ridge. "All the rivers around here disappear into caves," he said. "There's one that goes into a cave just above the municipal center and re-emerges twelve kilometers away in Chenalhó."

"How did you know where it came out?"

"My friend bought a load of dried red chilis and dumped them into the river. They came out in Chenalhó."

A few minutes more of steep climbing took us over the valley wall. It was as if we'd reached the top of the world. Mountains and valleys rolled off like waves on the sea. Tony appeared stunned.

"One of the reasons that I had to return," he said, "was that I kept coming back here in my dreams."

The path leveled off, skirting a rolling milpa on the left. On the right the land dropped into a deep, grassy sinkhole, from whose lower slopes we could hear the voices of some unseen farmers. A melodious birdsong sounded from a thicket. Looking closer, I saw a bright yellow oriole. This seemed appropriate, for according to the archaeologist Sylvanus Morley's list of Yucatec Maya folk beliefs, hearing an oriole's song means that a visitor is about to arrive.

Tony stopped by the edge of the milpa. He showed me how the squash vines spread laterally across the ground while bean plants, which were covered with delicate red blossoms, climbed up the corn stalks. He pointed out a rampant yellow-and-white composite.

"That's a medicinal plant," he said. "We used that flower for something, but I just can't remember what. I used to work in these fields when I was seven and eight years old. We never heard an engine then. There were no airplanes overhead, no trucks in the valley."

I looked at Tony and had to laugh. The United States had transformed him. He was wearing Levis, a pair of heavy hiking boots, and a bright blue T-shirt that had a picture of a surfer riding an enormous wave under the word MAUI. Draped over his shoulder was a Nikon camera, and in a little backpack that he had asked me to carry was a Sony Super-8 movie camera. As we set off again I asked him to tell me what had happened to his rock band after he returned to San Cristóbal.

"During the time I had the band I was having an affair with a Ladina girl, a *coleta* [woman from San Cristóbal]. Her parents hated me because I was an Indian, and made it very hard for us to see each other. Her mother was especially bad. She wanted her daughter to marry a doctor, or a lawyer, or an architect. She used to say—to my face—that I'd never be anything but a farmer, that if her daughter were to marry me, she'd wind up eating dirt.

"One night I was supposed to play a dance at a working man's club. I wanted my girlfriend to come, but her father wouldn't let her. I had a big argument with him, but after it became clear that he wasn't going to change his mind, she told her father that she was going out somewhere else with some of her Ladino friends. He said fine, and the whole group of them came to the dance anyway. My girlfriend was angry at me that night because she had heard that I was seeing someone else—which in fact I was, because I saw so little of her. To get back at me, she began making up to one of her Ladino friends right in front of the stage on which I was playing. During a break in the music I went up to her and said, 'Let's try to work this thing out.' But the people in San Cristóbal don't like to work things out. She went into a rage. She started throwing bottles and chairs. The dance was in the kind of club where a fight is part of the evening's entertainment, so it quickly developed into a riot.

"It was just my luck that her parents had figured out where she'd gone and had sent her maid to get her. The maid arrived just as the fighting started. I had gone up on the stage to try to calm things down when I saw a woman charge into the middle of the fight. It was the maid, but I thought it was my girlfriend, so I went to try to rescue her. By the time I got to the woman and discovered that it wasn't my girlfriend, half her clothes had been ripped off and she was in hysterics. I took her outside and put her in a taxi. I didn't recognize her because I was never allowed in my girlfriend's house. Later my friends told me who she was.

"The next day, my girlfriend's father started telling everybody that I had assaulted his daughter. He sent me a message saying that if I wasn't out of town within twenty-four hours, he'd kill me. I knew an American anthropologist who lived in San Clemente, California. I left for California that same night."

This all took place in the fall of 1980.

What had he done in California, I asked.

"I worked as a waiter and as a busboy for a while," he continued, "but I didn't really fit in. So I moved to New York, which is where I've been for the last eight years. For two years I worked in a car wash in Coney Island. However, my stepmother, Frances, is from the Bronx. She introduced me to her Polish-Jewish stepbrother-in-law. He taught me wiring. From there I got a job as a maintenance manager in a restaurant. Eventually I became the manager."

Had he ever seen his San Cristóbal girlfriend again?

"I passed her on the street a few years ago. She married the kind of man her mother wanted her to. We saw each other, but we pretended we hadn't."

After we'd walked in silence for a while, we saw a tiny, wizened Indian man coming toward us along the trail. When the man reached us, Tony stopped and spoke with him in Tzeltal. The man stepped aside and let us go by. I asked Tony what the man had said.

"He thought we were teachers, and since he was a farmer, he let us go first. He said to me, 'Go, ahead, sir.'" To which I responded, 'Thank you sir, I will go by.' The man then said, 'Thank you sir. I am leaving now, sir.' and I responded, 'Go ahead, sir.'"

Apparently this was a normal pattern of greeting for two Tzeltals meeting on a path. What would have happened if both parties had been farmers?

"They'd have looked at each other and decided who was older. The younger one would step aside."

"And a woman?"

"The woman would step aside."

I reflected on how much more complicated the Maya landscape is than our own. The Maya landscape is a Swiss cheese of strange transformations, hostile forces, different spiritual planes. The Maya need constant vigilance simply to occupy the little niche of creation granted them. As a result, every action—even something as simple as the protocol of passing someone on a path—is charged with significance. My retreat from San Andrés still on my mind, I wondered what would have happened if I'd been on the path alone. Would they have thought I was a spirit?

"Probably not," Tony said. "With the roads, people are more accustomed to seeing white people. What they've always been afraid of are the winged black creatures that they say live in the caves. These creatures kidnap women and eat children. However, the old people say that those creatures don't exist anymore. The last ones were seen forty years ago."

Late in the afternoon, we completed a long descent into Kulaktik. Kulaktik means "marsh grass place" in Tzeltal, and the hamlet— just a scattering of buildings, really—lies along one side of a wide valley, considerably lower in altitude than Tenejapa. The foliage was noticeably more tropical. Kulaktik is what local people call *tierra templada,* "temperate country," as opposed to Tenejapa, which, like the rest of the highlands, is *tierra fría,* "cold country." Together with *tierra caliente,* "hot country," the categories represent a Spanish system of landscape division said to date back to the separation of the earth into cold, temperate, and hot zones by the ancient Greeks.

Tony couldn't remember the way to his father's house, so we

asked some neighbors for directions. They pointed to a path leading into a grove of thick, waxy green coffee bushes six to eight feet high. We followed the path and emerged at a long, narrow shed in the middle of a grove of fruit trees. The shed was set in a packed-earth yard. Its roof was corrugated metal and its walls vertical planks. It looked like a miniature tobacco barn. Alonso and his family had not yet arrived, but their bus was due soon. Tony seemed preoccupied. He began pacing and then said that he was going to go out to the road and wait for the bus. After he left, it occurred to me that Tony was probably uneasy about this reunion with his father, that he'd invited me along on the trip to Kulaktik because he'd been too nervous to do it on his own. I, however, was exhausted from our walk. I found a plank under the eaves, dusted it off, put my hat over my face, and fell asleep.

Half an hour later, the whole family came through the coffee grove. Antonia and her three youngest children—Carolina, Norma, and Esther—were first. Tony was next, carrying some bags. Last came Alonso, his face red, his neck muscles bulging, the seventy-pound tank of propane suspended from his forehead by a tumpline. Someone ran to a store to get sodas, and Tony, Alonso, and I sat in three small wooden chairs in the late-afternoon sun. I looked out over the yard. Chickens were hunting for bugs. Scrawny dogs skulked through the shrubbery. Alonso turned to me suddenly and asked if I found it *triste*—sad. It was as if he'd been reading my mind. For a moment I was speechless. Then I told him that no, rather, I found it strange, but that was why I had come.

Alonso seemed to accept this answer, but his question stayed with me because I didn't feel that I'd responded adequately. In a way I did feel sad, but I think it had less to do with the poverty of Alonso's house than with its remoteness from my own experience. I remembered a professor with whom I'd studied Dante and who had pointed out that when Dante reached the upper levels of *Purgatorio,* he began to lose conciousness as he moved to each new level. Dante was trying to demonstrate a theological point about divine grace and free will, but it had always struck me that what Dante had really created was a singularly appropriate metaphor for how the mind behaves when the world with which it is confronted becomes too strange. I can only imagine how the Indians felt when they were first confronted with the Spanish. Their first difficulty was deciding whether the Spanish were mortals or gods. In *The Conquest of America: The Question of the Other,* the French structuralist Tzvetan Todorov makes the interesting argument that this confusion varied in direct proportion to literacy. The Incas, who could not write at all, were convinced that the Spanish were gods. The Aztecs, who had pictograms, initially thought that the Spanish were gods but soon changed their minds. The Maya, who could read and write, knew from the beginning that the Spanish were men. The Maya, therefore, were the most difficult to conquer.

Alonso suggested we walk around his land. We headed out behind the house through a wall of coffee bushes, their green berries just ripening to red. Coffee is an understory plant that grows best in filtered light; in the overstory were blossoming peach trees, lime trees, a huge, spreading avocado, several bananas, and something I had never seen before—a twenty-foot-tall tree tomato hung with red, egg-shaped fruit.

Alonso's garden struck me as a wonderful metaphor for the complex roots of present-day Maya culture. Peaches, bananas, and citrus fruits were all Spanish introductions to the New World, though none was native to Spain. Peaches originated in China, spread to Persia, and from there were brought to Spain when Spain was part of the Roman empire. Citrus fruits were brought to Spain by the Moors, as were bananas. Avocados and tomatoes, on the other hand, are New World plants. Avocados are Central American. Tomatoes, including the tree tomato, originated in Peru but had spread to the Maya region and beyond long before the Conquest.

In some ways, however, the most interesting crop in Alonso's garden was coffee—Central America's greatest export crop. Coffee is a native of Ethiopia and was introduced to Europe by the Ottoman Turks. The interesting thing about coffee is the degree to which it supplanted a native American crop, cacao, as a favorite beverage in

Europe. Cacao, like coffee, contains a powerful stimulant—in the case of cacao, an alkaloid called theobromine. Mixed with chili powder, cacao was the drink of the pre-Columbian Maya elite. The Maya considered it so important that they used the beans as currency. The Spanish did not take to it when mixed with chili, but they soon learned to enjoy cacao with sugar and cinnamon and in this form it was the fashionable drink of Europe until bumped by coffee and tea in the late seventeenth century.

A newly planted coffee grove on the far side of Alonso's orchard overlooked the wide valley below us. Sounds floated up—the gobbling of turkeys, children playing games, a distant school announcement in Tzeltal. The peace was suddenly broken by the sounds of three helicopters passing overhead, an unusual event this deep in the country.

"*Puta gobernador!*" exclaimed Alonso.

Tony laughed. A newly elected governor had just taken office a few days before.

Alonso had on a T-shirt that had a picture of the Mexican revolutionary hero Emiliano Zapata on it and the words ME VALE MADRE coming out of his mouth. It was a colloquialism I hadn't been able to fathom. It seemed the right time to inquire. Tony and Alonso conferred in Tzeltal for a second and then laughed.

"It means, essentially, 'I don't give a fuck,'" said Tony.

It was dusk by the time we got back to the house. In our absence Antonia had prepared dinner. Alonso hooked up the tank of gas he had so laboriously transported from San Cristóbal and lit a lantern. We sat next to the open-hearth fire on foot-high chairs around low, mismatched tables. The smoke of the fire curled its way out through the plank walls and up into the eaves. Antonia put a metal griddle called a *comal* over the fire and began to heat and distribute the tortillas she'd made in San Cristóbal that morning. She passed a bowl of black beans, and gave everyone some scrambled eggs. There were plates of salt and of fresh chilis and, in the middle of each table, bowls of greens. Alonso explained that the greens were the shoots of the chayote, a climbing plant that later in the year would produce a squash.

After dinner, Antonia and the three girls went to a neighbor's to get some peanuts. When they returned, she made tea and we sat drinking it while we tossed the peanut shells into the fire. Tony was in a wonderful mood, teasing his half-sisters, who ranged in age from five to eight, by deliberately misunderstanding and mispronouncing everything they said. After the girls went to sleep, and just before the tools were whisked off the plank bed I was to sleep on, Tony produced a cassette deck and, in place of the ubiquitous *ranchero* music, put on a tape of his own. It was Santana: *Blues for Salvador.*

I noticed Alonso sitting quietly in the corner. I asked him if he was glad that Tony had come back to Kulaktik.

"I am," he said. "It's been seventeen years."

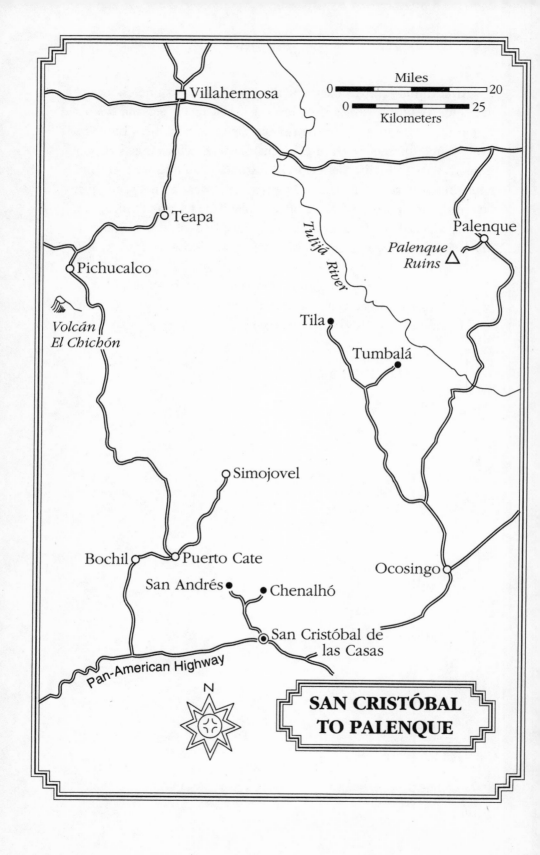

Miles
0 — 20
0 — 25
Kilometers

Villahermosa

Teapa

Pichucalco

*Volcán
El Chichón*

Tulijá River

Palenque

*Palenque
Ruins* △

Tila

Tumbalá

Simojovel

Bochil   Puerto Cate

San Andrés   Chenalhó

Ocosingo

San Cristóbal de
las Casas

Pan-American Highway

N

**SAN CRISTÓBAL
TO PALENQUE**

CHAPTER 3

Palenque

THE ANCIENT MAYA carved their hieroglyphic inscriptions in stone, set them in stucco friezes, and painted them on ceramics. But probably most important to the Maya were their hieroglyphic books, referred to as codices by European scholars. Maya books were made of pounded-bark paper coated with a plaster wash. This paper was folded like a screen and then encased in jaguar-skin covers. By all reports the Maya held these books in tremendous awe, and the first generation of Spanish friars in the New World felt understandably threatened by the books' unintelligible "characters," with which the Indians "taught ... the antiquities and their sciences." There is no evidence that any of the often brilliant friars who made up the first generation of Spanish colonial administrators ever learned to read hieroglyphs, but they nevertheless concluded that the Maya books contained nothing but "superstitions and falsehoods of the devil." As a matter of imperial policy, they set out to destroy them, and encountered little difficulty in this endeavor. Maya books were few, and the Spanish burned them when they found them. In one infamous sixteenth-century auto-da-fé, the Franciscan Bishop of Yucatán, Diego de Landa, burned twenty-seven hieroglyphic books, an act that the Maya, the bishop noted, "took most grievously" and that "caused them great pain."

Not satisfied with just eliminating the hieroglyphic books, the friars also determined to destroy the Maya ability to read and write their own language, a feat they accomplished through an ambitious program of social engineering. Literacy among the pre-Conquest Maya had always been limited to a small elite. The friars decided that by removing the children of this elite from their families and enrolling them in special schools where they would be carefully indoctrinated in Spanish culture, they might groom these Maya children into a class of native Catholic priests. The children were encouraged to inform on those of their parents who persisted in their ancestral religion. But both the children and their parents proved more attached to the old ways than the friars had anticipated, and after several rebellions the Spanish authorities became nervous. Educated Maya might become a focal point of native resistance. Having destroyed the Maya ability to read and write hieroglyphs, they now decided to deny the Maya the knowledge of Spanish as well. Subsequent Maya generations were allowed to lapse into ignorance.

Maya hieroglyphs were forgotten for the next three hundred years, until, late in the nineteenth century, a handful of pioneer scholars became interested in the ancient Maya writing system. These pioneer Maya epigraphers started by taking stock of what they had to work with. Despite the best efforts of the friars, parts of three Maya books turned up in European libraries: the Dresden, Paris, and Madrid codices. (A fragment of a fourth, the Grolier Codex, was later found in a dry cave in Chiapas.) All four are almanacs and of limited value, although, as the epigrapher Linda Schele has observed, this is "probably historical accident."

The bulk of what epigraphers had to work with were not books at all, but rather the political statements of Maya kings and queens on the walls of long-abandoned palaces and temples. A typical such statement consists of a long calendrical introduction prefacing a much briefer statement concerning what happened on that particular date. By the turn of the century, the early epigraphers had deciphered the calendrics but had come up short with the remaining noncalendrical glyphs. At first the epigraphers continued to be optimistic, but as the decades passed and scholars made no further progress on the noncalendrical glyphs, they began to argue that the undeciphered glyphs could only be "calendrics on top of more calendrics." This fueled a view of the ancient Maya that first appeared in the 1920's and gradually grew into the accepted orthodoxy during the '50's and '60's: the Maya were the "Greeks of the New World"; in contrast to the warlike Aztecs, the Maya were entirely peaceful people who eschewed conquest and empire in favor of charting the skies and ruminating on the mysteries of time. This argument was championed by the greatest Mayanists of the day, including, among others, J. Eric Thompson and Sylvanus Morley, of the Carnegie Institution in Washington.

The first significant progress to be made on the noncalendrical glyphs was made in 1952 by a little-known Soviet epigrapher named Yuri Knorosov. For decades, those who were trying to decipher Maya glyphs had been divided into two camps. One camp included those who, like Eric Thompson, believed that Maya glyphs were logographs, where each glyph stood for an individual word or concept. The other camp included those who argued that although some of the glyphs represented individual words, others consisted of clusters of phonetic signs that collectively spelled out words. If only because those who believed in a phonetic approach had nothing to show for their argument, the logograph argument had won out.

In a series of articles beginning in 1952, however, Knorosov revived the phonetic argument by going back to the most famous record of colonial-era Maya life, the *Relación de las Cosas de Yucatán,* (*Relation of the Things of Yucatán*), and reexamining a passage that had long puzzled scholars. The *Relación* (translated and annotated by Alfred Tozzer and published in 1941) was written by Diego de Landa, the sixteenth-century Franciscan bishop of Yucatán who had conducted the infamous auto-da-fé in which twenty-seven hieroglyphic books were burned. After this act, Landa was accused of conducting an illegal inquisition and was ordered back to Spain to stand trial. His *Relación,* an encyclopedic description of sixteenth-century Maya life in Yucatán, was meant to justify the measures he had taken against the Maya and was the basis of his legal defense. Knorosov focused on a section of the *Relación,* in which Landa recounts the conversation of a Yucatec informant, Gaspar Antonio Chi, on the subject of Maya hieroglyphic writing. Landa tells of sitting down with Chi and asking him to give the Maya equivalents of the Spanish ABC's. Chi was not able to oblige the bishop because the Maya did not compose their words out of letters, but rather out of syllables. Landa apparently could not understand this, and so Chi obliged him as best he could. When Landa asked for the Maya equivalent of the Spanish letter B, which a Spaniard would have pronounced "bay," Chi gave him a glyph showing a footprint on a road. The Yucatec word for road is the monosyllabic word *be,* also pronounced "bay." Chi apparently went along with this confusing exercise reluctantly. Amid all the syllables that Chi volunteered in response to Landa's requests for letters is Chi's glyphic exclamation, "I don't want to!"

Knorosov was the first to recognize the true nature of the misunderstanding between Landa and Chi. On the basis of his analysis, Knorosov argued (correctly, as it later turned out) that at least some hieroglyphs were constructed of phonetic elements and spelled-out words. Despite the essential core of truth in Knorosov's argument, however, other aspects of it were riddled with errors. Furthermore, living as he did in the Soviet Union under the shadow of Stalinism, Knorosov had prudently prefaced his argument with an attack on Western bourgeois scholarship. This preface infuriated Eric Thompson, who was not only the leader of the logograph school of Maya glyph interpretation, but also a deeply conservative man. In his treatise, Knorozov mistakenly described a Maya rendition of a deer as a jaguar, and Thompson retaliated with a stinging rebuff referring to Knorosov's "Marxist-Leninist jaguar."

Owing in part to Thompson's scorn and in part to Knorosov's own obscurity, Knorosov's arguments were all but ignored by Western scholars. As a result it took several more breakthroughs before Mayanists began to absorb Knorosov's theories. A corollary of the then-prevalent theory of the Maya as peaceful stargazers was that Maya hieroglyphic inscriptions were entirely concerned with calendrical observations and had nothing to do with the achievements or ambitions of individual Maya. As Eric Thompson put it in 1950, "To add details of war or peace, of marriage or giving in marriage, to the solemn roll call of the periods of time is as though a tourist were to carve his initials on Donatello's David."

Nevertheless, in 1958 an independent Mexican scholar, Heinrich Berlin, pointed out that certain glyphs around the rim of a tomb deep inside the Temple of the Inscriptions in the ancient Maya city of Palenque also occurred on a panel of glyphs on the temple facade above. Berlin argued that these glyphs referred to historical rulers of Palenque; shortly afterward, he proposed that another series of glyphs, which he called emblem glyphs, alluded to specific Maya city-states. Four years later, an American architectural artist named Tatiana Proskouriakoff went back over some detailed drawings she had made of a series of stelae (inscribed stone monuments) in the ancient Maya city of Piedras Negras and noticed that the dates on the stelae fell into patterns corresponding to human life spans. Within each life span, moreover, were further recurrent patterns of glyphs; these, she theorized, corresponded to historical events— events such as an accession or a taking of captives. Proskouriakoff argued that the recurrent glyphs were, in effect, verbs, and that the combination of these verbs with Heinrich Berlin's nouns implied historical subjects—i.e., Maya rulers and Maya nobility writing about their own activities.

At the time she wrote her Piedras Negras paper, Proskouriakoff was at the Carnegie Institution in Washington, where she was a colleague of Eric Thompson's. The epigrapher Peter Mathews tells the story that Proskouriakoff showed Thompson her Piedras Negras paper before it was published. Thompson, whose word was the word of God in the world of Maya scholars, read it and told her that what she was saying couldn't possibly be true. There was no historical element to the glyphs. Overnight, however, he changed his mind. He found Proskouriakoff the next day, apologized for his erroneous judgment, and told her that what she was arguing made perfect sense.

In retrospect, it is hard to understand how radical Proskouriakoff's proposal seemed at the time. Despite his gracious apology, Thompson never really accepted the historical argument, nor was he alone in his conviction. The supposed peacefulness of the Maya had been a source of solace for a whole generation of scholars weary of wars, depressions, and revolutions. People both inside and outside the scholarly community wanted to believe in the peaceful Maya, and although the theory asked the ancient Maya to be unlike anyone else in history, it died hard. Thus it was not for another decade that the combined arguments of Knorosov, Berlin, and Proskouriakoff came into their own.

The event at which this took place was a landmark December 1973 Mayanists' conference in the ancient city of Palenque. On the final afternoon of the conference, most of the participants went on an excursion to a nearby Maya site. Three, however, stayed behind. The three were Linda Schele, a painter from Alabama who had arrived in Palenque three years before and had become obsessed with the site; Peter Mathews, a long-haired undergraduate from the University of Calgary who had spent most of his savings to make his first trip to Palenque and, in four notebooks, had copied every glyph ever recorded there; and Floyd Lounsbury, Sterling Professor of Anthropology at Yale and then one of the world's leading Maya epigraphers. Schele and Mathews wanted to try to construct a dynastic history, combining their own encyclopedic knowledge of the site with Heinrich Berlin's ruler glyphs and Proskouriakoff's event glyphs. No one had ever done such a thing before, and Lounsbury was at first skeptical. But gradually he was drawn in. By four in the afternoon, the three epigraphers had identified all the Palenque kings between A.D. 612 and 783, along with their birth and accession dates. They pasted up their findings on the walls of the conference room and presented them to the other conference participants at dinner that night. Their presentation was greeted with a stunned silence and then wild applause. The ancient Maya were speaking again.

I decided I wanted to visit Palenque, and in the company of someone knowledgeable. So when I heard that Nick Hopkins and Kathryn Josserand, well-known linguists and epigraphers from Austin, Texas, were in San Cristóbal and planning to drive from there to Palenque, which lies on the edge of the Coastal plain, about seventy miles south of the Gulf of Mexico, I asked if I could go along. Nick and

Kathryn are experts in Chol Maya, the language of a small but historically significant Maya group who have lived in the hills above Palenque since they were removed to there during the Conquest but whose ancestors were once the dominant force throughout the whole of the Classic Maya lowlands. "It's the people who know the modern Maya languages who are now making the most significant contributions to the understanding of Maya glyphs," Kathryn explained just a little immodestly.

As we angled our way over a series of descending ridges, gradually dropping down out of the highland oak-and-pine forests into the hot country below, I talked with Kathryn and Nick about the modern Chols and how, if Chol had once been the language of the whole of the Classic Maya lowlands, the present-day Chol had come to be concentrated in a small area above Palenque.

Kathryn explained that it wasn't quite so simple. The ancestral form of Chol was referred to as "Cholan," and it was Cholan that the Classic Maya spoke.

"During the collapse of Classic Maya culture there was a severe population decline across the Cholan area. Previously unified populations became isolated enough from each other so that over time they evolved different languages. Modern Chol is just one of those evolutions. Eventually Chol and the other modern Cholan-derived languages diverged sufficiently so that speakers of one could no longer understand speakers of another."

Nick, who was driving, said that in the century prior to the Conquest many highland Maya towns had begun trading with the Aztecs, and that Nahuatl, the language of the Aztecs, became a lingua franca on the western edge of the Maya area. Nahuatl was spoken by the elite of each Maya town and bridged the differences between the Maya languages.

"This was so much the case that the sixteenth-century friars in Mexico City gave serious consideration to making Nahuatl, not Spanish, the administrative language of New Spain. In considering this, they essentially adopted an ideology that persists in Mexico today—that Mexico City is the center of the universe and that everything else is meant to serve it."

We had been on the road for two or three hours since leaving San Cristóbal when we descended into a Chinese landscape of steep mountains, dramatic cliffs, and deep canyons. The road, which had not been good to begin with, took a turn for the worse. Potholes, washouts, eroded culverts, and landslides awaited us around every corner.

"The road is degenerating," Nick said. "It's becoming geologically active." He pointed out a tree with clusters of big-fingered leaves surrounding beanlike fruits. "Looks like it wants to be jungle. That's *guarumbo—Cecropia peltata,* or trumpetwood, the first tree to colonize damaged land."

"Kinkajou love *guarumbo* fruit," Kathryn said; kinkajou are *Potos flavus,* the only member of the raccoon family with a prehensile tail. "They climb way out on the ends of the branches to get them. The Chol word for kinkajou means 'yellow monkey.'"

We had been traveling through Tzeltal country, but shortly after we spotted the *guarumbo* tree we ascended a steep ridge and looked down over a wide valley drained by a winding, twenty- or thirty-foot-wide river.

"That's the Tulijá," Kathryn said, "which means 'rabbit river' in Chol. It's the boundary between the Tzeltals and the Chols."

Along the river Brahman cattle grazed amid the blackened, buttressed stumps of what had once been jungle trees. White egrets were poking for insects in the spiky grass around the cattle's hooves.

Kathryn explained that at the time of the Conquest most of the Chols lived farther east, deep in what is now the Lacandón jungle. The Spanish knew the Chols as Lacandóns, a name derived from the words Lacam Tun, "great rock," the name of a fortress in the middle of Lake Miramar, a remote jungle lake. The Chols were unyielding in their opposition to the Spanish and for years after the Conquest continued raiding the Christianized towns around the periphery of the jungle. The Spanish finally decided that the only way to pacify the area was to depopulate the jungle altogether.

"They did this both by force and by persuasion, as was their custom," Nick said. "The force was a military incursion. The persuasion was a single, unarmed Dominican friar, Pedro Lorenzo de la Nada, who went into the jungle alone, lived with the Lacandón Chols, learned their language, converted them to Christianity, and persuaded them to move to the Tumbalá Hills above Palenque. From there, they've gradually expanded back down into the lowland area we're now entering. The irony, of course, is this is where their ancestors lived when they built Palenque more than a thousand years ago."

On the other side of the Tulijá we passed a group of Chol men walking home along the side of the road, returning from the fields. They had machetes on their shoulders and were wearing the uniform of all lowland male Chols—black rubber boots, a shoulder bag, a cheap, long-sleeved synthetic shirt, and a straw hat. I observed that they looked a lot less Indian than the colorfully dressed Maya around San Cristóbal.

"But they *are* Indian," Kathryn said. "A lot of them don't speak anything but Chol."

"They look just like the Classic period friezes we'll see at Palenque," Nick said.

"Except that they don't flatten their foreheads," Kathryn added, referring to the Maya nobility's practice of binding the foreheads of their infants to give them their distinctive profiles.

Not long afterward we reached the area outside Palenque where Kathryn and Nick had done their linguistic studies. Nick suggested we stop at one of the Chol *ejidos,* collective farms that the Mexican government has been granting to landless peasants since the Revolution. Nick explained that *ejidos* were the means by which the Chols had expanded out of the limited land area granted them by *Fray* (Friar) Pedro and the colonial authorities.

At a hand-painted sign that read BELISARIO DOMÍNGUEZ (the town was named for a Chiapas senator and proponent of free speech gunned down during the early years of the Revolution), Nick turned onto a dirt road. One side of the road was low forest thick with an understory of bird-of-paradise flowers. On the other side was a cornfield enclosed with a fence of Spanish dagger cacti.

"A winter crop," Nick said, looking at the corn. "It would freeze in the highlands—and down here it might not get enough rain, but it's worth a try."

It was approaching dusk when our Volkswagen van lurched down Belisario Domínguez' single, rutted, street. We turned around in the yard of the lemon-yellow cinder-block schoolhouse. One of the walls displayed a portrait of Belisario himself—starched collar, goatee, pince-nez, the very picture of a turn-of-the-century Mexican intellectual. It seemed appropriate to find him immortalized here, the welfare of impoverished, deracinated Indians having been one of the prime issues of the Mexican Revolution.

Driving back out of town, we pulled up in front of a bunch of metal-roofed shacks clustered around what looked like a family compound. Each of the houses was raised above the collective mud yard on its own stone foundation. I thought of the often-made point that all Mesoamerican temples were essentially magnifications of just this kind of house—a simple rectangular dwelling on a flat stone mound.

A group of Chol were gathered in the yard around a small, red, hand-powered mill.

"A coffee-cleaning machine," Nick noted.

We got out to take a look. At one end of the mill, coffee beans, looking like giant cranberries, were being poured into a hopper. At the other, after some strenuous hand cranking, they emerged looking like white, slightly flattened peanuts. A group of pigs were contentedly chewing on the residual pulp. No doubt they'd be awake for weeks.

The Chols stared, astonished, as we stepped out of the van. We might as well have dropped from Mars. Nevertheless, they courteously invited us into the yard. The men were shirtless. The women wore standard Chol issue: lustrous high-waisted dresses with puffed sleeves, decorative hair clips, mounds of glass bead necklaces, and ornate earrings.

Nick and Kathryn produced a Polaroid camera and, like seasoned diplomats, began taking photographs and handing them to their subjects. After we had each cranked the coffee mill for a while, we got back in the car and drove out of Belisario Domínguez. Behind us, we could see the Chols admiring their Polaroid portraits. Nick chuckled to himself.

"They'll be the envy of the whole town tomorrow," he said. "Someone will practice witchcraft on them."

We spent that night in the town of Palenque and headed out to the ruins early the next morning. The ancient city of Palenque, five or six miles from the modern town, is one of the most beautiful in the Maya region. Located just where the first wave of mountains rises out of the Gulf plain, the central city once covered at least four square miles and was the capital of a kingdom that may once have had fifty thousand subjects. Very little "dirt archaeology" has been done at Palenque. The city has had no systematic site surveys and only one probe into a major pyramid interior, but one of the reasons that Palenque is so well known (and one of the reasons it has been the site of so many glyph-reading breakthroughs) is that its two greatest kings left unusually articulate and unusually complete hieroglyphic accounts of their reigns. These two kings were Pacal, "Shield," who ruled the city from the age of twelve in A.D. 615 until his death at eighty in 683, and his son Chan Bahlum, "Serpent Jaguar," who ruled from then until his own death in 702. Pacal's and Chan Bahlum's buildings still dominate the site, and thanks to their hieroglyphs, and to those of several later inheritors of their hieroglyphic fluency, epigraphers now have identified sixteen generations of Palenque kings and queens who reigned between 431 and 799. But that's not all: From reading the king lists against iconographical representations, Mayanists have been able to infer the ideology that formed the Maya worldview at the time.

As I walked into the central plaza with Kathryn and Nick, the sun had just crested the steep, jungle-covered mountains. Parrots were screaming from the treetops and a heavy dew was beginning to burn off the grass. On our right, Pacal's Temple of the Inscriptions loomed a hundred feet overhead, its nine stone terraces reflecting the nine levels of the Maya underworld. On the left, a wide stairway rose to the low facade of the Palace, the dwelling place of generations of Palenque kings and queens. Ahead, on the periphery of a natural amphitheater ringed by steep hills, sat the three temples of Chan

Bahlum's Cross Group—the Temples of the Cross, the Foliated Cross, and the Sun—each one sitting on top of an as-yet-unexcavated pyramid.

The glyphic inscriptions on the three temples of the Cross Group make it clear that each of the temples represented a different aspect of Chan Bahlum's kingly obligations. Because of this, glyphers feel that the Cross Group conveys an unusually good picture of how Maya rulers saw their place in the cosmos. While Kathryn climbed to the Temple of the Foliated Cross, the temple describing Chan Bahlum's obligations to ensure the agricultural fertility of his subjects' land, Nick and I scrambled up a steep, stony path to the Temple of the Cross, which commemorates Chan Bahlum's accession and ancestors.

Like the other two temples of the Cross Group, the Temple of the Cross is a compact structure that sits atop its pyramid on a raised stone platform perhaps thirty by forty feet. The facade is interrupted by three doors. Overhead, a low mansard roof slopes up toward a roof comb, covered with the remains of sculpted stucco that had once depicted the entire temple as the ornate head of a Cauac Monster, also known as a *witz* monster—*witz* being the ancient Maya word for mountain. The temple doors, Nick explained, were the Cauac Monster's mouth. Because they led into the interior of the *symbolic* mountain, they were regarded as caves and thus as symbolic entrances to the underworld.

We entered through the center door into the temple's vaulted antechamber. The back wall was pierced by three more doors. The middle one led us into an inner sanctum—a tiny room, perhaps eight by twelve feet—that Nick said was referred to hieroglyphically as the *pib na,* the "underground sweat lodge." In the *pib na,* the most important ceremonies took place.

"The name of the Temple of the Cross refers to a carved limestone panel which used to be fastened to this back wall," Nick said. "It's since been removed to Mexico City, but it shows two figures, one full sized and one two-thirds sized, facing each other across a large, leafy cross. The cross is sprouting from the head of a sun god, marked on one side with signs of day, and on the other with signs of night."

He explained that the larger of the two figures, on the eastern side of the cross, was Chan Bahlum dressed in a simple white loin-cloth. The fact that he was wearing only a loincloth indicated that he had not yet become king. The smaller figure, on the western side of the cross, represented either the young Chan Bahlum, or Pacal returned from the dead. There was debate on the issue. In either case, the small figure was reaching over the cross, offering a scepter to the large figure. The scepter displayed the same sun sign that marked the deity head below the cross.

"Now look at this," Nick said, backing me out into the antechamber again. He pointed to two full-sized figures on panels mounted on opposite *pib na* doorjambs. "We know from dates that the action you see on the outer doorjamb panels takes place ten days after the action depicted on the panels inside *pib na*."

On the antechamber doorjambs, Chan Bahlum's figure had switched from the eastern to the western side of the door. He was now magnificently dressed as a Maya king, with an elaborate feath-ered headdress, a pectoral, a royal belt, and ceremonial sandals. He was also now holding the sun scepter that was being offered to him in the *pib na*. On the opposite doorjamb stood a stooped old man. He had goggle-eyes and was smoking a tobacco cigar wrapped in corn husks. A jaguar pelt was slung over his back, and a supernatural owllike bird was perched on his enormous hat. This strange figure was one of the principal underworld gods, a deity referred to only as "God L," because hieroglyph readers don't yet know his correct name.

"What happens between the inner panel and the outer door-jambs," Nick explained, "is Chan Bahlum's accession. Between the inner and outer panels Chan Bahlum has accepted the sun scepter, a symbol of royal authority, made a ten-day transforming trip through the underworld, and been reborn as Palenque's new king. Maya kings were addressed as mah k'ina—'great sun lord.' Chan Bahlum has become Mah K'ina Chan Bahlum."

* * *

What Nick had just shown me—the image of a Maya King trans-forming himself into a symbolic sun, traveling through the under-world, and being reborn as the guarantor of his people's well-being, is now thought of as perhaps *the* central dynamic of ancient Maya life. Linda Schele and others have pointed out that this dynamic has an echo in modern-day Maya villages, where, during healing cere-monies, shamans pray at the mouths of caves in order to enter the realm of the Earthlord and reclaim lost parts of their clients' souls.

That ancient Maya kings made such journeys—at least in ritual terms—is indisputable. The question of how they conceived of these journeys is another matter. However, thanks to a book known as the Popul Vuh, the "Book of Council," (or, as some call it, the "Book of Time") Mayanists have some idea. The Popul Vuh is an extraordi-nary colonial-era document written between 1554 and 1558 in a Spanish alphabet version of Quiché Maya, the language of the most powerful group of Conquest-era Guatemalan Maya. Judging from internal allusions, the Popul Vuh seems previously to have been transcribed from a concealed hieroglyphic text and, as such, is per-haps the best argument that ancient Maya books were far more than just almanacs. It contains a body of mythology that Mayanists believe was central to the whole belief system of the Classic period. The Yale art historian Michael Coe compares it to the Ramayana and Mahabharata of Hindu literature, to the *Iliad* and the *Odyssey,* the Norse sagas, the mythic cycles of the kings of early Ireland, and writes that "just as the gods and semidivine kings of the Hindu epics provided charters for the nascent royal houses of India, so the doings of Hunahpu and Xbalanque [the Popul Vuh heroes] would have been the paradigm for new elites in southeastern Mesoamerica."

The Popul Vuh contains five sections. The opening describes the creation of the present world, and the two concluding sections con-tain the history of the Quiché people. But the middle two sections—the heart of the book—tell the story of the journey of Hunahpu and Xbalanque, the Hero Twins, into the underworld and back. In a nut-shell, the central story goes as follows: The Hero Twins are players of the Maya ball game. Their playing on the surface of the earth annoys the Lords of the Underworld (the Quiché word is Xibalba, the "place of fear and trembling"). The Lords of Xibalba invite the Hero Twins to a game. The Hero Twins accept, entering Xibalba through a deep crevice in the earth. The Xibalbans have already tricked and sacrificed the Hero Twins' father and uncle and they hope to do the same thing to Hunahpu and Xbalanque, but the Twins are aware of the Xibalbans' intentions, and repeatedly outwit their hosts. Finally, the Twins permit the underworld lords to catch them, grind their bones—"just as corn is refined into flour"—and drop them in a river.

The Xibalbans think they've finally defeated the Twins, but the Twins first become catfish and are then reborn as humans after five days. They disguise themselves as vagabond performers and make their way back to the courts of Xibalba. Their special act involves a trick by which they kill themselves and then bring themselves back to life. The lords are fascinated. They ask the vagabonds, whom they don't recognize, to perform the trick on a bystander:

"Then they took hold of a human sacrifice.

"And they held up a human heart on high.

"And they showed its roundness to the lords ... and now that person was brought right back to life. His heart was overjoyed when he came back to life and the lords were amazed."

At the Lords' request, the vagabond Twins then sacrifice a dog and bring it back to life:

"That dog was really happy when he came back to life. Back and forth he wagged his tail when he came back to life."

Finally, the Lords of Death can stand it no longer: "Do it to us! Sacrifice us!" they say to the disguised Hero Twins.

The Hero Twins oblige the Lords of Death by sacrificing them, but they then refuse to bring them back to life. The other Xibalbans beg for mercy. In response, the Twins enjoin the Xibalbans from interfering with the mortal world except in the case of "the guilty, the violent, the wretched, the afflicted," and then banish the rest of the inhabitants of Xibalba to the bottom of a deep canyon. Afterward, they rescue their father and uncle and ascend "straight into the sky," where they become celestial bodies: Hunahpu, most likely the sun, and Xbalanque, possibly Venus (although the issue is debated).

"Such was the defeat of the rulers of Xibalba," the passage concludes. "The boys accomplished it only through wonders, only through self-transformation" (all from the recent translation by Dennis Tedlock).

It is impossible to know how directly the story described in the Popul Vuh, a sixteenth-century Quiché document, reflected the imagination of the eighth-century Cholan kings of Palenque. Judging from the iconography of funerary ceramics—which tend to show underworld scenes, many featuring twins and some directly depicting Popul Vuh incidents—the connections seem to be strong. The thinking now is that the Popul Vuh is probably a significant fragment of a much larger corpus of Classic-era mythology but that the central journey it describes—that in which the Hero Twins descend into the Underworld and outwit the Lords of Death—is a journey that all Maya Kings symbolically emulated.

I wandered back into the *pib na* and wondered what it was like for Chan Bahlum to make such a ritual journey thirteen hundred years before. The walls would have been painted in lurid polychrome. The air would have been thick with incense, and Chan Bahlum, having fasted and let blood, would have been surrounded by priests, hidden from his subjects by curtains and wooden doors. Linda Schele has argued that whenever the membrane that separated the living world from the underworld was breached, as Chan Bahlum would have done when making a ritual journey into the underworld, a potent spiritual residue was left behind. She describes the points at which this breaching took place as "power points" and says that the residual energy is one of the reasons the Maya built their pyramids one on top of another. The space had become permanently sacred.

But Schele has also argued the energy released by such spiritual breaching also had a physical manifestation, which, at Palenque at least, was glyphically referred to as a *wacah chan,* literally a "raised-up sky." The *wacah chan* is the life force created when the underworld and the living world are joined, and it is cabable of manifesting itself in different symbolic forms. The most usual form was a cross, a coincidence that delighted many an early friar. In the case of Chan

Bahlum's *pib na,* the *wacah chan* is represented by the leafy cross that was fastened to the back wall and across which Chan Bahlum is shown accepting the sun scepter from his father, Pacal. The cross, in other words, symbolized the life force created when Chan Bahlum returned from his journey into the underworld. On a more general level, however, the *wacah chan* is also what Mayanists refer to as the World Tree, the *Ceiba pentandra,* the giant rain forest tree that the Maya considered to be at the center of the world. The *Ceiba* grows to a height of 140 feet and can have a trunk diameter of eight feet. Certain *Ceiba* species have blood-red sap.

What the World Tree meant to the Maya is clear in the significance of the World Tree's glyphic name "raised-up sky." The reference is to the original creation of the world, an act recapitulated each time the membrane between the physical and spiritual world was breached. At the dawn of the present era the world was a featureless primordial sea, a place without sun, wind, rain, or the passage of time. Only when the World Tree came into existence was the sky raised up and the underworld depressed. Only then was the space created within which the sun could begin its rounds. Only then did human time begin.

I glanced out of the *pib na* and spotted Nick examining a block of glyphs carved into a panel on the antechamber wall. He pointed to a single glyph containing a shieldlike emblem.

"That's Pacal's glyph," he said. "Just a few years ago, glyphers thought this temple was Pacal's, but that was because they only recognized his glyph. Now they can read the remainder of the text and what it actually says is 'son of Pacal,' in other words, Chan Bahlum."

Nick explained that these particular glyphs were part of another larger panel that had been removed to Mexico City. The panel traced Chan Bahlum's ancestors all the way back to the original gods: the First Father and the First Mother (whom glyphers refer to as Lady Beastie). The Maya believed that the "present creation," the period of historic time that started when the current creation was differentiated out of the primordial ooze, began on the Maya date of 4 Ahau 8 Cumku, or August 13, 3114 B.C. Lady Beastie and the First Father had been born during a previous creation, one of three others. This, in Maya eyes, endowed them with great power.

From Lady Beastie and the First Father, Nick explained, Chan Bahlum's tablet skipped to their children, the so-called Palenque Triad, who were the patron saints of Palenque and were born in 2360 B.C., 754 years into the present creation. After the Palenque Triad, the tablet mentioned the birth 1,367 years later (993 B.C.) of a mythical Palenque ruler from the Olmec period named U Kix Chan. U Kix Chan served as a bridge to historical time. The next of Chan Bahlum's ancestors mentioned is Bahlum Kuk, the first historical ruler of Palenque, a king who acceded in A.D. 431. The glyphic panel then traced all the historical kings of Palenque from Bahlum Kuk to Chan Bahlum—but not what Nick called, "our Chan Bahlum," rather a namesake who was Chan Bahlum's great-great-great-grandfather.

From the Temple of the Cross, Nick and I walked through a patch of forest to the top of the Temple of the Foliated Cross, where we caught up with Kathryn. The Temple of the Foliated Cross is architecturally identical to the Temple of the Cross, and I went into the *pib na* to examine its central panel, which in this case is still attached to the back wall. Like its Temple of the Cross counterpart, the Foliated Cross panel shows large and small figures facing each other from opposite sides of the *wacah chan*, but this time the *wacah chan* is represented as a corn plant sprouting human heads, a reference to the Maya belief that the original humans were composed of corn and water. (In the Popul Vuh, the corn sprouts only after the Hero Twins defeat the Lords of Death.) On the Foliated Cross panel, moreover, the *wacah chan* is shown growing not out of the head of a sun god but out of the head of a lily-pad monster with froglike eyes. The Maya believed the surface of the water to be another entrance to the underworld and saw the lily pad as another symbol of the fertility that resulted from the intersection of the world of the living and the underworld. The Maya referred to their kings not just as *mah k'ina,* "great sun lord," but also *ah nab,* "he of the lily pad."

As I was looking at the figures on the Foliated Cross panel, Nick wandered in and pointed out a series of calendar glyphs commemorating the dedication of the Cross Group over a four-day period in July 690. The residents of ancient Palenque, he explained, identified the Palenque Triad (the city's patron gods, the children of Lady Beastie and the First Father) with certain planets. The dedication of the Cross Group had been timed to take place during a spectacular triple planetary conjunction. Leading up to it, Jupiter and Saturn sat unmoving on the horizon for forty days. Mars then moved into the same space to form a triad. Finally, the moon, whom the Maya associated with Lady Beastie, rose in the same sector of the sky. The Maya apparently interpreted this conjunction as Lady Beastie being reunited with her three children, the Palenque Triad. At the same time that this celestial reunion was taking place, Chan Bahlum had ritually brought the three gods of the Palenque Triad into human space animating the *wacah chans* of his three new temples.

"It must have been quite a party," said Nick.

The morning was getting on, and in the interest of seeing Pacal's tomb before the tourists packed in, we skipped Chan Bahlum's Temple of the Sun, with its references to his martial prowess, and headed back to the Temple of the Inscriptions. Although Pacal ruled Palenque from the year 615, when he was twelve, he built nothing of his own until his mother, Lady Zac Kuk, died in 640, twenty-five years later. What this says about Pacal's relationship to his mother is anyone's guess, but from 640 until his own death in 683, Pacal built with a vengeance. He experimented with thinner supporting walls and different vaults and gave his structures more interior space and more light than any earlier buildings. His crowning architectural achievement, however, begun when he was in his seventies, was his own tomb, the Temple of the Inscriptions. The Temple of the Inscriptions became instantly famous in 1952, when the Mexican archaeologist Alberto Ruz Lhullier discovered a hidden, rubble-filled staircase descending eighty-five feet down into the temple's interior. At the bottom, Ruz Lhullier discovered a vaulted chamber that contained Pacal's grave. Unlike most Maya pyramids, which are built one on top of another so that each covers—and is more magnificent than—its predecessor, Pacal's equally massive pyramid was built from scratch. His remains lie inside a huge limestone sarcophagus at the pyramid's very base, five feet below the level of the outside plaza floor.

As we walked, toward the Temple of the Inscriptions, Kathryn described some peculiar medical conditions that ran in Pacal's family. One was agromegaly, a hormone disorder resulting in excessive growth of the soft tissues. Pacal's mother, Lady Zac Kuk, is routinely portrayed with swollen, clubby fingers, and Pacal himself is thought to have had a clubfoot. Another of the royal conditions was polydactyly: being born with too many digits. In several places Chan Bahlum is shown with six toes on one of his feet. He may also have had six fingers on one of his hands. Kathryn told me the Maya considered such deformities divine.

"This is a representation of Pacal presenting six-year-old Chan Bahlum as his heir designate," she said, noting a badly eroded frieze when we reached the top of the Temple of the Inscriptions. "Pacal is shown holding Chan Bahlum in his arms while Chan Bahlum's six-toed foot metamorphoses into a serpent, a symbol of both divinity and royalty."

"The heir designation ceremony took five days," Nick added, "and culminated on the summer solstice."

Kathryn and I headed into the temple interior. On the back wall of the antechamber were two huge blocks of glyphs. On the center panel of an inner room was a third. I knew that altogether in this temple there were 640 glyphs and that they constituted, after the hieroglyphic stair in the ancient city of Copán, the longest series of glyphs in all Mayadom. Like the glyph panels in Chan Bahlum's Temple of the Cross, they are largely about Pacal's ancestors. Looking at them, I thought of Linda Schele's argument that the reason Pacal and Chan Bahlum went to such lengths to describe their ancestry was that they'd had trouble establishing the legitimacy of their claims to the Palenque throne. The problem stemmed from the fact that the Maya succession was patrilineal, but that Pacal had inherited the throne through his mother, Lady Zac Kuk, Lady "White

Quetzal." On his Temple of the Inscriptions panels, Pacal addressed this problem through an ingenious sleight of hand. Like Chan Bahlum, Pacal traced his ancestry all the way back to Lady Beastie and the First Father and, also like Chan Bahlum, implied that Lady Beastie was the prime creator of the present world. However, Pacal took the logic one step further. The glyph he used to represent his mother, Lady Zac Kuk, was the same he used for Lady Beastie, thus implying that his own matrilinear succession paralleled an original matrilinear creation.

From the temple's inner chamber, a stairway descends sixty-seven narrow, damp, limestone steps to Pacal's crypt far below. As Kathryn and I started down, she paused to show me a stone tube running up the side of the staircase.

"That what's referred to as the psychoduct," she said. "It's represented as a snake, and runs all the way down to the crypt. It allowed Pacal's spirit, after his death, to communicate with the living."

Pacal's crypt is thirty feet long, thirteen feet wide, and twenty-three feet high. After Pacal's burial in the year 683, the door was plastered over, five captives were sacrificed, and the staircase was carefully backfilled with tons of rock. So densely packed was this rock that it took Ruz Lhullier three seasons to remove it all. All his work was rewarded, however: he found Pacal's tomb just as it had been left almost thirteen hundred years earlier. Pacal's bones were wrapped in the remains of a red burial shroud (red is the color of the east, the direction of the reborn sun). His face was covered with a mask of jade, white shell, and obsidian. He wore a cape, earflares, and rings. A royal belt of jade with flint pendants lay on top of the sarcophagus.

The most striking feature of the crypt, however, is the sarcophagus lid: a single piece of limestone 12½ feet long, seven feet wide, and ten inches thick, and carved with one of the most wonderful images in Maya art. Pacal is falling backward down the trunk of a giant *wacah chan* growing out of the open maws of the underworld. He is weightless. His hair, his loincloth, and his pectoral are all floating away from his body. Just below him, also falling into the underworld, is the head of the same sun deity being handed to Chan

Bahlum across the central panel of the Temple of the Cross. At the instant of his death Mah K'ina Pacal is depicted slipping, like the setting sun, into the underworld.

Magnificent as the Cross Group had been, it paled before Pacal's grave. I mentioned my impression to Kathryn.

"You have to remember," she said, as we climbed back up from the crypt, "that Pacal ruled for over sixty years while Chan Bahlum ruled for less than twenty."

"What happened after Chan Bahlum's death?" I asked.

"Chan Bahlum was followed by Kan Xul, 'Precious Animal,' his younger brother," Kathryn said. "Although by A.D. 702, when Chan Bahlum died and Kan Xul became king, Kan Xul was no longer young. He was, in fact, almost sixty. We don't know much about him, even when to end his reign. The last mention of him at Palenque is in the year 710, eight years after his accession. What we do know is that there's a carving at the neighboring site of Tonina which shows him bound as a captive. The carving bears the date August thirtieth, 711. Poor man, he was close to seventy when he was captured."

We descended the Temple of the Inscriptions, crossed the plaza, and advanced up the front steps of the Palace, the residential complex of Palenque's royal family. The Palace is a low sprawling compound with several courtyards, a three-story tower, and even plumbing. Kathryn and Nick led the way into the interior and stopped in front of a low building with a mansard-style stone roof that had been carved to look like thatch. This was House E, a venerable and sacred building that had once belonged to Pacal's grandmother, Lady Kanal Ikal. House E was also known as the "white house": in a city that was largely painted red with polychrome detail, it bears some sixty coats of white paint.

Accession ceremonies took place on the arcaded porch of House E and an oval tablet on its wall depicts Pacal being anointed king. Seated cross-legged on a double-headed jaguar throne, he is receiving the Palenque crown—referred to as the "drum-major headdress" by glyph readers—from his mother, Lady Zac Kuk, who is seated on the floor next to him. The jaguar throne apparently remained on the porch of House E until the late eighteenth century, when Captain Antonio del Rió, commissioned by the Spanish crown to investigate accounts of a lost Indian city at Palenque, smashed it to bits while searching for gold.

From House E, we wandered back to the courtyard of the captives, so-called because of its oversized carvings of prisoners, hands clasping opposite shoulders in gestures of submission. The courtyard of the captives is thought to have been a receiving area. It is sunk below the porches that surround it, and its steps, steep to begin with, become progressively steeper as you descend. The effect makes you feel progressively smaller and humbler. From the bottom of the courtyard I looked up at a crumbling frieze of seated kings around the roof entablatures. I could still see the remains of bright colors where the friezes had been sheltered from the elements.

"There was a lot more paint on the walls before the eruption of El Chichón volcano in 1982," Nick said. "The eruption covered Palenque with tons of white ash. When it rained afterward, the ash acted like scouring powder. Fortunately, Merle Greene Robertson had just completed a detailed documentation of all of the artwork at Palenque."

We walked out of the back side of the Palace and down to the banks of the Otolum, a stream running under the central plaza through a vaulted, thirteen-hundred-year-old aqueduct. Nick picked some leaves from a shrub covered with panicles of white flowers and held them out for me to smell. They had a peppermint scent.

"The shrub is from the genus *Pepperonia*," he said. "Around here the leaves are referred to as *momo* leaves, but in Oaxaca they're called *hierba santa* and are used to flavor yellow *mole* sauce."

Farther downstream we sat down around the edges of a shaded pool. "This is known as the Queen's Bath," Kathryn said. "Down here in the late afternoons I've seen trogons sitting on branches over the water." Trogons are lustrously plumed tropical birds that include among their number the beautiful long-tailed Quetzal.

Nick pulled a snail shell out of the pool.

"A *xute* snail," he said. "The Chols boil them with *momo* leaves.

There's a Chol verb just for the sound you make sucking the snails out of their shells."

On our way out of the ruins we came upon a group of Maya men dressed in white smocks and with hair down to their waists. They were selling bows and arrows. These were modern Lacandóns, a small group of Yucatec-speaking Maya whose ancestors drifted into the Lacandón jungle from the east after Pedro Lorenzo de la Nada convinced the Chols to leave the forest. The Chols had been ruled by kings and had built cities and jungle fortresses. The successor Lacandóns lived at a more primitive level, avoiding outsiders and camping out in family compounds in the middle of hidden milpas. In the last thirty years, however, these once-isolated Yucatec speakers have been beseiged by outsiders: missionaries, logging contractors, filmmakers, and spiritual seekers. In Spanish, I asked one of the Lacandóns if he was from Nahá, the last of the non-Christian communities.

"No," he responded sarcastically, "I'm from California."

We watched as a hippie with baggy white pants, a bright Guatemalan vest, and a purple kerchief around his long hair sat down cross-legged in the middle of the Lacandón bow-and-arrow arsenal, pulled out a bamboo flute, and began to play "The Sounds of Silence."

"That's what I'd like to hear," Kathryn said.

Nick and Kathryn wanted to return to San Cristóbal by a different route, one that would take us through the city of Villahermosa, where they wanted to spend the night. Late that afternoon we left Palenque for Villahermosa. At the edge of town we passed a low green building bearing the words CASA DE HUÉSPEDES ALICE. Underneath, in English, was the translation, HOUSE BOARDING ALICE.

Nick drove up behind a truck with the words IN GOD WE TRUST ON painted on its bumper. We followed it out onto the great flat coastal plain. After the hours we'd spent winding down from the highlands, it seemed as if we'd been launched onto an ocean. Great seas of waving savanna grass surrounded low islands of tree-shaded ranches. Brahman cattle grazed amid a spider's web network of rivers, creeks, and bayous.

"No more Maya north of Palenque," Nick said, then immediately corrected himself. "Well, maybe a few Chontals."

Nick was referring to the mysterious group of maritime Maya whose trade routes penetrated to the heart of the Classic Maya world just before the collapse and who may have been instrumental in overrunning Palenque. The Chontals, also known as the Putún Maya, had developed powerful commercial ties with Central Mexico and had adopted Central Mexican methods of military organization. The latest date so far discovered at Palenque is A.D. 799. It was found painted onto a Chontal-style pot.

We passed a town called Manatinero. A murky stream was lined with a grove of coconut palms, the bottoms of their trunks painted white as if they'd been outfitted with waders.

"There used to be manatees here," Kathryn said. "There still might be. There's an early king of Palenque whom the glyphers call Casper because his glyph looks like a ghost. The archaeologist Alfonso Morales proposed recently that the glyph might represent a manatee surfacing out of the water."

Night fell as we approached Villahermosa, capital of the state of Tabasco. The horizon was lit with the dull orange glow of oil fires. In the middle of a traffic circle we passed an immense, muscular, socialist realism–style statue of an Indian labeled TABS COOB.

"Tabs Coob is a legendary chief of the local Indians," Nick said. "He's supposed to be the namesake of Tabasco. As far as I can tell, however, he's an invention. A woman commissioned by the McIlhenny family of Louisiana to write a book on chili peppers once consulted me on the origin of the word 'Tabasco.' I searched for historical references to 'Tabs Coob,' but didn't find any. I then decided on a different approach. Most of Tabasco is in the Nahuatl area, so I consulted a Nahuatl dictionary. I found a Nahuatl noun meaning 'shell midden.' Using a combination of local spelling and the locative form, it became 'Tabasco.' That was the explanation she finally used."

We spent the night in a hotel in Villahermosa and, the next morning, drove south towards San Cristóbal on a road that followed a low swampy river. We saw a caracara, a Mexican eagle, wheeling low over a marshy lagoon. On the side of the road people were holding up strings of fish for sale. For miles we drove through a banana plantation, each bunch of green fruit already draped with its own plastic bag. Just before we reached the city of Teapa, where the mountains rise out of the coastal plain, we passed a gringo in hiking boots and shorts trudging along the side of the road. He wore a set of placards that proclaimed CRISTO VUELVE—"Christ is coming."

As I pondered this message, I thought about how the Maya have been the victims of not one but two apocalypses. The first was the ninth-century collapse, about which little is still known. The second, both more severe and less well recognized, was part of the general collapse of the New World under the impact of the Old. In 1492, the year Columbus stumbled upon the New World, an estimated eighty million indigenous people lived in the Americas. A hundred years later only ten million survived. Indian urban centers that had once compared favorably with the great cities of Spain had been destroyed, and a once proud, accomplished people had been reduced to sullen poverty.

The agent of most of this decline, however, was neither the rapaciousness of the conquistadors nor superior European military technology, but diseases that the Europeans inadvertently transported to the New World. The plague, smallpox, measles, cholera, tuberculosis, yellow fever, typhus, and typhoid all arrived with the Europeans. The indigenous people of the New World had no immunity to any of them. Epidemics raced ahead of the conquerors, halving Indian populations and halving them again before the inhabitants ever laid eyes on a Spaniard.

The Annals of the Cakchiquels, a post-Conquest document compiled by descendants of the royal family of one of the major Guatemalan Maya groups, describes the effects of one of these epidemics, which struck three years before the arrival of the Spanish:

> Great was the stench of the dead. After our fathers and grandfathers succumbed, half of the people fled to the fields. The dogs and the vultures devoured the bodies. The mortality was terrible. Your grandfathers died, and with them died the son of the king and his brother and kinsmen. So it was that we became orphans, my sons! So we

became when we were young. All of us were thus. We were born to die!

It is worth keeping in mind that these diseases had the effect they did on the New World largely because the New World was epidemiologically so isolated from the Old. In *The Columbian Exchange: Biological and Cultural Consequences of 1492,* the historian Alfred Crosby writes that the indigenous population of the Americas was "more different from the rest of mankind than any other major group of humanity." The Europeans themselves were acting as unwitting agents for a complex of diseases from Asia that, beginning with the Black Death one hundred and fifty years earlier, had devastated Europe to nearly the same degree that it did the Americas. The Europeans were merely relaying this plague to the last corners of the globe.

On the far side of Teapa, the road began to climb up a wide green valley that took us through a town called Pichucalco to Puerto Arturo, where the mountains began to close in around us. A pass or gap is called a *puerto* in Spanish, and sure enough, the valley soon became a deep canyon. A sparkling river full of boulders, rapids, and deep pools rushed along the side of the road. On the other side of a hammock bridge, a sign for an unseen *ejido* pointed up a footpath that disappeared into a cut in the mountains. At the narrowest part of the valley, we pulled the car over and walked down to the water. A kingbird, perched on a rock in the middle of the rapids, nervously flicked its brown tail. Butterflies fluttered in the wind above a cobblestone beach. Kathryn glanced down at the rocks strewn along the river bank.

"Basalt!" she exclaimed. "Granite! A geode!" She began to gather rocks.

Nick, who was looking on, said, "Kathryn has this problem— rocks call her name."

The back of the van loaded with rock samples, we drove on. The canyon opened into another wide valley. Rich green pastures stretched to a distant line of high limestone cliffs around the valley rim. It was fertile-looking land. The fence posts lining the fields had all sprouted. The farmers had been forced into mass pollarding to keep them to size.

"El Chichón was just over that ridge," Kathryn said, referring to the volcano that erupted in April of 1982, burying Palenque and much of the rest of the region in ash.

"Central American volcanoes put out lots of ash and not much lava," Nick said. "There was a major eruption of Ilopango volcano in El Salvador in 150 B.C. The ash buried the Guatemalan highlands, and some people think it forced the Cholans to migrate to the lowland forests."

"The Cholans were originally from the Guatemalan highlands then?"

"The Cholans were from the area around Alta Verapaz, in present-day Guatemala," Kathryn said. "But they had been preceded into the lowlands by Yucatec speakers, who were also originally from the Guatemalan highlands but had migrated down to the jungle at the time they'd developed maize agriculture fifteen hundred years earlier."

"That's what Classic Maya culture was," Nick said. "The Cholans brought the idea of an elite social structure, which they in turn had probably acquired from the Olmecs, an earlier culture along the Pacific coast, and fused it onto a substratum of Yucatec speakers already living in the lowlands."

We climbed through the towns of Ixtahuatán, Tapilula, and Rayón. Beyond Rayón the air turned noticeably colder. We passed a sign saying RANCHO SIBERIA, and then another saying LA SELVA NEGRA, "the Black Jungle."

"La Selva Negra is the name of this whole region," Kathryn said. "Until not too long ago, it was cloud forest."

A cloud forest is a dense high-elevation forest sustained by the moisture of constant clouds. I asked when it had been cut.

"After they put the road through," Kathryn answered, "whenever that was."

"Roads are often a factor in de-Indianizing an area," Nick said. "It's something the Indians understand. When I was doing research in Guatemala in 1964, I heard of a group of Indians above Huehuetenango who were resisting a road. An army colonel came in, lined up all the Indians, and said, 'If anyone speaks against the road, I'll cut his tongue out.' The road went through."

Near the valley ridge the land became too steep even for grazing. We snaked our way under limestone cliffs and dodged rockslides. Suddenly we were in cloud forest. Tree ferns, wild fuchsia, and bromeliads with three-foot-wide leaves crowded the sides of the road. Dense fog scudded off the ridge above us and tumbled down onto the road.

"The Tzotzils think that the Earthlord makes clouds in mountain caves," Nick said. "It's not hard to see why."

I thought of what the botanist Dennis Breedlove had told me a few months before. During the Eocene, when North America was covered with tropical flora, Chiapas and adjacent Guatemala were continental islands off its southern coast. In North America, this ancient tropical flora was almost entirely destroyed by the subsequent ice ages, but isolated examples are still to be found on Chiapas mountaintops.

"I knew Dennis when I was working in Guatemala in the midsixties," Nick said. "We went into the cloud forests above Huehuetenango together. It was the first time Dennis had been in a cloud forest and he was interested in, among other things, composites. In the United States composites are roadside herbs, shrubs, and flowers, including the goldenrod and the daisy. In the cloud forest they grow sixty feet tall. In order to identify them, he had to chop them down. I remember him quoting from his graduate school textbooks as he whacked away with his ax: 'The composites ...' *thwack* 'are typically ...' *thwack* 'herbaceous plants ...' *thwack* 'that achieve a maximum height ...' *thwack* 'of twenty to thirty feet.

"'Timber!'"

We continued climbing until suddenly we were over the top of the ridge. The landscape immediately underwent a startling transformation. In place of the cloud forests and luridly green pastures of La Selva Negra, a familiar landscape of dried cornfields interspersed with pine and oak forests rolled away before us. We were back in the highlands. A Chamula woman wearing a heavy, black wool skirt and a royal-blue shawl stood by the side of the road.

"The Chamulas pioneered this land back in the fifties," Nick said. "It was mostly forest back then. I was out here working on a survey for the University of Chicago, trying to establish the linguistic boundaries between the Tzotzils and their non-Maya neighbors to the west, the Zoques."

We drove on through Pueblo Nuevo, Jitotol, and several other towns before we finally reached Puerto Cate. At Puerto Cate the road crossed a narrow saddle between two mountains and then, just beyond a supremely ugly roadside monument consisting of a stack of intersecting concrete planes, divided into two branches. The left branch plunged down into a deep mountain valley and wound its way toward the amber-mining town of Simojovel. The right branch, which we were going to take, continued south through the towns of Bochil and Soyalo. There were views in both directions, but the one toward Simojovel was particularly spectacular. We got out of the car to take a look. Rugged ridges crossed each other at right angles. Invisible rivers had cut deep creases in the landscape.

I wandered back to look at the concrete monument. A plaque fastened to its base commemorated the completion of the Selva Negra road to Villahermosa and answered my question about the year in which the road went through—it was completed in 1974 at a cost of 274 million pesos. I walked around to the other side of the monument. Someone had painted in blood-red letters, LLANO BAMOS APERMITIT QUE ENTRE OTRO UN GRUPO CAMPEZINO. After some puzzling, and with Nick's assistance, I turned this into *"Ya no vamos a permitir que entre un otro grupo campesino.* Now we're not going to permit the entry of another peasant group."

We were in a region that I knew had been plagued by an active land war between ranchers and highland Maya, and other slogans made it evident that the painted statement was a reference to the assassination, only a week or two before, of Sebastián Perez Nuñez, a peasant leader and Socialist state deputy. The San Cristóbal papers had been full of the story. Perez was gunned down at midday in the Bochil gas station. His assailants were a landowner and his three sons, with whom Perez had had a long-standing dispute. According to the newspaper accounts, the rancher and his sons stepped out of a white pickup, pistols in hand, and shot Perez twelve times in the back. They then stepped back in their truck and drove away. The newspaper account added that Perez had long been a defender of the state's poor and that his activities had once led to his having been personally threatened by the state's governor, a former army general from a prominent ranching family. Most recently Perez Nuñez had supported Indians in a land conflict with the rancher who had shot him.

We got back into the van and drove on toward Bochil, the next town on our route. The center of town was occupied by soldiers wearing helmets and carrying automatic rifles. It was a Ladino town. There wasn't an Indian in sight. At the gas station I looked, morbidly, for blood but didn't see any. Hard-eyed men lounged outside the office.

"A tough-looking bunch," said Nick, avoiding their stares.

"It's a frontier," Kathryn said, "the Wild West."

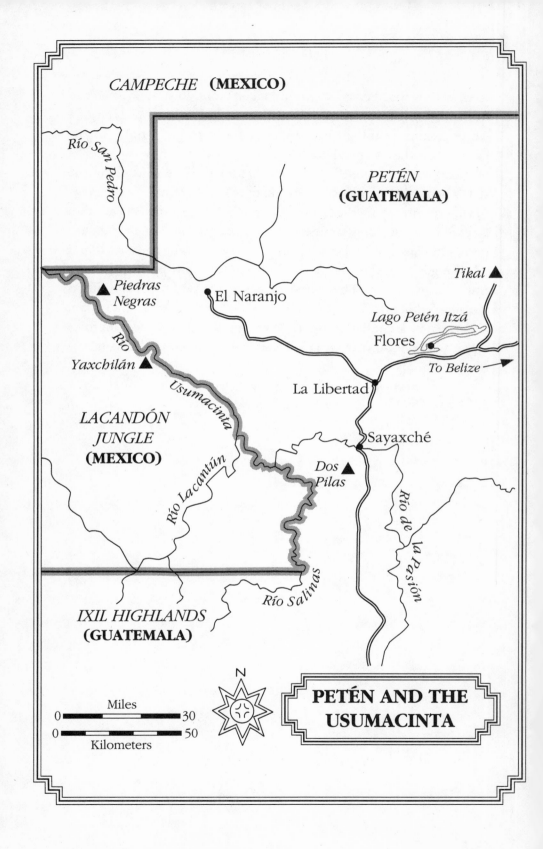

CAMPECHE **(MEXICO)**

Río San Pedro

PETÉN
(GUATEMALA)

▲ *Piedras Negras*

● El Naranjo

Tikal ▲

Lago Petén Itzá

Flores

Río Usumacinta

Yaxchilán ▲

La Libertad

To Belize →

LACANDÓN JUNGLE
(MEXICO)

Sayaxché

Río Lacantún

Dos Pilas ▲

Río de la Pasión

IXIL HIGHLANDS
(GUATEMALA)

Río Salinas

Miles
0 ————— 30

0 ————— 50
Kilometers

N

PETÉN AND THE USUMACINTA

CHAPTER 4

The Petén

At least four million Maya, more than half the total, live in Guatemala, but in the aftermath of a violent wave of repression in the early eighties, they live under the watchful eye of an army alert to every imagined nuance of subversion. Since being labeled a subversive in Guatemala is the equivalent of getting a death sentence, and since talking to an Indian might, under the wrong circumstances, be construed as subversive, I had decided not to go to Maya Guatemala until I was thoroughly on my feet in Maya Mexico.

This, at least, was the plan, but it was not to be. While in San Cristóbal I received a telephone call from an acquaintance in Guatemala, an American who worked in some mysterious capacity for the United States Agency for International Development (A.I.D.). The acquaintance, who knew of my interest in the Maya, told me that he knew of an ecologist who was taking a boat down the Usumacinta River through the rain forests where the river flows northwest along the Mexican-Guatemalan border. The Guatemalan national congress had just passed a sweeping piece of legislation designating fifteen percent of the country as a national park, and one of the parks was planned to include this stretch of the border. The problem was that no one knew what was happening there. The

Guatemalan side of the river had once been lined with cooperatives formed by landless highland Maya transplanted there by the government in the 1960's, but it had subsequently become an active guerrilla zone. In the early eighties, the army had chased most of the cooperatives out in an effort to eliminate the guerrillas' support. It was still a guerrilla zone, but there were rumors that some of the cooperative members were returning. In order to consider the question of the park, the government's Commission of the Environment, with whom this ecologist worked, needed to know what was happening along the river—at least this was the story the acquaintance gave me.

"You'll know what no one else knows!" he said enthusiastically.

I briefly wondered to myself why, of all the proposed parks, the one in guerrilla territory needed to be the first one investigated, but decided to set the question aside. The truth was that I'd been hoping to visit the Petén region in Guatemala's north, once the heartland of Classic Maya civilization, and hadn't been able to figure out how to do it. I hated to go under such strange auspices, but invitations like this didn't come easily. I could tell I was hooked. I asked about the ecologist I'd be accompanying down the river.

"His name is Santiago Billy. He's French, but he was born in Guatemala and he's married to a Guatemalan. He lives in Antigua Guatemala, which is about forty-five minutes from Guatemala City and was the capital until the late eighteenth century, when it was destroyed by one too many earthquakes. Santiago, however, used to be the director of flora and fauna for the national park around the Maya ruins at Tikal, in the Petén, the northern rain forest section of the country, and he knows the Petén better than anybody. He's been exploring it for ten years. His friends call him Petén Billy. When he's in the jungle he wears a pith helmet and a kimono with lions on it."

"Will the trip be dangerous?" I asked blandly.

"Bring your passport," my acquaintance said. "Leave your other documents behind. If you get in any trouble hold your passport in the air and shout, 'Gringo! Gringo!'" He began to laugh and hung up.

* * *

A week later I found myself in the living room of Santiago and Milena Billy's large colonial mansion a few blocks from Antigua's central square. The room was filled with modern furniture and expensive electronic equipment. The stark white walls were hung with blow pipes, arrows, and the colorfully feathered, splayed, and mounted carcass of a Petén turkey. Outside in the courtyard my belongings— a hammock, a mosquito net, a Panama hat, a few articles of clothing, and some malaria tablets—were stored in two woven maguey-fiber bags I'd bought in San Andrés Larraínzar. The plan was to take a flight early the next morning from Guatemala City to Flores, the capital of the Petén, and in preparation for the trip I was wearing my jungle clothes: a lightweight royal-blue work shirt, a pair of baggy green khakis, and some light boots.

Santiago, a small, dark, intense man, had returned from work a few moments before wearing an off-white linen sports coat and had changed *into* a suit. His wife, Milena, a stylish woman who runs a textile business, had changed into what looked like a one-of-a-kind designer dress. "Did we forget to tell you? We're going to an art opening." Milena looked at my clothing and winced. I'd be fine as I was, she assured me unconvincingly. I felt like a delegate to a forest rangers' convention.

On the way into Guatemala City, Santiago announced that he wanted to stop briefly at a friend's house, near the American Embassy. It was dusk when we arrived. The house was surrounded by a high concrete wall, rimmed with barbed wire. Santiago announced our arrival through a speaker on the street. Heavy metal gates swung open by remote control. We drove in and parked the car in a darkened courtyard between an Audi and a BMW. Snarling, snapping, and barking, six Doberman pinschers came drooling up to the car to meet us.

Milena explained that Santiago's friend was a Petén logging baron—one of the biggest in the country—and although I might think it peculiar that her husband, an ecologist, was visiting a man who was responsible for destroying as much rain forest as anyone in Guatemala, that's just the way it was.

The logger met us at the door. A bull-necked man of perhaps

forty-five, he had an angry look that was accentuated by a handlebar mustache. A tight leather jacket encased his barrel torso. Santiago introduced him as Jorge. We followed Jorge into the house, which I noticed was made entirely of exotic woods, down even to the lamp-shades, which were thin strips of mahogany veneer. Jorge's wife, Miriam, appeared wearing silk harem pants and a striped silk jacket with oversized padded shoulders. Her hair was frizzed into a wild mane. In English, she offered me a choice of Johnny Walker Red or Johnny Walker Black. When I complimented her English she explained that she'd learned it during the several years she'd spent in Toronto at a convent school from which the nuns had permitted her to leave only an hour each weekend and then only to go to a specific shopping mall.

Jorge had invited Santiago by to see a slide show about a Costa Rican door-making operation. The hook was that the door company made responsible use of Costa Rica's rain forest resources. The slide show was accompanied by a sound track, and while harps played, we watched foresters spray-painting tree trunks and using terms like "diameter at breast height." Sawmills sawed. Carpenters carpentered. Whenever there was a shot of undisturbed rain forest, the sound track swelled to the strains of "Danny Boy." In the end, we saw the shiny new doors being affixed to the fronts of ranch houses in suburban American developments.

When the show was over, Bruno, a Rottweiler with a spiked collar, let out a loud yawn. I looked over at Santiago. He seemed glazed with boredom and said it was time for us to go to the art opening. A black cloud seemed to settle over Jorge's head. He and Miriam said they'd join us at the opening later.

The opening was in an industrial-looking building downtown. The show was called "Urban Anthropology," and the paintings, fragments of faded Guatemalan advertisements given skim coats of whitewash, were by a New Jersey native who had been living in the country for six years.

The gallery was filled with beautiful people. A woman from Colombia with copper skin and screaming red lips told me that she was a dancer and a fashion model. She'd been in Guatemala for six months and although she had everything she wanted, she thought that one day she would just go out to the airport and get on a plane. "Maybe for the beach," she said, "maybe for the jungle."

A writer from *Crónica,* a weekly Guatemalan newsmagazine, told me that she wanted to introduce me to a friend of hers who was an anthropologist. "You might find it interesting," she said. "Anthropology is not a very popular subject here, but since the papers don't write about what's happening in the mountains, it's the best way to find out."

I asked why the papers didn't write about what was happening in the mountains.

"They can't," she said.

"Don't they think it's important?" I asked.

"Look," she said, "I write about economics. Before I was a writer I was an economist. The friends I worked with back then have risen to important posts. When I need a story, I call them up."

She walked away indignantly.

After a while Santiago came over and told me that we were going to a restaurant for dinner. "We" seemed to be the whole party. Santiago's car was full, so I got into another one. I wound up sitting next to a woman with cropped black hair wearing a black bowler and a horizontally striped tube dress that fell off her shoulder. As we drove off she draped her arm over my shoulder, spread her hand across my chest, and exclaimed, "*Qué pechuga!* What a breast!" Someone produced a joint. After a few puffs my neighbor began to laugh and shout with a Spanish lisp, "*Estamos volando!* We're flying!"

Our car pulled up in front of a chic Italian restaurant in the Guatemala City's tenth zone. An orange hibiscus was in bloom by the door and through a plate-glass window facing the street I could see the gleaming-white tablecloths within, each with a red carnation in a vase. I sat down opposite some Americans who lived in Panajachel, an expatriate town on Lake Atitlán. The man was a writer, at least he said he had a drawer full of unpublished novels. His hair was snow white and his eyes had the burned-blue look of someone who'd taken the hard route through the sixties. He spoke about a new book of photographs of Guatemala by the American human rights activist

Jean-Marie Simon. He volunteered that if she ever appeared in Guatemala, he, personally, would lead the lynch mob.

"Why?" I asked.

"Every photograph has a member of the army in it," he said. "It's a complete and ridiculous representation."

I said that surely something horrible and important had happened to the Maya of Guatemala, something that few people knew anything about, and that she was right in trying to communicate it.

The writer looked at me savagely. "Whole villages were massacred," he said. "No one witnessed it. If you'd witnessed it, you'd be dead."

I didn't quite get his point, but chose not to pursue it.

More and more people came in. The place got louder and louder. Wine bottles emerged from the kitchen in unending procession, soon followed by plates of squid, bowls of pasta, roasted quail.

I began talking with a tall blond woman with a very short miniskirt who introduced herself as Clara. "I don't know what I am," she told me. "I'm part Swedish, part gringa, part Guatemalan. I guess I'm the Central American woman."

Clara told me she'd grown up in Guatemala but her father had sent her to finishing school in Massachusetts, to a school called House in the Pines. After four years there she'd returned to Guatemala and her father had asked her what she had learned. "To smoke cigarettes," she'd said, and had pulled one out and lit it in front of him.

"He was appalled," she said, "but there was nothing he could do about it."

Clara said that while in the United States she'd dated a hockey and tennis star from Dartmouth. His family lived in Fairfield, Connecticut. "He pinned me," she said, "but I didn't know what being pinned meant, so I laughed at him. He was offended. Maybe I made a mistake. They were wonderful people. They had lots of money, but they didn't make a big thing about it. His family called me 'coffee bean, golden coffee bean.'"

The owner of the restaurant put on some music by Sade. People started to dance. As I continued talking with Clara, I noticed out of the corner of my eye that Jorge and Miriam had arrived. Jorge was scowling.

As the evening went on, Santiago consumed his share of wine. At close to two in the morning, he got up and began singing the Marseillaise. Everyone joined in, so, smile on his face, eyes unfocused, he sang it again. After he'd sung it a third time someone put the Sade music back on. Clara began dancing by herself. She turned to me, glared, shouted that life had to be led to the full, and, with a sweep of her arm, sent all the glasses on a table crashing to the floor. A tremendous shattering sound filled the restaurant. No one seemed particularly concerned, but I noticed the contents of a glass of red wine dribbling down the front of my forest ranger outfit. A movement on the street beyond the plate-glass window caught my eye. I looked and saw two tiny Indians, members of Guatemala City's legion homeless, staring.

At four in the morning the surviving revelers arrived at Clara's condominium. Her bookshelves were filled with art history books, and photographs of her beautiful teenage daughters hung on the walls. Santiago lay down on the floor and went to sleep. Others staked out couches and chairs. Clara alone was wide awake.

"It was the earthquake of 1976 that brought me back to Guatemala," she said. "*Mi páis lloraba, lloraba.* My country was crying, crying. I had to come back."

She got up to put on a record of Cuban-sounding jazz. "This man never left Cuba," she said approvingly. "Not many leave Cuba."

"Would you ever go there?" I asked.

"My mother did," she said. "But I'm too—how do you say?—high society." She laughed.

The only plane for Flores was leaving at seven that morning. I had watched the progress of the party throughout the evening wondering whether Santiago was going to get us to the plane or not. Finally I decided that I should let things follow their own course and, like the others, fell asleep on Clara's floor. Milena was the first to wake. It was ten past seven. Rumpled and bleary-eyed, the three of us drove to the airport. Santiago kept urging Milena, who was at the wheel, to hurry. When we arrived at the terminal Santiago and I ran in. All was quiet. The plane had gone. Santiago nevertheless turned to me and asked me to run out to the car and get our luggage. I asked him why. "*Hay que impressionar,*" he said. "We have to make an impression."

He pleaded, joked, flirted, wheedled, and cajoled, until finally, after a gringo turned up looking for a flight to Tikal, we found ourselves on a little Cessna six-seater headed for Flores. I don't know how we paid. I didn't ask.

Santiago fell asleep soon after takeoff, but I stared out the window, watching the landscape unfold beneath us. We flew up out of Guatemala City's volcano-rimmed valley and then headed northeast toward the Petén. Our flight path took us directly across the middle of the Guatemalan highlands, a dizzying disorder of mountains, sheer cliffs, meandering rivers, and only a few roads, which clung to the deep valleys. Despite the infrequency of roads, however, the mountains were heavily settled. A maze of footpaths connected milpas and tiny hamlets on even the least accessible land.

Almost all Guatemala's Maya live in the highlands and I knew that this was at the root of most of the country's problems. It was not so much that the Maya were unhappy with the land that had been allocated them by the Spanish almost five hundred years before—poor though it is. It was rather that during the nineteenth century half of that land had been taken away by the government and given to coffee growers in order to bolster the nation's exports. By leaving the Maya permanently land-poor, this act of expropriation had, by design, forced them to seek out migratory work to supplement what they eked out of their remaining milpas. Since the land expropriations, the situation had only worsened. The growth of the Indian populations and the rise of huge foreign- and Ladino-owned coastal agricultural plantations meant that most Indians were forced to do ill-paid migratory work for a third to a half of every year.

After we'd been flying an hour or so we crossed the last of the mountains and saw the great, forested plain of the Petén stretching out before us. Bounded on the north by the Yucatán, on the east by

Belize, and on the west by Chiapas, the Petén covers fourteen thousand square miles, a full third of Guatemala. Once the very heart of Classic-era Maya culture, it includes the ruins of ancient cities from Tikal to Uaxactún, El Mirador, and Dos Pilas and was at one time densely populated. After the Classic-period collapse, however, the population of the Petén gradually decreased, until the area became what it is now, an abandoned frontier of rain forests, swampy *bajos,* and natural savannas.

After another twenty minutes of flying, I caught a glimpse of a large lake, in the middle of which I could see a city attached to the mainland by a causeway. I knew that the lake was Lake Petén Itzá, the largest in the Petén at twenty miles long and three miles wide. The city on the island was Flores, the departmental capital, built on top of a Maya city named Tayasal, believed to have been founded around the year 1200 by Itzá Maya fleeing south from Chichén Itzá after its defeat by the neighboring city of Mayapán.

Tayasal was remote enough from anything of interest to the Spanish to remain largely unaffected by the Conquest. In 1524, however, Cortés stumbled on Tayasal while in the midst of a grueling cross-country trek to punish a rebellious subordinate in Honduras and paused to rest there for a few days. Upon his departure he left behind his horse, which had become lame while crossing a mountain pass. Cortés apparently neglected to leave the Itzá instructions on how to take care of the horse, because, never having seen a horse before, the Itzá attempted to sustain the creature on the same diet of flower sprigs and ceremonial poultry dishes that they fed to important Maya lords when they became sick. When the horse died, the Itzá built a stone replica of a horse, sitting on its haunches, legs bent and raised over its forefeet. They named their effigy horse Tizimin Chac. Tizimin means "tapir," the closest New World approximation of the horse. Chac was the god of thunder, lightning, and rain, whom the Maya associated with the horse because they had seen mounted Spaniards shooting off their guns.

It was not until a hundred years after Cortés, in 1618, that the next Spaniards arrived in Tayasal. Fathers Fuensalida and Órbita, two intrepid Franciscans, braved miles of rain forests to bring the

word of Christ to the Itzá. When Padre Órbita saw the Itzá worshiping the stone effigy of Tizimin Chac, he became so incensed that he
grabbed a nearby rock and, according to Juan de Villagutierre Soto-
Mayor, a Spanish chronicler, "filled with the spirit of the Lord,
climbed onto the statue ... and broke it to pieces." The two padres
had to flee the city for their lives. Four years later, the next Franciscan to visit was not so lucky. He and the fifteen soldiers with him
had their heads cut off and set up on stakes around the town. This
incident ended Spanish attempts to convert the Tayasal Itzá for many
years.

We flew over the modern city of Flores. Rows of pastel houses
with red corrugated-metal roofs rose toward a church in the center of
the island. A crushed stone causeway some two hundred yards long
connected Flores to the sprawling towns of Santa Elena and Santo
Benito on the south shore. Santiago pointed out our hotel in Santa
Elena, at the foot of the causeway, as well as a huge military base east
of town. As we banked for landing, I could see neat rows of military
aircraft, small tanks, and howitzers.

We were met at the airport by Carlos, a foreman for Jorge, the
logger we'd visited the evening before. Carlos was driving a Toyota
Land Cruiser pickup and offered to take us to our hotel. Santiago sat
up front so that he could confer with Carlos about the political situation in Flores. The legislation creating the parks had only passed the
national congress a few days before. All the largest parks were in the
Petén, and Santiago was concerned about the local reaction. While
he and Carlos talked, I leaned back in the heat and humidity and
marveled at the scene around us. Pigs squealed on the main street.
Girls with pastel-colored parasols picked their way around dusty
potholes. Abandoned machinery sat rusting in vacant lots.

Our hotel doubled as the bus station and consisted of three horizontal slabs of concrete separated by two levels of vertical concrete
walls. There was rudimentary plumbing and lots of mildew. After
we showered we went downstairs for a breakfast of eggs and *frijoles*.
Carlos had told Santiago that there was a great deal of hostility
toward the national parks bill in Flores.

"They're scared," Santiago said. "We're lucky they know me well, because if they didn't, they'd run us out of town."

Suddenly I realized that although it seemed as if I'd been with Santiago for an eternity, I barely knew the first thing about him. The acquaintance who'd telephoned me about the trip had told me that Santiago was born in the Petén but raised in Brittany and that he hadn't known about his Guatemalan origins until his twenty-first birthday, when, against the wishes of his parents, his grandmother told him. He'd left for Guatemala the next day. After telling me this story, however, the acquaintance confessed that he wasn't sure he believed it. He was hoping I'd find out what I could. So I asked Santiago why the people of Flores knew him so well.

"I lived here for many years," Santiago answered. He then mumbled something about an American murderer, a lake called "Laguna Misteriosa," and a bar he'd owned on the far shore of Lake Petén Itzá.

I couldn't follow what he was saying. I don't think I was supposed to, but remembering that I'd been told that Santiago had once been the director of flora and fauna for the park at Tikal, I asked how he had gone from owning a bar to being the director of flora and fauna for Guatemala's most famous national park.

"Because," Santiago answered, "I have a degree from the École Cynégétique, a school in France at which they teach you everything from ecological management to dressing game."

I thought of the turkey carcass on Santiago's living room wall and decided to drop the subject.

The genesis of the cooperatives we were planning to visit was intimately tied to a demographic explosion that has taken place in the Petén in the last forty years. As recently as 1950 the total population of the Petén was only fifteen thousand, approximately one person per square mile. Most of the residents were loggers or *chicleros,* itinerant collectors of the sap of the sapodilla tree, which was boiled down and exported to the United States as a base for chewing gum. But during the Alliance for Progress years of the Kennedy administration, the A.I.D. cooked up a program to develop the Petén. The idea was to kill two birds with one stone: to open the resources of the Petén to commercial exploitation while simultaneously defusing the discontent that was building in the Maya highlands. The A.I.D. plan designated for settlement a strip of land that included the northern slope of the highlands and the lower part of the Petén. The strip was named the Franja Transversal del Norte, "the Transversal Strip of the North." With help from A.I.D. and the Peace Corps, the Guatemalan government built roads, recruited landless highland Indians, organized cooperatives, and granted them patches of jungle. The cooperatives were supposed to be supported for the first critical years by a network of government assistance programs. After that they'd be self-sustaining.

The United States' motivation to undertake this program at that particular point in Guatemalan history is no doubt related to the fact that a few years earlier, in 1954, the United States had organized and financed the overthrow of Jacobo Arbenz Guzmán, the only president in recent Guatemalan history to seriously address the maldistribution of land that is at the heart of the nation's problems. This overthrow, and a subsequent series of harsh military dictatorships, had given rise to a guerrilla movement that had shown possibilities of winning the allegiance of Guatemala's poor, before it was defeated with the help of American Green Berets. The development of the Petén was therefore also designed as an alternative to insurrection, a less volatile way to alleviate the plight of the landless.

Unfortunately, it didn't turn out that way. The support programs for the cooperatives never materialized. What happened instead was that the Guatemalan military discovered that grazing cattle on newly cleared rain forest land could be a profitable enterprise: the first thing many of the rain forest immigrants heard from the government was in the form of an army officer challenging their title to the land they had painstakingly cleared. The Tranversal Strip of the North became known as the "generals' strip" and the resentment caused by this land grab created a fertile source of recruits for a reformed and relocated guerrilla movement that, in the early seventies, began to infiltrate over the Mexican border and into the Petén.

* * *

That afternoon, in a bar in a thatched hut on the edge of town, Santiago and I met the regional cooperative officers. Santiago produced maps and pointed out where the proposed border park was supposed to be and where we were planning to go. Where the park and the cooperatives overlapped, he asked about the numbers of families in the various cooperatives, how many had been killed, how many had fled, and how many had returned. When he inquired about the political situation, the cooperative officials characterized it as "very bad." They indicated a stretch of river inside the park that the officials said was "theirs," referring to the guerrillas.

"It's where they rest and recuperate," one explained.

"Maybe we can at least tell them that they're part of a park," Santiago said. "It will be to their advantage since there'll be no bombing permitted in the park."

Everyone laughed, but I already knew that Santiago was serious.

As we sat in the raggedy bar downing beers and discussing the parks and the hordes of dollar-toting tourists they would no doubt produce, things began to get pretty mellow. I stepped outside to get some air, and although it was the middle of dry season, a black cloud moved overhead and began to dump rain on me. Simultaneously, a ray of sunlight slanted under the edge of the cloud, producing a full rainbow on the horizon. I commented on this phenomona when I went back into the hut. "Ah," exclaimed one of the cooperative members, "a rainbow, the symbol of the cooperative movement. The seven colors, the total unity of the universe!"

Later that afternoon, on what was rapidly becoming a lobbying tour, I accompanied Santiago to another bar across the causeway in Flores proper. Santiago was describing to an old friend the Ruta Maya, a proposed international tourist route, backed by the *National Geographic* in Washington, that was intended to offer tourists a combination of visits to ruins and the newly created parks. An army captain came into the bar and sat down uninvited at our table. The captain, who wore a hearing aid, began to barge into the conversation, leaning forward and touching the person he was addressing and then talking in a hushed, exaggeratedly gentle voice. It soon became apparent that he was drunk. We were trying to ignore the man, when he suddenly flared into a rage.

"Do you know what I think about your Ruta Maya?" he shouted. "It's *la Ruta Mierda.*"

We got up and left. The army captain followed us out the door, got on a motorcycle, and fell off.

"Those are the ones you have to watch out for," Santiago said.

It was a Friday and that afternoon Jorge the logger, his wife, Miriam, and a son named Jorge flew up from Guatemala City to spend the weekend at a house they had along the lake. We had dinner with them and with Carlos at a Flores restaurant called El Gran Jaguar. Having consumed a fair amount of beer over the course of the afternoon, I was not that hungry, but I felt it would be impolite to turn down the *tepescuintle* that Santiago was urging on me. I didn't have any idea what *tepescuintle* was, but its description—a jungle rodent somewhere between a rabbit and an oversized rat—did not make it seem particularly palatable. I consented though, and found it good. Later I discovered *tepescuintle* was agouti paca. Of course!

Over dinner, Jorge became belligerent. For a while he tried to provoke Santiago. When Santiago refused to rise to the bait, he turned to me. What was I, beyond being a playboy? I had to laugh, which was not, I think, the reaction Jorge had hoped to elicit. Well, he said, since I wasn't a playboy, I must be an ecologist and what did ecologists know? Switching his attentions to Santiago, he declared in a loud voice that the whole system of parks was really camouflaged land reform. Santiago tried to quiet him down. This only made Jorge louder. So that the whole restaurant could hear him, he practically shouted that the Mexican peasant leader Emiliano Zapata had died for agrarian reform. Santiago knew who Zapata was, didn't he?

Carlos gave us a lift back to the hotel. It was well past midnight and drizzling when we got out of his pickup, but Santiago wanted to make one more stop. I followed him along the Santa Elena lakeshore until we crossed the line into Santo Benito. From the dilapidated shacks and the look of people on the street it wasn't hard to guess that this was the wrong side of the Flores tracks. A soldier carrying an automatic rifle stepped out of a shadowy alley and followed us up the street. Santiago told me to keep my eyes straight ahead and we wouldn't have a problem. At the next corner we turned onto a wide street lined with prostitutes in red-lit shacks. There were soldiers everywhere. A cattle truck was parked in front of one of the bars. The soldiers with the automatic weapons were herding recruits into the back of the truck. The recruits were just boys—Indian boys, many of whom, I knew, were drafted into the army by forced conscription. The recruits' heads were shaved. Their eyes were bugged out with excitement. The Ladino officers, a foot taller than the Indian recruits, were blooding their hounds. Santiago Billy and I walked home. I think he just wanted me to see.

The next day we packed, checked out, and loaded up for the trip to Sayaxché where we'd pick up a launch on the Rió de la Pasión. Almost as an afterthought, we stopped at a grocery store to buy provisions. Our purchase consisted of two tins of pork luncheon meat, three cans of *frijoles,* two cans of asparagus soup, one can of mortadella, two cans of frankfurters, several packages of crackers, five two-liter bottles of mineral water, two two-liter bottles of Pepsi, three bags of Bubble Yum, ten candles, and a box of mosquito spirals. At the last minute, Santiago asked if I'd seen his pith helmet. He couldn't find it anywhere. I told him I hadn't since the day we'd arrived, but reminded him that he was still wearing the same thin Italian loafers he had been wearing at the art opening in Guatemala City.

"I forgot my other shoes," he said. "I always forget something."

Founded in the late nineteenth century by friars trying to assert Guatemalan sovereignty over a wild section of rain forest, Sayaxché sits high on a gravel bank along the western shore of the Rió de la Pasión, one of the Usumacinta's major tributaries. Its ramshackle buildings, painted in bright colors, either are or seem to be up on stilts. Below, the water's edge is littered with river craft ranging from one-person dugout canoes to thatched wooden launches that serve as public transportation to the communities downriver.

We dropped our bags in a spare room in the Sayaxché cooperative office and went out for dinner. Soldiers with Galil automatic rifles patrolled the streets. A man stepped up to Santiago and said, "Señor Billy?" I thought it was the secret police. But no, it was Enrique Ortego Velásquez, foreign editor of the Guatemalan newsweekly *Crónica,* who was doing a piece of what *Crónica* calls *"grande reportaje"* on the Petén. He was traveling with a woman named Ana Arana, a Salvador-born, U.S.-raised stringer for CBS-TV based in San Salvador. Enrique had previously spoken to Santiago about interviewing him in Sayaxché, but Santiago seemed to have forgotten. We all went to dinner together, along with several local cooperative officials. After Ana regaled us with television-journalist stories of guerrilla prowess in El Salvador, Santiago observed that the guerrillas didn't have that much support here. The local Guatemalans disagreed. Not only did the guerrillas have support, they said, but they were local people.

That night Santiago dreamed that he was being strangled by a *"niña diabla,"* a devil child, and sat up shouting on his cot. In the morning, feeling unrested, we went down to the river the next morning to meet Julio, our *lanchero,* or boatman. It was actually our boat*men,* since at Santiago's invitation Enrique and Ana had decided to accompany us downriver and had arranged a launch of their own. When we arrived, Julio was busy preparing the sixteen-foot aluminum skiff that he, Santiago, and I would be traveling in, cleaning its forty-horsepower outboard and balancing the seventy gallons of gasoline we were taking along. He was a small, rugged-looking man of sixty-two with a white mustache and a straw hat that he fastened under his chin with a cord. Santiago told me that he'd been a *chiclero* and a crocodile hunter.

Next to our boat was a similarly laden one in which Ana and Enrique would be traveling with their boatman, Julio's son, Israel.

The Rió de la Pasión, below Sayaxché, is low and swampy. In January, not long after the end of the rainy season, it was thick and muddy and filled to its tangled green banks. Once we had shoved off, I sat in the bow and watched the foliage go by. Trees with mangrovelike roots supported an upper story of vine-draped, bromeliad-laden branches. Patches of filigree-leaved, thirty-foot-high wild grasses alternated with an understory of tree palms. The river traffic we encountered consisted mostly of one- or two-person dugouts. Every so often we'd pass clearings on the banks, where Indian families were smoking split fish over open fires.

Santiago pulled out binoculars and a pad of paper and began making a wildlife survey. He noted the countless turtles sunning themselves on logs. Wading stealthily along the river edges was an infinity of herons, gray, blue, and white. Santiago spotted a three-and-a-half-foot river otter and then a pair of white hawks soaring overhead. In a tree set back from the river, Julio pointed out a family of howler monkeys. I saw three different types of kingfishers—ringed, Amazon, and pygmy—sitting on branches over the river. When one of them spotted a fish, it would launch itself, hover for a second, and then plunge. I recalled that the word for kingfisher in Quiché Maya means "water hummingbird."

Late in the morning, we reached a cooperative called Buena Fe, "good faith," and put in for lunch. A group of barefoot children were just getting out of their thatched schoolhouse. They watched our boat approaching the shore and, when we got close, scattered in nervous giggles. Since this cooperative was not within the limits of the proposed park, Santiago made only a minimal explanation of our mission before getting to the point. Did they have any *carne del monte*, wild game, *bifstek?* There was something so French in the contagious enthusiam with which he posed this improbable question that I had to laugh. So did the schoolteacher to whom he'd posed it.

"Yes," said the schoolteacher, "we have *bifsteks* of tortillas and *bifsteks* of *frijoles*."

Over our beans and tortillas, we asked one of the cooperative members if they'd had any trouble during the violence. No, he said, everything had been very quiet. They'd all stayed. They'd had no problems.

Afterward, Ana, Enrique, and I sat down by the water and I asked what kind of support the guerrillas had had among the people. Enrique explained that the guerrillas had spent years organizing among the poor before they'd undertaken their first military action.

In 1980, before the major army offensives, they'd had a quarter of a million people, mostly highland Maya, under their control. When, shortly afterward, the army counterattacked, it went after what it perceived to be guerrilla supporters rather than the guerrillas themselves. The result was a bloodbath. A hundred thousand Indians were murdered.

One thing that had long puzzled me, I said, was why the Salvadoran guerrillas had been so successful and why the Guatemalan guerrillas had been, relatively speaking, such a failure.

"That's easy," Enrique said. "The Salvadoran movement was military from its inception. The Guatemalan movement, by contrast, was very idealistic. It had lots of priests in it. The guerrillas gave each town a few antiquated rifles and said it was the beginning of popular power. They never dreamed the Guatemalan army would kill as many people as it did. All that has changed, though. The guerrillas now think of themselves in military terms. The area we're now in is their rearguard, and for the most part the army's not attacking them here. When the guerrillas are ready, they'll try to move back into the highlands."

An hour or so after we got back on the river, we reached the point where the Usumacinta is created from the confluence of the Pasión and the Salinas, or Chixoy, another major river flowing down from the highlands. The major artery of the Classic period, the Usumacinta is the biggest river in the Maya region. For many miles below us, it formed the border between Mexico and Guatemala. Because the guerrillas are said to have used the jungles on the Mexican side of the river as a rear base, it was Usumacinta cooperatives that bore the brunt of the government's reprisals.

At the end of the day we pulled in at a cooperative called Flor de la Esperanza, "Flower of Hope," which sat on a steep, muddy bank high above the river. The current had picked up and when we approached the shore, I jumped out of our launch and tied the painter to a dead tree root. Although we had a lot of gear, no one volunteered to help us carry it up the riverbank. A few residents merely lined up and stared blankly as we worked. The president of the co-op was a fair, blue-eyed man from the *occidente,* the Pacific coast. He was an evangelical, he told us, and had nineteen children. No, he said, there hadn't been any trouble. Everything had been "*muy tranquilo.*"

After we left him, I asked Ana and Enrique if they didn't find it peculiar that in an area that was supposed to have experienced so much violence, everything was so "*tranquilo.*"

"He's lying," Ana said. "There was a massacre here."

"How do you know?" I asked.

"Because Julio, your *lanchero,* said so when you were tying the boat up. Santiago knows about it too."

The cooperative's *presidente* had given us a schoolhouse with a thatched roof and a concrete floor in which to sleep. While we were hanging our hammocks and our mosquito nets, I asked Santiago about the massacre.

"It's just stories," he said, refusing to elaborate.

At dinner we ate beans and tortillas at the *presidente*'s. He told us that he belonged to an evangelical sect called Centroamerica and had studied in Costa Rica at a Centroamerica seminary. There were thirty others of the same persuasion in the co-op, and other evangelical sects as well, and Catholics, though the Catholics didn't have a church.

"Of all the families in the cooperative, only two families don't have any religion," said the *presidente*'s wife, somehow managing to sound like the Jean Stapleton character in "All in the Family."

After dinner one of the evangelical groups was holding a hymn service in the cooperative's schoolhouse. The pastor sang the hymns over a loudspeaker set to a volume that made it audible a half mile away. The few participants in the service, mostly children, screeched along at the top of their lungs. "*Hay una gran cosecha que viene, una cosecha por el cielo.* There's a big harvest coming, a harvest from heaven."

"It's like Jonestown," said Ana.

The next morning we left for El Arbolito, the first of the cooperatives inside the proposed park. The atmosphere couldn't have been more different. As we landed the whole town lined up and stared with grave curiosity. Santiago produced a stack of colored nature cal-

endars from his gear and, like a seasoned salesman, scrambled up the
bank, asked for the cooperative's president, and presented him with a
calendar. He then presented calendars to the first three people who
had the nerve to ask for them. As the residents led the way into the
co-op, Santiago explained the park to them. They could be included
or not, as they saw fit. If they chose to be in the park, they'd continue to have a right to their land, but they couldn't convert any further
land into cornfield and there would be restrictions on cattle grazing.
In return, the government would help them establish ecologically
sound businesses. As he explained all this, we walked through the
center of the co-op and across a meadow before coming to a stop in
front of a low line of waxy-leaved shrubs in front of the pink-and-
white plastered foundation of an abandoned building. Bits of charred
wood lay around the edges of the foundation. One of the residents
absentmindedly picked up a couple of bent, rusted nails and
straightened them with the dull edge of his machete.

"This was our school," the *presidente* said, "but the army burned
it down."

The co-op members fled to Mexico in 1980. A few days before
that the army had killed a group of guerrillas and found three boys
from the co-op among the dead. The army then came and murdered
the families of all three boys, about fifty people in all, and burned
down the school.

"After that we all left," the *presidente* said, "because the army considered us all subversives. We only returned six months ago."

As we left the cooperative, I said "See you later" to one of the
co-op members.

"*Si Dios lo quiera.* If God wishes it," he responded morosely.

A little way downriver we pulled the launches up at a circular
limestone pool that had formed where a reef had been deposited by a
stream flowing out of the jungle. Outside the reef, the Usumacinta
was rainy-season muddy. Inside, the pool was clear and brimming
with minnows. Wild lilies grew around its rim. We went for a swim.
Ana had wandered off on her own at El Arbolito and I asked her
what she had learned.

"They spoke about a Belgian priest named Father Hugo," she

said. "He helped them buy a tractor. The day the residents left was the last day they saw him. The army was pursuing him and had gotten close enough to have shot a hole in his hat. They don't know what happened to him, but they think he escaped."

At Bethel, the next cooperative downriver, Santiago's request for *carne del monte* produced venison steaks—Bethel had been swallowed by a large army base and had its own restaurant. Santiago took photographs of boy soldiers gathered around their sandbagged M-60 machine gun. He gave away nature calendars and lectured the soldiers about properly disposing of their trash: "Otherwise the tourists won't come." The soldiers looked confused. As we were casting off, one of them came down the riverbank toting his rifle and demanded one of our two-liter bottles of Pepsi. We handed it to him. He didn't offer to pay.

Bethel was the last settlement on the Guatemalan side. Beyond it the river was lined with abandoned fields rapidly reverting to jungle. Santiago had been down this stretch of river before the violence, and seemed awed.

"This all used to be populated," he said. "There's no one left. There weren't a thousand people who fled from here, there were thousands."

I said something about how terribly the Guatemalan government treated its Indians.

"As opposed to the United States," Santiago said sarcastically, "where you killed them all."

We planned to spend that night at Yaxchilán, a huge Classic-era Maya city occupying the middle of an oxbow on the Mexican side of the Usumacinta. Late in the afternoon, as we were approaching our destination, the river narrowed, the current picked up, and an eight-foot crocodile slid off a gravel bank and into the water. Across the river from Yaxchilán was the site of what had been one of the biggest cooperatives, Centro Campesino, now completely abandoned. As we pulled the launch up on the bank below the ruins Julio said quietly, "Padre Hugo used to live there."

Yaxchilán, inaccessible by road, has a grass airstrip and, along the river, some palapa huts—shelters with thatched roofs and no walls—for the use of visitors. We strung our hammocks in the huts and wandered over to the ruins, which rise out of the river on a series of steep bluffs. Once painted white, the city faces due east, toward the rising sun. For nearly five hundred years Yaxchilán was ruled by the descendants of a king whom the hieroglyph readers call Penis Jaguar or, more politely, Progenitor Jaguar. Like Palenque, it reached the apogee of its power in the Late Classic, most notably during the reigns of a king named Shield Jaguar and his son, Bird Jaguar. Bird Jaguar died around the year 771, and not long afterward the city went into decline. The last Maya date recorded there is nine years later than the last date at Palenque: 9.18.17.13.14 9 Ix 2 Zec on the Maya calendar—April 13, 808, on ours. (The string of numbers is a transcription of a Maya "Long Count," a system whereby any date can be placed in relation to all of time, past and future.) Although Yaxchilán was inhabited for another fifty years, no new buildings were put up and no stelae were erected. No one really knows what set off its precipitous collapse.

I subsequently asked Sylviane Boucher, an archaeologist and ceramicist who had worked at Yaxchilán, how she explained its collapse. She said that around the time of the last dates, the site was suddenly flooded with a lighter, finer style of ceramics. The new ceramic style was a type associated with Gulf Coast sites and with the Putún, or Chontal, Maya who lived there. It seems likely that if Palenque, which is near the Usumacinta delta, was invaded at around this time, the invaders may simply have followed the Usumacinta into the interior, toppling Maya states as they went.

"One of the styles associated with this type of ceramic," Sylviane said, "is a tripod-type mortar and pestle with grooved sides. It's a style commonly found in Central Mexico, where its Nahuatl name is *mol cajete,* and where it is commonly used to grind chilis. Writing about Altar de los Sacrificios, a site farther up the Rió de la Pasión, the archaeologist Richard Adams has even suggested that the invaders may have introduced the consumption of chili to the Maya area."

Yaxchilán's resident caretaker, a jovial, good-humored man named Manuel, invited us to eat with him that evening. As we wandered toward his quarters in the twilight, parrots chattered from the tops of the trees and keel-billed toucans made froggy croaks from the undergrowth. It was hard to imagine that we were on the edge of a war zone. Manuel lived in a bamboo-and-thatch structure not far from our camp. He sat us down at a corner table made of three planks of wood. From my seat, I had by the light of a kerosene lamp an unobstructed view of a wall calendar illustrated with a photograph that, while purporting to be of Hawaii, showed three Mexican-looking women in grass skirts standing in a Mexican-looking landscape.

Dinner was subdued. Julio didn't know the river below Yaxchilán and was not at all enthusiastic at the prospect of running it. We all knew that there were large rapids below us, but we didn't know where. Moreover, the stretch downstream was outside the zone controlled by the army. In fact, this stretch was the area the cooperative members in Flores had identified as "theirs," meaning the guerrillas'. To make matters worse, Manuel began describing an aerial bombardment of Centro Campesino only six months before. The strafing of government jets had been met with rocket fire from the ground.

"You know," he said, "they won't get the guerrillas out easily. Look at the jaguar. The jaguar minds its own business until you corner it, and then watch out. The guerrillas are the people from over there. They're fighting for vengeance. Vengeance for their sons and daughters."

It was raining lightly when we went to bed. Ana produced a portable cassette player and put on some melancholic Catalan folk music of Enrique's. I got into my hammock and listened to the water roiling below. As I dozed off to sleep I imagined that the river's sounds were crocodiles surging up the riverbanks.

The next day we were hoping to travel all the way down to another Classic Maya river site, Piedras Negras, and back again. It was an ambitious distance, and Julio wanted to be on the water by six-thirty. At six-thirty, however, the river was so shrouded in fog that we could barely see in front of us. While we sat around waiting for the fog to lift, Santiago stashed his government credentials and military maps under a bag of lime by our campsite. In the war zone, it was illegal for civilians to possess military maps.

By eight the fog had lifted enough for us to set off. Almost as soon as we rounded the Yaxchilán oxbow, the current quickened and we were swept into a deep canyon lined with limestone cliffs and tall, undisturbed jungle. A flight of toucans, collared aracaris, passed overhead. They were followed by a lineated woodpecker with its lurid red head, and then a white-crowned parrot. A family of howler monkeys curled into tight furry balls hung like oversized fruit in a tree along the Guatemalan bank. In front of us, a black and white hawk dove into the river, emerged with a large fish in its talons, and flew to the beach. The hawk's mate was sitting on a branch nearby. Santiago directed Julio to drive the boat up on the beach and jumped out to look at the fish. Reluctantly, the hawk abandoned its prey and flew off with its mate. The fish was an iridescent-gray cat-fish a foot long. We put it in the boat to bring to Manuel for dinner.

We had been led to believe that the worst of the rapids were below Piedras Negras, but not long after stealing the hawk's break-fast we rounded a bend and saw a huge, turbulent rapid ahead of us. With a forty-horsepower engine, we probably could have fought the current to the riverbank, but that would have meant risking being swept sideways through the rapid, which would have been much worse. Anyway, I don't think Julio ever really considered pulling over. The closer we came to the rapid, however, the worse it looked. Santiago and I knelt down on the bottom of the boat in order to lower the center of gravity. No sooner had we done so than we were in the thick of it. The boat nosed up over the top of a huge standing wave and slammed down into a deep trough. Up it went over anoth-er even bigger wave and then slapped down again. I don't know how Julio hung on, but he did, and we emerged stunned but intact. Julio's face had lost all its color, but when he saw that we were through and that Israel and his launch had also made it through, he let out a wild, exultant shout.

Below the rapid, the river widened into a still pool. On the Mex-ican side someone had cleared a patch of jungle and built a tiny thatched hut that was dwarfed by the huge buttressed stumps of felled trees around it. Julio's shouting brought some Indians out of the hut, and we pulled the boats up on the beach and went to talk to the people about whether there were more or worse rapids ahead of us. The settlers were Tzeltals, from a region of the highlands north-east of San Cristóbal. I tried out a few of the Tzeltal phrases I'd learned from Tony Mendez. They laughed stiffly. In answer to our questions about the river they said that, yes, it got much worse downstream. There were bottomless canyons, terrible rapids, and dangerous waterfalls, but it seemed clear that they were only telling us what they thought we wanted to hear, so after some debate, we decided to go on. Julio, however, was determined to find a guide.

We hadn't seen anyone on the Guatemalan side of the river since we left Yaxchilán, but a mile or two below the rapids we spotted a narrow path covered with freshly cut palm fronds leading up from the shore. We circled in to take a closer look, and caught a glimpse of a number of men gathered inside a primitive lean-to. Santiago wanted to stop, but Julio was afraid they were guerrillas. We circled uncertainly, watching as the men seemed to confer among them-selves. Finally, one of them detached himself and came down to the water's edge. He was about twenty years old, had a goatee, and was wearing a pair of patched corduroy jeans and flip-flops. We told him we were going to Piedras Negras and asked about the river.

He ran back to the camp. There was more conferring, and a moment later he returned carrying an AM/FM two-band stereo radio with cassette player. He'd guide us.

His name was Umberto. He said he was Mexican, originally from Tabasco, but now he lived in Tenosique, a river town to our north. He was a *chatero,* an itinerant collector of the fronds of the chaemaedora palm, or *chate,* which are sold to florists in the United States and Europe. Since chaemaedora palms grow wild, Umberto's profession took him into the jungle for weeks at a time, and we asked him if he ever saw any guerrillas. He said that on the Guatemalan side of the river he hadn't seen a soul in two years. He wasn't very convincing, but then he didn't know who we were.

It turned out that there weren't any significant rapids between ourselves and Piedras Negras, which we reached about an hour later.

Umberto pointed to a high, sandy beach, which he said was the landing spot for the ruins. We ran the boats up on the beach and tied them next to some black rocks along the water's edge. As I was tying, I noticed that the top of one of the rocks was carved with a three-foot-wide disk containing the figure of a seated Maya lord. Piedras Negras: "black rocks."

A shallow furrow with footprints on either side ran up the beach. Umberto told me it had been made by an iguana. I knew that the ancient Maya had kept iguanas as a captive food source, capturing them by lassooing them off tree limbs and then storing them as a special food for their *nacomes,* or war chiefs. But what really struck me, looking at this strange track, was how different the flora and fauna of the New World must have seemed to the first Europeans to arrive on its shores. When Amerigo Vespucci first came upon an iguana he was terrified, although the iguana is quite harmless, and declared that except for its lack of wings, it reminded him of the flying dragon of legend. The iguana may have been Vespucci's Tizimin Chac, although the Maya had somewhat better grounds for being afraid of the Spanish horses.

From the top of the beach we followed a winding path into the jungle. Julio stopped along the path and pointed into the underbrush at a ten-foot-tall platform made of poles lashed together. He said that it was a jaguar-hunting platform but that it wasn't built high enough off the ground.

"The jaguar would smell you at that height."

The University of Pennsylvania mapped and partially excavated Piedras Negras in the 1930's, but since that time no major archaeological work has been done on the site. The rain forest can grow a lot in sixty years. Piedras Negras was in shocking condition. Everywhere there were cracked, eroded, overgrown temples. Inscribed stelae lay face-down, covered with moss. A blank mask, its eyes empty, stared at us from under a tree root. A stone altar lay broken in three pieces on the ground, a barely discernible ring of glyphs around its circumference. In the bushes sat a forlorn, 1930's-vintage Fordson tractor, vines creeping around its engine block. Everywhere were the shallow excavations of grave robbers.

The archaeological neglect of the Piedras Negras site notwithstanding, it has played an important role in the evolution of modern thinking about the Maya. One of the people working on the University of Pennsylvania excavation in the thirties was the American architectural artist Tatiana Proskouriakoff. Thirty years later, while going over her drawings from the thirties as part of a study of the historical evolution of Maya artistic style, Proskouriakoff reached the conclusions that led to her famous paper on event glyphs.

After touring the ruins, we got back into the launches and started back upriver. Umberto snapped a cassette into his deck, cranked up the volume, and began playing what Enrique, rolling his eyes, referred to as *rock duro*. We dropped Umberto off at his camp and then nervously clutched the sides of the boat as Julio and Israel, gunning the engines, guided us up the side of the rapids. By the time we arrived back at Yaxchilán, Julio was flying. His launches were safe. He hadn't knowingly encountered any guerrillas. To anyone who asked what the trip had been like, he graphically demonstrated the launch soaring up over the top of the rapids and slapping down again. After a dinner of *tepescuintle* fillets at Manuel's, Julio and Manuel began telling hunting stories. After a while, Manuel raised his finger for a second, went out of the room, and returned with a gourd sliced open at one end and covered with a thin, tightly stretched piece of leather at the other. A piece of waxed cord dangled from the leather down through the middle of the gourd. It was a jaguar caller, Manuel explained, and handed it to Julio. Julio began stroking the waxed string until the caller began emitting a strange, low, vibrating sound. Julio said it was the sound of a female jaguar and that with a similar caller, in the right place, he had once attracted three male jaguars.

Santiago began to look upset, as if something were slowly dawning on him. He asked Julio how many jaguars he had killed in his life. Julio didn't answer.

"Fifty?" asked Santiago.

"Maybe forty," Julio responded, his eyes lowered.

"You were a guide for hunters," Santiago said.

Julio nodded in assent.

"Gringos?" asked Santiago.

Julio nodded again.

Santiago had his hunting knife out and had been feeling the blade. He leaned across the table and, in the flickering kerosene light, put the knife to my throat.

"Gringos, gringos, gringos," he said.

The next morning I woke early. Swaying in my hammock, I watched through my mosquito net as some hummingbirds worked the blossoms of a lime tree a few yards away. After a while the others began getting up. Ana, who did not have a hammock and was sleeping on a sheet of plastic spread over a table top, discovered a large scorpion under the plastic. Santiago struggled out of his hammock and began digging his maps and credentials out from under the bags of lime. He hadn't shaved for days and had developed a pronounced limp as a result of a bruise he had suffered coming through the rapids. Dark and intense-looking, he pulled on a worn, zippered vest, spread out his maps, and began to study. I told him that he looked like Napoleon. He tried not to look pleased, but I knew that he was. He was working for the effect.

After Manuel fed us a breakfast of crested guan stew, we got on the river and began the long grind back to Sayaxché. Just above the confluence of the Pasión with the Usumacinta, we came upon a four-foot-long fer-de-lance swimming across a wide section of the river. This snake, *Bothrops atrox,* is responsible for more deaths in the Americas than any other snake. A pit viper from the same family (Crotalidae) as the rattlesnake and water moccasin, the fer-de-lance grows to a length of eight feet or more. It has long hinged fangs, quick-acting venom, and a reputation for being aggressive, hunting largely by sensing the heat emitted by its prey. In the water, however, it is quite helpless. Since it was swimming toward a cooperative on the far bank, Julio wanted to kill it with his machete. Santiago wouldn't let him. We circled the snake for a while in the launch. Its local Spanish name is *barba amarilla,* "yellow beard," and we admired the yellow under its chin, the diamond pattern on its back, and its vertical, elliptical pupils.

In the late afternoon, farther up the Pasión, we saw a tree along the side of the river whose branches were entirely filled with muscovy ducks. For me, seeing a single perching muscovy duck, let alone a tree full, was a first, particularly because muscovy ducks, along with turkeys and a species of small, hairless dog, were the only animals domesticated by the ancient Maya. The muscovy ducks had since naturalized, and the ones we saw were descendants of those ducks that had reverted to the wild state.

Below Sayaxché, we came upon a turtle fisherman in a dugout canoe. Santiago had Julio stop the launch and we bargained for two turtles. We bought the large one for three dollars and the small one for a dollar fifty. Afterward Ana scolded Santiago for calling himself an ecologist, yet consuming so much wild game.

"You don't understand," Santiago said. "It's not hunting I'm against. It's the destruction of the environment."

After our time on the river, Sayaxché seemed like a big town. Reggae-inflected salsa blared out of corner cantinas. Funky, ramshackle houses rose out of muddy streets in which sewage dribbled, pigs wallowed, and roosters fought. While we unloaded the canoes, Santiago marched with our turtles up to a restaurant and asked the owner to prepare them for dinner.

Over turtle in broth with tomatoes and baby potatoes, Santiago announced that everyone he'd spoken with felt that we'd been through the heart of the guerrilla zone.

Ana and Enrique nodded. The owner of their hotel had told them that the *chateros* worked the Guatemalan side by arrangement with the guerrillas.

"The guerrillas were checking us out to see who we were," Enrique said.

Ana added that their hotel owner had told them that the four cooperatives organized by Father Hugo—including El Arbolito and Centro Campesino—had borne most of the violence.

Just before we got up from dinner, a *lanchero* friend of Julio's sat down with us. We idly asked him a few questions about the co-ops. Suddenly, as if to unburden himself, he launched into a story.

"I'm an evangelical," he said. "One morning near one of the co-ops which is now abandoned, we were having a breakfast and a prayer service. It was at the height of the violence and three or four people were disappearing every day. I looked out of a window in our church and saw a man in camouflage coming out of the jungle. Another man followed and then another."

"Guerrillas?" asked Santiago.

"Army," answered the boatman.

"They asked what we were doing. We told them that we were studying the word of God. They told us to come with them. I was certain we were going to be killed so I asked if we could finish eating. That way, if we died, we'd at least die on a full stomach. They led us to a boat by the river. There were picks and shovels in the boat. They told us to get in and we started downstream. Soon they pulled the boat over. They pointed at the body of a woman. She was naked and covered with blood. They told us to put her in the boat. We did what we were told. Then we picked up another woman in the same condition. Soon there were four. They told us to get out and dig a hole. We dug a big hole and buried them all. From there they took us on to where we found more bodies. By the end of the day, we had buried fifty-nine corpses."

When the boatman finished his story, his eyes were rimmed with red. It was as if he were stuck in a nightmare from which he couldn't escape. After a moment, however, he regained his composure, mumbled apologies for having interrupted our dinner, and left.

Back in Flores, Ana and Enrique went their own way, heading southeast to Poptún, the next stop on their reporting tour. Santiago and I crossed to the north shore of the lake, where Jorge the logging baron had a weekend house. The house sat high on a limestone bluff. The rooms, up on pilings, were all on different levels. Their thatched roofs were supported by beautifully turned columns of tropical hardwood. There were no walls. The place was open to the jungle. Jorge, the logger's son with whom we had eaten dinner in Flores days before, was there. A handsome, sophisticated young man who had studied in Mexico City, he was playing Tracy Chapman on a cassette deck. Santiago and I strung our hammocks from hardwood pillars and went down to the lake to swim. From its blue waters we could see jade-backed trogons in the trees above and hear pieces of heavy fruit falling in the forest. A servant was sweeping the beach.

While I lolled in the lake, I reflected on the demise of the Petén Itzá. After they murdered the Franciscan missionaries in 1621, the Itzá were left alone for many years. But their continued presence— unconquered and un-Christianized—was a constant irritant to Spanish ecclesiastical and military authorities. The Spanish had consolidated their hold on the Maya to the north of the Petén in the Yucatán and farther south, in Guatemala, but the persistence of the the Itzá city of Tayasal, which as late as the seventeenth century had a population estimated at between twenty and twenty-five thousand, provided a sanctuary for Maya recidivists fleeing from Spanish mission towns. In 1695, the governor of Yucatán resolved that the only way to subdue the Itzá was to build a road south into the Péten from the coastal city of Campeche.

In connection with this project, three Franciscans, headed by Father Andrés de Avedaño y Loyola, departed for Tayasal on a mission to convince the Itzá that the time had come for them to renounce their pagan faith. Father Andrés was a clever, highly educated priest who not only was fluent in the Yucatec Maya that the Itza spoke, but also was familiar with the *chilam balam*s, books of history and prophecy kept by Maya priests and scribes long after the Conquest. Father Andrés knew that Katun 8 Ahau, a date that came up every 256 years on the Maya calendar, was an apocryphal one for the Maya, and that Fathers Fuensalida and Órbita, the Franciscans who had visited Tayasal in 1618, had mentioned the date to the then King Can-Ek and argued that it was only a question of time until the Itzá would have to renounce their faith. Apparently Can-Ek was intrigued by the argument but told the two priests that the time had not yet arrived before chasing them from the city. Father Andrés hoped to point out to the new Can-Ek that Katun 8 Ahau was imminent.

When Father Andrés and his fellow Franciscans arrived on the shores of Lake Petén Itzá, they were met by Can-Ek himself and a large Itzá escort. Quoting a Spanish manuscript recently discovered by the Mayanist George Stuart, Linda Schele and David Freidel described the scene in their book A *Forest of Kings: The Untold Story of the Ancient Maya:*

> The three Franciscans emerged from their hut in the morning to see a wedge of flower-adorned canoes emerging from the glare of the rising sun. The canoes were filled with resplendent warriors playing drums and flutes. Sitting in the largest of the canoes at the apex of the wedge rode Can-Ek, whom the Spanish chronicler described as "a tall man, handsome of visage and far lighter in complexion than other Maya."
>
> Dressed with all the elegance of his station, King Can-Ek wore a large crown of gold surmounted by a crest of the same metal. His ears were covered with large gold disks decorated with long dangles that fell to his shoulders and shook when he moved his head. Gold rings adorned his fingers and gold bands his arms. His shirt was made of pure white cloth elaborately embroidered with blue designs, and he wore a wide black sash around his waist to mark his status as a priest of the Itzá. His sandals were finely wrought of blue thread with golden jingles interwoven. Over everything else he wore a cape made of blue-flecked white cloth edged with a blue embroidered border. It bore his name spelled in glyphs.

Perhaps because he was intrigued by Father Andrés' knowledge of Yucatec and the Maya prophecies, Can-Ek briefly tolerated his presence in Tayasal, and even allowed himself and other Itzá to be baptized before jealous Itzá lords under him finally drove the priests out.

The road from Campeche reached the shores of Lake Petén Itzá in 1697. However, the road builders were met not by Itzá ready to convert, but by Itzá ready for war. The Spanish fortified themselves on the lake shore and, while they waited for reinforcements, spent their time constructing a galley and a pirogue with which to attack the island fortress of Tayasal. The attack took place on 12.3.19.11.14 1 Ix 17 Kankin in the Maya calendar—March 13, 1697. The 128 Spaniards in their two newly constructed craft took on two thousand Itzás in canoes. The Itzá were armed with bows and arrows. The Spanish had arquebuses. The Spanish prevailed. When they secured Tayasal, they planted a royal standard on its highest temple and renamed it Nuestra Señora de los Remedios y San Pablo de los Itzaes. There were so many idols in the city that it took the Spanish from nine-thirty in the morning to past five in the afternoon to destroy them all. Among the artifacts they discovered was the thigh bone of Tizimin Chac, the horse Cortés had left with the Itzá 172 years earlier.

Tayasal was the last independent Maya city of any size to fall and it is worth considering that it fell at a time when further north, in J. Eric Thompson's words, "many of the thirteen colonies had struck deep roots [and] graceful steeples were rising with the yeast of Wren's inspiration." In his book *Maya History and Religion,* Thompson notes that there is a record of a red-haired man who was living among the Itzá in 1695 and speculates that he may have been an Englishman from the old buccaneer settlement of Belize. "When one recalls," Thompson writes, "that the writing of books on native life was for long a leading British occupation, one regrets that this sojourner among the Itzá never returned to civilization to indulge in the national pastime; his observations would have been of inestimable importance."

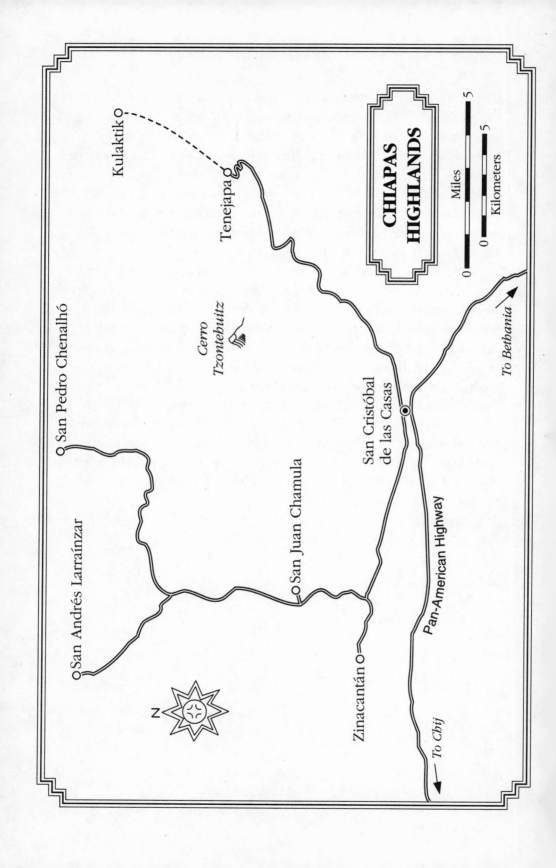

CHAPTER 5

Chenalhó

THE FOUNDATION OF ANCIENT MAYA TIME was the sun, which was believed to be born, mature, and die not just every day, but also every year. The proto-Maya word for the sun was *k'in,* which also meant "day" and had the connotation of divinity. The Maya believed the sun had been set in motion at the creation of the present world, and from its diurnal movement and its annual migration between the solstices were derived all the other subdivisions of ancient Maya life: the separation of the heavens and the underworld, the agricultural and religious cycles, the seasons, and the divisions of the day.

We think of time as an objective standard of measure that has an existence independent of the people that created it. In other words, time continues even when we cease to exist. To the ancient Maya, time was perceived differently, as a set of shared obligations by which each element of the Maya universe made sacrifices to support all the others. The ultimate object of this sacrifice was the sun, whose daily and annual rounds were the source of all life in the present world. But the sun was jealous of its beneficence and would not move of its own accord. Its daily and seasonal rounds were broken into periods of time, each of which was supported by a patron god. These gods in turn were supported by humans, organized by Maya priests into a system of ritual obligation that was the basis of the divine order. These ritual obligations formed the essence of the ancient Maya sense of time and also of the ancient Maya calendar. The calendar was the key to coordinating all the interlocking obligations, and knowledge of its workings was sacred because it meant understanding the sacred workings of the universe.

To this day, many Maya towns retain the idea of time as a set of religious obligations. Across the highlands of Chiapas and Guatemala some seventy Maya towns still follow one or both of the two concurrently running ancient Maya calendrical cycles known as the *tzolkin* and the *haab*. The *tzolkin,* a 260-day ceremonial year, consists of thirteen months of twenty days each. The *haab,* a 365-day solar year, is made up of eighteen twenty-day months plus five "lost days," dangerous days in which the sun is reborn and evil spirits from earlier creations are let loose on the earth.

Even in the seventy towns that still follow the ancient calendars, however, their use is discreet. You don't walk into a corner store and see a calendar of twenty-day months hanging on the back wall (although such calendars do exist). After the Conquest, the Maya deities presiding over parts of the ancient calendar were assigned the names of Catholic saints, and the ancient Maya calendar rounds became a round of ostensibly Catholic religious festivals. But because there were so few Catholic priests, who were able to visit Maya towns only occasionally, the organization of these festivals was left to Catholic-endorsed religious societies referred to in Guatemala as *cofradías* ("brotherhoods") and in Chiapas as *cargos* ("loads" or "burdens"). During the colonial period *cargos* and *cofradías* evolved into a means of self-government for Maya towns and have persisted as such to the present. Anthropologists refer to them as "barrier institutions" because although on the outside they have been carefully designed to fit the demands of non-Maya society, on the inside they provide the means by which the Maya can hold on to their ancient worldview and continue to fulfill their calendar-based obligations to the sun.

In modern Maya villages there are both civil and religious *cargos.* Each consists of a hierarchy of offices through which, over a lifetime, a Maya can serve his community. A Maya who "takes" a *cargo* borrows money, leaves his rural *paraje,* and moves to the municipal center for a year, where he assumes responsibility for some aspect of community life. If the *cargo* is a civil one, the Maya might start as a *regidor,* a ceremonial policeman, and may aspire eventually to become the *holteklum,* the "head of the land," the *presidente municipal.* A religious *cargo* holder might start as a *mayordomo* or an *alferez,* tending to a lesser saint or to that saint's belongings, and aspire eventually to become the head of a major saint's *cargo,* thus bearing full responsibility for carrying the sun through that saint's part of the sun's annual cycle. Maya who have worked their way up through the *cargo* hierarchy and have held major *cargos* eventually become *principales,* respected elders who are consulted on all matters of community importance. Such individuals accumulate enormous spirituality. An American friend who spent many years living in Tzotzil villages compared them to Zen priests.

The pre-Columbian conception of time shows through the disguise of Catholic saint's day festivals most clearly in the Tzotzil carnival celebrations in the Chiapas highlands. This is because the roots of the Tzotzil carnivals are the five lost days at the end of the Maya *haab*—perhaps the most difficult part of the Maya calendar to translate into Christian practice. In Tzotzil, the five lost days are referred to as the *ch'aik'in*—the "superfluous, the nonexistent, bitter, evil, unholy days." Some people connect them to the five days that the Hero Twins of the Popul Vuh spent underwater after the Lords of Death ground them up and dumped them in a river. Occurring in late February, between the Maya months of Sisak and Muktasak at a time of drought, frost, and agricultural dormancy, the five lost days mark a part of the year in which the sun's path across the sky, "the path of the holy father," is beginning to rise out of the depths of the winter solstice. The Tzotzils refer to the sun as Htotik, "our father" or "the father god," and during the five lost days they commemorate not just Htotik's rebirth but also the creation of the present world out of the evil and chaos of earlier worlds.

The carnival celebration in San Pedro Chenalhó isn't the most

famous one in Chiapas, but that may be because Chenalhó is relatively inaccessible. Isolated from its neighbors by high passes and
deep ravines, the municipal center of Chenalhó is located at an altitude of five thousand feet along the eastern bank of the San Pedro
River, which flows north from the spurs of Tzontehuitz—"moss
mountain"—a nine-thousand-foot dormant volcano that is the
tallest mountain in the region. The road to Chenalhó north from San
Cristóbal is only twenty-two miles long, but it deteriorates rapidly
after the San Andrés cutoff and can take two or three hours to negotiate. The final stretch plunges steeply downward into the San Pedro
valley and then follows the river to the site of the town, just below a
dizzying, nearly vertical seventeen-hundred-foot ridge.

I arrived in Chenalhó on the second day of the five-day carnival.
The town was packed with thousands of *pedranos,* as its residents are
called (after the patron saint imposed on the town by Spanish friars), the women in indigo blue skirts and white *huipiles,* intricately
embroidered in red, and the traditionally dressed men wearing belted white fingertip-length cotton tunics over white shorts. As I
approached the town square, I could hear firework explosions, the
cries of hawkers, *rancheros* blaring out over competing loudspeakers.
I thought of the late Cuban anthropologist Calixta Guiteras-Holmes's
observations—in her wonderful 1961 ethnographic work, *Perils of the
Soul: The Worldview of a Tzotzil Indian*—that when a *pedrano* was away
from home, he expressed his longing to return by thinking of "the
hum of the market place," which to him represented "the gathering
of his people, a joy equaled only by that of reunion with his immediate family."

My plan was to find Francisco Gomez Luna, a sixteen-year-old
pedrano whom I'd met the year before through an anthropologist,
Christine Eber, who had been working in Chenalhó. Francisco was a
bright kid whose natural good humor seemed unaffected by a string
of personal misfortunes to rival Job's. His father had died the year
before after a routine wound had become infected for lack of an
antibiotic. Over the years, eight of his nine siblings had died, and
Francisco himself was struggling to stay in school on a dollar-a-
month government scholarship while trying to support his mother

and remaining sister, who was partly paralyzed, by spending the afternoons working his milpa. When I had last seen him, Francisco had told me that he would be playing the flute in the carnival musical ensemble, and had invited me to visit. He said he would introduce me to Padre Miguel Chanteau, a highly regarded French priest who had been working in Chenalhó for almost twenty-five years and in whose parish house Francisco thought I might be able to stay.

A carnival *cargo* is the most expensive of all the *pedrano* religious *cargos* and the four principal *cargo* holders are referred to as *pasiones*. Like *cargo* holders elsewhere, the *pasiones* set up households in the municipal center, which become the loci of much of the carnival activity. Wandering around town looking for Francisco, I came upon a *pasión* house. The tile-roofed mud house was free-standing, wreathed in the smoke of cook fires, and hung with fruit and bromeliads for the occasion. Three groups of carnival figures were seated around a table outside the front door. I had studied a description of the carnival in *Ritual Humor in Highland Chiapas,* an anthropological text by Victoria Bricker, and from her description I recognized four *pasiones,* wearing flat black hats, bright red britches, and black, red-trimmed capes; four *k'oh,* or "masked men," wearing leather masks on the backs of their heads that made them seem to be looking two ways at once; and four "black men," or "monkey men," dressed in white tunics and white shorts, their faces darkened with greasy soot, and wearing tall, conical monkey-fur hats.

As I watched, one of the *pasiones* grasped a clear bottle of *pox* and poured some of it into a small gourd. He raised the gourd to the sky and drank. He then refilled and passed the gourd until everyone at the table had drunk from it. When the circuit was complete, the black men gave a strange high-pitched howl, got up from the table, and began to move off down the street. The *pasiones* stood up, grabbed tall wooden staffs hung with ribbons, and followed the black men. Bells tied below their knees rang with their every movement. Inside the *pasión* house a drum and pipe began to play. From the darkened interior my friend Francisco emerged. I stopped him for long enough to say hello and ask him where I could find Padre Miguel.

Francisco asked me what time it was. I looked at my watch and told him.

"Padre Miguel will be eating at one of the Ladino restaurants just up the street," Francisco told me. "You'll find him there."

After Francisco had rejoined the procession, I walked to the restaurant he'd described. It lay behind a stucco cinder-block wall painted the color of pistachio ice cream. I walked through a gate and entered a garden that consisted of two lime trees and a concrete sink. Two picnic tables protruded from a blackened, open kitchen. Three elderly Ladina ladies were slumped down on chairs in the kitchen. Their Indian servant, Dominga (whom I later discovered was Francisco's mother), was clearing the table in front of a small, solidly built man of perhaps sixty. He was dressed in motley olive-colored army trousers with cargo pockets on the thighs, a tan shirt with the sleeves rolled up, and a faded brown vest. His longish hair hung just over his ears and he wore glasses.

I knew that this had to be Padre Miguel, but for some reason, I walked up to him and asked if Padre Miguel was in the restaurant.

Padre Miguel looked amused. *"Parece que yo soy Padre Miguel.* It seems that I am Padre Miguel," he answered cheerfully.

When I explained what I wanted, Padre Miguel put aside his coffee and walked with me to the parish house. He had a dormitory, but at the moment it was filled with *pedranos* in for carnival. However, I was welcome to stay in the parish house office.

The parish house was next to the church, just off the main plaza. We entered through what seemed to be a combination kitchen—medical dispensary. Adjacent to it, an alcove was almost entirely filled by Padre Miguel's large, old-fashioned wooden bed. In the office, which had the look of a room in provincial France, Padre Miguel pointed to a couch on which he said I could sleep. I put my bag down and looked around the room. One wall was covered with a voluminous wooden armoire. On a table sat a huge, old-fashioned shortwave radio. Next to the fireplace a grandfather clock solemnly chimed the quarter hour. Framed black-and-white photographs on the mantel showed self-conscious young Frenchwomen in Sunday dresses and serious Frenchmen in ill-fitting coats and ties.

I asked Padre Miguel what part of France he was from.

"I was born in Normandy," he said, "but for five years before coming here, my parish was a Communist workers' suburb of Paris."

Padre Miguel had some business to attend to, so I left the parish house with him and set out to wander around the *pedrano*-packed plaza. I passed the town's ancient church, its facade recently refurbished, and beyond the church I came to the colonial-style *cabildo*, or town hall. Sitting on a bench under its arcade were the town's civil officers: the president and his assistants. Their faces were shaded by wide-brimmed palm hats festooned with ribbons, and they clutched silver-headed staffs, their badge of office. The Maya consider these staffs both a physical link to their ancestral gods and also a symbol of the divine aspects of holding a *cargo* office. The anthropologist Evon Vogt, a pioneer researcher in the nearby Tzotzil community of Zinacantán, has noted that Zinacantec *cargo* holders consider their staffs infallible. "If administrative errors have been made," Vogt observed in an unpublished paper he presented to a 1988 anthropological conference in Spain, "they are the mistakes of human officials who hold these batons while serving in high office." Vogt also noted that when a new *cargo* holder took office, he washed and censed his staff to symbolically rid it "of any mistakes made by a predecessor serving in the same position."

I walked past the *cabildo* to the west side of the plaza, where I found a small covered market. Vendors were selling everything from avocados to mangos to piles of dried red chilis and stacks of salted prawns. The variety of the produce reminded me of the size and diversity of the municipality of Chenalhó. There were some thirty thousand *pedranos* within its borders, and from where we were, the municipality descended another twenty miles north, where it finally ended amid hot country fields of pineapple and sugarcane.

From inside the market, I glimpsed a large crowd gathered on a side street and went outside to see what was happening. Just as I left the market, two men on horseback thundered by. They wore white turbans, red jackets, short red breeches, and flowing black capes. These I recognized as the carnival *capitanes*, members of the carnival *cargo* hierarchy. Up the road, in the direction from which they had come, I could see a pair of live turkeys tied to a rope stretched over the road. The two *capitanes* were clutching fistfuls of feathers they'd grabbed from the turkeys while galloping by.

The *capitanes* are supposed to make twelve passes at the turkeys, snatching feathers from the poor birds each time. I must have missed the first eleven, because I knew that on the thirteenth pass, which was made not by the *capitanes* but by the carnival black men, the turkeys met their fate. I looked up the road and saw it coming. Two of the black men approached, brandishing drawn machetes. Behind them, Francisco's string-and-drum band was playing a funereal tune. The crowd of *pedranos* craned their necks in anticipation. The turkeys looked around apprehensively. The black men reached the suspended turkeys, ruffled their remaining feathers, and swiftly chopped off their heads. Two men stepped out of the crowd, took the turkey carcasses, wings still flapping, and carried them off. The black men, meanwhile, began haranguing the crowds, stroking the severed turkey heads obscenely while shouting out a running commentary that made everyone laugh.

Bricker says that the black men identify one of the turkey-victims as Andrés Luis C'ut Tuluk, "Andrés Luis Turkey Belly" (C'ut Tuluk is a *pedrano* surname), and while using the severed turkey heads to mimic sexual intercourse intone, "If you behaved in this shameless fashion, just you wait and see! Your fate will be the same as Andrés Luis Turkey Belly's!" Bricker observes that this is part of a pattern of cautionary immorality that the black men carry through the festival. I was immediately struck with the parallels to Yucatec five-lost-days ceremonies as described in Diego de Landa's *Relación de las Cosas de Yucatán*. Landa not only noted that all lost-days ceremonies included the ritual sacrifice of turkeys, but also that the festival participants painted themselves with soot and fasted beforehand, "none for less than thirteen days."

My thoughts were interrupted by the reappearance of the mounted *capitanes*, this time carrying ecclesiastical banners, followed by the masked men mounted on hobby horses and parodying their every gesture. The black men with their turkey heads soon formed up behind, and, accompanied by a drummer and a flute player, the procession marched off toward the center of town.

Rather than following the procession back toward town, I followed the two men with the turkey carcasses in the direction of the river. I caught up with them next to a high, arched stone bridge. They had strung the birds up to a tree along the riverbank and were busy depluming the poor creatures. I walked out on the bridge and watched. Just on the other side of the river, in an unruly clump of trees, I could see the outlines of a one-room adobe house that belonged to one of my friend Christine's informants. The woman was a *curandera* who had developed a reputation as a *bruja,* "witch," when she put a curse on her husband and he died after he left her for another woman. Now, Christine had told me, she had a respectable practice casting spells on her fellow *pedranos* and had even picked up a few clients in San Cristóbal.

"It's no small matter learning the Tzotzil prayers that it takes to become a *curandera,*" Christine said. "If you want to learn the prayers to cure a snakebite, for instance, the first few times you say them, a snake will appear to test your abilities. If you get one word wrong, the snake will attack you."

I toyed with the idea of visiting the *curandera* but thought better of it. I watched until the turkeys were completely plucked. When two black men appeared and escorted the turkeys back toward the center of town, I joined in behind and followed the little group until they disappeared into one of the *pasión* houses—a large, single-roomed adobe building with a wide tile roof.

Standing at the door, I could see that the members of the turkey-decapitating procession were also inside. Ordinarily non-*pedranos* would not be invited in, but Francisco saw me standing at the door and beckoned for me to enter. *Pasiones* provide food and liquor for five days of carnival banquets, and the interior of the house was crammed with people and with food. Several cook fires were burning simultaneously. Firewood lined the walls. Baskets of tortillas, tamales, bread, fruit, and chilis were everywhere. An entire side of beef hung along one wall. The two turkey carcasses had been placed on a low table. The black men put two flaming torches of resin-filled pine in front of them and began to keen in high staccato voices while striking the turkey carcasses mournfully with the flats of their machete blades. Everyone laughed. The black men then picked up the two severed turkey heads and began to conduct a mock argument.

"They're saying, 'Here you are still fighting in death, just like the sacristan who always hit his wife!'" Francisco told me. "They're pretending to mourn."

When the turkey conversation was over, Francisco departed with the band, and I walked down to the plaza. In a corner I came upon a group of *chicha* sellers. *Chicha* is a poisonous-looking sugarcane beer dispensed directly out of the wooden barrels in which it is fermented. *Pedranos* in various stages of intoxication were thick around the stuff, like bees around a hive. One of the *chicha* drinkers came up to me and asked if I was French and if I was related to Padre Miguel.

No, I told him, I was American and staying with Padre Miguel. He seemed pleased at my answer.

"I have one question for you," he said. "*Como está el ambiente de su páis?* How is the ambience of your country?"

I was wondering how to respond to this, when the man interrupted me.

"It's violent, isn't it."

This amused me, because, as frightened as Americans are of the perceived violence of Mexico, Mexicans are even more scared of the perceived violence of the United States, which many see as a land filled with depraved criminals and trigger-tempered warriors.

"In parts it's violent," I responded noncommittally.

"I want to go there to find work," he said. "How do I do it?"

"You need a visa," I told him.

"A visa?"

"A card from the government," I explained. "They're hard to get, and without one, you'd have to walk across the frontier, which is both dangerous and illegal."

"Dangerous? I'd bring my pistol. Pow! Pow! Pow!" he waved his finger in the air laughing.

I left the man with his guns blazing and wandered across the plaza. On my way, I was accosted by an inebriated *pedrano* official.

"Where can I get a machine to find treasure?" he asked.

I told the man that I was returning to my country soon. I'd look into the machine and, when I came back, bring him the details. This seemed to please him, and he let me go on my way.

On the other side of the plaza, I ran into Amber Past, an American poet who has lived in Chiapas for many years and can speak Tzotzil. I told her about the request for the treasure-finding machine.

"I was in Chamula once," she told me, "carrying a cardboard mailing tube with a map in it. People asked me what it was. I told them it was a machine for seeing treasure. In a flash I had a crowd of fifty people around me. The Tzotzils think that where meteorites fall there is buried treasure, but that you have to dig very deep to find it. There's a Tzotzil god called Me Tak'im—the "mother of money" or the "mother of metal." If someone suddenly becomes rich they think it's because that person struck a deal with Me Tak'im."

Amber and I sat down for a beer. She told me she was staying with the family of Manuel Arías Sohom, a *pedrano* who had died a few years before and had been Calixta Guiteras-Holmes's chief informant. As the Chenalhó representative of the revolutionary government in Central Mexico during the 1930's and '40's, Manuel Arías had been instrumental in enforcing the laws that had freed the *pedranos* from debt slavery. Amber characterized him as "Chenalhó's Martin Luther King" and said that many times he'd narrowly escaped assassination by Chenalhó's Ladinos.

"Debt slavery still exists in many areas of Chiapas," Amber said. "But even where it doesn't, it's amazing how people treat the Indians. A number of years ago I lived in San Andrés. One day, the Ladina baker there appeared with a baby girl. She hadn't been pregnant. She'd bought the baby from an Indian woman. It became a Cinderella situation. The baker didn't educate the child, and when the girl grew up they made her work all day long. This went on for a few years until suddenly the girl disappeared. She'd gotten pregnant by one of the men in the baker's family. They let her come back after she'd had her baby, but they tied the baby to a chair so that it wouldn't distract its mother from her work. They fed it scraps. It grew up retarded."

The sun had gone down as Amber and I talked, and by the time we'd paid our bill and wandered up the street, the moon was racing in and out of the clouds, casting dramatic shadows. We passed one of the *pasión*'s houses and, from inside, heard a group of musicians playing exquisitely beautiful music. Amber, whom the *pedranos* knew, led me into the house, and we sat down and watched the musicians playing on a harp, a small fiddle, and two clay-pot drums. Amber explained that the music was called *toy k'in* music, which meant "raising up music," and that it was only played during carnival.

"It's supposed to raise the level of *alegría*, happiness," she said.

As we sat around the embers of the *pasión*'s cook fires, listening to the *toy k'in* music, the house we were in seemed to take on a life of its own. The Maya, in fact, believe that a house is a living thing and, like a person, has a soul. The foundation is its foot. The walls are its stomach. The corners are its ears. Houses, like milpas, are sacred spaces. Guiteras-Holmes says that when a *pedrano* house is first constructed, permission has to be sought from the earth to live on that particular part of its surface and prayers are said in order to deflect the harmful powers inherent in the house materials, newly brought in from the wilderness realm of the Earthlord—the *te'tik*. It is important that these prayers be said by older people, since over the course of their lifetimes, older people have accrued "heat" from their exposure to the sun and this makes them relatively less susceptible to the evil forces inherent in untamed nature.

In the Tzotzil lexicon, the concept of "heat" is closely tied to the concept of taking a *cargo;* in fact, the Tzotzils believe that *cargo* holders acquire supernatural "heat" over the course of their lifetimes. The Tzotzil word for "fire," *k'ok,* is related to the word for "heat," *k'ak'al,* which also means "day." In *Chamulas in the World of the Sun,* the anthropologist Gary Gossen points out that in Chamula, which borders Chenalhó, the sun is sometimes referred to as Htotik K'ak'al— "our father sun," or "our father heat." By taking a *cargo,* a *pedrano* is, in effect, taking responsibility for maintaining part of Htotik K'ak'al's divine order and thus accumulates "heat." Those who have held office are considered *panwil,* meaning "they have heated their souls." Those who have never held office are referred to as *tse'il,* "defective" or "raw."

* * *

After we departed the *pasión* house, I left Amber and walked down to the church. In the middle of the church floor, in the flickering candlelight, a group of religious officials were dancing. They had shawls pulled up over their heads and over the shawls, palm hats cascading with colored ribbons. They shook rattles and shuffled in circles to the music of a pipe and drum in what seemed to be a trance.

I wandered around the dark, incense-filled interior. Offertory candles crowded the floor, and chanting, imploring *pedranos* were down on their knees asking favors from saints lined up along the church walls. I looked at the saints—stock Catholic figures with ghostly pale faces and vacant blue eyes—buried under layers of beautifully embroidered, intricately designed *huipiles,* which had claimed the saints' figures for the Maya. I remembered a story that Christine Eber had told me that demonstrated the way *pedranos* felt about traditional dress, or *traje.* When Christine first moved in with a Maya family in one of the *parajes,* she didn't know whether to wear *pedrano* clothing or not. She worried that if she did, the *pedranos* might think her pretentious. One day the family's four-year-old son asked her if she was going to marry a rabbit. When she asked him what he meant, he told her that because she didn't wear traditional dress, he wasn't sure whether she was human or not. Thereafter she dressed like a *pedrana* and her host family was conspicuously relieved.

I returned to the parish house shortly before nine and found Padre Miguel listening to a scratchy recording of a piece by Francis Poulenc. At nine he turned it off and switched on his shortwave to get the news on Radio France International. The reception was bad, and he finally settled on the BBC World Service, perhaps for my benefit. Afterward he switched on the only television channel he could get and watched highlights of world soccer. A gregarious man, he would, I think, have liked me to join him, but all I could manage was to crawl into my sleeping bag. As I went to sleep, I saw Padre Miguel, seated in a heavy, old-fashioned carved-wood chair, cheering "*Eso!*" "*Así es!*" and "*Bravo!*" at the most extraordinary shots of the week.

* * *

The carnival band came by the parish house at four-thirty A.M., accompanied by a series of loud rocket explosions. I managed to sleep until seven anyway, after which I went out to find breakfast. The sounds of strange rituals were still emanating from the *pasión* houses. Bleary-eyed Indians were sweeping the streets with leafy branches. I walked up to the restaurant, shooed the flies away from the remains of some earlier patron's breakfast, and ate tortillas, black beans, and scrambled eggs. Afterward I walked back down to the church. Padre Miguel had told me that he was saying Mass at eight and I thought I'd see how it was going. I stuck my head into the church. Even at this hour, *pedranos* were on their knees before their saints, praying and burning copal incense. Undisturbed, Padre Miguel was at the altar, cheerfully saying Mass to a congregation consisting of a single Ladina lady in a blue dress and matching cardigan.

At nine, a stage was erected in front of the town hall and a banner reading CARNAVAL '89 was hung. Someone announced that the newly elected governor was coming, and at ten a helicopter set down on the road south of town. The governor marched into town behind a procession consisting of the black men, the *pasiones*, the masked men, the drummers and pipers, and, finally, a Ladino brass band. A big, jowly man whose shifty eyes seemed lost in his large face, the governor was, I knew, a great-nephew of the infamous governor of the state of Tabasco, Garrido Canabal, whose relentless hunting of priests during the 1930's had prompted Graham Greene to write *The Power and the Glory*.

At the foot of the stage, *pedrano* officials outfitted the governor with the woolen robe, beribboned palm hat, and silver-tipped baton of a municipal office holder. After the governor tied his hat under his pudgy chin with a piece of colored yarn, he stepped up to the microphone. His speech was brief. He alluded to his respect for Indian life and noted that other governors had been there before him and had promised many things. Despite this, life for the *pedranos* had remained the same.

"I, by contrast, am not going to promise anything," the governor said grandiloquently, "except that everyone will work together to build a better Chiapas."

At least there'd be no disappointments.

Afterward the governor's wife made a short speech in Tzotzil and then sat down looking pleased with herself. At the conclusion of the ceremony, a Chenalhó Ladino sang the Chiapas state anthem. A handful of Ladinos followed along. The *pedranos* stared blankly. The governor shook a few hands and helicoptered away.

After lunch, I was sitting in the marketplace when I heard music and saw Francisco's pipe, drum, and harp ensemble marching into town. Following the group was a trio of new carnival figures. In the middle of the trio a somber-looking man dressed in *pedrana* woman's clothing was being escorted by two barefoot men clad in white loincloths. Large X's were painted on their chests and backs. On their torsos and faces were yellow and white circles, made, according to Bricker, from a paste of ochre, annatto, and lime.

The female impersonator was Me Cabnal, the wife of Cabnal, the legendary chief of the Lacandóns. During the one hundred and fifty years that the Cholan-speaking Lacandóns held out against the Spanish, they periodically sallied forth from their rain forest redoubts to raid Christianized highland Maya towns like Chenalhó for salt, women, and, at least according to lore, sacrificial victims. The *pedranos* therefore considered the Lacandóns cannibals, and since cannibalism is regarded by the *pedranos* to be one of the vices of the earlier creations, the carnival figure of Me Cabnal acted as a reminder of the depravity of Maya life before Htotik initiated the present era.

Me Cabnal's partners were jaguars, which the *pedranos* associate with night, darkness, and evil and which, on a supernatural level, are *poslob,* devourers of men's souls. Guiteras-Holmes says that in ancient times, Cabnal's daughter married a *pedrano* culture hero named Ohoroxtotil, who rid the world of jaguars, thus making it safe for humans. Bricker argues that Ohoroxtotil derives from the Tzotzil title Ahau Rios Totil, which she translates as "Lord God Father," Totil being Htotik, Father Sun. The jaguars, therefore, were another reminder of the dangers of ancient times, before the sun made the world safe for *pedranos.*

According to Gary Gossen, the Chamulas, like the ancient residents of Palenque, believe that the world is now in its fourth creation. The Chamulas don't say much about the second and third creations, which were terminated when the people didn't behave properly, but during the first creation, monkeys and demons lived on the earth and did such amoral things as eating their own children. In fact, the monkeys were so bad that they finally killed the sun itself, forcing it to leave the earth and ascend to the heavens, thereby initiating the current existence.

Gossen points out that in Chamula today, newborn unbaptized infants are considered to be dangerously cold, a quality that the Chamulas associate with both infancy and earlier creations, and are referred to as *max* (pronounced "mash"), or monkeys. Their baptism represents a first step away from the coldness of the earlier world, to which they are still related, and toward the sun-related heat to which a respectable Maya aspires over a lifetime of *cargo* service. During their research, Gossen and his wife were frequently asked such questions as "Do people bite and eat one another in your country?" The reason for these questions only gradually dawned on them. As *hrinkos*—gringos—they came from the far reaches of the earth, from a place far from the enlightening power of Htotik, from a place where the bad habits of earlier existences still prevailed.

As Me Cabnal and her jaguar escorts crossed the plaza, they waved bundles of weeds mimicking, according to Bricker, one of the curing ceremonies practiced by shamans when a patient experiences *shi'el,* or "soul loss." Among the causes of soul loss are moments of extreme fright; as I followed the mock shamans I remembered that Evon Vogt, one of the first anthropologists to work among the Maya of the Chiapas highlands, had reported that in the 1940's the first airplane to fly over Zinacantán, the town in which he was working, had caused an epidemic of *shi'el.*

On the other side of the plaza I ran into Barry Norris, a friend from San Cristóbal. Barry suggested we have a glass of *pox.*

"It makes you more a part of the festival," he said.

We sat down at a table, where we were soon joined by several severely sloshed *pedranos.* At a Maya festival, drinking performs several functions. At one end of the spectrum, the *cargo* holders, who fast and don't sleep for the length of the festival, use alcohol as a means to put themselves in a trancelike state and get closer to Htotik. On the other end, for the ordinary Maya a festival is a release from the pressures of daily life and frequently an occasion to simply tie one on. Our tablemates were from the latter category.

Barry gave one of the table crashers a thousand pesos, and soon he returned with a bottle of *pox* and a little plastic shot glass. As *ranchero* music blared, the bottle started making the rounds. Barry began singing along to the music—something about a pain in his *corazón*. One of the drunks, whose head had slipped down on the table, lifted himself up and shouted "*Viva Jalisco!*" which made everyone laugh.

Striving to maintain my journalistic sobriety, I was pouring every other drink onto the ground at my feet. As I dumped the contents of one of the glasses, one of our tablemates suddenly jumped up and glared at me. I glanced under the table. The man was wearing sandals. The *pox* had splashed over his feet. I'm not sure he thought it was *pox*.

Later in the afternoon, after Barry had left, four ragged-looking cowboys carrying ancient flintlock rifles appeared, herding a bull up the street. One of the cowboys had on a beige uniform with dark brown epaulets. A patch above one of the pockets said SERVICIO POSTAL MEXICANO. The bull consisted of a man inside a stick frame covered with a woven reed mat; its tail was bailing twine; its head and horns, lightly painted papier-mâché. On one of the horns, through the wash of paint, I could still make out a newspaper advertisement: GOODYEAR ME RESPONDE: "Goodyear is responsible for me."

I joined hundreds of young kids pursuing the figure of the bull through the streets. People laughed to see me among the tots, but I didn't mind. Every so often the bull would turn on its followers. The kids screamed and ran in terror. Several clutched sticks and even nails to defend themselves from this dread creature. One little boy was so frightened by one of the bull's charges that he reached up to hold my hand without even looking to see who he was holding onto.

That evening, the black men wandered the streets making spectral howls. They were in search of Me Cabnal and her jaguars, who had hidden themselves in a *pasión* house. From just outside the door,

I watched as Me Cabnal and the jaguars rolled themselves under a mat in the middle of the floor. Soon the black men came banging and howling into the house. Shuffling around the room, they sniffed like dogs at the women and goosed a man sleeping off too much *pox*. Finally one of them found their quarry. Pulling up the mat in triumph, he turned and made a ritual Tzotzil address to the members of the *pasión* household: "Watch carefully how this is done!" he says, according to Bricker. "Look children, so you will know how to do this when you grow up!"

The three black men then lifted the six sandal-shod feet of Me Cabnal and her consorts, spread their legs, and went through the motions of having sexual intercourse with them. They then switched positions, Me Cabnal and the jaguars on top and the black men underneath. The occupants of the house, young and old, screamed with laughter. In the end, Me Cabnal stood up, picked up a gourd full of *chicha*, drank most of it, and spat the rest on the black men and the surrounding crowd. A good part landed on the *hrinko* at the door.

When I returned to Padre Miguel's afterward, he poured me a drink.

"People think it's so peaceful here," he said, "but look at these."

He pulled out a folder full of newspaper clippings and handed it to me.

"Testimonies to my character," he said. "For when they canonize me in the Vatican."

I pulled out one of the clippings. It was from *Excelsior*, the paper of the Mexico City establishment. The article was about Ladino-Indian conflicts in the highlands of Chiapas, and explained that Padre Miguel had denounced certain Chenalhó Ladinos for selling diplomas and teaching positions in the local school. One of those Padre Miguel had accused had been convicted of the charges, but not before spreading the rumor that Padre Miguel was directing a group of catechists—natives who do Christian teaching—to arm themselves and drive the Ladinos from the highlands.

There was no date on the clipping, but Padre Miguel told me that it was from the mid-seventies—the same period during which the Ladinos were being driven out of San Andrés, just over a mountain ridge. But, Padre Miguel's problems ran deeper than simple racial conflict. The catechists to which the article alluded were the foot soldiers of a widespread religious revival that had been underway among the highland Maya for several decades and that, over time, had taken on the overtones of a struggle between the poor Maya and the rich—not just Ladinos, but certain Maya as well. Because the bishop of San Cristóbal, Don Samuel Riúz García, was a liberation theologist—one of only two in Mexico—the churches in his diocese had addressed themselves largely to the poor.

"They accused me of hiding machine guns," Padre Miguel said. "I had to leave for a few weeks."

Reaching for the folder, Padre Miguel pulled out another clipping.

"This is one of my favorites," he said. "It came out after the *Excelsior* story."

It was from a Mexico City tabloid called *Alarma*. The headline read, EL PADRE MIGUEL CREE EN LOS JIPIS, "Padre Miguel believes in Hippies." It began, "It's really scandalous, the comportment of the French priest Miguel Chanteau, alias 'Padre Miguel. ...'" and went on to describe how Padre Miguel had turned his church into a way station for hippies who took drugs and slept on the altar. "He is also a drinker, and he dances in the modern style," the article continued, and accused him of having a personal collection of *francesitas,* "French girls."

"Here's a copy of a letter I received after the *Alarma* article was published," said Padre Miguel, handing me another sheet of paper.

The letter was from Monterrey: "I am a man who believes that people's private lives are their own business. I speak perfect French—and English." After a while, the letter got to the point. If Padre Miguel had so many *francesitas,* could he perhaps send one to Monterrey—although only a "*pura francesa*" would do.

Many of Padre Miguel's more recent clippings contained references to conflicts between traditionalists and evangelicals in Chenalhó. I asked him what was at issue between the two groups.

"In recent times the Catholic church has stood for change and evolution, while the evangelicals have been a force of conservatism," he answered. "But, as to specific issues, the evangelicals are adamantly opposed to the worship of saints, and they don't want to be obliged to contribute to the festivals. This makes the festivals more expensive for the rest of the people."

"And why do people become evangelicals?"

"One reason is the amount of drinking during festivals. It's an integral part of the festival system. However, the evangelicals forbid drinking, and for some people, becoming an evangelical is the only way they can stop. Another reason people become evangelicals is to avoid the expense of taking a *cargo*. It costs more than a million pesos [more than four hundred dollars] to become a carnival *pasión*, for example. It's a source of great prestige, but it's also a tremendous financial burden, and when the evangelicals refuse to contribute their share, it costs everyone else more."

That night I had trouble sleeping. I lay in bed and thought about the creation stories as they are related in the first section of the Popul Vuh. The Quiché creation began when the gods, confronted with a featureless, water-covered world, decided to separate the land from the sea and to populate it with creatures who would be "providers and nurturers" for the gods. The gods created the earth by simply pronouncing the word *earth*. In return for this act, they wanted to hear their speech echoed. The gods' first attempt at peopling the earth, however, produced only animals; rather than praising the gods, the animals only chattered and howled. The gods' second attempt at populating the earth yielded mud creatures, but the mud creatures merely crumbled into dust. The third attempt resulted in effigy humans, carved out of wood. The effigy humans spoke, but had nothing in their hearts and minds and didn't remember their creators. As a result of their godlessness, their world turned against them. Cooking pots, hearthstones, tortilla griddles, all rebelled. Their houses collapsed. They were attacked by jaguars. Eventually they were forced to flee into the forest, where they were transformed into monkeys. Given that the black men, the monkey men, of the carnival seemed to stand for godless, immoral behavior, I was willing to believe that the Chenalhó monkeys, like the Popul Vuh itself, were a local variation on what had once been a larger, more pervasive body of creation myths.

Once the monkeys were banished to the forest, it took the gods two attempts to get the fourth, the present, creation right. Their first attempt at the fourth creation produced four original people: Jaguar Quitze, Jaguar Night, Mahucutah, and True Jaguar. These people saw everything on earth perfectly. "As they looked, their knowledge became intense. Their sight passed through the trees, through rocks, through lakes, through seas, through mountains, through plains. ... [They] were truly gifted people." The gods, however, found their new creation threatening and decided it needed alteration. The eyes of the first four people were therefore weakened. "They were blinded as the face of a mirror is breathed upon. ... Now it was only when they looked nearby that things were clear."

It was the nature and duty of the Maya to try to recover this sight through accumulating knowledge and enlightenment over their lifetimes. The Lords of Quiché passed on this knowledge through the Popul Vuh and other hieroglyphic texts like it. In this context it is easy to imagine the pain it caused the Maya when the Spanish friars burned the Maya hieroglyphic books. Once the hieroglyphic texts were gone and the Maya scribes and priests were shorn of the knowledge of what the texts had once contained, it fell to the villages to preserve what they could of the accumulated clarity of vision. The ethnohistorian Ralph Roys says that at Indian festivals in colonial Yucatán, the fables, stories, and histories that were once found in the hieroglyphic books were chanted out loud to the beating of drums. It isn't hard to see that carnival *cargo* holders, the guardians of *pedrano* tradition, performed this same function for Chenalhó. Calixta Guiteras-Holmes writes, "He who serves the people and the saints is uplifted, enhanced, exalted; he becomes greater and sees the world in an ever clearer light."

The next morning I woke up early, feeling as if I were done with carnival. I left the parish house to make a round of the town before the sun rose over the steep eastern valley wall. At the end of main street I ran into Francisco, who asked me if I wanted to see the black men being painted. I followed him through the low door of one of the *pasión* houses. The interior of the house was lit by a single light bulb and crowded with people. Francisco beckoned me toward a corner, where a man poured me a large juice glass full of a clear liquid. It was *pox*. I didn't feel it appropriate to refuse. I drank it in several gulps, felt it burn down my throat, explode into my empty stomach, and immediately begin radiating toward my nerve endings. I graciously tendered the glass, thankful that I'd paid the admission fee, when to my dismay the glass was refilled. I looked at Francisco plaintively.

"It's the custom to drink three," he said cheerfully. "It makes you feel *fuerte*—strong."

I drank the three glasses, but *fuerte* I did not feel. My gums went numb. My stomach felt bombed. Someone offered me a stool, and gratefully I sat. Once I was settled, the world seemed very cheerful. Colors were brighter. Time seemed to stand still. I felt at one with the overcrowded, mud-walled house. A fire smoldered on the floor in the center of the room. Two of the masked men sat between me and it, their masks staring at me off the backs of their heads. One of the masked men leaned forward, thrust a few sticks of resinous pine into the fire, and balanced a *comal,* a flat metal griddle used for frying tortillas, over the hearthstones. The fire flared, burned brightly, and began emitting black, oily smoke, which curled its way around the *comal* and then disappeared up into the rafters. Standing on the far side of the fire were the six black men. After a while, one of them picked up a bunch of leaves and, using the leaves as a potholder, removed the *comal* from the fire. He let it cool for a minute and then with his free hand scooped the black resin off its underside. One of the other black men knelt in another pile of leaves and presented his face to the black man holding the *comal.* As the resin was applied, the other black men began a keening chant.

While this was going on, a young *pedrano* boy of four or five came and stood directly in front of me. Because I was on a low stool we were eye to eye. He wore a belted tunic and looked like a diminutive forty-year-old, an impression augmented by someone having inked a rakish mustache on his upper lip. I found his stare disconcerting, so I pointed and said, *"bigote,"* the Spanish word for mustache.

"Isimil," the boy corrected, offering the Tzotzil equivalent with the tone of someone long put upon by non-Tzotzil-speaking fools like myself.

He waited for a moment, continued staring at me, and then pronounced the word *"k'in,"* while indicating that I should repeat the word after him.

I couldn't believe it. *K'in* was not only the word for "day," it was also the word for "sun," and the oldest word ever found on a Maya inscription.

"K'in," I repeated.

"K'in," he said, demanding a more glottalized *k*.

A *pedrano* nearby took pity on me and explained that in Chenalhó, *k'in* was the word for carnival.

We were interrupted when the black men's chant suddenly rose in volume. They had finished painting their faces and they began running in and out of the house in pairs—three times each. Someone signaled for the flute and drum. The *pasiones* stood up and began a shuffling dance around the fire, pounding the earth with their beribboned staffs. Gradually the company formed a procession, poured into the street, and headed toward the plaza. I followed along. The sun was just coming over the valley wall, and as I emerged from the darkened *pasión* house, the outside seemed witheringly bright. Blinking, I looked at the world as if I'd never seen it before. People stared at me. I wondered if they could tell what I was feeling, or whether I had simply not previously noticed. We passed Padre Miguel, who had stepped out of the restaurant to watch the procession go by. I stopped and told him I'd had three glasses of *pox*. He waved his hand dismissively and headed back to his breakfast. I turned to rejoin the black men, but in the few seconds I had tarried, the little group of ceremonial figures I'd been following had receded down the street. I wanted to catch up with them, but it suddenly struck me as futile. I belonged, inevitably, to another world.

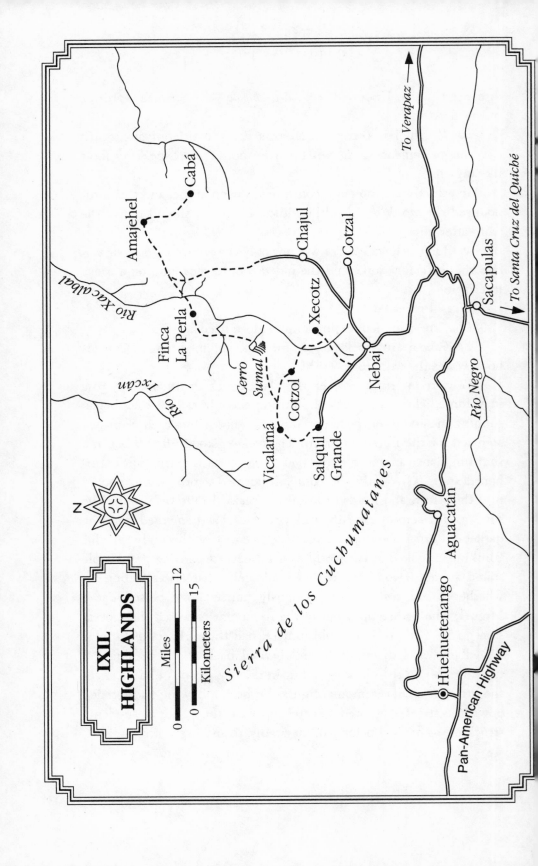

CHAPTER 6

Nebaj

AT THREE-THIRTY IN THE AFTERNOON, the wheels fell off my progress toward Nebaj, one of three towns forming the so-called "Ixil Triangle," the region perhaps hardest hit by the violence of recent years in Guatemala. I had been riding buses since leaving San Cristóbal in Mexico at seven that morning, but had managed to get only as far as Aguacatán, "place of the avocados," in the northern Guatemalan highlands. Aguacatán lay hard under the Cuchumatanes, the nation's highest mountain range, with peaks to almost thirteen thousand feet. Nebaj was still across the mountains, and my prospects of getting any closer that day seemed bleak.

"*Ya,* that's it," the bus driver said when I asked him if we were going farther.

His assistant climbed up on the bus roof. He pulled my dust-covered duffel from under a mound of onions and lowered it down onto the sidewalk, next to a basket of cabbages. I looked around me. The bus had come to a stop in front of an ancient colonial church. A jagged crack, looking like a knife slash across someone's face, ran across the church facade. The windows were boarded up. It was Saturday afternoon, the eve of market day, and the town's central plaza was already jammed with Indians, the women wearing a brocaded cloth, a symbol of water and fertility, wound into their hair in such a way that two bright pompoms emerged at the back. These were *aguacatecos,* some sixteen thousand in number, who constitute one of the smaller of the twenty-one groups making up the linguistically shattered world of the Guatemalan Maya.

For two quetzales, seventy-five cents, I took a room in Aguacatán's only *pensión.* A naked light bulb hung over a saggy cot in a windowless concrete cell. I put my bags in the corner and lay down on the cot. I felt as if I'd checked into jail.

Back in the center of town, I learned that "Civil Patrol Day," culminating in the election of "Miss Civil Patrol," was about to be celebrated. The Civil Patrol is the means by which the army, in the aftermath of its successful counterinsurgency campaign of the early eighties, has perpetuated its control over rural Guatemala. In the contested zones (which is to say the Indian areas) all able-bodied men between the ages of eighteen and sixty-five are required to spend a day every week or two doing paramilitary work. In the beginning this work included such duties as forming a human shield for army units advancing into guerrilla territory or making the choice between murdering one's subversive neighbors or being murdered oneself, but in recent years it has more typically consisted of standing guard duty or checking identification cards. This is the face that the Civil Patrol presented in Aguacatán. While evil-looking Ladino policemen with dark glasses and pump-action shotguns toured the town in an expensive Mercedes jeep, a couple of discouraged *aguacatecos* sat on an adobe wall slumped over bolt-action rifles.

The honking of car horns announced the arrival of the beauty contestants. Three Japanese pickup trucks drove down the main street with three dazed-looking Ladina girls sitting on the hoods. The contestants' frilly dresses and profuse makeup made them look like dolls. Banners proclaimed that the girls represented two government agricultural banks and a government-sponsored farmers' organization. The pickups pulled up in front of the municipal building. The three contestants climbed down from the truck hoods, disappeared inside, and then reappeared on the roof, where concrete reinforcement bars sprouting nakedly skyward indicated that another

level of government offices was forthcoming. There, a master of ceremonies ripped open envelopes and over a loudspeaker posed such
questions as "What can young people do to help Aguacatán?" and
"What, with specific reference to the San Juan [a local river], is the
best way for the town to promote tourism?"

I watched all this from a bench on the edge of the plaza. Gusts of
wind sent a grit of fine dust swirling into my teeth. Air plants hung
from the telephone wires. A crowd gathered around a man drawing
pink strands of sugar into cotton candy. The wind caught several of
the strands and blew them past a family of *aguacatecos,* the women
dressed in bright *huipiles.* They watched the drawn sugar float by as
if watching the flight of an exotic butterfly.

My plan in going to Nebaj was to get some sense of the violence
inflicted on the Guatemalan Maya, which in the early 1980's
resulted in the deaths of perhaps a hundred thousand people, most of
them Maya, as well as the eradication of more than four hundred
Indian communities. Beyond the body count, however, what interested me was the degree to which this violence seemed to echo issues
in the relations between Maya and non-Maya that had plagued the
region since the Conquest. In fact, some anthropologists have argued
that the recent wave of violence has brought about changes in Maya
life greater than any since the Conquest.

I had little time in which to accomplish this mission, and after
passing the night in my *pensión,* I was starting to find "the place of
the avocados" a serious impediment to my plans. There were plenty
of buses going back toward Huehuetenango and the Mexican border,
but none going farther down the valley toward Sacapulas, from
which a road crossed the twenty-three miles over the Cuchumatanes
to Nebaj. I took to stopping every moving vehicle, of which there
were few. None were going in my direction.

Finally, at nine, two motorcyclists rode into town. They looked
like something out of *The Road Warrior.* One was a huge, unshaven
man with close-set blue eyes. The other had a black tinted visor on
his helmet that completely hid his face. They were German and
Dutch, had met on the beach in Belize, and had rented the bikes in
Antigua, Guatemala's former capital.

Sure, I could ride with them to Sacapulas. The German biker slung my duffel across his back. I hopped on behind the Dutchman, and we roared up out of town, kicking clouds of dust up into the cold, early-morning mountain air. As we left Aguacatán we traversed a mountain ridge, gradually gaining altitude. It had been well below freezing overnight and it was still cold. The bikers had gloves, but as we skidded on loose gravel, snaked around switchbacks, and dodged landslides, my hands turned stiff with cold. Then the terrain changed. The road leveled off on a high plateau. The green of Aguacatán disappeared and we were looking down into a wide, dry interior valley. Cacti studded the slopes. Distant, flat tablelands were dissected by dizzyingly precipitous ravines. Far below, in the valley bottom, a sparkling river wound through green fields and groves of graceful palms.

We got off the motorcycles to admire the view. The land that stretched out beneath us belonged, at the time of the Conquest, to the Quiché Maya, then the most powerful group in Guatemala. The Quiché took on the Spanish almost as soon as the conquistadors entered the highlands. The decisive battle was fought in 1524 outside what was then Xelahuh—"under the ten"—and is now the city of Quetzaltenango. The Spanish were commanded by Pedro de Alvarado, a notoriously cruel captain of Cortés' whom the Indians referred to as Tonatiuh, or "Sun," for his blond hair and beard. In his account of the battle Alvarado mentions drawing a Quiché army down out of the mountains and onto a plain, turning on them with his cavalry, and making "a very severe pursuit and punishment." His account continues: "In this affair one of the four chiefs of Utatlán was killed, who was captain general of all this country." Utatlán was the Nahuatl name that Alvarado's Central Mexican auxiliary used for the Quiché capital, Chi Gumarcaah, "place of the rotten cane."

The Quiché version, recorded in a post-Conquest document in support of Quiché land claims referred to as the *Títulos de la casa Ixquín-Nehaib* (edited by Adrían Recinos), is very different. In preparation for war, the Quiché captain, Tecum Uman, grandson of the great Quiché king Quicab, put on wings with which he flew and his two arms and legs were covered with feathers and he wore a crown, and on his chest he wore a very large emerald which looked like a mirror, and he wore another on his forehead. And another on his back. ... This captain flew like an eagle. He was a great nobleman and a great sorcerer.

The Quiché chroniclers note the death of many Indians when the battle was joined, until

Captain Tecum flew up, he came like an eagle full of real feathers, which were not artificial; he wore wings which also sprang from his body. ... That captain Tecum came with the intention of killing Tonatiuh who came on horseback and he hit the horse instead of the *adelantado* ["provincial governor"] and he beheaded the horse with one lance. It was not a lance of iron but of shiny stone and this captain had placed a spell on it. And when he saw that it was not the *adelantado* but the horse who had died, he returned to fly overhead in order to come from there to kill the *adelantado*. Then the *adelantado* awaited him with his lance and he impaled this Captain Tecum with it. Immediately two dogs ran up ... those dogs seized this Indian in order to tear him into pieces, and as the *adelantado* saw that this Indian was very gallant and that he wore these three crowns of gold, silver, diamonds, and emeralds and of pearls, he came to defend him from the dogs and he stood looking at him very deliberately. He appeared covered with quetzal [feathers] and very beautiful plumes, for which reason this town of Quetzaltenango was given its name, because here is where the death of this Captain Tecum came to pass. (English translation by Victoria Bricker from her book *The Indian Christ, The Indian King*)

After the defeat of the Quiché armies, Alvarado advanced on their capital, Chi Gumarcaah, the ruins of which are now located just outside the modern city of Santa Cruz del Quiché. There, Alvarado discovered a plot to trap and burn him inside the capital. In revenge, he seized two of the Quiché kings, Oxib-Queh and Beleheb-Tzy, and burned them alive. The date was April 4, 1524, and it effectively marked the end of Quiché power in the Guatemalan highlands.

Twenty-five years later, an unnamed Spanish traveler described an encounter with the grandsons of the kings of the Quiché: "Those who were at one time the lords of Utatlán are as poor and miserable as the poorest Indian of the village, and their wives made tortillas for their meal ... and they carried wood and water for their houses. ... All were extremely poor; they left children all of whom were destitute and miserable." (Quoted in the introduction to Adrian Recinos' version of the Popul Vuh)

We got back on the motorcycles and made a skidding descent into the valley. Sacapulas lay along the river below us, the Negro, near the site of an important pre-Columbian saltworks. The motorcyclists left me off on the east bank of the river at the foot of a bridge that crossed over to the town. I walked out to the middle of the bridge and looked down at the sparkling blue-green water rushing over shallow sunlit gravel banks below. The bridge was a recent construction, but built on the site of a much older bridge put up in the mid-sixteenth century, when Sacapulas had been the site of the preeminent Dominican friary in the Guatemalan highlands and the administrative center of an amazing sixteenth-century attempt to accomplish a second, spiritual, conquest of the Maya.

In the initial decades after the Conquest, the conquistadors themselves were the primary organizers of the defeated Maya. The king granted the conquistadors *encomiendas,* feudal estates on which they were given unrestrained use of Indian labor in exchange for supposedly providing the Indians with a benign example of the Spanish-Christian way of life. In practice, life on most *encomiendas* translated into unredeemed slavery for the Indians.

The philosophy behind the *encomiendas* was the then prevalent Aristotelian notion that humanity was divided into natural freemen and natural slaves. In the context of the New World, the Spanish, needless to say, were the freemen and the Indians the slaves. This was seen as a more or less permanent condition. Any improvement in the Indians' condition would come only gradually, through prolonged exposure to their Spanish superiors.

At the time of the Conquest of the New World, the king of

Spain was Charles V, emperor of the Holy Roman Empire. Raised in Flanders, he was an intelligent, conscientious man who spent a good deal of time worrying about what was the right thing to do with his millions of New World subjects. Although he was a grandson of Ferdinand and Isabella, the Spanish considered him a foreigner; when he assumed the crown of Spain in 1516, he brought a retinue of liberal-minded Flemish advisers with him. One of Charles V's principal advisers on New World policy was a Dominican named Bartolomé de las Casas. Las Casas, who later came to be referred to as "the apostle of the Indians," had been a slaveholder himself until, disgusted by the abuse he saw, he became an advocate of a more humane treatment of the New World Indians.

Rather than directly attacking the Aristotelian conception of Spain's role in the New World, Las Casas turned the argument on its head by agreeing that there were freemen and slaves, but arguing that the Indians were not natural slaves. He maintained that the Indians fulfilled Aristotle's requirements for leading the virtuous life. The Indians were religious and monogamous; their temples compared favorably to those of the ancient Egyptians. The Indians were, in effect, "infants of the faith." They were open to God, he argued, and they therefore needed to be introduced to Christianity responsibly, by men of God, not by *encomenderos* whose interests ran contrary to those of the king. Las Casas' idea was that rather than congregating the Indians in *encomiendas,* where they would be abused and never would receive proper religious instruction, they should be congregated around churches, under the auspices of friars who had a genuine interest in their religious well-being. Las Casas essentially argued that friars, not conquistadors, should administer the New World empire.

In 1537, Las Casas convinced Charles V to experiment with his approach. Although *adelantado* Alvarado had been able to conquer the Quiché and the other large Maya groups of the central highlands, ten or fifteen years after his arrival in Guatemala he had still made little progress with the wilder, more dispersed Maya of the eastern highlands. The conquistadors called this region the *tierra de guerra,* "land of war," and had more or less given up trying to conquer it. Las Casas told Charles V that if he would ban all civil and military authority from the *tierra de guerra* for five years (a time frame that was later extended), Las Casas and his fellow Dominicans would conquer the Indians by peaceful means. They would turn the *tierra de guerra* into Verapaz, "true peace."

After receiving the king's endorsement, the Dominicans set to work. They began by composing ballads telling the Bible stories in Quiché couplets, and trained four Christianized Maya merchants to sing them. They loaded the merchants down with knives, scissors, bells, mirrors, and other trinkets and sent them off into the Maya regions. Their first destination was Sacapulas, where, because the Maya of this region had never heard Spanish harmonies before, the merchants were a hit. Their reputation spread, and they were eventually invited to perform for the lords of the *tierra de guerra* on the far side of the Cuchumatanes. As planned, this welcome led to invitations being extended to the friars themselves. The first to go, in the summer of 1538, was a friar named Luis Cáncer. Las Casas himself joined Luis Cáncer later that same year. They were well received and began preparing the way for the next phase of their project, which was to congregate the Maya into Dominican-controlled towns.

At this point, Las Casas returned to Spain, where he not only recruited more friars for the project, but also arranged to have the *tierra de guerra* attached to the diocese of San Cristóbal de las Casas and to have himself appointed bishop. While making these arrangements, however, he became involved in a far greater controversy concerning Spain's policy toward its colonies—the promulgation of the so-called New Laws. The New Laws codified much of Las Casas' vision of the New World and thus represented a temporary triumph of his ideas on a universal rather than an experimental level. Instituted in 1542, they essentially made Indians citizens of Spain and gave special privileges to the friars who were to be their tutors. They also abolished the *encomienda* altogether, thus disenfranchising the very Spaniards who had conquered the Indians.

The New Laws caused a sensation when they were published in the colonies in 1543. In Peru, enraged colonists severed the head of a royal viceroy and then dragged it around town by its hair. Because

Las Casas was perceived to be the moving force behind the New Laws he became, according to the historian Lewis Hanke, "the most fiercely hated man in all the Spanish realms." When, in 1545, Las Casas returned to San Cristóbal (then known as Ciudad Réal) to take up his new bishopric, riots broke out and his parishioners threatened his life. After three months under siege in his cathedral, Las Casas managed to slip out of town to make a brief visit to the Verapaz. Shortly afterward, he discovered that his enemies at court had had the New Laws gutted. Las Casas promptly returned to Spain. He was already over seventy, and never came back to the New World.

The Verapaz experiment continued in Las Casas' absence. By 1547, the highland areas had been successfully congregated, and Las Casas' Dominicans began to turn their attentions to the wilder areas farther north, an area where the slopes of the highlands descended to meet the Lacandón and the Petén—land that belonged to Cholan-speaking descendants of the Classic Maya. There, the missionaries ran into trouble. With great difficulty they succeeded in converting a group called the Manché Chol, but no sooner had they done so than the Manché towns were raided by unconverted Lacandóns and Itzás. In 1555, Lacandóns surprised two of Las Casas' friars and thirty of their Christianized followers in a Manché town and murdered them all. Since there were few friars to begin with, this was a severe blow to the Verapaz experiment—especially severe since one of the murdered friars, Domingo de Vico, was a scholarly Dominican who had mastered seven Maya languages. Panicked when they saw that the friars could not defend them, the Manché Chol began to desert the mission towns and return to their former religion. As they did so, the Lacandóns extended their raids all the way into the highland heart of the Verapaz. In 1558 the Dominicans were forced to petition for military protection, to the great satisfaction of the Guatemalan civil authorities.

As I stood along the Sacapulas bridge rail, I glanced up and was startled to see a fully armed military patrol in camouflage gear marching toward me. The line grew until I could see fifty or sixty soldiers, armed with everything from machine guns to mortars. The irony of their marching across the bridge to the Verapaz was not lost on me. The 1960's and '70's, leading up to the worst of the recent violence, had been the first period of church idealism in Guatemala since the Verapaz experiment. Foreign priests, many of them Spanish and North American, had evangelized among the Indians, founded cooperatives, and taught literacy. The civil and military authorities in Guatemala had apparently found the resulting Indian political consciousness threatening, because in the late seventies, as a preface to the more generalized violence to come, thousands of religiously inspired catechists, cooperative members, and community leaders were selectively assassinated. Nor did the violence stop with the lay religious. Between 1976 and 1981 sixteen priests were murdered. The situation got so bad in the Indian highlands that in 1980 the bishop of Quiché, a largely Indian department that includes both Sacapulas and my destination, Nebaj, sent his priests into temporary exile.

I followed the soldiers up the hill and into the center of town. Just off the main plaza, they filed through a gate bearing the words DECAMPAMENTO MILITAR SACAPULAS. To one side of the gate was painted the base motto: SOLO EL QUE LUCHA TIENE DERECHO A VENCER. SOLO EL QUE VENCE TIENE DERECHO A VIVIR. "Only he who struggles has the right to conquer. Only he who conquers has the right to live."

It was Sunday and a market was underway beneath two huge ceiba trees in the central plaza. Despite the presence of the military, the leafy shade of the trees and the bright colors of the Indian *huipiles* created a festive atmosphere. I walked around the plaza looking for traces of the Dominican monastery, but could only find some foundations underneath market stalls and, to one side, a very old colonial church. Inside the church, a double row of carved wooden columns, painted pale blue, supported a cream-colored canopy ceiling. The walls were lined with wooden saints, cracked and twisted with antiquity. A young bearded priest was saying Mass to a congregation of Indians, one of whom had a guitar and was leading the others in hymns. Despite the efforts of the army, this was definitely activist, post–Vatican II Catholicism, and I thought of the irony of the reform movement in the Guatemalan church. The foreign priests who had led the movement had been invited into the country by Mariano Rossell y Arelano, a conservative Guatemalan archbishop eager to counteract the liberalism introduced by the postwar regime of President Juan José Arevalo. Under the auspices of Catholic Action, an anti-Communist, anti-Protestant, and socially conservative church movement emanating from Rome, the archbishop recruited foreign priests to work in Guatemala. When the archbishop started recruiting, in 1948, there were only a hundred priests in the entire country. By the late 1960's the number had risen to above five hundred. Most of the foreign priest-recruits were promptly sent out to Indian areas. There, they experienced first hand not only the shocking racism toward the Guatemalan Maya, but also the right-wing military coup sponsored by Washington in 1954. Twenty years after the archbishop began his recruiting, the very priests who had been brought in to combat liberalism and reform became its chief proponents.

Recrossing the river, I found the Nebaj bus waiting in the shade of a small tree. A beefy Ladino man had set up a tepee in the river shallows nearby and was baptizing people and singing revival music over a loudspeaker. A group of Indian women sat nearby, listening passively. Apocalypse was in the air. The bus, like most in Guatemala, was a battered Blue Bird schoolbus with balding tires. It was largely empty when I climbed on board, but jackets and other articles of clothing were strewn all over the seats. I pushed someone's hat aside and sat down. Shortly the passengers began to file back on. When there were two people on each bench, a third squeezed on and, in some cases, a fourth. I had taken someone's place, but didn't offer to give it up. To me this was acceptable behavior in the cut-throat world of Guatemalan bus travel. Besides, the aisle was so full that it soon became impossible to move in any direction.

The bus started climbing the mountain at an angle so steep that I felt as if I were taking off in an airplane. Within a few minutes we had attained sufficent altitude to be inching along precipitous drops. The mountain itself consisted of loose scree, which seemed ready to avalanche at any moment. A thin retaining wall appeared to be all that held the road in place. A mile out of town the bus ground to a halt. Passengers started pouring off. I asked my neighbor what was happening.

"They're going to sit on the roof," he told me.

My neighbor assured me that I was foolish to give up my ill-won seat, but for me there was no hesitation. I climbed up to the bus roof and sat down on top of a sack of corn at the very front of the luggage rack, directly over the driver's seat. I felt content. The sun was hot. The air was cold. The view was spectacular. Even better, if the bus rolled I could jump for it.

The northeastern slopes of the Cuchumatanes differ radically from the southwestern. Climbing up from Sacapulas, you reach a ridge from which, within a short space, you can look down on both sides of the range. Behind you, particularly in the dry season, everything is desiccated, hardscrabble. Ahead, a turbulent sea of green mountains, watered annually by up to nine feet of Caribbean moisture, drops off toward the jungles of the Lacandón and the Petén. This is Ixil Maya country.

During the Classic period the Ixil Maya were a prosperous people who acted as middlemen in the exchange of Lacandón rubber, feathers, skins, and copal for highland salt, obsidian, and pyrite. With the Post-Classic decline of Maya rain forest culture, however, the Ixils fell into a wild isolation, maintaining close contact only with the even wilder Lacandóns. In the fifteenth century the Quiché king Quicab, grandfather of Tecum Uman, conquered the Ixil all the way down to the foothills of the Lacandón. A century later, in 1530, the Spanish managed to conquer the region on their second attempt. Their vanquished opponents were branded and shipped south as slaves, where they died as cargo bearers on the isthmus of Panama or while supporting the Spanish conquests in the Andes.

The Ixil region was not part of the *Verapaz,* but it was part of the Sacapulas parish, and the friars were able to use the assistance of civil and military authorities, rather than the power of simple persuasion, to accomplish the first part of their mission, which was to flush the Ixils out of the mountains and congregate them in Spanish-controlled towns. The Ixils, however, rapidly developed a reputation as a stubborn people who were reluctant to leave their own lands or give up the dispersed existence to which they were accustomed. The colonial records are full of complaints about their propensity for slipping back into the mountain wilds, their lack of respect for priests, and their persistence, in the face of fines and whippings, in burning copal at their own shrines. According to *Ixil Country*, an anthropological study by Benjamin Colby and Pierre van den Berghe, the maximum extent of Spanish control came in the early to mid-seventeenth century. This was a time when, among other things, Ixil names such as Batz, Pop, Icom, and Yax were abolished in favor of Spanish names such as Hernandéz, Mendoza, and Guzmán.

There were several reasons for the subsequent decline in Spanish control, but prominent among them was the decline in the evangelical zeal of the priests. The first generation of New World friars—Las Casas' contemporaries—were men aflame with idealism. Among the most highly educated people in Europe, they approached their missions in the New World with millennial fervor. Europe was decadent, debauched, hopeless. The Indians were children of God who had not yet been corrupted and therefore had the potential for spiritual perfection. In going to the New World, many of the friars hoped for nothing less than a religious utopia, the creation of an Augustinian city of God.

Within a few years it became apparent that the Indians weren't interested. The Maya may have been defeated by the Spanish armies and baptized by the friars, they may have taken Spanish names and attached Christian saints' names to the names of their own gods, but in most other ways they remained stubbornly Maya. Their intransigence was frustrating to the friars. William Hanks, a University of Chicago linguist who has worked extensively in the Yucatán, explains Bishop Landa's auto-da-fé of 1562 this way: After more than a decade of painstaking efforts to ideologically remake a select group of carefully chosen students, the bishop discovered that his charges were still practicing "idolatry." It was too much for him. Bishop Landa went into a rage. Fueled by confessions exacted under torture, he conducted an unsanctioned inquisition which culminated in the infamous burning of twenty-seven hieroglyphic texts.

In more remote outposts like the Ixil country, disillusionment must have set in in less spectacular fashion, but it set in nevertheless. As years went on, initially idealistic friars and priests woke up each morning to find themselves not the spiritual leaders of Christian utopian communities, but beleaguered administrators alone in a sea of sullen Maya hostility. They began to cut corners, make compromises. In return for publicly acknowledging certain Spanish Catholic norms, the Maya up until the nineteenth century were conceded a large measure of independence.

What finally changed this equation was the arrival of coffee, in the mid-nineteenth century. Coffee, which grows on mountain slopes up to five thousand feet, was the first crop ever to show real commercial potential in Guatemala, and it suddenly made large areas of Indian land, previously of no interest to the Ladino world, extremely valuable. Coffee growing also required large quantities of seasonal labor, for clearing and planting the fincas, for harvesting the beans, and for building the roads that allowed the coffee to be transported to its markets.

The problem was that the Maya simply weren't interested. Inducements were offered, but the Maya had better things to do than leave their families and their milpas for underpaid work on coffee fincas. To the rulers of Guatemala, this was an intellectual as well as an economic affront. Laboring on the coffee fincas would have a civilizing effect on the Maya. The Maya could improve themselves by their increased contact with Ladino society. It was the old Aristotelian argument all over again. To most Guatemalans, the measure of the level of civilization attained by a Maya was still how much he or she wanted to live according to "European" norms.

When various inducements failed to produce either sufficient land or labor to get the coffee economy off the ground, the government took measures to force the Maya into the economy. It started by expropriating fallow Maya land and reviving the long-dormant colonial practice of labor drafts. Maya who fled into the mountains were brought down tied like criminals. Wives were held hostage against fugitive husbands. When even this didn't produce enough workers, the Maya were bound into a web of debt. The government imposed new taxes and forced the Indians to carry identification cards showing their debt status. Indian village authorities were made legally and financially responsible for the debts incurred by individual Indians.

The anthropologist Carol Smith estimates that the Guatemalan Maya lost fifty percent of their land during the nineteenth century. Since this was also a time when the population of the Maya was beginning to rebound after centuries of decline, the Maya gradually fell into the situation in which they find themselves now: forced by an insufficent land base to spend large parts of every year doing seasonal work on large agricultural plantations. In the late 1960's, Colby and van den Berghe discovered, a third of the Ixil men were forced into migratory work each year, and the situation has worsened dramatically since then. In recent years finca work has expanded beyond coffee to seasonal work on big coastal agricultural plantations. There, laborers are sprayed with pesticides, housed in unsanitary conditions, fired when they get sick, and paid virtually nothing.

The resentment this situation caused among the Maya fueled the rise of Catholic Action. In the Ixil country, the arrival in Nebaj of Sacred Heart missionaries from Spain in 1955 marked the revival of the old conflict between the Catholic church and the civil authorities over who should control the Indian population. With the help of the Sacred Heart missionaries, the Maya began to learn to read, to write, and to question their condition. They bought and colonized unused land, set up cooperatives, and began to organize unions, actions that proved profoundly threatening to Guatemala's ruling class. Soon the assassinations started. The targets in rural areas were people in the Catholic Action leadership, regardless of whether their involvement was political, educational, or religious. Between 1976 and 1979, three hundred and fifty Catholic Action activists are said to have been kidnapped and killed in the three principal towns of the Ixil alone, Nebaj, Chajul, and Cotzal.

In a refugee camp in Mexico, I talked with an Ixil catechist, part of a group that with the help of one of the Spanish priests had bought and colonized land in the jungles in the north of the Ixil country, land from which they were later driven by the army. The murders and kidnappings first started back in the highlands, he told me. He'd gone back to his old village and found that the people there had become so angry after several of their leaders were killed that they'd fortified themselves with drink, picked up their machetes, and killed the army lieutenant who was responsible for the death squads.

"But why did the army start the assassinations in the first place?" I asked.

The catechist smiled bitterly. "We were learning to help ourselves," he said. "We were buying our own land, organizing unions. One day the *patrón* would have asked for people to cut his sugarcane, to harvest his coffee, and no one would have come."

Nebaj, the capital of the Ixil, lies at approximately sixty-two hundred feet at the head of a high valley ringed with conifers. Wood smoke hangs in the air and the sun glints on creamy stacks of new-split pine in a way that makes you think that you're in a mountain resort. It's not an impression that lasts. Soldiers are everywhere. There's an air of sullen resignation about the place.

I checked into the Pensión Tres Hermanas and for the same two quetzals I'd spent in Aguacatán got the same cot-and-concrete-cell combo. After I'd put down my bags, I set out to find Mike Shawcross, an Englishman in his mid-forties who ran a bookstore in Antigua and, in Nebaj, the Shawcross Aid Programme for Highland Indians, an organization devoted to rebuilding Indian villages destroyed during the violence. I had discussed traveling into the Ixil mountains with Shawcross in Antigua, and he had suggested we meet in Nebaj.

"Are you up for a stiff walk?" Shawcross asked when I found him in his office. He was a bearded man with the knotty muscles of an inveterate hiker. He explained that he had some English volunteers who for the last four months had been building a water system in the *aldea* (the Guatemalan word for "hamlet") of Cotzal, a six-hour march into the mountains. "It's real backcountry," Shawcross said.

"I've never been there myself, but I'm going for the inauguration of the water system tomorrow. Would you like to come?"

I said that I would, and we arranged to meet at his office at six the next morning.

That evening I had dinner at the Tres Hermanas with a Stanford anthropologist named David Stoll. When I asked him about the history of the Ixil, he told me that the Ladino coffee growers had arrived in the 1890's and had stolen a great deal of Ixil land north of Nebaj, where the mountains sloped away toward the tropics along the border with Mexico. The region's most famous coffee finca, Finca La Perla, was in this area, on land that the Indians felt rightly belonged to the Ixil municipality of Chajul. The loss of the land had left a legacy of bitterness among the Ixils, and it was probably not coincidental that the first significant guerrilla military action in the region had been the execution, in June 1975, of the much-hated owner of Finca La Perla, Luis Arenas Barrera, the so-called Tiger of the Ixcán.

Were the guerrillas still a viable military force in the area?

"There was a fire fight on the far side of town last night," David said. "It started with a short burst of automatic weapons fire. That was the guerrillas. They're very conservative with their ammunition. The automatic weapons fire was followed by a series of single shots. That was the Civil Patrol. Then a grenade was thrown, followed by heavy, sustained machine-gun fire and finally a few mortar rounds. That was all, presumably, the army. However, beyond the first few shots, I'm not really sure what happened. I'm not in a position to go to the local military commander and ask him about the previous night's engagement."

The guerrillas who carried out the execution of Luis Arenas Barrera and who, no doubt, had attacked Nebaj the night before were members of the Ejército Guerrillero de los Pobres—the "Guerrilla Army of the Poor," or the EGP—one of four guerrilla groups that took up arms against the government in the seventies. The EGP was created by Ladino survivors of the disastrous guerrilla campaigns in the south a decade earlier. The guerrillas of the sixties had been a peculiar combination of romantic insurrectionist and rigidly text-book Marxist, which is to say that their primary interest was the "workers," their goal was the city; they had shown only marginal concern for the Indians.

In the aftermath of their crushing defeat, however, the guerrillas apparently rethought their premises, decided that the Maya were "the people," and, in the EGP, arrived at a strategy of Vietnam-style popular war with both rural and urban fronts. The urban front was soon wiped out, but the rural front was a different story. In 1971, twenty-five EGP members crossed into the northern Ixil from the Lacandón jungle in Mexico. Initially the little band created a base for itself among the rain forest colonists in the border area, but it gradually extended its range into the heavily populated highlands. An account of the group's first four years, *Days of the Jungle,* was written by Mario Payeras, now living in exile in Mexico City. Payeras speaks of sleeping on beds of moss and pine needles, of discovering ancient Maya cities, of watching comets cross the sky, and of singing guerrilla anthems with lyrics such as this:

> Today when our country, cradle of Tecum Uman,
> Is governed by thieves and assassins,
> The fighters who will guide its destiny
> Are found along the road. ...

But Payeras also mentions that it was mounting pressure from the Indians among whom the guerrillas were recruiting that prompted the decision to execute the Tiger of the Ixcán in 1975. The guerrillas approached Arenas Barrera, whom the Indians hated, by joining a crowd of peons lined up on payday. They caught him, Payeras says, "standing in front of the manager's office and looking like a bird of prey, the lord of the manor was counting his coins and unfolding some crumpled bills." When Arenas Barrera saw his assailants, he reached for his gun, but the guerrillas shot first. Afterward the guerrillas gave a speech explaining their action in Ixil, and then led the workers in a chorus of "Long live the poor, death to the rich!"

At the time of the execution of the Tiger of the Ixcán, the EGP's rural military wing consisted of fifty combatants. Within five years, however, their support had mushroomed to the point where, with the exception of a few garrison towns, practically all the central highlands were under EGP control. Several things accounted for this extraordinary growth. Among them was that the EGP made a point of addressing the Maya in their own languages and respecting their customs as far as possible. Their message, that the Indians were oppressed and that something ought to be done about it, contained an irrefutable core of truth. The problem was that recruits began to come in faster than they could be either armed or politically absorbed. In any event, many of the Indians were joining the guerrillas not because of ideological commitment but because it was the only way that they could be safe from army death squads, then running at full tilt.

The guerrillas became overconfident. Seeing the success of the Sandinistas in Nicaragua and the near success of the Faribundo Martí Liberation Front in El Salvador, they began to provoke the army, inviting retaliation on Indian communities who were wavering in their commitment and at the same time pressing for an overly optimistic timetable for insurrection.

One of the reasons the army is said to have struck the Ixil in late 1981 was because it had correctly observed that the EGP was vastly overextended. And when the army struck, it struck not at the guerrillas, who were elusive and capable of fighting back, but at the Ixils, who weren't—at least not with more than slingshots, booby traps, and an occasional .22-caliber rifle. To the army, the question of whether the particular Ixils they found themselves attacking had been allied with the guerrillas or not was irrelevant. In response to what the Guatemalan leadership perceived as a Maya rebellion spreading across the highlands, the army color-coded a map of Guatemala according to the alleged degree of guerrilla sympathy. The Ixil was colored red, which meant maximum sympathy. In the red zones, anything that moved was the enemy.

The first stage of the army's campaign, called *tierra arrasada*—literally, "razed earth"—lasted eighteen months and was clearly intended to traumatize the Maya so that they would never again entertain the idea of asserting their rights. Women were raped, children machete'd. Populations were herded into churches and burned alive. Villages whose inhabitants had never seen a helicopter were first strafed or napalmed from the air and then bombed out of existence. Huge areas of the highlands were depopulated. Those Ixils lucky enough to survive either fled to Mexico or, in smaller numbers, into the army-controlled towns of Nebaj, Chajul, and Cotzal, the three Ixil communities for which the army had coined the term "Ixil Triangle."

There, many were settled into model villages collaboratively run by the army and various American evangelical Protestant missionaries. Identical houses were laid out in neat grids fronting on "Street of the Army," or "Development Avenue." Supporting funds from the United States were raised through an organization called "International Love Lift," backed by such fundamentalist luminaries as Jerry Falwell and Pat Robertson. Ixils started becoming evangelicals to save their lives.

I asked David if he felt the model villages represented another effort at a spiritual conquest of the Maya.

"In my opinion," he said, "the model villages have one overriding purpose, which is to isolate the people from the guerrillas."

I had begun to advance another theory, that the model villages represented an attempt to break the age-old bond between the Maya and their land, when Mike Shawcross walked in. Mike takes a conservative view of the Guatemalan situation, and he apparently picked up, and did not approve of, my use of the term "model village."

"What you are about to say is wrong," he told me. "The Miami Herald just ran an article in which it discussed the 'model cities' in Nebaj," he continued. "There are no cities in the Ixil, and none of the new settlements is 'model.'"

"What would you call them then?" asked David.

"They're relocated," Mike said.

"And concentrated?" asked David.

"I would agree with 'concentrated relocated,'" said Mike.

I had the sense that I was witnessing an argument that had been replayed more than one evening at the Tres Hermanas, so I pleaded our early departure the next morning and returned to my room.

The door of my Tres Hermanas cell closed from the inside by propping up a six-foot log. No sooner had I wrestled the log into place than I heard a light tapping on the outside. I asked who it was. No one answered, so I removed the log, opened the door, and looked down to see two big-eyed, rail-thin Indian boys standing shoeless in the forty-degree cold. They were sorry to bother me, the older one said, but they didn't have anything to eat and their mother was sick and could I help them out?

"Where is your father?" I asked.

"He's been gone for years," the older boy said.

"Where did he go?"

"They dragged him out of the house and we never saw him again."

"Who was 'they'?" I asked.

"The army."

I gave the boys some money to buy some corn and then a few aspirin—the only medicine I had on me—for their mother. Perhaps I was being suckered, but it didn't matter to me. The boys had an appealing dignity to them. I closed up the door and went to sleep.

A low fog hung over Nebaj as we followed the new army road out of town early the next morning. We were in the Shawcross Aid Programme's rattletrap van, bound for Salquil Grande, an Ixil town in the process of being resettled after having been leveled by the army in May 1982. The plan was to walk from Salquil Grande, which was the end of the road, to Cotzal, where the water project was to be dedicated. Five people besides me were in the van: Mike Shawcross, the office's Ixil secretary, Marta, a Ladino field assistant named Dionisio, a German volunteer named Tomás, and a Canadian premed student named Mark.

The scenery as we left Nebaj was spectacular. The road plunged into steep valleys and wound its way up sharp ridges. Rushing torrents cascaded over mountain faces and disappeared, far below, into ravines filled with tropical-looking foliage. David Stoll had told me that two long river valleys reached down from the Lacandón almost as far as Nebaj, and that within an hour and a half's walk from the town one could reach rain forest flora.

Seven or eight miles outside of Nebaj we passed a sorry-looking collection of houses with identical wooden-slat walls and corrugated-metal roofs gleaming as the sun began to burn through. I was surprised when Mike, who was riding in the front seat, turned around, waved his hand, and identified "the model village of Tzalbal." Before it had been destroyed during the war, I knew, Tzalbal had been a several hours' walk from Nebaj. The trip by car, on a road that had been built with the forced labor of the Civil Patrols from the model villages, took fifteen minutes. The circumstances under which the model villagers had been permitted to return to their homes were evident on a roadside sign that loomed out of the fog just above Tzalbal: below the words GUARDIANS OF HONOR was a white skull and crossbones painted over a blood-red background.

"The army base," explained Mike.

After forty minutes of driving we reached Salquil Grande, perched high on a mountain ridge at an altitude of eight thousand feet. Once the fourth-largest town in the Ixil, it was now a collection of shacks. Tomás parked the van on the edge of some packed dirt surrounded by piles of scavenged construction material. As we shouldered our packs and prepared to start walking, I asked Mike if the area into which we were traveling was still a zone of conflict.

"Until a year ago a hundred soldiers were stationed in Salquil," he said. "They wouldn't have been here if they weren't needed."

Before the violence Salquil Grande had been the center of Ixil potato production. The potato originated in the Andes, and as we left the town and climbed higher into the mountains, I became convinced that we'd been transported to the Andean *altiplano*. Small mountain streams gurgled through scrubby pastures. The bleating of sheep and the ringing of their bells wafted through the thin mountain air. From the far side of a distant valley we could hear the sounds made by a tiny figure of a man wearing a straw fedora as he turned the soil with a heavy adzelike hoe.

After two hours of hard walking, we ascended a bare ridge to a fortified settlement. A sign, in Spanish, welcomed us to VICALAMA, CONSTRUCTED JUNE 10, 1987, PEOPLE AND ARMY WORKING TOGETHER. Beyond the sign were foot-high strings hung with tin cans and, behind them, coils of barbed wire, trenches, and finally sandbagged machine-gun emplacements. Two soldiers armed with Galil automatic rifles took our identification papers and ran off with them toward a command bunker on the top of the hill.

As we waited, Mike told me that the Galils were about to be replaced with M-16's from the United States. "The crates are already on the docks," he said.

The original *aldea* of Vicalamá had been destroyed during the army's razed-earth campaign in the early eighties. This new version was part of a string of army base—towns (including Cotzal, our destination) constructed the year before in connection with a 1987–88 army offensive in the wild mountainous area just north of us that had once been the center of guerrilla operations in the region. Before the war, this area, known as Sumal Grande, had been largely uninhabited, but in the early eighties thousands of Indians fled there to avoid attacks on their villages. The 1987–88 offensive had been carried out by three thousand soldiers and two thousand Civil Patrollers from the model villages around Nebaj. The army had used the Civil Patrollers to burn the houses and destroy the crops of their refugee cousins. The operation had flushed something like three thousand Maya out of the mountains. The army then ran them through reeducation camps and enlisted them in the Civil Patrol, and was now permitting them, under close military supervision, to return to the military-controlled versions of their original towns. This was the nature of settlements such as Vicalamá.

After the soldiers came back with our passes, we walked through the army base to the town on the far side of the ridge. The town had been a logistical and operational center for the army offensive, and had the treeless look of a Vietnam firebase. Low houses made of construction scraps had been dug, seemingly without logic, into the hillside. There was no shelter from the sun anywhere. Mike apparently caught me staring at a pile of gray wallboard, pieces of which I could see had been incorporated into people's houses.

"We think it may be asbestos board," he said. "An American lawyer was up here recently and took a sample back to have it tested."

The population of Vicalamá seemed to consist largely of women. Wearing the beautiful traditional costume of Ixil women, they stared at us in silent dignity. I asked one of them where she had been before the town had been resettled. The question clearly made her uncomfortable.

"When they burned our houses," she answered, "we fled into the mountains."

She refused to elaborate, even after I got Marta to question her in Ixil.

At the far end of town, our path took us by two Civil Patrolmen standing guard next to a bell made from the shattered jacket of a five-hundred-kilogram bomb, and then up a ridge line covered with head-high bracken, burned golden brown by a killing frost several nights before. After a long ascent we reached the top of the ridge, which Mike's map showed to have an elevation of nine thousand feet. Views extended in all directions. In the valley to our south, we could see the military airport, La Pista, and beyond, the uniform, boxy dwellings of the model village of Acul, its regularly spaced metal roofs in shiny contrast to the earth-colored tiles clustered around Nebaj's colonial church.

Mike pointed a mile or two north to the mass of a looming, forest-covered mountain; this, he said, was Cerro Sumal, the highest mountain in the region and, not long before, the guerrilla command base. At its foot just across a valley was the village of Sumal Grande, resettled by the army only two months previously.

I asked Mike how many villages had survived the razed-earth campaign of the early eighties.

"As far as I know all the villages were destroyed," he said. "There may have been one village somewhere, but I don't know of it."

And what did he think of the army's tactics?

"You have to understand that Guatemalan soldiers are brainwashed into being fanatical anti-Communists. They also assume that if you're not with them, you're against them. Therefore, in 1981, when the army began its campaign to depopulate the Ixil, they assumed that anyone who ran from them was their enemy. They bombed and strafed people from the air. If they caught Ixils on the ground, and the Ixils were lucky, they were taken back to Nebaj. If not ..." He didn't finish his sentence.

I asked how many people had been killed in the Ixil.

"Impossible to say," he answered.

I prodded him.

"Five thousand, ten thousand, even more."

I later heard informed estimates that ran as high as thirty thousand, but given that the population of the Ixil before the war had been estimated at seventy or eighty thousand, and taking Mike's guess of ten thousand killed, this meant that the army had killed perhaps one of every seven or eight Ixils. I asked if he had any qualms about working in military camps in light of this record.

"What are we supposed to do, abandon the Ixils just because their country is occupied by the army? They need help. Besides, the current military is better than the past military."

I asked what he thought of the guerrillas' campaign.

"They themselves have said that they were overextended. They got too many recruits too fast. They didn't have the weapons or the organization to consolidate their gains. That's when the villages were destroyed. The people who suffered were the people whom the guerrillas had sworn to help."

What source of discontent had the guerrillas tapped to gain so many recruits?

"We're talking several hundred years of grievances," Mike said. "Land stolen by Ladinos or by the government, finca owners paying subminimum wages, people treating them like animals. The guerrillas promised them a better life. They believed it, and that's what set it all off."

What was his estimate of the guerrillas' current strength?

"They've got a thousand or twelve hundred combatants, and they're mounting consistent harassing attacks. However, they're also beginning to stop buses and trucks again asking for food and donations. That's probably because the army is gradually pushing north into what was their territory."

As we looked north toward Sumal Grande and the contested zones, I thought about the Ixils who were still out there, the so-called "internal refugees" who, after seven or eight years, were still hiding out in the mountains. Some of these were no doubt the *pueblo en resistencia,* highly organized, frequently religious groups tied loosely to both the Catholic church and the guerrillas, but others were simply people so traumatized by army brutality that they had been living for years under sheets of plastic. David Stoll had told me that the best estimates were that there were still five or six thousand Ixils living thus, outside army control.

Although Mike was no doubt correct in observing that "the current military is better than the past military," it wasn't saying much. It seemed to me that two wars were going on. The military conflict continued—only away from the centers of population and against a more elusive "enemy." At the same time another campaign was being fought behind the lines, a campaign to control and monitor every aspect of Indian life. Ken Anderson, a human rights lawyer with whom I'd spoken in New York, told me that before the war, the army didn't even know where most of the Indian hamlets were. "Now," he said, "not just the hamlets are on army computers, but everyone in them." The army was resettling the Ixils when and where it was ready and then controlling the resettled villages through the Civil Patrol. He offered the example of a group of Ixils—internal refugees—who on their own initiative came down out of the mountains and resettled their village in the Cerro Sumal area. These Ixils had cleared their fields, planted crops, and built rudimentary shelters before the army found them. When it did, the army gathered together the Civil Patrols from the nearby villages, made them surround the new settlement, and burned it down. Anderson quoted a Guatemalan colonel speaking admiringly of "the Cambodian solution," of how the Khmer Rouge had "totally reformed" its country's population.

Shortly after we crossed the height of the ridge, we caught a glimpse of Cotzal, our destination. Like the other army resettlements, it sat on a ridge top shorn of trees. The military command was at the highest point and the flat roof of the command bunker was sharply outlined against a dropoff behind. Mike explained that Cotzal consisted of forty-five Ixil families whom the army had permitted to return just over a year before. Before the violence, the families had lived in the same general area.

I spotted a piece of paper on the side of the trail, picked it up, and found it to be an army propaganda leaflet. It showed a burning church with the initials of the various guerrilla groups written on the puffs of smoke emerging from the fire. A repentant EGP guerrilla was throwing down his rifle, while next to him stood an idealized Civil Patrol couple. The caption read, "Abandon the sterile struggle. God and your brothers await you." On the flip side, Jesus Christ was shown emerging out of a cloud, striking down two armed EGP members and protecting a soldier in combat fatigues and a Civil Patrol member carrying a machete. The caption read, "God our father guides and blesses those who struggle as brothers to maintain the peace and defense of their homes."

Another leaflet showed a depraved-looking EGP member eating leaves off a tree, with the caption "Terrorists of the EGP! Take the Amnesty! Your family awaits you!"

A little farther on I began to notice curious deep pits dug into the path. I was idly wondering what they might be, when I noticed one still partly covered with a layer of sticks, bracken, and grass. The bottom of the pit was filled with sharpened bamboo spikes. Punji traps! Although these might have seemed a product of the EGP's Vietnam War inspiration, such traps had a long history of use among the Maya. In the Yucatán Caste War in the mid-nineteenth century, when the Maya came close to taking over the whole of the peninsula, a group of American mercenaries fighting against the Indians was turned back with the help of such pits. Nelson Reed, in his book on the conflict, *The Caste War of Yucatán,* quotes one of the American survivors: "The Indians there played us a trick; they made concealed pitfalls in the path and placed sharp pointed stakes at the bottom; then they appeared and dared us to come on; we rushed after them with hurrahs and many of our bravest men fell into the pits."

Cotzal was an inhospitable-looking place, so exposed to wind that the roofs of its squat houses had to be held down by rocks and heavy logs. As we trudged up the single street of the settlement five hours after we had left Salquil, powerful little whirlwinds kicked up dust and sent leaves and trash spiraling into the sky. Even an innocent-looking beehive had a catch to it. African bees, like some inexorable Third World conspiracy working its way toward the United States, had taken over the colony.

The Shawcross potable-water–system volunteers in Cotzal were five Englishmen and women from an agricultural college in Bedfordshire. They greeted us with a conspicuous lack of enthusiasm. They had been at Cotzal for four months and during that time had dug a trench almost a yard deep and more than a mile long—sections of it through solid rock. They had laid pipe in the trench and then built taps and holding tanks. Owing to various unforeseen complications, the project had taken considerably longer than anyone had anticipated and although the day of our arrival was the official opening, more work was needed to complete the system.

Since we had arrived behind schedule, the dedication ceremony proceeded promptly. The volunteers had hung the concrete wellhead, with its protruding metal spigot, with paper streamers and pink and pale blue balloons. The Cotzal Civil Patrol drew up in front—five rows of four ragged-looking men, every third one with an antique weapon. After a moment in formation, they shuffled off down the road and joined a contingent of twenty-eight of the hundred or so soldiers on the base. They marched back in unison, saluting as they passed the balloon-covered fountain. At the wellhead, while the Civil Patrol stood by, the army did some drill work, slapping their rifles, pounding their feet, and looking convincingly martial. Afterward the lieutenant in charge of the base stood up to speak. In a hectoring voice he said, "Now you have water. One day you'll have electricity ... maybe even cars."

This unlikely vision reminded me that, according to the Chilean anthropologist Beatriz Manz, the army had contemplated as a solution to their Ixil problem a proposal for "the Ladinoization of the

Ixil population so that it will disappear as a subgroup distinct from
the national mode." This proposal, ultimately not accepted, would
have included the forced imposition of the Spanish language and
"eliminating the distinctive dress and other visible differentiating
signs of the group." The Ladinoized Ixils would then accept the concepts of "nationality, fatherland, etc."

After the lieutenant was done speaking, an Ixil member of the
town's potable water committee stood up and made a formal speech
that was full of sincere gratitude. In the middle of it, the lieutenant
started barking orders. The soldiers rattled their Galils, shouted in
unison, and marched off. After they had gone, the man resumed his
speech. I found myself looking at the Ixil women standing around
the well. I realized how much, with the Ixil men largely gone over to
Ladino clothing, the women embodied Ixil tradition. They wore
long red skirts with irregular thin yellow striping, red-and-white-
striped sashes, and pure white *huipiles* embroidered with flowers,
quetzal birds, and, around the neck, a design symbolic of the sun.
Their hair was knotted up with a striped yellow, red, green, white,
and blue cloth that ended in pompoms of the same colors behind.
Around their shoulders they wore shawls of similar colors embroidered with abstract shapes representing animals and other figures.
They were beautiful. That they all dressed in the same fashion I
knew to be a mark of respect for their ancestors.

Afterward I spoke with one of the English volunteers about life
in Cotzal. She told me that the lieutenant only let the residents of
Cotzal farm milpas near the base because he was afraid they'd come
in contact with the guerrillas if they went farther out. The people,
therefore, didn't have the use of all their former milpas and there
wasn't enough land to go around. Because there wasn't enough land,
the residents couldn't make a living, and the men all wanted to go to
the coast to work on the plantations. However, the lieutenant hadn't
been letting them go. He had to keep enough of them in Cotzal to
fill the Civil Patrol.

"We try to help out some by donating our spare rations," she
said, "but it's a problem. Five men left last night without the lieutenant's permission. Today, he's very angry."

That night the villagers celebrated the opening of the potable-water system with a fiesta. Outside a low straw hut, the only structure large enough to accommodate all their visitors, they lit a bonfire, tossed in strings of firecrackers, and shot off rockets. Someone hooked a loudspeaker to a cassette deck and began broadcasting strange Guatemalan country music. Bottles of rum appeared from nowhere. Parents began to laugh. Little children began to dance. After a while the Ixils summoned all of us foreigners plus the lieutenant into the communal straw house. The villagers sat us down and presented us each with a soda and a *tamal* wrapped in a banana skin. As we ate, they waited attentively. When we finished, they sat down at the places we had vacated and themselves ate. The lieutenant was at the center table. When he was finished eating, instead of getting up to make room for one of the Ixils, he leaned back, put his arms over the shoulders of two blond women volunteers, and began complaining that all Guatemala's best coffee was sold to foreigners. "*Basura,*" he said of the domestically available coffee, "*pura basura.* Garbage, pure garbage."

I went outside. It was a cold, moonless night. A brisk wind was blowing from the west and the sky was full of blindingly bright stars. In the distance, north of us, an escaped milpa fire was burning its way down the shoulders of a cone-shaped peak. The fire looked like a luminous necklace. It was bizarrely beautiful.

I had neglected to roll out my sleeping bag before dinner. It was the kind of night in which you have trouble seeing your own feet, and I was dismayed to discover that I could locate no level ground anywhere. Snooping around the volunteers' hut, I found a rough-sawn wooden plank. I dragged it over to a relatively level patch of earth between a vacant palapa hut and a coil of barbed wire, propped up the downhill edge with a line of stones, and got into my sleeping bag. Below, the fiesta continued. Above, I could hear the coughing of soldiers on sentry duty. One of them heard me getting into my sleeping bag. Out of the darkness he called out, warning me that I'd be cold where I was—something that was already becoming apparent. He said that he'd be there all night and if there was anything he could do, to please let him know.

* * *

The next morning, after the rest of the crew headed back to Salquil Grande, Mike and I left by a slightly longer path, one that would deliver us to La Pista, the military air base. The path dropped down an incline below the command post. At the bottom of the hill we came across what had once been Cotzal's school. Like the school at El Arbolito, it had been burned to its foundations. I asked Mike who'd been responsible for destroying the school.

"The army," he answered morosely.

As Mike trudged on ahead, I asked him when he'd first come to Guatemala.

"Nineteen sixty-nine. I was on the point of leaving England to hitchhike to India when a friend in Canada suggested that I go caving with him in Mexico and Guatemala instead. I flew to Toronto and four hours later left for Mammoth Cave, Kentucky. From there, we hitchhiked south."

Mike explained that, as a caver, he'd found the karst region of Mexico and southern Guatemala so engrossing that he'd spent the next nine winters there, returning to Canada in the summers, where he had a job as editor of a biannual publication, *Canadian Caver.* After nine years, he moved permanently to the region—first to San Cristóbal de las Casas in Mexico, and then to Antigua, Guatemala.

I asked what he'd been doing before leaving England.

"I was the office manager of a lime quarry in the Yorkshire Dales," he said. "I ordered oil for the kiln, sold the lime and limestone, and did the wages. It was a nice bloody job—in the middle of nowhere, good walking country. My house was a seventeenth-century cottage twenty yards from an eighteenth-century pub. People said I could crawl home in a minute. I never timed myself."

Was he from Yorkshire then?

"I grew up near Manchester. My father was a manager of Virtue & Company, a publisher mostly of Bibles, but also of encyclopedias and medical books."

Was he himself of any particular religious persuasion?

"No."

For a while our path traversed the mountainside, then dropped steeply downward into a pine forest. The air was aromatic. The light slanted through the trees in shafts, illuminating the little clouds of dust created by our footfalls. At the valley bottom, we came upon a beautiful blue-green river. We were two thousand feet below Cotzal and the plants along the riverbank were from a different world. Instead of highland pine and oak, we found a sycamore tree, a grove of bananas. Blue, pink, and white flowers filled a wild meadow. On the side of the path twenty yellow butterflies clustered on a rock.

We crossed the river on two huge tree trunks laid side by side and then started up a steep mountain on the far bank. One of the interesting things about the highland Maya is that they don't believe in switchbacks. When confronted with an incline, they go straight up it, which is what the path did. Soon we were back in the filtered light of a pine forest, panting and sweating and scaring up grasshoppers, which made crackling flights through the dry grass of the forest floor. After perhaps half a mile's ascent, we met an Ixil descending the path. He was wearing tattered Ladino clothing set off by a red Ixil sash and, incongruously, calf-high yellow rubber boots. He sat down to talk, thrusting his machete into the earth and carefully setting his battered fedora on the ground next to it.

Where had we been? he asked, as if we were next-door neighbors who'd been away for a few days.

"In Cotzal," we told him.

He nodded silently.

And where was he going? we asked in our blunter Western style.

"To Xecotz," he responded, waving his hand in the direction of a ridge on which, on our way down, Mike had pointed out a few houses.

"Are people living there?" Mike wanted to know.

Not yet, "—but for the past three weeks they'd been building shelters and preparing their milpas. They hoped to move back soon.

"From where?" Mike asked.

"From Nebaj," he answered. He'd been in Nebaj since 1987. Prior to that, he'd hidden in the mountains—ever since the army entered Xecotz in 1980, shot his brother and a number of other residents, and burned the *aldea* to the ground.

What had he done after his house was burned?

He'd rebuilt it, and after the army burned it a second time, he rebuilt it again. When it was burned a third time, he gave up and, along with the rest of the village, moved farther up into the mountains, where they lived in huts made of leaves and branches.

"What did you eat?" I asked.

They'd surreptitiously worked their milpas and fled whenever they saw the army. When the army saw them, it shot at them or bombed them. That's how he'd lost his second brother. They'd lived this way for six years, people had died of cold and hunger and some had fled farther north. He himself had always stayed in the vicinity of Xecotz.

Had they seen much of the guerrillas?

"We saw them," he said, "but they were usually just passing by. Sometimes they came and spoke to us. When they did they were polite and they told us that everyone should be at *el mismo nivel*— 'the same level.'" He paused, then with an almost imperceptible flash of humor, added, "But the army didn't agree."

"Did the guerrillas give you any assistance?" asked Mike.

"They only gave us *política,* 'political lectures.'"

Mike looked pleased.

"And when the army came," he continued, "the guerrillas weren't there, only we were."

Mike looked even more pleased.

"But the guerrillas never killed anyone," the man added.

"Do you still see the guerrillas?" I asked.

"We see them all the time, but only in groups of two or three. They're still amiable."

"Why did you wait so long to surrender?" Mike asked.

"Because we were afraid the army would kill us."

"And why did you change your mind?"

"Because the army is better now. They no longer just shoot the people when they see them."

"There!" Mike wagged his finger at me as if he'd scored a debating point.

* * *

The path continued its brutal ascent. While Mike sat down for a cigarette, I went ahead. After an hour's climb my knees had begun to feel like rubber. I found a boulder overlooking a precipice and sat down. The view was spectacular. I could see the whole of the valley we'd been circling for the last two days, from Salquil Grande in the west, through Vicalamá, Cotzal, and, in the east, Xecotz. I couldn't help being struck again, however, by how much the ridge-top army resettlements made it look like occupied territory. I thought of what Adolfo Zinser Aguílar, a Mexican specialist on the Guatemalan situation, had told me: "The Indian areas are completely militarized. All economic aid goes through the army. If you don't have a relationship with the army, you're in trouble." But then again, although the form of this domination was new, the substance was not. Anthropologists talk about the Maya "heritage of conquest" and, in Guatemala at least, try to understand Maya culture as an evolving response to four hundred fifty years of ongoing colonization. In "Surviving Conquest," an article he wrote for *Latin American Research Review*, the Canadian geographer George Lovell postulates three cornerstones of Maya culture: land, community, and attachment to place, and observes that "persistent defense of this trinity has been, and will remain, fundamental to the maintenance of Maya identity." The question seemed to be not "Will the Maya survive?" but "How will they survive?"

I was startled by the sound of someone coming down the path. I looked up and saw two nuns in conservative brown habits. I asked where they were from. They were attached to the church in Nebaj. One was Guatemalan, the other Costa Rican. The Guatemalan was wearing a straw hat tied with a ribbon under her plump chin. She looked medieval. They were going to Xecotz, they explained. A Xecotz resident had brought them a petition concerning malnutrition. They were on their way to evaluate the problem and to try to get the residents in touch with the appropriate agencies.

Perhaps because it was such a relief to find the Catholic Church concerned with something beyond restricting people's reproductive rights, I told the nuns how happy I was to see them in a region so full of evangelicals.

"Oh, but there're only four of us!" the Costa Rican exclaimed bashfully.

The nuns went on their way. Shortly afterward Mike came trudging up the mountain. I asked him if he'd seen the nuns. He said that he had.

"They didn't waste any time getting to Xecotz," he said sourly.

The man from Xecotz whom Mike and I had met on the path had told us that before the army permitted him to return to his village, he had been processed through a camp called Xemamatze. Xemamatze, located on the outskirts of Nebaj, was the place to which recently captured Indians were brought; according to our informant, the army had just brought in a group of twenty-five from the guerrilla zone a week before. The next day, after a good night's sleep, I asked around for directions to Xemamatze, and was directed to a road that led south out of Nebaj's main plaza. After twenty minutes of walking, I arrived at the camp—a dusty, heat-baked soccer field surrounded on three sides by low plywood barracks. A sign over one of the barracks said CEARD: COMISIÓN ESPECIAL DE ATENCIÓN A REPATRIADOS Y DESPLAZADOS. A building to one side of it was labeled CLÍNICA PSICOLÓGICA, and a building on the other, CLÍNICA MÉDICA. I had been warned that there would be soldiers guarding the camp, that I might be refused entry or, at the very least, would have to surrender my passport. But there was only a small shelter at the gate with a few Ixils in it. I told one of them—a short, tough, barrel-chested man with a goatee—that I wanted to speak to the people who'd just been brought in from the mountains. He seemed surprised but, after a moment's hesitation, shrugged as if to say "Why not?" and led the way.

We entered the nearest of the barracks. The sight was an extraordinary one. The outer wall of the building was lined with knocked-together wooden bed frames, and each bed frame was draped with a family of hollow-cheeked, pale Ixils. It was as if we'd entered the level of the Inferno reserved for the tired and the resigned. My escort told me that refugees were generally brought into the camp for three months and then either sent on to other camps or, if their town had been resettled, allowed to return there. He himself had been in the camp for longer than three months. He didn't explain why. Nor did he seem to have any plans to leave.

At the far end of a second barrack, my guide waved his hand at a group of Ixils and said that they were the ones I was looking for. The first thing I noticed was how small they were. Almost all of the women and most of the men were under five feet. I suspected that this had something to do with nutrition, although the average height of pre-Columbian Maya men was five feet. The second thing I noticed, after I'd introduced myself, was that few in the group spoke Spanish. These were real backwoods Maya. Finally someone directed me to a gentle-looking man of about thirty lying sideways across a mattress. I was told that he could speak *castellano*—Spanish.

I asked when they'd been brought to Xemamatze.

"We were captured on February twentieth," he answered, listlessly propping his head on his elbow, "and then they marched us from where they found us to the army base at Cabá. There were twenty-five of us and we were all from the *aldea* of Bajchocolá, near Finca La Perla. They kept us at the army base for five days before flying us here in a helicopter."

It was March 2. That meant that this group of refugees had arrived at Xemamatze five days earlier. It must have been a bizarre scene around Finca La Perla. The current owner, Roberto Arenas Barrera, had reportedly joined an ultra-right-wing evangelical group from California, the Full Gospel Businessmen's Association, and he had turned the finca, now protected by three military garrisons, "over to the Lord," whatever that meant.

"What were you doing prior to your capture?" I asked.

"We left our home in Bajchocolá six months ago. The army base at Finca La Perla had become too strong and we were afraid that if they found us they'd kill us. So we left our homes and went to Cabá, in the *aldea* of Amajchel. That's where the army found us. It was the middle of the night and we were asleep at the top of a ravine, under the trees, very close to our milpas. It was a patrol of about a hundred soldiers."

I asked whether Bajchocolá had been guerrilla territory up until the time they left.

"We saw the guerrillas passing by all the time, and they told us we had to keep growing food or we'd starve. But they always paid for what they took. Once, in 1980, a few of them came into the village and said they were from the EGP. They said they wouldn't harm us. We didn't know them, but they spoke to us in Ixil. There were Quichés with them also."

Had the refugees had any problems with the army prior to their departure from Bajchocolá?

"The army came from Finca La Perla in 1981 or 1982. We didn't think we had any reason to fear them, but they burned our village and shot seven people who were just standing there—including my mother and father. We rebuilt the houses after that, but whenever anyone approached we'd hide. We'd hide not just ourselves, but everything we had—the dogs, the animals, even down to the roosters. Then they burned our houses again. We rebuilt them again. Ten times. Where else did we have to go? At first, we rebuilt the houses in wood, as they had been, but after a while there was no wood left and so we just made little *ranchitos* of leaves and branches near our milpas. Every week or so they'd come over and bomb and whenever they saw us, they'd shoot."

"Were they big bombs?" I asked.

"*Rompieron toda la montaña.* They tore up the whole mountain."

"Why was the army trying to kill you?"

"*Quien sabe?*" he answered. "*No teníamos culpa.* We weren't guilty of anything."

What had life been like in hiding?

"We had very small milpas," he replied, "and we never had enough food. We didn't have enough clothes. We didn't have any salt, any axes, or even any machetes. "We're very happy to be in Xemamatze. They gave us clothes"—he indicated his jeans and a sweatshirt proclaiming NEW YORK YANKEES—"and they say we can return to our lands in ninety days."

My escort had disappeared after introducing me to the refugees, but at this point he reappeared. He walked up and stood right next to me—one step too close. There was an unmistakable belligerence in his manner, but I couldn't tell if it was because he disapproved of my being there or because he wanted to be interviewed as well. As much to defuse the situation as to learn something from him, I asked him where he was from.

"Salquil Grande."

And when had he left?

"My parents left in 1982."

Nineteen eighty-two was the year the army destroyed the town. But when did *he* leave?

"I left in 1980," he answered, "when I joined the guerrillas."

I was so taken aback that I asked him to repeat himself. He repeated himself.

"*Los guerrilleros! Que bueno!*" I exclaimed, and then immediately caught myself. You don't say things like that in Guatemala—particularly in the middle of a war-zone reeducation camp.

It was too late. Both men had heard me. Fortunately, they laughed.

"I fought the soldiers," the man said proudly, while mimicking the motions of firing an automatic rifle. He was still standing too close. I half expected him to pull out a machete and slash me.

"You were a combatant then?" I asked.

"No. I was in security."

"Security?"

"Protecting one of the *jefes,* chiefs." He went through the motions of firing his imaginary rifle again.

Who was his *jefe?*

"He was a *viejo,* an old man, like yourself. Maybe forty-five."

I winced, but remembered that the average life span of a Guatemalan peasant was forty-nine, a milestone that for me was only ten years distant.

"Was he Ladino?"

"He was. All the *jefes* were tall, like you, and *castellanos.*"

All this seemed consistent with what I'd heard: that as the Maya had incorporated themselves into the guerrilla movement, they'd risen to the level of field commanders but that the political leadership had remained largely non-Indian.

"Where was your *jefe* from?" I asked.

"I won't say," he answered, "because I don't know who you are."

"And the guerrillas themselves, were they Ixils?"

"Ixils, Quichés, Kekchi, Cakchiquels, Kanjobals, Chuj, Mam, everybody," he replied, waving his hand expansively and naming a number of the major Guatemalan Maya groups.

"After the army burned Salquil Grande in 1982, I went with my family to Batzumal, near Vicalamá, in the Cerro Sumal region. But later, I went all over the highlands—all over the Quiché and Huehuetenango departments."

Did he ever go to Mexico?

"No."

How and when did he leave the guerrillas?

"In 1985. I decided to *reunir con la gente,* rejoin the people." I understood him to mean that he became a campesino again, a process that, given his presumed knowledge of the guerrilla command, must have been complicated.

Why?

"Because the guerrillas weren't what they said they were."

What did he mean by that?

"They told us they were going to take power. By 1985, I could see that they weren't."

He suddenly held out his hand. There was something weird about the gesture, but I shook it anyway. "If there's nothing else," he said.

There was plenty else, but he was already walking out the door.

Back at my hotel, I was told that the man I'd been speaking with was almost certainly an *oreja*—a government informer, literally; an "ear"—and therefore a dangerous man. I thought of Falstaff: "The better part of valor is discretion." I had no reason to suspect I was in any trouble; anyway, I'd already accomplished what I wanted. There was a bus leaving town at 12:30 A.M. I was on it.

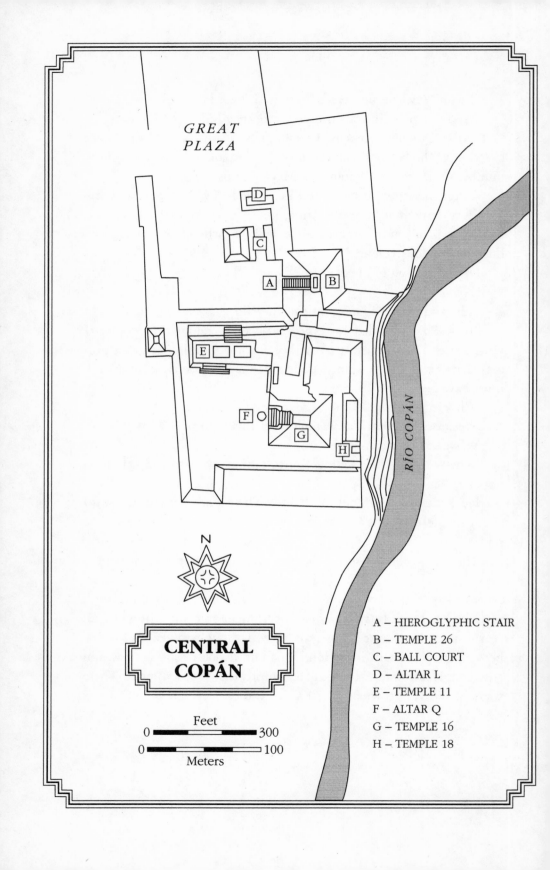

GREAT
PLAZA

RÍO COPÁN

N

CENTRAL
COPÁN

Feet
0 ⊨━━━━━ 300
0 ⊨━━━━━ 100
Meters

A – HIEROGLYPHIC STAIR
B – TEMPLE 26
C – BALL COURT
D – ALTAR L
E – TEMPLE 11
F – ALTAR Q
G – TEMPLE 16
H – TEMPLE 18

CHAPTER 7

Copán

O F ALL THE CLASSIC MAYA archaeological sites, Copán, in western Honduras, has been the most thoroughly excavated. Located in an alluvial pocket of the Copán River, ringed by rolling, green mountains, Copán is the southernmost of the Maya cities, far from the great Petén sites such as Tikal, Uaxactún, and Yaxchilán, and light-years away from the Yucatán. Copán's geographical marginality, however, seems to have stimulated rather than inhibited its Maya-ness. William Fash, an archaeologist from Northern Illinois University who has worked at Copán for close to fifteen years, says that the Copánecs, almost as if to compensate for their isolation, became "super-Maya" and made their city into a center of arts and learning. The famous Carnegie Institution archaeologist Sylvanus Morley used to refer to Copán as the "Athens of the New World."

It is appropriate therefore that Copán should have played a significant role in the nineteenth-century rediscovery of the Maya. Copán was the first site visited by John Lloyd Stephens, the American writer, lawyer, and diplomat whose account of his 1839 Central American journeys, *Incidents of Travel in Central America, Chiapas, and Yucatán,* published in 1841, contained the revolutionary proposal that not only were the abandoned cities he found the remains of an indigenous American civilization (and not, as others had suggested, the product of wandering Celts, Vikings, or lost tribes of Israel), but also that the hieroglyphs associated with these ancient cities were the written record of that civilization. Stephens, who had previously published a best-selling description of a trip to the Egyptian ruins, was not the first to visit the abandoned Maya cities, nor even the first to suggest that they represented the remains of an American civilization, but he was the first to take the proposition seriously enough to bring it before the world at large.

Stephens had become acquainted with the existing accounts of the abandoned cities of Mexico and Central America through an antiquarian bookseller in New York. The accounts were sketchy, ill substantiated, and sometimes fantastic, but there was enough in them to grab his imagination. One such account was a brief description of Copán published in the 1835 *Proceedings* of the American Antiquarian Society, written by Colonel Juan Galindo, an Englishman who was killed shortly thereafter in Central America. It contained a description of Copán so stirring that Stephens placed it first on the list of sites he wanted to investigate. In 1842 he arranged to be appointed United States ambassador to the newly re-formed Central American Federation, a political grouping of the republics of Guatemala, Honduras, Costa Rica, Nicaragua, and Salvador that coalesced and then fell apart several times in the decades following the region's 1821 separation from Spain. (There was not a lot of competition for the post of ambassador—Stephens's four predecessors had died in office.) After recruiting an illustrator, an Englishman named Frederick Catherwood, he set out. Stephens and Catherwood landed on Lago de Izabal on Guatemala's Caribbean coast and promptly found themselves in the midst of a raging, recently rekindled, civil war between conservatives and liberals. The war prevented Stephens from locating the government he was supposed to be the representative to, let alone presenting his credentials, but it did free him to go in pursuit of his real interests.

He and Catherwood hired mules and undertook the several days' ride to Copán. While approaching the ruins, they were captured by a band of rebel soldiers, imprisoned as spies, and threatened with execution, but they managed to escape and eventually reached Copán, which they found covered in six hundred years' rain forest growth.

The site was both larger and stranger than anything Stephens had imagined, and while monkeys and parrots chattered overhead, the two men sat on an ancient wall and contemplated the ruined, jungle-girded metropolis below them. "Who were the people that built this city?" Stephens asked.

> In the ruined cities of Egypt ... the stranger knows the story of the people whose vestiges are around him. America, say historians, was peopled by savages; but savages never reared these structures, savages never carved these stones. ... Architecture, sculpture, and painting, all the arts which embellish life, had flourished in this overgrown forest; orators, warriors, and statesmen, beauty, ambition, and glory, had lived and passed away, and none knew that such things had been, or could tell of their past existence. Books, the records of knowledge, are silent on this theme. The city was desolate.

Harrassed by the nearest rancher, the owner of the site, Stephens quickly assured himself access to the ancient city by buying it. About this transaction he wrote:

> The reader is perhaps curious to know how old cities sell in Central America. Like other articles of trade, they are regulated by the quantity in market, and the demand; but, not being staple articles, like cotton and indigo, they were held at fancy prices, and at that time were dull of sale. I paid fifty dollars for Copán. There was never any difficulty about price. I offered the sum, for which Don Jose Maria thought me only a fool; if I had offered more, he would probably have considered me something worse.

Stephens and Catherwood stayed long enough to survey the site and record what they found there. Afterward they packed up and began an overland northward trek that eventually took them all the way to Yucatán. Just before leaving Copán, however, Stephens observed of the ancient city, "One thing I believe, that its history is graven on its monuments. No Champollion [the French Egyptologist who, using the Rosetta stone, laid down the principles for deciphering Egyptian hieroglyphics] has yet brought to them the energies of his enquiring mind. Who shall read them?"

Stephens's story reveals how much the world had forgotten about the New World civilizations in the course of the few centuries since the Conquest. Although the story of the subjugation of the Maya existed in detail in the Spanish archives, the world knew so little about the contents of these archives that when Stephens postulated New World creators of Copán, he no longer had a name for his proposed people.

But by the nineteenth century, curiosity about Latin American pre-Columbian civilizations was in the North American air. Stephens's book on his Central American travels became a best-seller. Two years after its publication, in 1841, William Prescott's magnificent *History of the Conquest of Mexico* followed. Prescott was a Boston lawyer who had lost the sight in his left eye after he'd been hit by a crust of bread as a student at Harvard. When his good eye began to fail, he abandoned his law practice, shut himself into a darkened room, and spent the remainder of his life gathering manuscripts and writing histories of Spain and its New World colonies. Although Prescott's work reintroduced the story of the conquistadors to the English-speaking public, its most important consequence for Mayanists was indirect. A young French priest, Charles Étienne Brasseur de Bourbourg, honorary vicar general in Boston at the time Prescott's *History* was published, read the book, was inspired by it, and subsequently devoted his life to research on the Maya. It was Bourbourg who, in 1863, discovered Bishop Diego de Landa's *Relación de las Cosas de Yucatán* in the archives of the Academy of History in Madrid.

It so happened that my approach to Copán followed the same route that Stephens and Catherwood had taken one hundred fifty years earlier. The route, however, was the beginning and the end of the similarity between my trip and Stephens and Catherwood's. The owner of my Guatemala City hotel overheard me planning my bus route to the ruins. He had a friend from the United States who was living in Guatemala and had to leave the country to renew his car papers. This friend had been planning to go to San Salvador, but he might be persuaded to go to Copán and Honduras instead. Should he inquire?

"Sure," I answered.

The ride showed up the next morning. Let's call him Larry.

He had blow-dried hair, aviator glasses, round cheeks, white tennis shorts, Top Siders, and a polo shirt bearing the logo of a Florida diving club. We loaded up Larry's car, stopped briefly at an American-style convenience store to buy American-style junk food, and took the Atlantic Highway east, along with what seemed to be half the trucks in Guatemala, in the direction of Puerto Barrios on Guatemala's Caribbean coast.

After we'd gotten through the outskirts of the capital, I thanked Larry for giving me a ride and for switching destinations from El Salvador to Copán.

"Oh," he said, "I don't mind. I go to El Salvador all the time. I've got a buddy down there who's a diving instructor attached to the Salvadoran armed forces. When we want to go diving, the Salvadorans take us out to the offshore islands in one of their PT boats. Can't beat that—a private PT boat! The only thing is that I was talking with my buddy the other day when there was a boom in the background. 'What's that?' I asked him. 'A bomb,' he answered. 'About two blocks from here. The presidential transition is about to take place, and it's going to be hot here for the next week or two.'"

As he talked, Larry reached under his seat and pulled out a little cassette case. He chose a Quincy Jones tape, put it on the cassette player, and began conducting in the air with one hand while nervously strumming the wheel with the other.

I asked him how he liked living in Guatemala.

"Nice country," he said. "*Muy tranquilo.*"

I pointed out that there had been a coup attempt the previous week.

"Just a little exercise from some provincial commanders," he said. "The real coup was a month or so ago. The American press said that President Cerezo called his top military commanders to a meeting in the National Palace. In fact it was the *military* who summoned *Cerezo.* They told him to get in line. They told him they were sick of his messing around with the Soviet Union. Their helicopters hovered overhead the whole time. When it was over, Cerezo went to his country estate and stayed drunk for a month. He's only just started appearing in public again."

Larry alluded several times to friends in the A.I.D. office. I asked him what kind of work he did.

"I'm into import-export marketing," he answered.

What did he import and export?

"I don't import-export anything in particular," he answered. "I build people networks. I'm in ten countries. Networking today is where franchising was twenty years ago. Eventually it'll account for ten to twenty percent of the market."

"What market?" I asked.

"I try to target the upper five percent who have all the money," he said. "Say, maybe you and I can have lunch sometime, compare notes. I'll tell you more about my network."

At Zacapa, we turned off the Atlantic Highway and picked up Stephens and Catherwood's route to Copán. A sign by the side of the road read BIENVENIDOS A ZACAPA. ALTITUD 220 METROS. CLIMA CÁLIDO." We had dropped more than four thousand feet from Guatemala City and it was, in fact, *cálido.* Larry pulled the car over at a roadside restaurant and we went inside to get sodas. We sat down on a terrace shaded by a mango tree heavy with unripe fruit. The terrace looked down over a wide, gravel-bottomed river. Below, a group of men in their underwear had driven a bus up to its hub-caps in the river shallows. As we drank our sodas, we watched them scrubbing it clean inside and out. After a while one of them lay back in the river and blew a stream of water out of his mouth.

Stephens noted the richness of the Zacapa valley and related that it was cultivated for corn and cochineal. We could still see the corn, but the cochineal was long gone. From the 1820's to the 1860's, cochineal, a beautiful scarlet dye made from scale insects raised on the leaves of the nopal cactus, was Guatemala's major export. The process of making it, which the Spanish had learned from the Indians, was tremendously time-consuming. The wingless females of the insect, *Dactylopius coccus,* were brushed by hand into a receptacle and then dried in the sun. Seventy thousand insects were needed to make one pound of dye, so it was very expensive. When aniline dyes were perfected in Germany in the 1860's, the market for cochineal disappeared overnight. It was after the demise of the cochineal market that coffee took over as Guatemala's major export.

Since Stephens's time, the road has been diverted around Zacapa, and the only evidence we saw of the town was a series of billboards advertising such institutions as the MOTEL AMÉRICA, and the fact that we had entered the TERRITORIA DE PEPSI. These signs seemed to cheer Larry.

"There's a melon business out of Zacapa now," he said. "It's a new honeydew hybrid called Mayan Sweet. The only problem was that twenty percent of the crop was losing its premium grade because of the brown spots left where the melons ripened on the ground. We were able to get the growers in touch with the producers of a chemical called O.L.C. that eliminated the problem."

"What's O.L.C.?" I asked.

"Organic Liquid Cleanser," Larry answered.

"What's in it?"

"Oh, they wouldn't divulge *that*," he said. "They'd lose the secret of how it's made!"

After crossing a mountain pass that separated Zacapa from the departmental capital of Chiquimula, we rounded a bend and were confronted with a large billboard bearing a picture of Woody Woodpecker and the slogan SOLDIERS PROTECT YOU. Shortly afterward we passed a military base.

"That's one of the bases that rebelled last week," Larry said. "The commander told his troops that Guatemala City had been taken over by subversives, then marched on the capital." I knew that the rebellious troops had beseiged the home of the defense minister and briefly held him and his wife hostage. Wild country.

Our road continued toward Esquipulas, a famous pilgrimage site, but long before the town, a sign directed us onto a dirt road that wound into the mountains toward Honduras and Copán. We climbed past orange-flowering acacia trees hung with long brown seed pods, past hillside plots filled with pineapples, and past little mountain towns whose fields, delineated with cactus fences, were sprouting the new year's corn. We forded stream beds, and eased our way past two bulls that had locked horns in the middle of the road.

Despite repeated explanations, Larry seemed unclear about the purpose of my visit to Copán. He kept referring to me as "the archaeologist," as if he were in the middle of an *Indiana Jones* episode. At one point, amidst the jumble of mountains we were traversing, we came upon a sheer stone column protruding surrealistically out of the landscape. Larry turned serious.

"In some of my reading," he said, hesitating as he carefully chose each word, "the ancient Maya ... they've seen pictures ... they think maybe ... extraterrestrials?"

I had met William Fash, an archaeologist who has worked for many years at Copán, several months earlier at a symposium focusing on new findings at the site. Fash had outlined the century of archaeological research done at Copán, noting especially the degree to which environmental and site surveys had added up to a knowledge of the rise and fall of the city of Copán more comprehensive than that of almost any other Maya city. He went on to describe the Copán Mosaics Project, which he and his wife, Barbara, had initiated in 1985. The purpose of the project was to reconstruct a number of temple facades, many of which had collapsed, and then to try to correlate the glyphic messages found on them with various stages of the city's growth.

Fash began his talk with some comments on the geology of the Copán region. Limestone is rare in the vicinity of Copán; as a result, the structures in Copán are made of a volcanic tuff instead of the limestone used for most other structures elsewhere in Mayadom. Tuff is harder than limestone, and individual carvings were therefore better preserved. But the lack of limestone caused problems—for both the original Maya builders and, later, archaeologists. Elsewhere, Maya pyramids typically consist of a plastered, cut-stone exterior laid over a core of rubble, normally fused together with limestone-based mortar. The plaster sheathing on top of the cut stone is also generally limestone-based, serving the dual purpose of providing a paintable surface and of protecting the underlying structure from water seepage. In Copán, however, where limestone was scarce, the rubble core of the pyramids was fused with clay, or even mud. In some cases, even pyramid exteriors were set in mud. This was fine as long as the building was protected from water seepage—and the Copanecs did save what limestone they had for exterior plastering. While the city was active, the limestone sheathing was renewed regularly. Once Copán was abandoned, however, the building maintenance ceased and the plaster began to break up. Water, followed by vines and tree roots, penetrated the building shells and began to erode the rubble core. In many cases this led to entire facades simply collapsing off building exteriors.

The task of reconstructing these facades would have been challenging under any circumstances, Fash noted, but it was made all the more formidable because earlier generations of archaeologists had picked up pieces of sculpture from where they'd fallen and stacked them, unsorted, off to the side. The first phase of Fash's project consisted of taking an inventory of these pieces, during which he, his wife, and their colleagues discovered close to twenty thousand pieces in such piles.

Other factors worked in the project's favor. Unlike many other Maya sites—particularly Yucatec ones where the sculptural elements of a building were mass produced and then applied to the building—the sculpture in Copán was carved in place. Pieces therefore either fit or didn't—there was only one possible correct placement for each piece. Second, each building at Copán had its own sculptural motifs, which meant that the piles of sculpture could at least be sorted by building.

Fash originally came to Copán as a graduate student of Gordon Willey's at Harvard. Willey, known in Maya archaeological circles as "the grand old man of settlement pattern archaeology," had worked over the ten square miles of the Copán valley, mapping and making representative excavations of the house mounds left by non-kingly families in order to get a sense of how the use of the valley had evolved over time. Because Classic Maya culture evolved in the middle of a rain forest region, site surveys of lowland Classic Maya sites are prodigiously difficult to accomplish and, accordingly, quite rare. However, a site survey is the only way to find out information such as a city's size, its economic base, and how it evolved through history.

Since Willey's work made this information available for Copán, Fash decided that the next logical step was to try to correlate Willey's findings with the history of Copán's kings and their ideology, to try to understand each facade as a statement made to his subjects by whichever king had erected it. To accomplish this, one more element was necessary—epigraphers. As part of the Copán Mosaics Project, Fash invited two epigraphers, Linda Schele, of the University of Texas, and David Stuart, now of Vanderbilt, to work with him at Copán. Schele and Stuart accepted on the condition that they be permitted to disseminate the resulting information to other interested epigraphers. The result, Schele says, has been "an explosion of information and understanding" about the history of Copán.

It was late afternoon when Larry and I reached Copán Ruinas, the nearest town to the ruins. Copán Ruinas is built around a tiny rectangular park that features a neat lawn and a fountain and gives the town a tidy European feel. The town church is at one end of the park, and a post office and museum are at the other. Immediately upon arriving, I spotted Bill Fash slumped down in the front seat of his car in front of the post office. His eyes were red and he looked exhausted. "I've got conjunctivitis," he said when I went over to greet him, "and the flu, and I've been trying to reach *National Geographic* all afternoon on the radio phone."

National Geographic?

"We've been tunneling inside Temple 26, and just a few hours ago we found a tomb under the Hieroglyphic Stair. Through an opening between two of the capstones we can make out what looks like a mosaic on the floor. But before we open the tomb, we need to get hold of a snake-mounted video camera so that we can get some idea of its contents."

Temple 26 was one of the main pyramids in Copán's acropolis, the central grouping of royal Copán. The Hieroglyphic Stair, which contains the longest hieroglyphic inscription yet discovered in Mayadom, runs up its facade. In some twenty-two hundred glyphs, the stair tells the story of Copán's kings from A.D. 565 to 756. Temple 26 was thus an important building, and if it contained a tomb, the tomb was probably a significant one.

"As you know," he continued, "the Maya built their pyramids successively one on top of the other. There are, for example, at least six earlier pyramids under Temple 26. Tunneling is controversial. But all the buildings you see at Copán are from the eighth and ninth centuries, and for us, tunneling is an economical way to get some idea of what the city was like at earlier points in its history. That in turn gives us better insight into the purposes of the final structures. What we're doing in Structure 26, for instance, is trying to locate the superstructures of each of the temples underneath it. By locating the superstructures, we hope to be able to figure out who built them and why."

I asked which of the structures underneath the Hieroglyphic Stair contained the tomb they'd discovered.

"There are two structures between the one that contains the tomb and the existing Temple 26. We're not sure yet, but the two intervening temples may have been built by the same king."

I asked if he had any idea of who was inside the tomb they'd discovered that day.

He explained that at the entrance they'd found an offering consisting of five pots and a figurine. "They date to the seventh century A.D., which puts it during the reign of either the twelfth king, Smoke Imix God K, or his predecessor, the eleventh king, Butz Chan, 'Smoke Sky.' Butz Chan ruled from A.D. 578 to 628. Smoke Imix, who was one of Copán's greatest kings, was a contemporary of Pacal's at Palenque, and, like Pacal, lived into his eighties. He ruled from 628 until his death in 695."

Fash, a handsome, bearded man of thirty-four, and his eight-year-old son, Nathan, picked me up the next morning on the Honda 550 motorcycle with which Bill commutes between his house in town and the archaeological site, a mile or so away. I got on behind Bill, and Nathan, who was wearing a baseball-style hat labeled PROFESSIONAL FOOTBALL HALL OF FAME, CANTON, OHIO, got on in front. As we rode out of town through the fresh morning air, we passed lines of low alluvial fields dotted with two-story barns. Bill explained that they were tobacco-drying barns and that the Copán valley was famous for its tobacco.

"The soil here is extremely rich," he shouted over his shoulder, "which is why the Maya settled here in the first place. This valley's been occupied since at least 1000 B.C."

We parked the motorcycle inside the gate and walked out into the Great Plaza, radically transformed since Stephens's day. The stelae that he and Catherwood had hacked out from under roots and vines were now standing eight and ten feet tall in imposing array across a wide, close-cropped greensward. A series of low stone platforms defined the northern end of the plaza; the southern end, 150 yards away, was defined by the massive ceiba-topped structures of the acropolis.

I was amazed by this huge panorama.

"You can never catch Copán's size in a photograph," he said.

As we walked toward Temple 26, which was part of the acropolis, Bill explained that the thirteenth king, known as Eighteen Rabbit, had built the plaza between A.D. 695 and 738.

"Eighteen Rabbit's stelae are done in a style that, when seen in the rest of Mayadom, is considered Early Classic," he said. But here, perhaps because of Copán's distance from other sites, it persisted into the Late Classic."

Bill pointed toward the acropolis. "From the fifth century A.D. on, the basic arrangement of the acropolis buildings, as well as their purposes, stayed the same. Structure 11 was always the lineage, or rulership, house. Structure 26 contained the dynastic temple."

I asked him about a complex of low buildings to our left as we approached the acropolis.

"That's the ball court," he said. "Talk about sacred space, there were four hundred years of ball courts in that same spot. There are two ball courts under the existing one, and each of them was reconstructed twice."

Bill explained that there were ball courts on every Maya site, but their function was not well understood. "There's little question that ball players emulated the Hero Twins' victory over the Lords of the

Underworld and that the central purpose of the game was to perpetuate the natural cycles—specifically the movement of the sun, the moon, and the heavenly bodies. But beyond that, we don't have much detail. We don't know, for instance, how many people watched, how many people played, what people bet, if anything, or which players, if any, were sacrificed."

We reached the foot of Temple 26, Copán's dynastic temple, where Bill had discovered the tomb. The famous Hieroglyphic Stair ran up the front of the temple. It was fifty feet wide and had seventy-two steps, each of which was eighteen inches high. A line of free-standing martial figures ran down the middle. Glyphs many badly weathered, ran across each of the risers.

Bill indicated a door at the base of the stair and together we entered the tunnel. Stooping to avoid the string of naked light bulbs overhead, we proceeded forty or fifty feet into the temple interior before turning sharply right and scrambling five or six feet up through a pile of loose dirt. The air was incredibly close, and when I paused to catch my breath, I noticed that the tunnel walls weren't in any way braced. Basketball-sized pieces of gray-green tuff were suspended in a thousand-year-old medium of hardened mud—all that prevented tons of rubble from cascading down and turning us into relics to be unearthed by future generations of archaeologists.

At the top of the pile of loose dirt, Bill stopped in front of a plywood box set into the tunnel wall. He explained that the section of the tunnel we had come through had been dug in the thirties by a Norwegian engineer-turned-archaeologist, Gustav Stromsvik. Under the box was a Petén-style plaster mask Stromsvik had discovered and Bill had boxed in for protection. The mask was on the outside of the buried temple, and Stromsvik's tunnel continued horizontally across the face of the pyramid, on the other side of the mask.

"In the hopes of discovering more such masks, we decided to dig vertically above the mask," Bill said. "We discovered a set of stairs and followed them last season as far as we could. This season, we continued the excavation until, six weeks ago, we reached a door-jamb and a plaster floor on the other side of it. It was on the plaster floor that we found the ceramic offerings."

The plaster floor indicated to Bill's crew that they'd reached the top of the buried pyramid; then, while clearing the edges of the tunnel, a workman dislodged a rock that exposed the line of a corbeled roof vault. Further clearing revealed a vault fifteen feet long and nine feet wide, filled with rubble. It took three weeks to clear the rubble as far down as the level of the temple floor. Instead of arriving at plaster floor, though, they found what seemed to be only more rubble. Considerable sentiment had built for giving up, when Bill noticed a ring of plaster around the edge of the vault. This indicated that the temple floor had been broken through, vaulted over, and then filled with rubble—something that neither Bill nor any of the archaeologists working with him had ever seen before. On the afternoon I arrived, his crew had come across a line of rectangular capstones covering a trench that ran down the length of the vault. The joints between the capstones had been sealed with plaster, but some of the plaster had broken, and through one of the cracks they had made out the bright colors of what Bill thought might be a mural.

We scrambled through some more loose dirt to the temple top. It was unbelievably humid. Two electric fans worked to little avail. The Honduran excavators were bathed in sweat. Below us, in the tomb, the harsh electric light reflected green off the glistening stone walls. A trench had been dug down the middle of the vault, exposing the capstones. The workmen were wrestling with the remaining rubble, gradually widening the trench toward the vault walls and carefully removing any pottery shards they found among the debris.

I asked Bill what he expected to find.

"I'm most concerned that there might be a codex in there," he answered, referring to the bark-paper Maya books. "The air inside that tomb was twelve hundred years old, and now that we've broken the seal, a lot of moisture is entering very suddenly."

Was there any reason to suspect there might be a codex?

"A few years ago, I found the tomb of what was probably a fifth-century shaman. In it were the remains of a codex. Unfortunately, the tomb was wet, and although I could see traces of pigment and traces of foliation, the codex had turned into an unreadable mush. What was interesting about that tomb, however, was that in addition to the remains of the person who'd been buried, it contained deer and caiman bones. My idea is that they were the shaman's *naguales,* the animals through whom he entered the spirit world. There were also five quartz stones of a type that are still used in divinations today. Word of the shaman's tomb got around town quickly. After we got him to the town museum, I fell off my motorcycle and broke my leg, and people began to refer to him as *el brujo,* 'the witch.' At one point, when we tried to remove him to a temporary exhibit in Tegucigalpa, the townspeople nearly rioted. We had to cancel the Tegucigalpa exhibit. *El brujo* has stayed in Copán ever since."

Early the next morning, one of Bill's foremen stopped by in a car to pick me up. His name was Juan Ramón Guerra, but Bill had told me that he was known as Moncho, or Super-Moncho, for his prodigious strength in moving rocks.

Bill and I had been discussing the degree to which Maya cities recapitulated the surrounding landscape. Pyramids were *witz,* symbolic mountains, stelae were *te tun,* literally "stone trees."

"If you're really interested in the sacred geography of Copán," Bill had said, "you might like to see some of the stelae put up by Smoke Imix, the twelfth king. During a two-hundred-sixty-day period in A.D. 652, he surrounded the entire valley with stelae. It was as if he was on a crusade; as if he wanted to make the whole valley sacred. I can get someone to show you the valley."

I had taken Bill up on this offer, and he had arranged for Moncho to be my guide.

Moncho and I drove out of the river bottom mists and up into the clear air and oak and pine forests of the surrounding mountains. After a few miles, we parked the car at the bottom of a wide, rough path and continued climbing on foot.

"This was the first road to Copán," Moncho told me as we walked. "Don Gustavo Stromsvik built it, and my father helped him. Don Gustavo wanted to bring a car to Copán, so he and my father built the road. They'd level a few yards, drive the car forward a few yards, level a few more yards, and then drive the car forward again. They traveled like that all the way to Copán."

From 1935 to 1942, Gustav Stromsvik, whose tunnel Bill had expanded, had been the reigning archaeologist at Copán. "Don Gustavo," as Stromsvik is still affectionately remembered by townspeople, seems to have been a character. Having shipped out aboard a Norwegian naval vessel as a young man, Stromsvik got so drunk off Yucatán one night that he fell overboard. The next day, the story goes, his shipmates found a body washed ashore and, assuming that it was his, buried it under a tombstone with his name on it. In fact, Stromsvik had swum ashore and taken the first steps in what was to become a life-long AWOL from engineering into archaeology. Although he knew nothing about Maya civilization, he made his way to Chichén Itzá, where Sylvanus Morley was then trying to erect the fallen columns of the Temple of the Warriors. On the basis of his engineering background Stromsvik was hired by Morley, and managed to reconstruct a section of the colonnade in a fraction of the time that Morley's crews were putting up other sections. Because of this and subsequent successes at Chichén Itzá, Stromsvik was accepted as a full member of the then small world of Mayanists. From Chichén Itzá, he moved to Copán. At Copán, he not only laid out the European-looking park in the center of the town but also restored several of the principal Maya structures and constructed a dike that held back the river that was then eroding the acropolis.

Following Don Gustavo's road, Moncho and I passed a farmyard, scattering dogs, chickens, and ducks. A green parrot perched in the underbrush alongside the path squawked at our approach and flew away like a shot. After a half mile's climb, we reached the ridge top. The whole of the Copán valley opened below us. The valley was still partly shrouded in mist, but it was easy to see that, except for a few pockets of trees, the rain forest that Stephens had found in 1839 had been eradicated. To be sure, there'd been a ranch or two in Stephens's time, but the real clearing didn't start until the 1860's, when immigrants arrived from Guatemala. Bill had told me that the oldest settlements of the valley dated to 1000 B.C. I thought about this. Two thousand years of settlement, the better part of a thousand years of abandonment, and now intense settlement again. It certainly wasn't the steady progression that is our idea of history, but then our historical horizons are tiny, and I suspected that the booms and busts of the Copán valley had more to do with our own past and future than we cared to contemplate.

Moncho directed my attention to a pair of crosses, adorned with flowers, protruding from an immense pile of stones.

"This is the pilgrimage route to Esquipulas," he told me. "The Indians carry the stones from their *aldeas* and leave them at this site."

"The Maya concept of *cargo*—a load or a burden—" Bill said when I asked him about it later.

I followed Moncho out along the ridge line until we came to one of Smoke Imix's stelae. It stood about ten feet tall in the middle of a small meadow and glowed a warm reddish-brown in the morning sun. I went to examine it. The glyphs on its eastern face were worn away, but those on the western face were quite readable. Individual Maya stelae have glyphic names, and I knew from the conference at which I had first met Bill Fash that this one was named Chan Chac Bay Chan, or "Vision Serpent." The inscription on its western face began with the date 9.11.0.0.0 in the Maya calendar, or A.D. 652, the end of a twenty-year *katun* period, a significant date. The stela identified Smoke Imix, the twelfth king, as having erected the stela, and said that he was heir to Copán's first king, Yax Kuk Mo— "Resplendent Blue-green Quetzal Macaw." The stela noted that Smoke Imix had reached the second twenty years of his reign and that the occasion of the erection of the stela was a bloodletting cere- mony in which Smoke Imix had summoned his ancestor, the tenth successor, "Moon Jaguar," back from the dead.

The Maya believed that their rulers took on the qualities of divinity during rituals and then were capable of bringing the super- natural into human space. I wondered why Smoke Imix had chosen this spot and remembered that Bill had said there was a cave nearby. I asked Moncho about it.

"It's below that rise," he said, pointing to a grove of trees about two hundred yards away. "You go in the cave just a short way and then there's a drop of about thirty meters. Bill found a skeleton in there but he hasn't been able to date it. Around here they say that the cave was used to store arms during the nineteenth-century war between the conservatives and the liberals, so the skeleton could date to then."

The Copán valley is riddled with caves. One of the ancient city's hieroglyphic names is Ah Po Tzi, "Lord Bat." I had seen a drawing of the glyphs on a sleeping bench belonging to Copán's sixteenth and last king, Yax Pac, "Rising Sun." One of the glyphs showed Yax Pac letting his own blood and calling his ancestors out of a black hole. A still-readable glyph on one of the worn panels of this stela showed a black-hole-like entrance to the underworld. Another showed water welling up. Had Smoke Imix called up his ancestor Moon Jaguar through the nearby cave mouth?

"No way to know," Bill said to me later. "I got to the bottom of the shaft last year, but it's impossible to do any serious work in there without a lot of preparation. There's no light, it's hard to breathe, and it's full of bat shit, I didn't want to come down with histoplasmosis."

After Moncho and I had returned from Smoke Imix's stela, I found Bill at the ruins. The day before, when we'd been inside the Temple 26 tunnel, Bill had mentioned another Temple 26 discovery and I now asked if he'd show it to me. He preceded me to a door on the temple's southwestern corner, unlocked the door, flicked on a light switch, and led the way into a large room close to ground level. On one side of the room was the top of a broken stela lying horizontally across some stones. Against the back wall was a step inscribed with hieroglyphs.

"We found this room by accident," Bill said. "We were running a tunnel above the room, came across the top of the vault, and dropped down through. We call this the founder's temple. The stela you see over there was *Yax Kuk Mo's*—Resplendent Blue-green Quetzal Macaw's. He was founder of the Copán lineage. Not that he knew it at the time. There were certainly kings before him, but he was Copán's ruler at the end of a four-hundred-year *baktun* on the ancient Maya calendar—a date of millennial significance—and because of that, they retroactively selected him as the dynasty founder. If you look at his stela, you can see it's inscribed with the *baktun*-ending date. It's the earliest date we've yet found at Copán: 9.0.0.0.0, December 11, A.D. 435.

"Yax Kuk Mo's stela used to be set up along the back wall, behind that step. The step was placed there by the fourth successor, Cu Ix. Now if you look into that pit behind you, you'll see a series of horizontal white lines. Those are lines of plaster reflecting former levels of the outside plaza. You can see that none of them come above the level of this room. To us, that means that the room was open for between two hundred and two hundred and fifty years, the implication being that for all that time, people could go in and pay homage to the founder-king, Yax Kuk Mo.

"But then this temple was covered over. It happened during the reign of the thirteenth successor, Eighteen Rabbit, and before the temple was covered, they ripped up Cu Ix's step, broke Yax Kuk Mo's stela, and burned it. If you look at the step, you'll see that whoever destroyed the temple also chiseled off the date glyphs. Fortunately, they left Cu Ix's name, otherwise we wouldn't have known who the step belonged to. The really interesting thing, however, is what happened to Yax Kuk Mo's stela. They not only broke it, but when they did so, they struck it right on Yax Kuk Mo's name. It was as if they knew that the stela was extremely potent and they needed to deactivate it."

When we left the room, Bill locked the door behind us and we walked to the foot of the Hieroglyphic Stair.

"Eighteen Rabbit was one of Copán's most powerful kings," Bill continued. "And he was Copán's greatest patron of the arts. He not only built the Great Plaza, but he also commissioned all the stelae that are standing on it. Many people argue that Copán became a city state under Eighteen Rabbit. This is because Eighteen Rabbit managed to get a close relative, Two-legged Sky, installed on the throne of Quiriguá, the nearest Maya city to the north. He thus gained hegemony over Quiriguá. But this hegemony proved to be his downfall. Quiriguá rebelled. Eighteen Rabbit went to war, and he was captured and killed. David Stuart found the announcement of his capture and death at Quiriguá.

"The event seems really to have taken the wind out of the

Copanecs. Their response was to put up the Hieroglyphic Stair. It was built not by Eighteen Rabbit's successor, Smoke Monkey—an ineffectual man who ruled for only ten years and left almost no monuments—but by *his* successor, the fifteenth ruler, Smoke Caracol, who seems to have shared Eighteen Rabbit's vision of Copán as a premier Maya city. Among other things, Smoke Caracol sent all the way to the other end of Mayadom for his wife, a woman from the Palenque royal line. In any case, the Hieroglyphic Stair gives a detailed history of Copán's rulers from A.D. 565 to 756. Each is portrayed as a great warrior. The essential message is that everything is all right. However, the construction belies that message. The fill below the Hieroglyphic Stair wasn't even mortared. The stair was built on top of loose stone rubble. As a result, it's the only one of Copán's stairways to have collapsed.

"To put this all in perspective," Bill continued, "it's as if, when the desecration of the founder's temple was followed by Eighteen Rabbit's death, the rulers of Copán felt that they had a lot of explaining to do. Temple Twenty-six has always been a dynastic temple, but most of its earlier decoration had been on cosmological subjects. The Hieroglyphic Stair is different. It's almost as if Copán's kings were trying to create a personality cult."

The schedule for the arrival of *National Geographic*'s camera team and the opening of the tomb were set by the next day, and it had become apparent that it wasn't going to happen until after I had to leave. I went out to the ruins and found Bill inside the tunnel watching his workers gradually clearing the remaining rubble away from the edges of the capstones. Everyone looked tired. Bill was still fighting the flu, and he told me that he and his workers had been going straight out for three weeks—including weekends. Only the excitement of opening the tomb had kept them going.

I complimented one of the workers on his effort. Sweat pouring out from under his blue hard hat, he smiled and said that they were all working *con ánimo,* "with spirit."

I asked Bill if they were ready for the arrival of *National Geographic.*

There was plenty still to do, Bill said. They were trying to find an air conditioner. There were press releases to write. They needed to post an armed guard.

I realized that I was going to be in the way, that it was time for me to go. However, there was one more section of ancient Copán that I wanted to see. Bill had alluded several times to Yax Pac, "Rising Sun," Copán's sixteenth and last king, and I asked Bill to show me Yax Pac's temples on the south side of the acropolis.

As we left the tomb and crossed the plaza, Bill explained that by the time Yax Pac acceded, in A.D. 763, Copán was experiencing serious problems. In the three hundred years since Yax Kuk Mo had been king, the population had doubled, from ten to twenty thousand. House compounds had been built all over the valley bottom—not just on the alluvial land that historically had been the source of Copán's wealth, but also on the piedmont, the next-best agricultural land. Farming had been displaced to the upper slopes, and soil studies had shown that this had resulted in serious erosion.

"Deforestation also seems to have been a problem." Pollen studies done by a team of archaeologists from Pennsylvania State University indicate that by Yax Pac's time there probably wasn't a tree left within sight of the city."

"Despite all this," Bill said as we walked under the north end of the acropolis, "Yax Pac made some major expansions of Copán's buildings. He rebuilt the lineage temple, Temple 11, for example, into the largest structure ever seen at Copán. Across the top of its entablature he placed a thirty-foot-long crocodile resting on *bacab*, "sky god" heads. He then crowned the whole thing with an outrageous roof comb."

We walked around Temple 11 and into the western court of the acropolis. Rising up out of the courtyard was another pyramid, Temple 16.

"Yax Pac also rebuilt Temple 16, making it a deliberate echo of the dynastic temple, Temple 26. There are significant differences, however. Temple 26 has thirteen terraces. Thirteen is the number of lords of the Maya heavens. Temple 16 has nine terraces, the number of lords of the Maya underworld. The focus of Temple 26 is the

Hieroglyphic Stair, Mesoamerica's longest glyphic inscription. The focus of Temple 16 is a huge Tlaloc head."

The Tlaloc head sat on top of a row of skulls. It was entwined with sinuous ropes.

Bill explained that Tlaloc originated in Central Mexico as god of both war and rain. But when the Maya adopted the Tlaloc, they dropped the rain association and emphasized war. The ropes were references to the binding of prisoners, and the skulls below the head were associated with sacrifice.

At the foot of the stair running up the front of Temple 16 sits a four-foot-square stone altar. This is the Altar Q. Four figures are carved into each face of the altar, seated on glyphic thrones as if in lotus position. Before Mayanists could read the glyphs, they hypothesized that the sixteen figures were astronomers coming to Copán for a conference on the moon. But once the glyphs could be read, it became apparent that the sixteen figures were Yax Pac and his fifteen predecessors arranged in such a way that Yax Kuk Mo, first in line, was passing a scepter of authority to Yax Pac, the last in line.

Excavations below Altar Q had unearthed a sacrificial cache containing the bones of fifteen wild cats, thirteen jaguars, and two pumas. Though it had been hypothesized that one cat was killed for each of Yax Pac's ancestors, Bill said that the hole into which the bones were placed wasn't big enough for them to have been put there all at once.

"They must have been put in periodically. Perhaps they honored one ancestor a year. But what interests me is that there aren't fifteen jaguars. They had to resort to pumas. One of the jaguars, moreover, is a juvenile. I see this as a reflection of the retreat of the forest by Yax Pac's time."

We left Temple 16 and headed toward Temple 18, on the southeast corner of the acropolis.

"Yax Pac ruled for fifty-nine years," Bill said as we walked, "but he seems to have had trouble with the allegiance of the noble families in the valley. It might be a problem of sampling—the records of the most recent kings are the ones nearest the surface—but as far as we can tell, Yax Pac is the only king to have actively participated in bloodletting ceremonies in the compounds of the nobility. He also seems to have encouraged the noble families to erect monuments emphasizing their association with him. It was as if he needed to confirm his authority."

Temple 18 was a modest temple, carved into a wall overlooking the river, almost as an afterthought, it seemed—"As if the population wouldn't stand for the construction of another large temple. We think that this was Yax Pac's burial temple, but we don't know for certain. It has Yax Pac's stela outside and a relief panel showing Yax Pac as a warrior, but the tomb itself was looted during the Late Classic. All that was left were some tiny jades, a few pieces of pottery, and a few bone fragments. For good measure, the looters broke Yax Pac's stela when they left."

It was getting late. In the trees overhead the orioles were beginning their evening song. Bill had one more thing he wanted to show me. We walked back to the northern edge of the ball court, where he stopped in front of an inconspicuous altar.

"This is referred to as Altar L. To one side of this panel you see Yax Pac. On the other is a man identified as Smoke Flint. In the middle, there's a date—A.D. 822, the year of Yax Pac's death. After the date is a glyph for 'He is seated,' in other words, 'He accedes.' But then you go around to the back of the altar—my wife, Barbara, discovered this—and the figures are only outlined, not carved. The blocks of glyphs are laid out, but not filled in. Some people list Smoke Flint as the seventeenth successor, some don't. My own feeling is that central authority had collapsed at Yax Pac's death and that Smoke Flint was a pretender. It's as if a bunch of guys with spear throwers came running over the hill, found the artist carving Stone Flint's altar, and chased him away. It's as if he dropped his carving tools and ran. That's it. That's the last recorded date at Copán. After 822, settlement pattern surveys have shown, noble families continued to live in the valley until the end of the tenth century, and the common people staying in diminishing numbers for another two hundred years after that. By 1200 the forest had reasserted itself. The valley was abandoned. In the four hundred years between 800 and 1200 the population of Copán dropped from twenty thousand to zero."

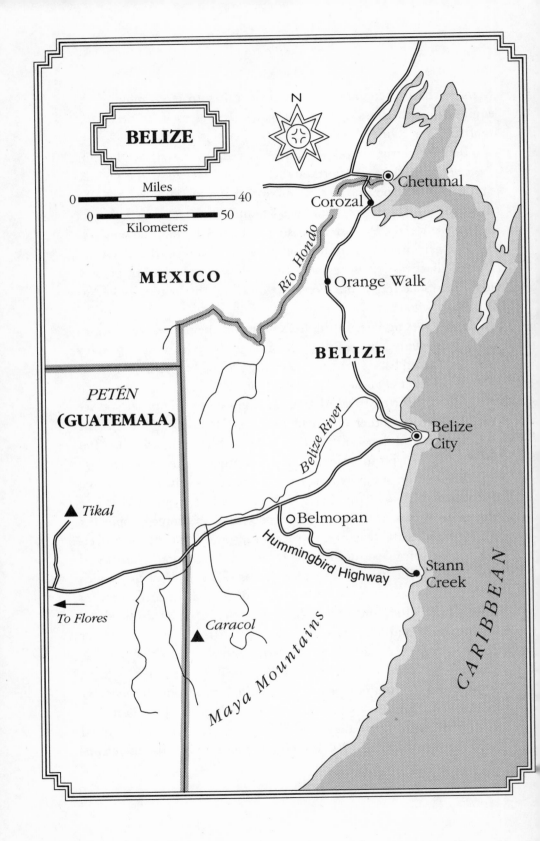

CHAPTER 8

Belize

FOR MONTHS I HAD BEEN CORRESPONDING with Barbara MacLeod, an anthropology graduate student at the University of Texas, but it was not until the Palenque Round Table that we met. The Round Table, held in Palenque more or less every three years, is a sequel conference to the famous Linda Schele/Peter Mathews/Floyd Lounsbury gathering, and it now draws Mayanists from all over the world. Barbara, a highly regarded epigrapher, had driven down from Austin.

Barbara's reputation had preceded her. I had seen the comic book about two New Age travelers who enter a cave deep in a Central American rain forest and cross a time barrier into the world of the ancient Maya. She had written and drawn the comic book herself. Some of its dialogue was in Cholti, an extinct branch of Cholan. The story reflects the several years Barbara spent with the Peace Corps doing archaeological surveys of caves in the Belize interior. And it was about her interest in caves that Barbara and I had corresponded. After the Round Table, I had arranged to travel to Belize with Barbara where she planned to show me through a cave that, she said, had been the site of an important Maya underworld cult a millennium ago. Barbara had been enthusiastic on the telephone, but even before she got to Palenque she seemed to be having second thoughts. Eventually, after arranging for me to visit the cave with an archaeologist friend who lived in Belize, she informed me that she wasn't going.

The night before the last day of the conference, we sat down under the thatched roof of a hotel terrace to talk about it. The dry season had just broken. Thunder was crashing, lightning was flashing across the sky, and rain was coming down in sheets, gusting across the hotel terrace in a fine mist that threatened to extinguish the little candle in the center of our table. Barbara was explaining that she had first gone to Belize in 1970 as part of a caving expedition and then had arranged to return the following year as part of the Peace Corps.

"I fell in love with the area," she told me. "The caves in Belize are great vaulted chambers connected by long underground rivers. The sense of enclosed space is the same that you feel in a cathedral. I was amazed at how beautiful the underground chambers were, and how far the Maya penetrated to get to them. In some cases I was the first person to enter the chambers since the Maya priests twelve hundred years before. That's a powerful sensation. You feel a bond."

The cave that Barbara and I were to have explored was in subtropical rain forest in the foothills of the Maya Mountains, a few miles from the nearest road. It was in a limestone region of razorback ridges in which the water had seeped down to form a network of underground streams and caverns. Where the roofs of these caverns had collapsed, they had formed cenotes (from the Yucatec Maya *dzonot,* or "well")—yawning, water-filled craters that pockmarked the jungle floor. Where the water had worked its way below even the cenotes, it had left behind dry-floored craters referred to as "sinkholes." This was the case with the cave Barbara had proposed we explore. The cave entrance was at the bottom of a very large sinkhole almost three hundred feet deep. One of the sinkhole's sides had collapsed, and you reached its floor by scrambling down over the loose stone and then roping the last twenty-five feet. The cave had been discovered in 1969 but hadn't been explored until Barbara and a friend went through it in 1971. She returned in 1978 to do a systematic archaeological survey and turned up obsidian blades, stingray-spine bloodletters, a pyrite mirror, and ceramics covering a five-hundred-year time span from approximately A.D. 300 to 800. The survey also turned up the remains of twenty-five skeletons, half of which were children three years old or younger. The children had been carefully laid in a series of shallow pools near the mouth of the cave, an area known as the Rimstone Dams. The pools had since dried up, fusing the infants' bones into the stone.

"Some of the pottery in the cave was from a long distance away," Barbara said. "As I see it, it was a ceremonial center focusing on the rain and earth gods. It may have been a site for initiations into a cave cult. There may even have been a priest, or priests, who lived there permanently."

Barbara had jointly directed the 1978 archaeological survey of the cave with Dorie Reents, a ceramicist now teaching at Duke University. In April of that year, Dennis Puleston, a young archaeologist from the University of Minnesota, joined them. Puleston had gained a towering reputation for, among other things, his argument that the great Classic-era Maya cities had sustained themselves not just with milpa agriculture, but by the use of sophisticated techniques of rain-forest silviculture and an extremely productive system of raised-field agriculture. Puleston argued that the Maya had built the raised fields above swamps and river floodplains with the muck obtained from their digging out a network of permanent canals. This had ensured constantly renewable fertility and a constant supply of water in a region where water is in short supply during the dry season each year.

Puleston's raised-field argument offered the first explanation of the disparity between the population of the ancient Maya that theoretically could have been supported with milpa agriculture alone, and what appeared to be a much larger actual population of Maya cities. His theories were borne out when traces of his proposed canals were detected at several sites with side-looking radar. By then Puleston had become interested in the iconographical association connecting royalty, water imagery, and the underworld. He suggested that the Maya saw the patterns made by the raised fields as similar to those on the ridged back of Itzam Na, the great crocodile on whose back the world floated. He and others noted that Maya kings were referred to as "water-lily lords" and that the surface of the water was often portrayed in Maya art as a membrane between the underworld and the surface of the earth.

Puleston's interest in underworld imagery led to his joining Barbara MacLeod and Dorie Reents's project. After several months of working together in the Belize cave, Puleston and MacLeod jointly presented a paper entitled "Pathways into Darkness" at the 1978 Palenque Round Table. In it they discussed the principle of fertility and renewal that connected stalagmites, stelae, and ceibas, the sacred World Trees at the center of the Maya universe, noting that one of the stelae at Yaxchilán was actually a carved stalagmite, and that a broken section of stalagmite had been carefully laid in one of the calcified pools of the Rimstone Dams. "Pathways into Darkness" was the last paper Dennis Puleston ever gave. Two weeks after the Round Table, he climbed to the top of the Castillo at Chichén Itzá during a storm and was struck dead by a bolt of lightning.

"It was a crazy thing for him to do," Barbara said. "It was very unlike him. His two kids were with him. They came screaming down the pyramid, but they were unharmed. I felt the lightning bolt was meant for me, as if my work in the cave had somehow led him to his recklessness."

I asked Barbara if she had any reason to believe this.

"I'd become convinced that whatever rituals took place within the cave involved sensory deprivation. As an earlier experiment, a friend and I had spent forty-eight hours in complete darkness deep inside one of the caves. We'd placed no restrictions on our behavior. For the first four or five hours we chatted away. But after that we suddenly ran out of things to say. It was as if the cave was demanding we listen. So we sat in silence. After a period of uncertainty and disorientation, we felt a presence that asserted itself first as a deep chill and then as a wave of energy. I began to feel as if I were everywhere in the cave at once; as if I were separated from it but part of it. Whatever it was, was older than the Maya. It was as old as the cave itself. It offered me a choice of time travel or apprenticeship. Time travel would have meant walking out of the cave into the ancient Maya world. It was something I fantasized about, but wasn't ready for. I chose apprenticeship, which is a choice I've maintained. My career as a Mayanist is a result of it.

"However, Dennis's death came as a real setback. I felt as if my dabbling with cave gods had angered them somehow and had resulted in Dennis's doing something he wouldn't ordinarily have done. It was crazy, really, his going up the pyramid in a storm. After he was killed, I went into the cave to make atonement. It was difficult. I thought I wouldn't come out alive. After I did, I gave up cave archaeology. To have continued would have been to perpetrate a violation."

When Barbara finished her story, we sat in silence for a while, listening to the storm raging around us. A movement caught my eye and I looked down beyond our table to the edge of the terrace. From out of the shrubbery, a toad hopped over, looked up at us, and hopped back off again into the night.

My departure for Belize two days later was not a smooth one. Although the cave was only some two hundred miles due east of Palenque, it also lay on the other side of the Petén, which no roads traversed. The only practical way to get there was to head northeast, cross the base of the Yucatán, and then cut south along the Caribbean coast. It was a long trip, and on Sunday, the day I wanted to leave, there were only evening buses. Since I did not particularly want to take an all-night bus ride, I began asking around to find out if any conference participants were headed for Belize. Someone pointed out a husband-and-wife archaeological team who, along with several graduate students, were leaving for Belize that morning in two shiny, new pickup trucks.

"No passengers," snapped the prematurely jowly husband-and-wife archaeologists, their eyes shrunken to hardened little beads by years of no doubt successful academic turf wars. "It's a government truck."

One of their graduate students, a long-legged blond woman, came over to sympathize. She suggested I hitchhike. "I spent three months hitchhiking through Mexico last year," she said, "and I never had to wait more than ten minutes."

I was about to point out the difference between her hitching and my hitching, when she cut me off.

"Of course," she said before turning away, "I'm pretty and you're not."

I walked to the road on the outskirts of Palenque and unfurled my thumb. Several hours of fruitlessly waving at cars got me as far as the bus station of Emiliano Zapata, a stone's throw northeast of Palenque, where I met Elder Mair, a missionary with the Church of Jesus Christ of Latter-Day Saints from Ogden, Utah. Elder wore a white short-sleeved polyester shirt and a thin black tie. Despite his title (or name, I didn't figure out which it was), which was inscribed on a little plastic badge attached to his shirt pocket, he appeared to be in his early twenties. He had a potbelly, short-cropped sandy-brown hair, a protruding lower jaw, and large, highly polished clod-hopper shoes. He asked when I thought the Maya had first come to the region and seemed genuinely interested in my answer. After I'd gone on for a while about the Formative and the Pre-Classic, he waited for a polite interval and said that the Mormons believed that the Maya had come to the New World from the Biblical lands around the time of Christ but that around A.D. 400 there'd been a war in which all the Christian Maya had been killed. In deference to the earlier dates I'd mentioned, however, Elder added that it *was also possible* that there'd been earlier Maya who'd migrated to the New World at the time of the fall of the Tower of Babel.

Elder and I were standing in the first-class ticket line. When it hadn't moved in half an hour and he noticed that I was beginning to get agitated, Elder said that if I held his place in line, he'd go over and check the second-class schedules for me. By the time he got back, I'd already decided to go out to the road and start hitching again. As I walked away, Elder thrust a Mormon Bible into my hand.

"Be sure to read the Tower of Babel chapter," he said to me. "You might find it useful for your work."

The road from Emiliano Zapata to Francisco Escárcega, a crossroads town with a bad reputation, traversed flat swampy grassland. While buzzards wheeled overhead, I watched Indians selling spider monkeys at roadside and the occasional tortoise, halfway across the asphalt, craning its neck at an oncoming semi. I had somewhat better luck hitching, but by the time I reached Escárcega, I'd resolved to give it up again and catch a bus to Chetumal, a port city just north of the Belize border. However, Escárcega had a reservations

system that made it impossible ever to get on a bus. An officious
clerk wouldn't sell tickets until the buses arrived, and the buses
always arrived full. The fare to Chetumal was eight thousand
pesos—a little over three dollars. After several buses had gone by, I
was standing at the ticket desk with a twenty-thousand-peso note in
my hand, discussing the prospects of my ever getting out of
Escárcega, when, out of the corner of my eye, I noticed a bus pulling
in. I knew without asking that it was full, but went over to talk to
the driver anyway. A man carrying a portable gas-powered generator,
also trying to get to Chetumal, followed me. The driver asked where
I wanted to go.

"Chetumal," I told him.

"How much are you willing to pay?"

"He'll pay twenty thousand pesos," volunteered the man with
the portable generator.

Without waiting for a reply, the driver snatched the bill out of
my hand and began waving me up onto the bus.

"*Rápido güero, rápido!*" he said, as I hesitated in confusion—
"Quick, whitey, quick!"

Behind me, the other man was frantically hauling his generator
up the bus steps. No one asked him for any money. A free ride to
Chetumal was his finder's fee.

As we traveled east from Escárcega, the road gradually climbed
into a region of low rolling hills and sparsely populated scrub forest.
This was the transition zone between the jungles of the Petén and
the dry bush of the Yucatán further north. My twenty thousand
pesos had bought me a stool at the very front of the bus, right next
to the driver, from which I could see so many colored birds perched
in the trees along the roadside that the trees looked as if they were
ornamented for Christmas. I particularly admired the motmots,
beautiful iridescent blue-green birds that pluck their long tail feathers until the central shaft is clean and the tips flair out in elegant
fans. At one point, however, outside an *ejido* called Justício Social, a
bright-orange oriole flew into the windshield directly in front of me.
I started. The people in the front seats giggled.

Oh, the funny gringo!

* * *

At Chetumal that evening, I sat on a sea wall, felt the sultry Caribbean breezes, and watched a near-full moon rise over the horizon. In a park behind me, palm trees arched gracefully over a bandstand. A band consisting of elderly gents in khaki uniforms and peaked hats was playing tropical tunes. When they'd finished, they trooped off, and the bandstand filled up again with a fifteen-piece string band from the Lopez Mateos Secondary School. The string band strummed and sang *Lagrimas de Amor*—"Tears of Love." When they were finished, their music teacher dedicated it to everyone in the audience, but especially to the fathers. It was *Dia de los Padres*—"Father's Day."

The next morning at the bus terminal, my request for a ticket to Belize was the cause of a loud argument between the representatives of two Belizan bus companies: Batty Bus and the Z-line. Each accused the other of lying. When I finally bought my ticket from Batty, the Z-line man looked at me sulkily and told me I'd regret my decision. The Batty bus would break down *long* before I ever got to Belize City.

When the Batty bus showed up forty-five minutes late, the Batty representative, as if to vindicate his reputation, personally escorted me on board. He pointed out that the bus was a Blue Bird which, as anyone knew, was synonymous with quality. He pointed out the stuffed, green vinyl seats—most of which were covered with tears and pieces of tape. Z-line, he assured me, had only hard benches.

After he'd left, I flicked a cockroach off a seat, opened a window, and sat down to wait for the bus to fill. Two Maya women across the aisle from me began to speak to each other in Caribbean-inflected English. One called the other "Mon." It was bizarre. A bus from Belize pulled into the spot next to ours. Leaning out my window, I watched two Mennonite couples get out. The two women wore long, floral-print dresses and wide straw hats. The two men had white beards, were dressed in overalls, and seemed to be discussing preaching. One turned to the other and in heavily accented English said, "When I look at the congregation, I don't see people, I see souls!"

* * *

The Mexico-Belize border lies along the Rio Hondo, a sluggish tropical river just south of Chetumal. From the Late Classic on, the Rio Hondo was a major trade artery between the interior of the Petén and the sea. The Maya were great seafarers—"just as maritime as the ancient Greeks," as one archaeologist put it. When the Spanish arrived, the whole of the eastern shore of Yucatán and Belize was dotted with harbors participating in a network of canoe-born commerce which stretched from Central Mexico all the way to coastal Honduras. Chetumal, for instance, a Maya port city of two thousand dwellings, had been the home of the renegade Spaniard Gonzalo Guerrero. At the time of his death in 1536, Guerrero had taken a fleet of fifty canoes south to Honduras to aid the Indians of the Ulúa River valley in their fight against the Spaniards.

Earlier, on Columbus's fourth voyage in 1502, he had come upon a Maya trading canoe off the coast of Honduras. This was probably the first contact between the Spanish and the Maya.

"It was as long as a galley and eight feet wide, made of a single tree trunk," Columbus's son Ferdinand Colon recalled in his biography of his father. "Amidships it had a palm leaf awning like that which the Venetian gondolas carry. ... There were twenty-five paddlers aboard."

The ship's cargo consisted of roots and grains, "wine made of maize that tasted like English beer," cotton mantles, brightly embroidered sleeveless shirts, copper hatchets and hawk's bells, and "long wooden swords with a groove in each side where the edge should be, on which were fastened, with cord and pitch, flint knives that cut like steel."

> They had as well many of the almonds [cacao beans] which the Indians of New Spain use as currency; and these the Indians in the canoe valued greatly, for I noticed that when they were brought aboard with the other goods, and some fell to the floor, all the Indians squatted down to pick them up as if they had lost something of great value—their greed driving out their feelings of terror and danger at finding themselves in the hands of such strange and ferocious men as we must have seemed to be.

The Maya of Belize and eastern Yucatán were also among the most unyielding of all the Maya. In the 1540's they rose up in one last massive pre-Conquest rebellion against the Spanish and, when they were defeated, paid dearly for their defiance. Bishop Landa relates how, after its final defeat, Chetumal was transformed from "the most settled and populous" province of Yucatán to being "the most wretched of the whole country." Landa describes the "unheard-of cruelties" that were inflicted on its captured residents: "cutting off their noses, hands, arms and legs, and the breasts of their women; throwing them into deep water with gourds tied to their feet, thrusting the children with spears because they could not go as fast as their mothers. If some of those who had been put in chains fell sick or could not keep up with the rest, they would cut off their heads among the rest rather than stop to unfasten them."

In the end, the Spanish completely destroyed all but the most remote Maya towns in eastern Yucatán and forced the remaining population to take refuge in the interior forests. There, the refugee Maya became known as *huits,* or "loincloths" (for the rolled-up white shorts they wore). It's hard to know how many *huits* there were—one historian says that counting them would have been like "counting the birds in the forest." But for administrative purposes, the Spanish discounted the *huits,* declared the region *despoblada*— "depopulated"—and retreated to the drier climate around Mérida. In many ways, this scorched-earth campaign against the sixteenth-century Maya accounts for what Belize is today. So underpopulated did the whole region become that, by the early seventeenth century, pirates—especially British pirates—began to use it for permanent bases in their campaign of pillage and looting against the Spanish. One of these pirates, a Scot named Peter Wallace, landed at the mouth of what is now the Belize River. Protected by an impenetrable complex of swamps, reefs, and shoals, Wallace built a camp, surrounded it with a palisade, and went to work preying on Spanish shipping. Wallace was only one of many such privateers. His name stuck, however. In Spanish, it became *Walis, Balis,* and, finally, Belize.

The first town south of the border was Corozal, Spanish for

"grove of cohune palms." Corozal seemed a world apart. Instead of the rounded thatched houses that you see in Yucatán, Corozal's dwellings were pastel clapboard structures with rusty galvanized-metal roofs. Some were on stilts. As the bus pulled into the center of town, a black man stood with a pushcart shouting "Ice Cream!" under a sign that read MINISTRY OF WORKS. Down at the end of the main street I could see the masts of fishing boats outlined against the bright turquoise of the Caribbean.

Corozal was founded in the mid-nineteenth century by refugees from Yucatán. The Spanish may have declared eastern Yucatán depopulated, but when royal protections for Maya lands were discarded after Mexico became independent from Spain in 1821, Mérida-based entrepreneurs began to grab frontier land, and they discovered it was anything but *despoblada*. The *huits* who had lived independently in Yucatán's eastern forests for hundreds of years led a Maya rebellion, referred to as the Caste War, that lasted for the next half century, killed hundreds of thousands, and sent refugees pouring over the border into British Honduras. British Honduras was spared the violence, not because the rebel Maya particularly liked the English, but because, in the best buccaneer tradition, the English authorities profitably sold the rebel Maya whatever armaments they needed.

South of Corozal we pushed on through Orange Walk, Gardenia, Coco Plum, Burnt House, Grace Bank, and Lady Ville. Finally we arrived in Belize City, a jumble of crooked houses built on dirty canals. Rasta men with dark sunglasses offered to shine my shoes, carry my bags, or "fix me up" in other unspecified ways.

In Belize City I switched buses for my final destination, Belmopan, Belize's inland capital. On the bus, I sat between two sisters named Sherry and Kim who were headed beyond Belmopan to Cayo, a town on the Guatemalan border. They were beautiful. I told them they were the first Belizeans I'd ever spoken with, although, recalling the Batty and Z-line bus representatives, this wasn't strictly true. Kim, who was seventeen, was about to go into the sixth form. She'd just missed a place in the country's best preparatory school,

Saint John's, and was now trying to choose between secretarial school, a course in business management, or modeling. Sherry, who was older, had been the third-place finisher in the Miss Belize contest. Kim's friends had told her that she should try for Miss Universe. Had I seen the Miss Universe contest? she asked me. In fact, I had seen part of it while traveling through Guatemala not long before.

"Did you see Miss Jamaica?" Kim asked. "She was *beautiful*."

When we reached Belmopan, I was a little confused. I expected a city that had been the capital of the country for the last twenty years to be a bustling place, but instead the bus pulled up in front of a terminal in the middle of an open field. Scattered around the edges of the field were a few discolored concrete buildings of the internationalist school of architecture favored by United Nations directorates. I asked Kim if this was in fact Belmopan. She assured me that it was. What had I expected?

"I don't know," I answered. "A little bit more."

After the bus left, I pulled out the address Barbara had given me, banged on a taxi until the driver woke up, and rode over a hill to a neighborhood of stuccoed, one-story houses. Each house stood in the midst of its own patch of industrial-strength crabgrass. Each patch of crabgrass merged with the neighbor's. Tract housing.

I got off at Sinsonte Street, walked until I found the right number, and knocked at a door decorated with a sticker that read A CAVER LIVES HERE. My knock was answered by a bearded, rail-thin Texan named Logan McNatt. Logan, who has lived in Belize for years, pieces together a living out of various archaeological projects interspersed with wilderness guiding and occasional archaeological contract jobs back in the States. The interior of his house was covered with wildlife posters, and the corners filled with camping and caving gear. A shelf was crowded with formaldehyde-filled jars containing gigantic beetles. Pictures of caving expeditions were everywhere, the participants posed with ropes strung across their chests like bandoliers.

Logan showed me to my room. It was already late afternoon. The tropical light was fading fast, and, after I'd gotten settled, Logan suggested we go to a place called the Bullfrog Inn for dinner. As we walked down the twilit, suburban streets, shadowy figures sitting on screened porches called out "Good night, Logan!"

"Good night!" Logan shouted back, including everyone's name. I asked Logan how he liked Belize.

"I love it," Logan said. "There're only two hundred thousand people in the whole country; there's not a single stoplight, and all the tallest buildings are pre-Columbian."

"How about Belmopan?"

"It's a very comfortable place," he said. "Very middle class."

I asked Logan about the open field where the bus had dropped me.

"Belmopan has only been the capital since 1970," he said. "After Belize City was destroyed by a hurricane in 1961, the government decided to move the capital to the interior. Belmopan was carved right out of the jungle. The plan was to build it in wedges, like the spokes of a wheel, emanating from the central plaza, where you got off the bus today. The original projections were for a population of thirty thousand by the year 1990, but most of the government continues to live in Belize City, and Belmopan's population has never exceeded five thousand. As a result, all that ever got built is the one wedge we're in now."

At the Bullfrog Inn we ran into two Fulbright scholars whom Logan knew. One of them was an anthropologist who had worked with the Kekchi Maya in southern Belize.

"The Kekchi only moved to Belize in the late nineteenth century," he said. "They fled the eastern Guatemalan highlands because of the land seizures and forced labor at the time of the introduction of coffee."

Had there previously been Maya in the region he'd worked in?

"It's not clear." At the time of the Conquest, the Manché Chol lived along the Petén-Belize border, but they were so rebellious that the Spanish finally removed them all to the highlands. Eric Thompson thinks that some of the Manché Chol escaped the Spanish and remained behind, living in isolation in the forest. The evidence he offers is that there are some Cholan loan words that occur in Belizean Kekchi but not in the Kekchi back in Guatemala. Where I worked there were also folktales about a mysterious forest people called the 'Chol Cuink,' 'the Cholan people.'"

Logan, who had been listening absentmindedly, suddenly began to laugh. I followed his gaze to a huge black and brown spider, the size of an open hand, crawling across the restaurant floor.

"Tarantula!" he said.

My hair must have stood on end, because Logan assured me that tarantulas weren't aggressive and that if one bit me, I'd *probably* only get sick.

Other diners soon spotted the creature and a shout went up from the bar, "Sam'll pick it up!"

Over came Sam, a black Belizean with hair bound into a pony tail by a white cloth. After several attempts, he managed to pin the tarantula to the floor with a drinking straw and then to pick it up by the bristly hair on its back. Someone asked him if it was dangerous.

"A snake is dangerous," Sam said, "but not if you know what you're doing. The same with a tarantula. Besides"—he put his finger about a quarter of an inch from the spider's mouth—"it's only from here that he can bite you."

That night I dreamed that tarantulas were pouring in my window and woke, unrested, at six-thirty. Outside, a neighbor was repeatedly stalling his mower in the thick grass of his lawn. Logan and I ate a breakfast of Mennonite bread and coffee laced with Mennonite milk. Afterward Logan got on the telephone and tried to recruit a third person to join our expedition.

"I always try to travel with three people in the jungle," he said. "That way, if someone gets injured, one person can stay behind while the other goes for help."

Logan didn't have any luck recruiting, but he did succeed in borrowing a stun gun, which, for reasons medical science has yet to explain, counteracts the effects of poisonous snakebites. Logan was worried about fer-de-lances, known as "tommygoffs" in Belize, which are common in the region—especially near cave mouths.

After breakfast we loaded our gear into Logan's 1966 VW microbus. It had a mandala on the rear window and a National

Speleological Society sticker on the bumper. As we headed out of town, Logan pointed out a large empty field next to the British High Commission building.

"You asked about the design of Belmopan," he said. "A few years ago, signs went up in that field saying that this was the future site of X embassy, this was the site of Y embassy. It was going to be Embassy Row. But the signs just stood there in the field until eventually they collapsed. That was all we ever saw of Embassy Row."

We followed a road called the Hummingbird Highway southeast out of Belmopan, until Logan pulled over at an abandoned cacao plantation. The caretaker was a wild-looking black man with flaming red hair and an amputated right hand. Logan introduced him as Pauline, told Pauline where we were going, and asked him to come look for us if we weren't back by sunset.

"Pauline blew his hand off dynamite fishing," Logan explained as we walked away.

Because Logan hadn't been able to get anyone to go with us, he had decided to enter the cave through a back entrance that Barbara had called *saatbe,* or "lost way" in Yucatec Maya. The *saatbe* entrance was closer and meant that we didn't have to rope down the sinkhole face of the main entrance. We walked up the valley of the former plantation until steep limestone hills closed in on both sides. We then cut through the tangled thorns and vines of a former cacao grove and proceeded over a ridge. On the other side of the ridge the jungle was higher. We passed the mounded red soil of a leaf-cutter–ant colony. The ants, each with a leaf fragment held high over its head like a banner, were streaming into holes in the ground.

I asked Logan what the ants did with the leaves.

"They grow fungus on them," he said, "and then eat it. You have to watch out for leaf-cutter colonies, though. Snakes often use them as convenient nests. I once saw an eight-foot boa constrictor disappear into one of the holes."

The landscape seemed full of portent as we approached the cave. Mountains looked like pyramids. Outcroppings seemed sculpted. The *saatbe* entrance to the cave, when we arrived, was no exception. A steep clay ridge dove under the base of a vertical cliff a hundred feet high. Where the two met, the surface of the earth simply disappeared, spiraling downward into a vortex of interior space. The light at the cave mouth was a weird green-gray. Stalactites beaded with moisture and covered with moss hung from the bottom surface of the cliff. I thought of a passage in Calixta Guiteras-Holmes's *Perils of the Soul* in which she describes one of the causes of soul loss as "daring to penetrate into the Earth by way of a cave or sinkhole."

Logan and I slid down the ridge until we reached the entrance to the cave.

"You can sometimes sense cave mouths even before you see them," Logan said. "You can actually feel the cold air."

We sat down and opened our packs. Logan produced two carbide lamps. They were brass, labeled PREMIER, BRITISH MADE. Logan unscrewed the tops of the lamps, separating the empty cylinder below from a reservoir on top. He filled the cylinders two-thirds of the way up with carbide chips and the reservoirs with water. After he screwed them back together again, he showed me the valve that when opened would allow water to drip slowly down into the carbide chips, producing the same acetylene gas that's used for welding.

"When I first started caving," he said, "I was surprised at how primitive these lamps were, but they work remarkably well."

Logan told me that there was a thirty-foot drop as we entered the cave, but after that it would be easy going. As he began unfurling the rope for the initial descent, I noticed claw marks disappearing into the cave.

"Those are coatimundis, kinkajous, and small cats," he said. "But they won't enter far into the cave itself. The little organic matter that's inside the cave is either washed in by the river or brought in by bats. With the exception of the bats and some fish, most cave life is invertebrate."

Logan fastened the rope to a boulder, lit his lamp, attached it to the front of his hard hat, and disappeared underground.

As I grabbed the rope, I took a last look around. The cave mouth arched above me like a palate. The stalactites hanging off the cliff bottom looked like dragon's teeth. I suddenly realized I had seen this image before. I was looking at the *witz* monster, the Cauac Monster, the remains of whose wide-open jaws frame the entrance to Chan Bahlum's Temple of the Cross at Palenque. The Cauac Monster is the god of stone, of the earth. His jaws separate the natural and super-natural worlds. Through the Cauac Monster's maw, Maya kings entered Xibalba, the underworld, the place of fear, terror, trembling, fright, and death.

After we had roped ourselves through the first steep, narrow passage, the cave opened up. The ceiling arched up and the floor pitched off into the darkness. Below, we could hear an unseen stream. Watery gurgles filled the air, eerily like human voices.

"Once I was working in this part of the cave with two other people," Logan said. "All three of us were simultaneously so sure that we heard human voices that we went down to the stream to find out who it was."

Logan and I slid down the clay dunes until, at the bottom, we reached a sparkling stream, its bed dotted with smooth little black stones.

"They're from a source several miles away," Logan said. "But because they're heavier and less soluble than limestone, they've been collecting on the stream bottom over the years. Their net effect is to decrease the drag on the water and therefore to accelerate its passage. The water can really rush through here. With just a few days' good rain, it can rise ten feet above its present level."

Rainy season was due at any time. I looked up. The cave ceiling was eight feet above us.

We walked along the stream bank until we came to what Logan referred to as a breakdown. Huge limestone boulders had collapsed off the cave ceiling, filling the streambed in front of us.

"Here goes," Logan said. He waded into the water up to his knees and then crawled into the jumble of collapsed rocks.

I took a deep breath and followed. As I was emerging from the last of the breakdown rocks, my lamp suddenly illuminated a soli-tary plant, its bone-white stalk growing out of a clay bank like a blanched asparagus spear.

Logan was ahead of me around the bend, and I shouted to get

him to come back and look. Logan answered that *I* should come to where *he* was. I walked around the corner and was confronted with a macabre garden of these plants. They all had spindly stems and sickly mouse-ear leaves. They grew in little clumps.

"Look," Logan said, pointing overhead.

I looked up. Thousands of bats wheeled noiselessly above. A bat's nest hung twenty feet above each clump.

"Fruit-eating bats," Logan said. "The plants have grown from seeds that have passed through the bats' digestive tracts."

As we made our way upstream, the river gradually deepened. We had started with water to our knees, but soon it was up to our crotches, then waists, and then chests. My jeans sucked at my legs and my water-filled boots felt like lead. Finally we reached a section where, even on tiptoe, the water was up to my chin.

"Be careful not to submerge your lamp," Logan warned. "Hold your pack over your head and be careful not to burn it with your lamp. Once I was crossing a stream with an extra lamp inside my pack. I didn't realize it, but the lamp was leaking acetylene. I held the pack too close to the lamp on my hard hat and the whole thing blew up."

After we'd made the crossing, the stream gradually became shallower again. We walked along the bank until we came upon a curtain of lacy, dripping limestone. Logan pointed at a stream of water spilling over the stone face onto a stalagmite below.

"This is the kind of place the ancient Maya collected *zuhuy ha*,"Logan said. "*Zuhuy ha* means 'virgin water' in Yucatec Maya. It's water that was used for ceremonial purposes, water gathered in a remote place, far from human activity. It's water that belongs to the realm of the gods, not to the realm of man."

I had been reading an essay by Eric Thompson in which he had noted that *zuhuy ha* ceremonies in the Yucatán required fire newly kindled by the stick-twirling method, and brand-new utensils that were smashed after one use. He also argued that it was the idea of *zuhuy,* "virgin," that lay behind the sacrifice of children to the rain gods.

* * *

After we'd walked another half mile or so, we rounded a corner and saw a faint glow of light ahead.

"You go first," Logan said.

I clambered around another bend and over a ridge and was brought up short by the sight in front of me. A subterranean amphitheater of enormous proportions opened before me, its arched ceiling a hundred yards over its water-washed, boulder-strewn floor. At the far end of the cavern, high on top of a cliff and two hundred yards away, was the cave mouth, itself opening into the bottom of the huge three-hundred-foot-deep dry sinkhole that Barbara MacLeod had described as the main entrance to the cave. The filtered light supported a few scrubby plants near the cave mouth, but as the light diffused farther back, there was only a wash of green, then a few blue-gray lichen, and finally only mud and stone.

On one side of the cave, halfway to the front and high on a slope, was a large, flat-topped boulder. Logan told me that Barbara had named it Nohoch Tunich, "great rock" in Yucatec Maya. Logan suggested we have lunch there. As we picked our ways toward the rock, I noticed that the sides of the cave had been terraced to form scores of little platforms. Some were connected by steps. Each seemed large enough to accommodate one, or at most two, people. Box seats for five hundred years of ceremonies to the underworld gods.

The base of Nohoch Tunich was sealed off with a curtain wall, its mortar as fresh-looking as if it had been applied one year ago, not twelve hundred. Logan reached behind the wall and pulled out a potsherd. Beautiful ropelike fluting lined one edge. The inner surface had been blackened by fire. Logan said that it had been ritually broken, as had almost all the pots that Barbara and Dorie had found. I looked behind the curtain wall. The ground was littered with pottery fragments. I thought of Eric Thompson's description of *zuhay ha* rituals and wondered if they'd been smashed after one use.

I walked with Logan around the side of Nohoch Tunich on a path strewn with millions of tiny *xute* snail shells. "The path continues all the way up to the Rimstone Dams at the cave mouth," Logan said. "Its entire length is covered with snail shells. Barbara thinks they're a symbolic road to the underworld. She cites the Temple of the Foliated Cross at Palenque in which the diminutive figure of Pacal, returned from the dead, is portrayed standing on top of a *xute* snail shell while he hands Chan Bahlum a bloodletting instrument."

On top of the rock we pulled out our lunch—cold beans and little Viennese sausages mixed with jalapeño peppers. From where we sat, we had a good view of the cave mouth. A hundred yards away, high above us, we could see the spiny palms and tangled lianas of the sinkhole floor. It looked like a primeval terrarium. Sounds projected strangely. The hooting of a motmot, one of the long-tailed birds I'd seen through the windshield of the Chetumal bus, filled the cavern. As we watched, a brief shower rustled the distant leaves. When the shower subsided, Logan said that he thought he could hear the croaking of *uo* frogs.

Uo frogs, of the genus *Leptodactylus,* are considered both harbingers of the rainy season and servants of the *chaacs*, the rain gods who live in caves and the cenotes that are the only source of water over much of the Yucatán peninsula. The association of *uo* frogs and the rain gods may come from the fact that young *uo* frogs hatch in muddy underground burrows at the bottom of seasonal ponds. The frogs begin to grow underground, so when the rains start and the ponds fill with water, they are suddenly, instantly, also full of grown frogs making the deafening collective roar from which their Maya name derives.

As to the rain gods, the *chaacs*, there are four of them, one for each of the sacred directions. They are old men, but dangerous in the way that the Maya underworld is dangerous. They are the source of lightning, tornadoes, hurricanes, and floods, but since they are also the source of the earth's fertility, the world could not survive without them. Therefore they must be constantly managed, constantly placated.

During a severe drought in the summer of 1930, the pioneer Mexican anthropologist Alfonso Villa Rojas witnessed what is referred to as a *cha-chaac* ceremony, a rain-bringing ceremony, in the Yucatec village of Chan Kom. A shaman conducted the ceremony. *Balche,* a ceremonial fermented drink, had been prepared from a mixture of *zuhuy ha,* honey, and the pounded bark of the *Lonchocarpus* tree. When the mixture had sufficiently fermented, an altar was constructed on which a feast was laid out for the gods. Four boys, representing *uo* frogs, were tied to the four corners of the altar. An old man was given a *lelem,* a lightning stick, and designated Kunku-Chaac, chief of the *chaacs.* While the boys croaked and the old man imitated the sound of thunder, the shaman invited the gods to the feast and asked for the favor of rain.

Because there were only two of us, Logan didn't want to climb the steep bank to the Rimstone Dams and the cave mouth. Instead, after lunch we headed back into the interior of the cave. A few hundred yards downstream, however, Logan turned and ascended the bank above the stream. We followed a rising passageway, until soon the ceiling opened up, the walls blew out, and we found ourselves in a cavern so huge that our dim lamps couldn't make out the edges. A gleaming white stalagmite stood in the middle of the cavern floor.

"This is the kind of place the Maya sought out," Logan said. "This is where they performed their rituals."

As we walked toward the stalagmite, my lamp illuminated two tiny, funnel-shaped depressions made by water dripping onto the clay floor. I stopped and looked more carefully. In one I could see part of a human-sized jawbone with three molars still attached. In the other the water had exposed what looked like the bleached curve of a cranium.

"I don't know what these are," Logan said when I pointed them out to him. "Barbara and Dorie didn't do anything beyond a surface survey."

The stalagmite in the center of the room was covered with fluffy extrusions of limestone, making it look like a northern conifer laden with fresh snow. The ground around it was littered with tiny sparkling stones that Logan referred to as "cave pearls."

We walked to one of the cavern walls where a huge limestone column ran from floor to ceiling.

"Do you see anything?" Logan asked.

I didn't.

"Look carefully," he said.

All I could see at first was another dazzling display of crystal-coated stone, but at Logan's urging I continued peering around, until, practically under foot, I noticed what looked like a pile of sticks.

"Bones," Logan said.

I looked more closely. I could make out a collapsed rib cage as well as arm and leg bones.

"And over there?"

He pointed to a stone shelf nearby. On it, a skull covered in crystallized limestone sat next to a stone column.

"The skull used to be right here too," Logan said. "It was fused to the floor until someone chipped it up. Bishop Landa says that the Maya sacrificed their victims and then dragged them, already dead, into caves. But because of the distance from the cave mouth, and because this person was deposited here in a seated position—presumably before rigor mortis set in—Barbara thinks he was probably sacrificed right here. They've found the remains of at least fifteen other people in this chamber."

I wondered to myself what kind of ceremonies had gone on. I knew that Barbara and Dorie had found snake skeletons cached in recesses along the cavern wall. Since snakes, like frogs, were servants of the *chaacs,* this was consistent with the idea of rain and fertility rites. They had also found obsidian blades. Obsidian is a volcanic glass that the Maya believed was created when lightning struck the earth. They no doubt used this obsidian for bloodletting as well as, presumably, dispatching sacrificial victims.

Barbara and Dorie had also turned up hollow-bone enema tubes. During certain rituals, the Maya, like many other New World Indians, made use of enemas containing hallucinogenic drugs: substances absorbed through the colon wall directly into the bloodstream. The preparation of these enemas started with *balche,* the same fermented honey-based drink that Villa Rojas had seen prepared for the *cha-chaac* ceremony in 1930. To the *balche* the Maya added a *Bufo marinus* toad, whose skin contains a cardiotoxin, bufotoxin, similar to digitalis, as well as a powerful hallucinogen called bufotenine. The effect of the mixture administered in this fashion can only be imagined.

A reproduction of a polychrome funerary vase I had seen in Yale art historian Michael Coe's *Lords of the Underworld* depicts a wild underworld ceremony presided over by a god sitting inside the open maw of the Cauac Monster. A *moan* bird, the supernatural underworld bird perched on God L's hat on the Temple of the Cross at Palenque, is perched on one corner of the cave. Facing it is a three-person orchestra, all of its members singing, apparently at the top of their lungs. One orchestra member is shaking a pair of rattles. Another is beating a turtle-shell drum with a drumstick made from a deer antler. The third is pounding another drum covered with jaguar skin. In between the orchestra and the presiding god is an audience of four men with stoned smiles and glazed eyes sitting cross-legged in front of four enema jars. The four men are tended by four female consorts and two servants.

Coe identifies the four men as God N's. God N was one of the principal Maya underworld gods. In the Yucatán he is known as Pauhatun, an old-man god associated with earth, water, and agricultural fertility. Pauhatun, like the *chaacs*, is a quadripartite god who supports the earth in each of the four sacred directions. In some of his forms he is shown with a reptilian ear. In others he is shown emerging from a shell. In his earth-bearing form, he wears water lilies and bears Cauac signs on his body. His female consort is Ixchel, goddess of the moon, the night, and the female, gestational, half of the universe.

Clearly, however, whatever rituals had taken place in the chamber where Logan and I found ourselves had involved more than just music and hallucinogens. They had also involved sacrifice. Not long before, I had met with Don Samuel Rúiz García, the bishop of San Cristóbal de las Casas, a man deeply involved in contemporary Maya life. I had asked Don Samuel about his predecessor Bartolomé de las Casas. Specifically, I wanted to know if Don Samuel did not agree that Las Casas, although sympathetic to the Maya, had been part of the machinery of conquest. Why did the Maya have to become Catholic at all? Didn't they have a right to their own religion?

This question was not guaranteed to endear me to Don Samuel, but it was one that I felt strongly about asking. I was surprised by

Don Samuel's response, which began with the subject of sacrifice.

"We know from colonial Yucatec sources," he said, "that Indians who were about to be dropped into cenotes as sacrifices to the rain gods went to their deaths happily. In a letter Las Casas wrote to his Dominican brothers in Guatemala, he asked which of them could explain why the willingness of the Maya to sacrifice human beings to their gods was any different from Abraham's willingness to sacrifice his son Isaac? The logic was that the Maya gave to their gods the best of what they had, even if it meant sacrificing people. None of Las Casas' Dominican brethren could answer his question."

Tzvetan Todorov, in his book *The Conquest of the Americas: The Question of the Other*, makes the point that sacrifice demonstrates the power of the social fabric and its mastery over the individual. He contrasts it to a world of massacres, where there is no social fabric, where anything goes. It is hard for us, in the West, to even contemplate the question of human sacrifice, but it seemed to me that Todorov's point was that sacrifice could only be understood in context. It is now widely acknowledged that the ancient Maya, once thought of as peaceful people, performed hideous tortures on their captives. But it's worth considering that as far as anyone knows the victims of this torture were exclusively the nobility of enemy city-states. Being tortured was a possibility that came with the noble turf. By contrast, the Maya seem not to have waged war against civilian populations. The sort of widespread violence we routinely inflict on the nonmilitary population of our opponents would have been anathema to the ancient Maya. Which form of violence is worse is not any easy question to resolve, but one thing is clear: If our own heads of state personally led us onto the battlefield, there would be many fewer, or at least much shorter, wars.

Logan interrupted my thoughts to ask if I'd ever experienced "total darkness." I said I hadn't. We sat on rocks thirty feet apart, placed our flashlights at hand, and doused the lamps. The blackness was at first thick, almost creamy. After fighting off an impulse to go to sleep, I began to think about the hollow eye sockets and collapsed bones of the skeleton nearby. I wondered what kind of person the sacrificial victim had been, and what his death had been like. Had he been drugged? What had he been thinking of as he was ushered by the light of a pitch-pine torch into this forlorn chamber. What had he thought about in the instant he was cut by the obsidian knife? I thought of the passage of twelve hundred years since the sacrifice, the body's slow decomposition, and then the gradual fusing of the bones to the cave floor. I felt the humidity of the cave around me and listened to drops falling into distant pools. It occurred to me that this must be what death is like—dark, featureless, and unchanging. No day, no night, no rain, no sun, no fluctuation of temperature. No hope. No future. Miasma.

"Are you awake?" Logan called out.

I groped for my flashlight and switched it on. When I adjusted my eyes, I found myself staring at the rock in front of me. Fragments of smaller rocks were frozen, swimming, in a larger stone medium.

"That's brecciated limestone," Logan said. "That rock went through a traumatic experience long before this cave ever existed."

That night, after we got back to Logan's house, the skies let loose. The first rain of the season beat down on his metal roof with a deafening roar. There were more leaks than Logan had pans to place under them. When the rain finally subsided, Logan stepped outside to smoke a cigarette. He returned shortly afterward.

"Do you want to hear something?" he asked.

I followed him out onto the street and we walked to the edge of the development. Someone had tried to drive a car across a footbridge spanning a sizable drainage ditch. The car lay abandoned, nosed into the side of the ditch like an unexploded artillery shell. We walked by until we arrived at the edge of a field.

"There," Logan said, "Do you hear it?"

From a swamp on the other side of the field, I heard what sounded like the roar of a factory. I looked at Logan questioningly.

"*Uo* frogs," he said. "Welcome to rainy season."

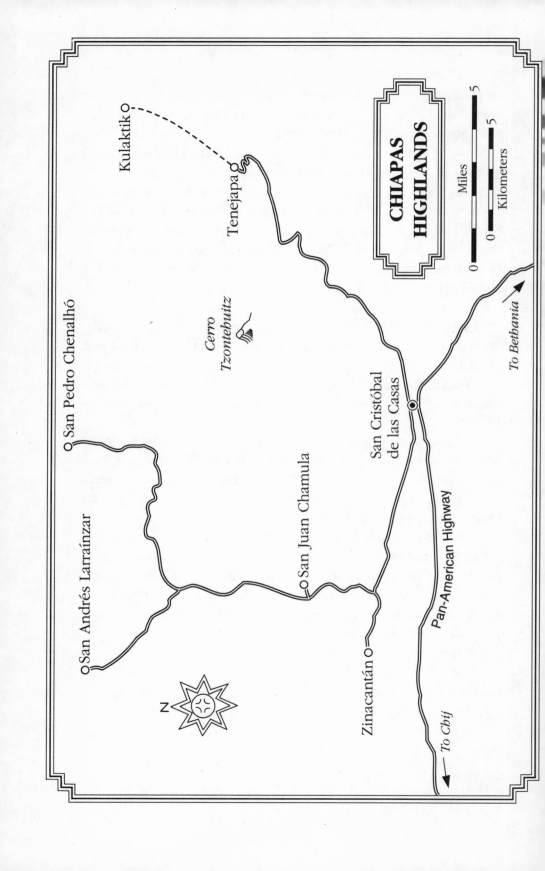

CHIAPAS
HIGHLANDS

Miles

Kilometers

Kulaktik

Tenejapa

Cerro
Tzontehuitz

San Pedro Chenalhó

San Andrés Larraínzar

San Juan Chamula

San Cristóbal
de las Casas

Zinacantán

Pan-American Highway

To Bethania

To Cbij

N

CHAPTER 9

Chij

Many people view the contemporary Maya as being in the process of absorption by the outside world. They see Maya villages as isolated outposts of pre-Columbian life gradually succumbing to modernity. The problem with this essentially gloomy perspective is that it assumes that the Maya are losing an isolation that they actually never had. Most colonial historians now agree that throughout their post-Conquest history, the Maya have been firmly in thrall to the outside economy and that village institutions that on the surface appear pre-Columbian owe at least their formal structures to the influence of the non-Maya world.

This distinction is important. In what might be referred to as the "dying-folk-culture" point of view, the Maya are an endangered species whose every small accommodation to the modern world is to be regretted. By contrast, if one looks at the Maya as a colonized people who have retained their identity by continually adjusting their institutions to meet the demands of the outside world, their culture can be regarded as a vital and even expanding one.

I went to George Collier, an anthropologist from Stanford, because I became interested in the latter point of view. A quiet, deliberate man, George is the grandson of Franklin Delano Roosevelt's commissioner of Indian affairs, John Collier. For thirty years George has been studying a *paraje* in the Chiapas municipality of Zinacantán, tracking the changes that have taken place in its relationship to the outside world, most notably those that have occurred in the aftermath of Mexico's oil boom. I was interested in George's work because it seemed to me that the ways in which the Zinacantecs were adapting to the changing demands of the outside economy should be a reflection of the adaptations that were going on among the Maya more generally.

Zinacantán is a Tzotzil-speaking municipality lying along the western edge of the Chiapas highlands, high above the Grijalva River valley. Before the arrival of the Spanish, Zinacantán's lands extended all the way down to the river, which defined both the edge of the highlands and the western boundary of the Maya region. The Zinacantecs took advantage of their peripheral position and prospered by trading jaguar pelts, quetzal feathers, amber, and other Maya commodities to Aztec merchants.

When the Spanish arrived in 1524, the Zinacantecs allied themselves with the conquerors, but as soon as the fighting was over the Spanish helped themselves to the best Zinacantec land anyway, notably the rich valley bottomland that lay between the foot of the highlands and the Grijalva River. Here, in the years after the Conquest, well-connected Spaniards built sugar plantations, started cattle ranches, and established a relationship to the Maya that has persisted to the present. The highland Zinacantecs became what anthropologists sometimes refer to as "sub-subsistence" farmers, tilling their rocky slopes for what they would produce, while being forced by the inadequacy of their land to search out supplementary work on hot-country Spanish plantations.

Like most of the other Maya, the Zinacantecs experienced a second great loss of land after Mexico's nineteenth-century wars of independence from Spain. Anxious to develop the country, the victorious Liberals passed legislation that outlawed corporate land holdings. On a national level, this legislation was aimed at the Catholic church and the large land holdings it had accumulated during the colonial period, but in Indian areas such as the Chiapas highlands, it applied equally to the collectively held Maya lands. As in contemporary Guatemala, the Chiapas Maya lost large stretches of their best land (although the incompleteness of land titles from the period makes it impossible to say precisely how much). By design also, this second loss of land once again forced many Zinacantecs to seek outside work, most notably on the coffee fincas that were then being developed in Chiapas as well as Guatemala. Other Zinacantecs took to roaming the state as muleteers, a skill for which, with their mercantile traditions, they became regionally famous.

The loss of Zinacantec land was not redressed until the 1930's and '40's, when President Lázaro Cárdenas, a former revolutionary general and himself part Indian, instituted a land reform program. Some thirty thousand acres of Zinacantec land were returned in the form of *ejidos*. This restitution temporarily alleviated Zinacantán's problems, but by the 1950's and '60's the Zinacantec population had already begun to strain the boundaries of the new *ejido* land.

George Collier happened to be in San Cristóbal while I was there and I asked if I could accompany him on a vist to the *paraje* he'd been studying, which I'll call Chij. George told me that he planned to visit his *compadre,* an honorary relative, in Chij soon. His *compadre,* whom I'll refer to as Xun, was an important man in the community and had helped the Zinacantecs win back a unique 7500-acre ranch in the hot country, almost on the banks of the Grijalva. If I was interested, George suggested, we could stay the night with Xun's family in Chij and then visit the lowland ranch, known as Colonia Santa Rosa, the next day. Not long afterward, I found myself driving toward Chij, talking with George about Zinacantec history. I asked him how the Zinacantecs had used up the *ejido* land awarded them by General Cárdenas so quickly.

"Thirty thousand acres may seem like a lot of land," George said, "but you have to remember that in the highlands, land can be planted for only a year or two before it has to be left fallow. Depending on such factors as altitude and incline, a highland milpa can take anywhere from five to twenty years to recover its fertility. Thus when

I started working in Chij in the early sixties, only twenty percent of the land was planted at any given time. The other eighty percent had to be left fallow."

George explained that the problem of landlessness among the Zinacantecs of the fifties and sixties had been alleviated when cattle ranching began expanding in the Grijalva River valley and land holders began to convert their forested land to pasture. They did this by hiring Zinacantecs, who cleared the valley land that their ancestors had once owned in exchange for the right to temporarily farm the cleared land. When the land lost its fertility after a few years, the Zinacantecs turned it over for pasture and moved on to another plot. This was a good arrangement for both parties. The ranchers got the pasture land they wanted, and, because the valley land hadn't been planted with corn for years, the Zinacantecs often got yields three times the size of what they got from their highland plots.

"The arrangement was so successful," George said, "that by the early sixties, eighty percent of Zinacantec corn came from the lowlands. The problem was that the land the ranchers wanted cleared was farther and farther away, and travel costs began cutting into profitability."

This was before the oil boom, which began in the early seventies and led many Zinacantecs to drop out of corn farming altogether. Before the boom, nearly all Zinacantecs had been corn farmers. Within a few years, huge construction projects were underway throughout the lowlands, and nearly three-quarters of the Zinacantecs had some kind of wage work. Less than half remained primarily corn farmers. People bought corn, or planted just enough for their own consumption.

When the Mexican economy collapsed in 1982, construction sites closed down. Jobs disappeared overnight, and the Zinacantecs were suddenly forced to become farmers again. However, the rising cost of gasoline made commuting to rented fields in the lowlands even more expensive than it had been before, so for the first time in decades, the Zinacantecs had to support themselves off their highland milpas. But in the preceding decades, Zinacantán's population had expanded enormously.

The only thing that allowed the Zinacantecs to survive was fertilizer. Using fertilizer, the Zinacantecs reversed the ratio of fallow to growing land. Whereas before, eighty percent of the land was fallow and twenty percent in crop, now with fertilizer, eighty percent is in crop and only twenty percent fallow.

I asked George if he thought this rate of cultivation was damaging to the land.

"I worry about it," he said, "but there's no going back to the old system. It would take fifteen or twenty years for Zinacantec land to recover its fertility. Where would the Zinacantecs go?"

"Does the situation worry them?"

"It does. The metaphor they use is of their land getting tired."

The *paraje* of Chij, population twelve hundred, occupies one side of a high mountain bowl at an altitude of seventy-five hundred feet. Above the town a few surviving patches of cloud forest, where horned guans once lived, cling to the highest, most inaccessible cliff faces, but otherwise everything else seems to drop downward along a network of footpaths toward the hot country five thousand feet below. Chij is not an old *paraje*. It was founded in the nineteenth century by Zinacantecs who walked the mountain ridges on their way to work as lowland sharecroppers. As we drove into the *paraje* late that afternoon, our van was pursued by a crowd of small boys excitedly shouting "Alemani!"—a generic term for white people used by the remote Chiapas Maya, whose first exposure to foreigners was the German coffee planters who moved into the region around the turn of the century.

Xun's house was a substantial brick structure, built into a steep hillside in such a way that it seemed to be suspended over the whole of the Chij valley. The road looped down beside the house, and George pulled the car into a packed-earth yard next to two trucks. Oil-boom money had enabled some Zinacantecs to buy their own trucks, and in the teamster tradition, these Zinacantecs were now trucking produce to markets as far away as Mexico City. But the wealth of the oil-boom years fell unevenly on the Zinacantecs, according to George's surveys. Those who prospered the most were the truckers and merchants, while those who fell farthest behind were those who stayed with milpa agriculture. The wage earners were somewhere in between. Xun, it appeared, belonged to the prosperous sector.

Xun's wife, Maruch, came out dressed in traditional Zinacantec women's clothing: an ankle-length black cotton skirt, a white, lightly embroidered *huipil,* and a red sash. Her gray hair hung down her back in long braids and her feet were bare. I thought about Gary Gossen's argument that Maya women always go without shoes because they want to be in touch with the earth, the female half of the universe.

Maruch told us that Xun was in the hot country but would be back soon. She led us around to the front of the house, where three green painted crosses, covered with cedar branches and flowers, leaned against a wall. I recognized the crosses as part of a curing ceremony. According to Evon Vogt, who was George's teacher at Harvard and did the first major ethnographic work in Zinacantán during the 1950's and '60's, crosses represented doorways into the interior of the mountains, the home of the Earthlord. People had thirteen parts of their souls and became sick when a witch, male or female, sold one or more parts of their soul to the Earthlord. During a curing ceremony, a shaman erected several crosses and prayed until he was able to pass through the crosses into the interior of the mountain. There he could bargain with the Earthlord for the return of the missing part of his patient's soul.

"One of Xun's granddaughters has just had a serious case of measles," George told me. "When she stopped eating—by which they mean eating tortillas—they began to be afraid she might die, so they had a curing ceremony performed."

We followed Maruch inside. She took a number of half-sized wooden Indian chairs from hooks on the wall and placed them in a circle around an open fire burning directly on the packed-earth floor. Smoke filtered upward, threading its way through strips of beef hung over the fire to cure. I looked around the room. It was lit with a single naked light bulb suspended from the ceiling by a wire. The walls were hung with gourds, net bags, plastic jugs, hats, and an assortment of clothing. Two beds were pushed up along the walls.

One was draped around with blankets and covered, overhead, with a sheet of plastic—apparently because of a leak in the roof.

"When Xun built this house in the early seventies," George said, "it was the first brick house in Chij and represented a revolution in Chij architecture. Since then, however, there's been a further revolution. The current fashion is concrete block. Masons who've worked on construction projects in the lowlands brought the style back to Zinacantán."

George explained that until the 1950's all the houses had been wattle-and-daub with high, peaked thatch roofs. Late in that decade, however, the first adobe houses with tile roofs were built, and by 1962, when George first arrived in Chij, only twenty percent of the houses were adobe and tile. Now only two thatched houses remained in town.

I asked him why the Zinacantecs had abandoned thatch.

"The pitch had to be so steep to shed water effectively," George answered, "that the houses were necessarily very small. A larger house would have required an unworkably high roof. With tile roofs, the pitch is less and the houses can be much larger. However, getting the first tiles to Chij was quite a project. There was no road then, so the tiles were brought in on mules. An old man here in Chij told me that his father had built the first tile-roofed house. At first, his father tried loading twenty tiles on each side of the mule—forty tiles per mule. But too many tiles broke, so he cut the load in half—ten on each flank. His father needed eight hundred tiles for his roof. It took forty mule trips for that house alone!"

George's observations were interrupted by the low growl of a truck engine accompanied by a loud blaring of *ranchero* music. We went to the door. A bright yellow two-ton truck had pulled up in the yard. EL TIGRE DE CHIJ was emblazoned in florid script across the top of the windshield. There were two men in the truck, or, rather, a man and a boy, because when the driver stepped down, he proved to be a very young boy wearing tight jeans, cowboy boots, a cowboy-style shirt, and a laughably huge hot-country hat.

"That's Xun's twelve-year-old son," George explained. "Xun's been letting him drive for years."

Xun himself stepped around from the passenger seat. He was a square-shouldered man of fifty-six, with rakishly long hair, a flowing mustache, and striking golden-brown eyes.

After George had introduced me, we went into the house. Xun pulled up a chair next to mine at the fire. While George and Xun talked in Tzotzil, I reflected on what I knew about Xun and Colonia Santa Rosa. The land had been mysteriously purchased by the Zinacantecs around the turn of the century, but illegally absorbed by the surrounding Ladino ranchers before the Zinacantecs had been able to take possession. The land was then forgotten until a deed proving Zinacantec ownership surfaced in a San Cristóbal land reform office during the Cárdenas era. The Zinacantecs tried to occupy the land in the late fifties, but the ranchers drove them off with gunfire. A decade or so later, Xun filed a legal claim in the state agrarian reform office. The Ladino ranchers bribed state officials to rule in their favor. In response, the Zinacantecs sent Xun to the federal land reform office in Mexico City, which ruled for the Zinacantecs. Eventually, in the early seventies, the case went to the Mexican Supreme Court, where the Zinacantecs finally prevailed.

George interrupted my train of thought when he turned to me and said that Xun wasn't coming with us the next day and that now was the chance for me to ask questions.

I asked Xun how long he'd worked in the lowlands.

"Since I was eight," he answered, "which was my age when my father died. We didn't have any money, and since I was the eldest, I rented a milpa in the hot country to help support my mother and my brothers and sisters. That's how I learned to work so well. If you don't learn to work when you're young, you never learn."

I knew that during the period when the ownership of the *colonia* had been under appeal to the Supreme Court, the Zinacantecs had occupied the land, fending off the ranchers with a small arsenal of antique shotguns, .22's, and a few larger-bore hunting rifles. I asked Xun about the difficulties they'd had during that period.

"We had ten or fifteen guns," he said. "Some were single-barrel. Some were double. The ranchers took shots at us every day. However, because we were armed, they kept their distance, stayed up on the ridges. Fortunately for us, that meant they were out of range for the most part. One day, however, one of the ranchers sent a Zinacantec sharecropper with a message for me. 'If you want to die,' it said, 'stay where you are. If you want to live, get off the land.' I sent the man back to the ranchers to tell them that whenever they wanted to meet us, they only had to name the date and the hour. If their luck held, we'd die. But if it didn't, they would. They never accepted the challenge, but years later, after we'd won the land, I wound up having a drink with the rancher who'd sent the message. He never even mentioned it."

George asked how the corn was growing in Santa Rosa.

"We were having a terrible drought," until we took the Virgin out of her chapel and walked her up to the foot of the mountains to pray. After that it poured, and the corn is fine."

Dusk had fallen, and I watched Maruch pour the corn for the next day's tortillas into a pot of water, add a spoonful of lime, and then hang the pot over the coals. A thunderstorm rolled up the valley, sending gusts of cold air into the house and making a staccato banging as hail pelted a nearby metal roof.

George said that he and Xun had to go to a meeting about opening a health center in Chij, and invited me to come. We walked up the hill to a muddy town plaza cut into the hillside. On one end of the plaza sat a small church. George pointed out on either side the offices of two rival political parties: the Partido Revolucionario Institucional (PRI), the traditional ruling party forged out of the Revolution by Lázaro Cárdenas and others; and the Partido de la Revolución Democrática (PRD), the protest party founded during the most recent elections by Cárdenas' son, Cuauhtemoc.

I knew George had argued that as a result of the changes that had taken place during the oil boom, the gap between rich and poor in Zinacantán was greater than it had been at any time since before land reform. On the one hand, truckers and merchants, largely represented by PRI, had prospered as never before. On the other hand, milpa farmers and wage laborers with little or no land to fall back on had seen their position erode and had banded together to form the opposition party, the PRD. Underlying this split, George has maintained, was a more significant transformation in the Zinacantec way of life: away from one emphasizing consensus and mutual obligation to one subject to wage economics and market economies. George referred to this as a process of "proletarianization." Previously, Zinacantán had been ruled by powerful men who, over their lifetimes, had bound other Zinacantecs to themselves through marriage and *cargo* obligations. People had taken care of one another and arrived at decisions collectively. Now that wages had lessened the Zinacantec's dependence on each other, the institutions of interdependency were also beginning to lessen in importance and Zinacantecs were beginning to split into rich and poor.

As we walked across the plaza, I asked George how the split between PRI and the PRD had come about in Chij.

"It used to be that everyone was a part of PRI," he said. PRI, after all, was the party that brought land reform in the thirties and forties. But then, a decade ago, there was a fight over a municipal president in Zinacantán center, and in protest over the outcome, Xun started an opposition party in Chij. Most of the town followed his lead. However, in the early eighties, Xun was trying to get authorization for a trucking route between Zinacantán and the lowland capital of Tuxtla Gutiérrez. The PRI told him that they'd authorize his trucks, but only if he rejoined PRI, which he did. Needless to say, this caused a great deal of resentment, and when Cuauhtemoc Cárdenas became a candidate in this last election, those who'd stayed in the opposition founded a branch of the PRD. The PRD has the majority in Chij, but PRI still holds the power because the municipal president in Zinacantán center runs all the government programs through the local PRI branches."

"What about the other *parajes?*"

"About half of them are split along the same lines as Chij."

The meeting about the health center took place in the inner room of the two-chambered, concrete PRI municipal building in Chij. The room, about fifteen feet square, was furnished with handhewn benches, two chairs, and a wooden desk. On the walls were hung portraits of Salinas de Gortari, Mexico's Patrocínio president, and Patrocínio González Blanco Garrido, the Chiapas governor whom I'd seen in Chenalhó. George and I took a seat on one of the benches and watched as the room filled up with Zinacantec men wearing their traditional red-and-white pin-striped tunics. Some still wore wide palm hats hung with ribbons, but others wore plastic versions, or Texas-style sombreros. None were wearing the tasseled scarves or rolled-up homespun cotton shorts that would have completed a traditional outfit twenty years ago.

The meeting didn't so much came to order as the conversation become gradually more shared. Since the meeting was in Tzotzil, George briefed me on what was being discussed. The materials for the health center were being donated from the outside on the condition that the community of Chij would provide the labor to build the clinic. The problem—and the principal subject of discussion— was how to get the "other side" to participate in the construction of what otherwise might appear to be a PRI clinic. Although everyone expressed his opinion—frequently all at once—the discussion always seemed to return to Xun, who sat with his elbows on his knees, his fingers running around the edge of the cowboy hat he held in front of him. Eventually it was decided to refer the question to the PRI municipal president in Zinacantán center.

As the meeting broke up, George said, "People say that communities such as Chij are dominated by Indian political bosses, people whose heritage is the deals made between the Maya and the national government during the land reform era. They call such people 'caciques.' People say that Xun is a cacique—although whether he is or not is another thing. But you can see that it's much more complicated than is usually made out. There's a lot of discussion and a lot of consensus behind it all."

We returned to Xun's house and pulled our chairs back around the fire. Maruch poured coffee. George asked about preparations for an upcoming Zinacantec religious festival; for some reason this set Xun off reciting the exact festival schedule of the remote Chol-speaking area above Palenque. He knew the patron saint day of Tila, of Tumbalá, of Yajalón. I wondered how he knew all these dates.

"I used to take mule trains to the coffee fincas over there," he said. "I used to go out for ten days at a time picking up coffee and bringing it back to buyers in San Cristóbal."

Xun's answer reminded me of a story of Nick Hopkins's, with whom I'd gone to Palenque, about how he'd once run across a herd of pigs being driven from San Cristóbal across the mountains to the railhead at Pichucalco.

"Oh yes," Xun said. "There'd be twenty or thirty pigs with dogs to herd them. But because they didn't want the pigs to lose weight before they were sold, they'd only travel at night. When there wasn't a moon, they'd use pitch-pine torches."

Maruch poked up the fire, made a tripod out of three stones, placed her flat metal *comal* on the stones, and began to cook tortillas. As she did, she threw pieces of smoked beef directly into the coals and, when they were hot, handed them to us folded into a fresh tortilla. As I watched her cooking, I noticed a *metate,* a grinding stone, on the floor behind her. Carved out of a single piece of basaltic lava, it was so worn from use that it had thinned out at one end. Xun said that this *metate* had belonged to his mother. When he was a boy, she'd used it to grind corn not just for her family, but also to sell to the neighbors. This was how she'd supported them after Xun's father died.

"My mother bought the *metate* from an outgoing religious *cargo* holder," Xun told me. "It used to be that the *cargo* holders had so many people to feed that they needed five or six *metates* for the corn alone. They'd buy the *metates* when they came into office and sell them when they were done. Now, of course, *cargo* holders grind their corn in gasoline-powered mills. Now they only need a single *metate* for the chilis, the tomatoes, and the other special ingredients."

That night, Xun, Maruch, and the rest of their family climbed into the beds along the walls of the main room, while George and I were given the extra room, which seemed to double as a barn. My bed, which traditionally would have been made of poles laid over a wooden frame, had been modernized to the extent of now consisting of wooden planks. A straw mat had been tossed over the planks. Overhead, a herbicide sprayer dangled from a hook on the wall. Xun had left the light on in his part of the house, and from where I lay I had a fine view of the strips of beef hanging over the fire. I had had one too many cups of coffee and the meat looked as raw and twisted as my stomach was beginning to feel. After a while I gave up trying to sleep, and stared at the tile ceiling, thinking about the changes taking place in Chij.

George has argued that there is nothing inherently out of balance in traditional Zinacantec milpa agriculture. In his book, *Fields of the Tzotzil: The Ecological Bases of Tradition in Highland Chiapas,* he wrote, "Felling and fallowing can be balanced to fit the needs of a stable population." The problem was that the population of Zinacantán hasn't been stable. In fact, in the twenty-five years between the early sixties and the late eighties, the population of the municipality as a whole has risen from eight to nearly twenty thousand, a pattern reflected throughout the Maya region.

George has argued that this growth is attributable less to a decline in mortality and improved medical care than to changes in marriage customs, which he felt were in turn part of the same process of "proletarianization" sweeping through Chij life. Marriage had once been closely tied to land use. Traditionally, petitioning a young girl's parents for her hand had in effect been part of a complicated negotiation for access to a share of the limited municipal land base— the primary means of support for a Zinacantec. Arranging a marriage had been a process that sometimes took years to accomplish. Ritual petitioners had to be hired, gifts presented, formal visits made. All this meant that the prospective groom had to go into considerable debt, to his own and his bride's family, and agree to work it off later. These protracted negotiations not only resulted in later marriages, and therefore fewer children, but also meant that before a young couple married and had children of their own, they were bound to help sustain their parents—a sensible arrangement in a world of scarce resources.

An alternative had always existed, however. Those who wanted to avoid the obligations of traditional marriage could elope and offer the bride's parents a smaller sum after the fact as a request for forgiveness. According to George, such elopements had been rare in the fifties and sixties, but were increasingly becoming the norm. With the rise of employment possibilities outside the community, the Zinacantecs were no longer locked into becoming farmers on a limited land base and therefore no longer needed to take on large debts to ensure their inheriting some land. This in turn made possible earlier marriages and, since work opportunities no longer were as limited as they once had been, more children. It seemed tragic to me that the Zinacantecs were just beginning to lose an ideology that emphasized consensus and living with limited resources—just what the world most needed at this point in history.

At four in the morning, great waves of rooster crowing broke over the still-dark town, and we got up to leave for the hot country. Xun's daughter, another Maruch, and her husband, whom I'll call Lol, were going to accompany us. Maruch wanted to take measurements in order to make a new set of clothes for one of the virgins in Colonia Santa Rosa's chapel. When they got into the van, George introduced me by my Tzotzil name of Petul and explained, in Tzotzil, that I didn't speak *Batz'i kop,* "the true language," but did speak *castellan,* "Spanish." They nodded sympathetically, but made no further effort to communicate. Speaking *castellan* doesn't get you far in the *parajes.*

In total blackness we bumped out of Chij, stopping periodically to pick up pink-tunicked Zinacantecs who leapt up from behind roadside bushes. By five-thirty we had made the steep, fifty-five hundred-foot descent from the highlands and reached the Grijalva River: muddy, swathed in early-morning mist, and swollen to its banks with rainy-season runoff. The road rose and fell over grassy hills, following the line of the base of the mountains. This was ranch country. Arched brick gates proclaimed the entrances to fincas, most of them no doubt swelling the pride of absentee Ladino owners in San Cristóbal or the state capital of Tuxtla Gutiérrez. I asked Lol if any of it was Zinacantec land.

"No," he answered, "but lots of Zinacantecs rent land from the ranchers."

The road to Santa Rosa was a narrow track that ran away from the river. We lifted a strand of barbed wire, drove the van through, refastened the wire, and followed the road up into the sandy hills. As we drove, we forded a small stream, skidded up a steep slope, stopped to clear away the debris of a small landslide, and scattered a bevy of quail. The road, such as it was, was covered with deep puddles from what had apparently been a heavy rain the night before.

At just after six we drove into the *colonia*, a scattering of huts clustered together in the middle of an immense rolling landscape of pastures and cornfields. The only tree of any size stood just in front of the small white church. George parked the car in front of Xun's house, an irregular pole-and-wire structure with a roof of bent pieces of corrugated metal weighted down with rocks and logs. I had expected something more substantial, but George explained that as a result of the heat and the insects, most of the Zinacantecs lived in the highlands and only came to the *colonia* to work their fields.

Lol and Maruch went to look for the church caretaker; when they found him, we all entered the *colonia*'s chapel. It had a poured-concrete floor and an altar covered with a bright oilcloth. In the center of the altar was a three-foot-tall virgin with a pleasant round face and big startled eyes.

"That's Santa Rosa," George said, "the patron saint of the *colonia*. Xun had her carved by a famous saint carver in Tila, where there's a huge cross shrine on top of a hill that he's always talking about."

Lol and Maruch put some copal incense in a censer, lit it, and began to pray. When they had finished, they set to measuring not Santa Rosa, but the Virgin of Rosario, a smaller saint so smothered with clothing that her tiny white face seemed like a ball balanced on top of a mound of cloth. Afterward we stopped at Xun's house for some tortillas and beans and headed out to Lol's milpa.

The importance of corn farming to the Maya is well summarized in a passage from the Popul Vuh (as translated by Dennis Tedlock). Before descending into the underworld and their contest with the Lords of Death, Hunahpu and Xbalanque, the Hero Twins, bring the first grandmother two ears of corn and say:

> "Each of us will plant an ear of corn. We'll plant them in the center of our house. When the corn dries up, this will be a sign of our death:
> "'Perhaps they died,' you'll say, when it dries up. And when the sprouting comes:
> "'Perhaps they live,' you'll say, our dear grandmother and mother. From now on, this is the sign of our word. We're leaving it with you.'"

When it seems that the Lords of Death have defeated the Twins, the corn dries up. The grandmother burns copal in front of the corn, and after the Twins finally prevail over death, the corn sprouts a second time.

> There was happiness in their grandmother's heart the second time the corn plants sprouted. Then the ears were deified by the grandmother and she gave them names.

The names were Middle of the House, Middle of the Harvest, Living Corn, and Earthen Floor.

After the Hero Twins defeat the Lords of the Underworld and ascend to the heavens, the grandmother, at the request of the gods, grinds the corn nine times (the number of layers in the Maya underworld), mixes the ground corn with water, and makes the first humans: Jaguar Quitze, Jaguar Night, Mahucutah, and True Jaguar.

> "And these are the names of our first mother-fathers."

The Popul Vuh story interested me on several levels. First, the domestication of corn, the defining act of Maya civilization, is metaphorically celebrated by the sprouting of corn inside the grandmother's house. Second, the corn that the grandmother sprouts and names Middle of the House, Middle of the Harvest, Living Corn, and Earthen Floor, represents the Maya principle of resurrection and clearly refers to the World Tree, which only grows after the Hero Twins defeat the Lords of Death.

A third level on which the story interested me was its remarkable echoes in traditional Zinacantec milpa techniques. According to Evon Vogt, the Zinacantecs believed that each kernel of corn, like each person, has an inner soul, a *ch'ulel*. At the end of the harvest, the largest, healthiest ears are selected to provide seed for the next year's crop. The ears of this seed corn are referred to as "mother-father" ears; whereas the rest of the harvest is stored in a corn crib, the "mother-father" ears are hung over the crib next to a flowery cross. There, they act as guardians for the rest of the corn.

In the spring, after the four directions are acknowledged and milpa ceremonies are conducted to appease the Earthlord, the "mother-father" ears are carried to the fields. The seeds are stripped and placed in an armadillo-skin pouch. Using a dogwood or a hawthorn planting stick, the traditional Zinacantec farmer made holes, into each of which he dropped five or six kernels.

According to Vogt, the principal labor after planting consists of two weedings, performed with a hoe or billhook. These weedings are among the major tasks of the agricultural year, and the Zinacantecs believe that if the weedings aren't performed, the souls of the corn will migrate to a cleaned field. In July, after the second weeding and just before the corn tassels appear, a shaman is sometimes called in to perform a field ceremony in which he prays for both rain and lightning. This is because the Zinacantecs believe that lightning rises from the earth, forcing the winds to stay harmlessly high over the fields. The wind not only flattens the corn, but also steals its soul.

As we walked toward Lol's fields, we passed a milpa with wind damage from the previous night's storm. I asked Lol if he'd ever had wind ceremonies performed on his fields.

"I had one performed once," he told me, "but shortly afterward the wind blew down all my corn. It was the last time."

Lol and Maruch seemed to have a foot in both the modern and traditional worlds. At the health center meeting the night before, Lol had been wearing the traditional red-and-white-striped Zinacantec tunic, but here, in the hot country, he was wearing a tight pair of trousers, running sneakers, and a bright red T-shirt that said PRI CHIAPAS on the front.

Maruch, a strikingly beautiful woman, was more traditionally dressed. She had on a long, blue-black cotton skirt held up by a woven red-and-black belt. Her white blouse was embroidered with colorful representations of chrysanthemums, and her thick hair, which hung to her waist, was braided with yellow satin ribbon. But even in the context of traditional dress—which most Zinacantec women still wear—there were changes. The chrysanthemums were a recent innovation, and George pointed out that the cloth of Maruch's blouse was not homespun cotton, but a polyester-cotton mix.

I asked Lol how long he'd been farming in the *colonia*.

"Three years."

"Before that did you have a highland milpa?"

"Before that I spent five or six years working in construction in Villahermosa, Tuxtla, and Villa Flores."

"Do you still work in construction at all?"

"No, for the past three years I've been farming full time."

Lol went on to explain that he'd planted four *almuds* (an *almud* is fifteen liters, or almost sixteen quarts) of seed corn in the *colonia* and another two *almuds* in his highland milpas. Since this is a prodigious amount of corn for any individual farmer, I asked if he'd hired anyone to help him.

"No. I can farm as much land as I do because I have a *bomba* [pump] and *líquido* [herbicide]."

At Lol's milpa I could see dying yellow weeds in between the rows of his corn. Lol's weeding, which would have taken him weeks by hand, had been accomplished in a few days with herbicides. Something was missing, however, and after a while I figured it out. The beans—not to speak of the squash, chilis, sweet potatoes, gourds, pumpkins, onions, and wild greens that traditionally grew among the corn plants—weren't there. This was monoculture.

I asked Lol if he had not planted beans because the herbicide would have killed them.

No, he said, the herbicide didn't kill beans. He hadn't planted beans because it was too expensive to hire people to plant them.

I asked George if he thought herbicides were damaging the land.

"There's no measurable damage from herbicides," he said. "In fact, in the highlands it's in some ways beneficial. With herbicides, there's less erosion than with hoeing. However, people's health is another matter. The Zinacantecs don't read the labels on the herbicide containers. They get spray on themselves. I've even seen paraquat containers being used as household water jugs."

By the time we got back to the *colonia*, the hot country had caught up with us. The heat and humidity were oppressive, and we decided to go for a swim. Lol led the way past a grove of Spanish plums to a ravine about half a mile from the *colonia* center. At the lip of the ravine it was witheringly hot, but down below was another world. There were leafy trees and flowers and vines, and several generations of Zinacantec women were washing their long hair in pools along the streambed. Lol pointed to a spring coming out of a small cave into the mouth of which a cross had been set. With considerable satisfaction, he told us that the priest, who visited every two months from San Cristóbal, had blessed it.

Maruch produced some laundry and began to scrub vigorously, pausing every so often to slap it down on a flat rock with a force that echoed through the narrow ravine like a rifle shot. George went for a swim in a thigh-deep pool. I lay down on a sunny rock, watched a bright red dragonfly balance on a blade of grass, and thought about this brave new Zinacantec world of fertilizers, herbicides, and monoculture. I realized that the Zinacantecs were now as tied into the global prices of oil, energy, and petrochemicals as the rest of us. But that was the point, really. Since the Conquest, the Zinacantecs had been tied into our world. It was only, perhaps, that we preferred not to see it.

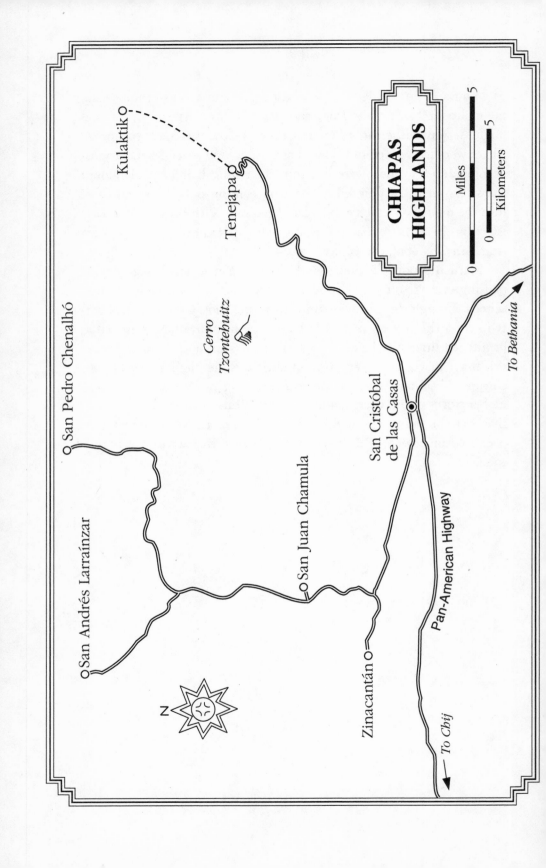

CHIAPAS
HIGHLANDS

Miles
0   5

Kilometers
0   5

Kulaktik

Tenejapa

San Pedro Chenalhó

Cerro
Tzontehuitz

San Andrés Larraínzar

San Juan Chamula

San Cristóbal
de las Casas

To Bethania

Zinacantán

Pan-American Highway

To Chij

N

CHAPTER 10

Evangelicals

THE CITY OF SAN CRISTÓBAL DE LAS CASAS, the capital of highland Chiapas, sits in a rich, well-watered mountain valley. Visitors to the city are sometimes told that the valley was uninhabited when the Spanish arrived. The Maya believed that it had once been a lake and would someday be a lake again. They had therefore located their milpas in the less fertile but safer uplands.

This story seems harmless enough until you begin to think about it. For one thing, like a number of similar stories that circulate in the Ladino community, it casts the Maya as foolish and superstitious, while portraying the Spanish as sensible and industrious. Second, according to the story, no one was displaced when the Spanish moved into the San Cristóbal valley, so its settlement seems a neutral or even benign act.

The real story of the settlement of the San Cristóbal valley is another matter. Cortés' chronicler, Bernal Díaz del Castillo, was among the first party of Spaniards to arrive in the Chiapas highlands. Before the Spanish began their ascent into the Maya region, they won a fierce battle over the Chiapanecs, the traditional enemies of the highland Maya. When the battle was over, a number of highland Maya tribes sought alliances with the Spanish. Among these were the Zinacantecs and the Chamulas, their powerful neighbors and sometimes rivals who, at the time of the Conquest, lived on three fortified hilltops around the San Cristóbal valley. The valley was the main source of their wealth.

The Spanish entry into the highlands might have been peaceful had not a Spanish soldier made an unauthorized trip to the Chamula capital demanding gold. Unsatisfied with what he was given, the soldier attempted to seize the Chamula chief. In response, the Chamulas rose up against the Spanish. With archers and two thousand lancers protected by "large shields with which they could cover their whole body," the Chamulas took refuge inside one of their forts. The Spanish laid siege to them there but, says Díaz del Castillo, "Our musqueteers fired upon the enemy, but with very little effect, whereas their missile weapons injured us who were uncovered." The Spanish eventually constructed a siege machine and rolled it up to the walls of the fort. Four of the Chamula chiefs then stood up on the walls and tossed "seven crowns of fine gold, together with a quantity of gold trinkets, and other things made of metal cast in the form of shells and birds," over the walls, saying to the Spaniards as they did that if it was gold the Spaniards wanted, they ought to come and pick it up. When the Spanish tried to do so, the Chamulas poured blood and boiling water over the walls, and pelted them with arrows, darts, and stones. Only when the Zinacantecs came to the aid of the Spanish were the Chamulas eventually defeated.

The Chamulas suffered dearly for their rebellion. They were exiled from their valley land and relocated six miles away, to the present town of Chamula in the highest and coldest part of the highlands. Arguably, this relocation determined the entire subsequent history of the Chamulas. Because their new land was too poor to support them, their fate was a life of migratory labor. In the nineteenth century, the Chamulas formed the mainstay of the Chiapas coffee industry, walking one or two hundred miles in a week to pick the coffee harvest in the Sierra Madre fincas near the Guatemalan border and then, several weeks later, walking back again. In time, people forgot that the Chamulas had ever lived any other way. They were just poor Indians who'd never known how to take care of their land.

* * *

Another oft-recounted Chamula story: Late in the year 1867, a
Chamula shepherdess named Agustina Gómez Checheb was tending
her sheep near the remote *paraje* of Tzajalhemel, when three stones
fell from the sky. When Agustina Gómez Checheb approached the
stones they began to speak. She took the stones back to her *paraje,*
where the people began to venerate them, and a cult developed
around them. The cult spread from Tzajalhemel to the surrounding
parajes and *municipios,* until the cult followers decided the stones
needed their own Christ and proceeded to crucify a young Indian
boy for that purpose. After that, they brutally murdered the parish
priest and then, in an orgy of hatred, laid siege to San Cristóbal,
threatening, as a contempory newspaper put it, "to ravage and kill
[the city's] tender wives and sisters." San Cristóbal survived this
onslaught only as the result of the timely intervention of troops from
the state capital.

The actual circumstances of this story are again somewhat different. The incident took place when conservatives and liberals were
vying for control of the Indian villages in the tumultuous years after
independence. The conservatives wanted the priests to continue
administering the villages, while the liberals wanted to ban the
Catholic church and have free access to Indian land and labor. The
two parties fought throughout the nineteenth century. During periods of liberal ascendancy, the Maya were told that they no longer
needed priests, that they no longer were obligated to pay the revenues the priests demanded, and that they could conduct religious
ceremonies as they saw fit. Then the conservatives would return to
power, the priests would reappear demanding overdue revenues, and
things would return to what they had been.

In 1865, during a period of conservative ascendancy, a new
priest, Father Miguel Martínez, arrived in Chamula. No priest had
been in Chamula in some time and, anxious to recoup lost ecclesiastical income, Father Martínez began withholding Mass until paid
for, whipping officials who refused to pay his fees, and illegally looting the coffers of Maya *cargo* societies. It was during Father Martínez'
tenure that the talking stones fell from the sky. Father Martínez sent

a Chamula religious official named Pedro Díaz Cuzcat out from the municipal center to investigate Agustina Gómez Checheb's allegation that the stones were speaking to her. Cuzcat was a *fiscal,* a lay priest who had performed priestly functions during the periods when there was no priest in Chamula. When Cuzcat arrived in Tzajalhemel, he examined the stones, declared that they spoke to him as well, ordered trumpets and a bell, and built a shrine. A market grew up around the shrine and began to eclipse the central Chamula market. When the Tzajalhemel market began to threaten Father Martínez' income, he sent soldiers out to arrest Cuzcat and take him to the San Cristóbal jail. This was done but the cult still continued. Not until Father Martínez rode out himself and confiscated the sacred stones, however, did the real hostilities begin. On his way back to Chamula, Father Martínez was attacked and killed. The Chamulas subsequently killed some Ladinos against whom they held grudges, and then marched on San Cristóbal demanding Cuzcat's release. Although they were not armed and did not attack the city, the San Cristóbal papers proclaimed a "war to the death between barbarism and civilization." The lowland forces came to the rescue and, swelled by Ladino volunteers from the city, marched out to Chamula, to which the followers of the talking stones had retreated. There, the Ladino army found the Chamulas huddled together, unarmed, on several hilltops and massacred more than three hundred of them, including women and children. The papers described it as a "valiant hand-to-hand battle." Not until twenty years later, when the first highly romanticized accounts of the incident were published, did the story of the crucified boy appear.

I became interested in the legends surrounding Chamula for a number of reasons. For one thing, Chamula is the largest of the twenty-one Indian municipalities in the Chiapas highlands, covering an area of some 140 square miles and having a population in excess of a hundred thousand. For another, the Chamulas are an appealingly truculent people with a reputation for throwing surprised tourists who transgress Chamula regulations into the municipal jail. Finally, a religious movement of a different sort had taken hold of Chamula during the previous twenty years, and I wanted to try to understand what it was about. A wave of evangelical religion had swept across the municipality, and Chamula's political bosses—widely referred to as caciques—had reacted by expelling upward of twenty thousand alleged evangelicals, or one out of every five Chamulas. For lack of anywhere else to go, many of these refugees had wound up living in a ring of evangelical slums around the edges of San Cristóbal. As slums go, these were the best you could hope for. The streets all bore biblical names and the residents went to church every night, but controversy swirled around the communities nevertheless. Some people argued that caciques were gangsters. Others claimed that the evangelicals were CIA-sponsored and a means of destroying Indian solidarity. Neither, or both, of these arguments might have been true. So might dozens of others. I had been dodging evangelicals throughout Mayadom. Confronted with the Chamula situation, I decided that it was time to get some sense of what it was all about, at least in this one instance.

I soon discovered that the evangelical movement in Chamula had roots going back at least to the 1910 Revolution and, in a larger sense, all the way back to the Chamulas' original eviction from the San Cristóbal valley. By the time of the Revolution, the priests had been thrown out of Chamula and, in their place, it was being run by the same *enganchadores*—Ladino labor contractors—who had figured so prominently in the history of San Andrés Larraínzar. This was because in Chiapas, unlike the rest of Mexico, the conservatives essentially won the Revolution in which the Indians had not participated to any significant degree. But by the 1930's, when General Lázaro Cárdenas became president, he decided it was time to break the *enganchadores*. To accomplish this he selected a San Cristóbal native, Erasto Urbina, who was the illegitimate son of a Ladino grain merchant and his Tzotzil-speaking maid. Using a group of idealistic young Chamula scribes who came to be known as "Erasto's *muchachos*," Urbina organized a finca workers' union and, after a sharp struggle, destroyed the *enganchadores'* power.

As soon as General Cárdenas left office, however, the staying power of Erasto's *muchachos* was tested. During the reign of the *enganchadores,* alcohol had been the prime means of drawing the Indians into debt. Production and distribution of alcohol had fallen into Indian, particularly Chamula, hands, but after the departure of General Cárdenas, the Ladinos in San Cristóbal declared Indian *pox* making illegal and sent in armed revenue agents to enforce the ban. There was little question that this was an attempt to reassert control over Chamula, and the *muchachos* responded by levying a secret ten-percent protection tax on all *pox* distillers and using the proceeds to raise a Chamula army. Battles raged over Chamula for more than a decade. Uncounted people were killed, but the *muchachos* eventually prevailed.

Victory, however, had its price. Because of their union-organizing heritage, the *muchachos* were already secretive. The *pox* war, as it came to be called, took them a step further and transformed them into what one anthropologist described to me as an "almost paramilitary organization." In the early fifties, the *muchachos* further consolidated their machinelike control of Chamula when the federal government created the Instituto Nacional Indigenista, or INI, which sought to bolster Indian economies by opening them to the outside world. INI's plan was to take bilingual Indians out of their communities, train them as *promotores*—teachers, health workers, and agricultural specialists—and then send them back as point men for government programs. In Chamula, the *promotores* were chosen almost entirely from among Urbina's *muchachos* or their families. The result was that the *muchachos* controlled the government programs. The *muchachos* had become caciques.

The seat of the newly created caciques' power was the Chamula municipal center. All the religious *cargos,* for example, were in the municipal center, as was the only school that reached sixth grade, the level necessary to become a *promotor.* The only road in Chamula, moreover, went only as far as the center of the town of Chamula, and this allowed the caciques to develop a trucking monopoly through which all the other hamlets had to channel their goods.

At the same time that the caciques were consolidating their power in the municipal center, however, the municipality as a whole was going in the opposite direction. During the Cárdenas administration, Chamula, like Zinacantán, had had some of the land it had lost during the nineteenth century returned in the form of *ejidos*. But, as in Zinacantán, this land represented a fraction of what the municipality actually needed and, by the fifties, landless Chamulas were spilling out of the municipality, making connections to the outside world where previously there hadn't been any. Naturally, the caciques tried to control this expansion for their own ends, and resentment of the caciques grew particularly strong in the eastern end of Chamula, where with new INI-sponsored educational opportunities, more people were beginning to speak Spanish and develop their own ties to San Cristóbal. The caciques repeatedly ignored petitions to extend the single road into the eastern end of Chamula, so in 1965 a representative of the east-end *parajes* went directly to Mexico City, over the heads of the caciques. Upon his return to Chamula he was murdered.

The struggle between the caciques in Chamula center and the landless Chamulas in the *parajes* soon took on another dimension: religion. People think of Mexico and Central America as overwhelmingly Catholic, and nominally they are. But there have never been many priests in the region, and their influence has in many ways been quite superficial. As recently as the 1950's, for example, the San Cristóbal diocese had only four priests covering its entire 17,000 square miles. Traveling by horse and mule, the priests were never able to make more than occasional and fleeting stops in Indian towns. Doctrinal understanding was sacrificed in the interests of nominal observance of the sacraments.

Things began to change, however, in the late 1950's. The frontier with Guatemala was then open, and Catholic Action Maya calling themselves "delegates of the word" began to drift over the border from Guatemala into southern Chiapas. The delegates came carrying Bibles and bearing the message of the Bible's relevance to daily problems—including the problem of landlessness. Padre Ramón Castillo, a Maya and the vicar general of the San Cristóbal diocese, recalls attending meetings of 20,000 and 25,000 Indians in his youth. "There were no priests," he told me, "just Maya—and Maya not just reading the Bible, but reflecting on it."

In 1962, the present bishop of San Cristóbal, Don Samuel Ruíz García arrived. Don Samuel was a conservative from western Mexico who evolved into a proponent of liberation theology after his arrival in San Cristóbal, a process no doubt hastened by his discovery of the widespread religious ferment already existing in his diocese. For whatever reason, however, Don Samuel soon put out a call for more priests. One of those who responded was a Mexican priest, Padre Leopoldo Hernandez, or Padre Polo for short. Padre Polo was sent to Chamula in the mid-1960's.

Other than during a brief period in the twenties, Padre Polo was Chamula's first resident priest since the ill-fated Miguel Martínez. Certainly, priests had stopped in to say Masses or to perform weddings or baptisms, but the anticlericalism and political chaos of the previous hundred years had broken the church's hold on Chamula. During that time the Chamulas had become much more independent in religious matters. Baptisms continued to be important to the Maya, but they had little interest in the Catholic Masses and virtually no knowledge of Catholic doctrine. One anthropologist said, "If you'd asked ten Chamulas who was the man hanging on the cross in the front of the church, nine would have identified him as San Juan, the patron saint of Chamula."

Padre Polo was a socially conscious priest, and he set out to re-Catholicize Chamula. Everything he did, however, brought him into conflict with the caciques. He started a credit union. It conflicted with the caciques' own loan business. He built chapels in the east end. They were burned down because they competed with the municipal center's religious monopoly. Soon rumors were spread that Padre Polo was having assignations with Indian women in the mountains. A mob gathered outside the church while he was saying Mass. The tires of his car were slashed.

Before long, Padre Polo was forced to move back to San Cristóbal. Although he had fought with the caciques, he had also garnered a large number of Chamula adherents, particularly in the east end, where religious ferment ran strong. And though he no longer lived in Chamula, he was determined to see justice prevail. Padre Polo's opportunity arose in 1973, when there was a municipal election in Chamula. He invited the Mexican conservative party, Partido Acción Nacional (PAN), to field a slate of candidates and organized his followers in the east end to back them. Elections aren't normally decided by vote in Maya communities. *Principales,* the respected elders, get together and choose a president by consensus. Padre Polo's maneuver, therefore, took the caciques by surprise, and simply by having several hundred supporters on hand, PAN's candidates legally won the election. This forced the caciques to steal it.

Not long after the election, the caciques organized a massive roundup of Padre Polo's followers. They put six or seven hundred of them in trucks, drove them to the edge of town, and dumped them by the side of the road. Within a few weeks, Padre Polo's followers had made their way back to their homes, but the following year they were rounded up again and incarcerated in Chamula center. Some were beaten with sticks. Afraid that they would be killed, the state Indian affairs agency intervened and brought them to San Cristóbal.

It was in San Cristóbal that Padre Polo's exiles met the evangelicals, and ironically, it was General Cárdenas who was responsible for their being there. During the thirties and forties, the head of Cárdenas' Indian affairs department had been a radical Presbyterian. Looking for ways to break the hold of the then conservative Catholic church, Cárdenas and his Indian affairs minister had invited the Southern California–based Summer Institute of Linguistics into Mexico. In association with the Wycliffe Bible Translators, the SIL had a program of translating the Bible into every language on earth. SIL members believed that the Second Coming of Christ wouldn't happen until this had been accomplished. In pursuit of this eccentric agenda, the SIL had turned out some workable Guatemalan Maya grammars, and Cárdenas decided that similar grammars for the Indian languages of Mexico might be useful in bridging the linguistic gap between the Ladino and Indian worlds. Although the SIL later became notorious for its alleged CIA connections, at the time the group's right-wing politics and apocalyptic vision must have seemed harmless quirks to Cárdenas.

The first Summer Institute of Linguistics missionary arrived in the Chiapas highlands in 1939, but not until the early 1950's did an

SIL missionary, a Presbyterian, go to work in Chamula. There he did bilingual work for INI while quietly proselytizing on the side. His efforts to convert the Chamulas were notably unsuccessful. In fact, by the late sixties he had converted only a handful of families—all from the east end. In 1968 this handful of families was expelled and took up residence in San Cristóbal.

Being a Maya in San Cristóbal at the time was no easy thing. Indians were not allowed on the sidewalks. They had to ride in the backs of buses and were jailed if they were found on the streets at night. The only acceptable means for an Indian to live in San Cristóbal was, essentially, to cease being an Indian: to give up native clothing, to desist speaking Tzotzil or Tzeltal, and to become a maid or gardener for a Ladino family. The small group of Chamula evangelicals who arrived in 1968 became the first exceptions to this rule because the North American SIL missionaries found them places to live, encouraged them to continue speaking Tzotzil and wearing Indian clothing, and eventually arranged for them to get jobs in the market. Because they were the only Indians working in the market, and because they had connections to the Chamulas coming into San Cristóbal to sell their goods, they prospered.

When Padre Polo's group arrived in San Cristóbal in 1974, the Catholic church made no permanent provisions for them. Don Samuel had spoken out publicly against the expulsions and had taken the position that the only acceptable solution to the problem was for the caciques to permit the exiles to return. The caciques were equally adamant, however, and eventually Don Samuel retaliated by withdrawing the Catholic church from Chamula altogether. It was the evangelicals, finally, who took in the exiles and found them jobs. Somewhere along the line Padre Polo's exiled Catholics ceased being Catholics and became evangelicals.

I heard the story of Padre Polo from Jan Rus, an anthropologist who speaks Tzotzil, works through a French-Mexican anthropological institute in San Cristóbal, and knows more Chamula history than anyone else. Jan's research had turned up the real story of the war of the talking stones, and Jan had made the point that the fate of the

Chamulas had been determined by the land to which they'd been exiled after the Conquest. I looked up Jan one day and asked if he would go with me to one of the evangelical communities. He agreed, but suggested that rather than visiting one of the immediate suburbs, we go to Bethania, an evangelical community eleven miles south of San Cristóbal on the Pan American Highway. Bethania had been founded in 1981, when, in response to growing alarm among the citizens of San Cristóbal at having so many unassimilated Maya in their midst, the municipal president had sold the evangelicals a piece of his own land far down the highway. Two hundred evangelical families were now living there, Jan said.

On a rainy afternoon several days later, we drove out of town toward Bethania. As we climbed over the San Cristóbal valley wall, clouds hung low and wisps of fog clung to the tops of the pines.

I asked Jan how many Chamulas he thought were now living in the San Cristóbal valley.

"My guess is between twenty and twenty-five thousand," he said.

"And how did the number grow so in the fifteen years between the time that Padre Polo's group was expelled and the present?"

"There've been three waves of departures, each bigger than the one that preceded it. The first was the handful of Summer Institute of Linguistics evangelicals. The second was Padre Polo's group. The third consists of economic refugees."

I asked Jan what he meant.

"The religious expulsions are continuing in Chamula, but the lines of authority are breaking and the caciques are now expelling nonevangelicals as well as evangelicals. I would say that now it's the poor, regardless of religious affiliation, who're either leaving or being expelled. At the root of it is the age-old Chamula problem of too many people on too little land. It's not that there isn't land in the state. The lowlands are covered with huge underused ranches. It's just that there isn't enough land in Chamula. My wife, Diane, did a survey of a Chamula *paraje* where she's worked and discovered that only forty percent of the families had any land at all, and only five percent had enough to subsist on. That means ninety-five percent of the people have to work outside. That's not new. What's different is that the outside work is no longer seasonal the way it was in the coffee-finca era. Construction jobs are year-round. Instead of going away to work for part of every year and then coming back, the men are going away and staying away. When they get established, they send for their families."

I asked Jan why this was happening.

"During the oil boom, the government wanted to industrialize Mexico quickly. In order to keep labor costs down, they held the price of corn artificially low. This got the Chamulas out of lowland tenant farming. When the construction jobs opened up, the Chamulas quit working on the coffee fincas as well. In 1982, when the crash came, public works jobs dried up overnight. Unlike the Zinacantecs, however, the Chamulas didn't have anything like a workable land base to go back to. They wandered back down to the coffee fincas, and, when they got there, discovered that the Guatemalan refugees, who were so desperate that they worked for half what the Chamulas made, had taken the jobs. Fortunately, there's been a tourist boom in San Cristóbal, and a lot of the Chamulas found jobs in the city."

After we'd driven for a while, I asked Jan what had happened to the Catholic church in Chamula.

"When Don Samuel refused to back down on the issue of the expulsion, the caciques invited a church called the Mexican Orthodox church to come to Chamula. The Mexican Orthodox church has nothing to do with the Russian or Greek Orthodox church. It imitates all the forms of the Roman Catholic church, but without any of the doctrine. The minister is a Ladino seminary school dropout. He dresses like a friar and has a tonsure, but he's married and has children. He does exactly what the Chamulas want—he uses tortillas and *pox* instead of consecrated wafers and wine—and, as I understand it, he pockets the proceeds from his work."

I thought about the Catholic church's dilemma in Chamula. Although Don Samuel had lost both the traditional Chamulas and their evangelical cousins, he'd held onto the moral high ground. And although he was wildly unpopular among San Cristóbal Ladinos, because he seemed to favor the Maya over his Ladino constituents, he still commanded an enormous respect among the Indians.

In an interview in 1990, I asked him Don Samuel about the ultimate compatibility of the Catholic and Maya outlooks.

"The Catholic church does not belong to any one culture," he told me. "People forget that the Catholic church isn't a Western religion, it's an Eastern religion that acquired its Western aspects after it arrived in Rome. The mistake most missionaries have made is to assume that to make someone Christian, that person has to be Christian in the missionary's image. God is a spirit, not a doctrine. It is our task to discover in what way God is manifested in a community. Saint Paul, for instance, discovered the manifestation of God among the Greeks. He sought out what we call *semillas del verbo,* the "seeds of the word." We need to find *semillas del verbo* among the Maya and, out of them, construct a Maya church."

I asked the bishop if it was acceptable to him if the Maya, under the guise of Catholic prayer, were actually praying to the sun.

"We have to be careful of accusations of polytheism," he answered. "Frequently such things as the sun or the rain are manifestations of a more general God. What we need to do is to work from inside a culture and find the seeds of God's presence within that community. After all, questions of orthodoxy are not as important as questions of praxis. When we are finally judged, after all, we will be judged not by our intellectual positions, but by our comportment in relation to others."

Not long after I spoke with Don Samuel, Pope John Paul II visited Mexico. During his swing through the southern part of the country, he not only boycotted the San Cristóbal diocese, the oldest and largest in the region, but also publicly attacked liberation theology, an attack that most people took to be personally directed at Don Samuel.

When Jan and I pulled into Bethania, he told me that the last time he'd visited, one faction of evangelicals had been threatening to secede from the other. Sure enough, in the center of town we came upon a new church, its concrete facade still faced with scaffolding. Across the highway, set back further, Jan pointed out the original church. He suggested that we check in with the American pastor, both as a courtesy and to ascertain the status of the feud between the two churches. We turned off the highway and drove up a narrow dirt lane. Bethania had the feel of a frontier town, freshly hewn out of the forest. The walls of the houses were rough-cut vertical planks sealed with mill-slab battens. The smell of fresh-sawn lumber mingled with wood smoke in the damp air.

The minister's house was like all the others except that it had a washing machine tucked under its eaves and was surrounded by a rough lawn instead of a farmyard. The minister, however, was in San Cristóbal. A neighbor told us services were beginning momentarily in both churches. He himself belonged to the newer church, and told us we would be welcome there.

By the time Jan and I got back down the hill, the service had already begun. We joined fifty or so other Chamulas on half-sawn wooden benches. The floor was dirt, the window frames still empty, and bits of wiring stuck out from the concrete walls. Four men with guitars were standing next to the altar singing hymns *ranchero* style.

As we sat down, the minister, a Chamula, interrupted the service to greet us. *"Aquí somos Christianos!* Here we are, Christians!" he exclaimed, handing us a Bible and opening it to the lesson. He tried to put us in the front row, but we demurred and took a bench a few rows back.

The lesson was Proverbs 30, 24–28:

> There be four things which are little upon the earth, but they are exceeding wise:
> The ants are a people not strong, yet they prepare their meat in the summer;
> The conies [rabbits] are but a feeble folk, yet they make their houses in the rocks;
> The locusts have no king, yet go they forth all of them by bands;
> The spider taketh hold with her hands, and is in kings' palaces.

This struck me as a rather unusual text, but the minister went right at it, and as trucks shifted gears along the highway outside, Jan translated his Tzotzil:

"Now you're going to hear the truth about the four animals. When we go down to the hot country to work, we're just like the four animals gathering food against the winter. Only we're not storing up food, we're storing up the word of God against the time to come. The word of God is like a milpa. It needs to be cultivated, nurtured. Out in the *parajes* they don't care for the word of God. All they do is drink and dance. Out in the *parajes* there's a spiritual hunger. Of course, these may seem like strong words, but strong words are what are needed."

The minister then proceeded to draw moral lessons from the behavior of the four animals. He got to the rabbits last. "Rabbits build their houses in the rocks for their own safety. We too must build our houses in safe places in order to protect ourselves from the rich who, like wild animals, can destroy our homes. But we also need to protect ourselves from the devil and to do that we must pray and pray without ceasing."

With that the congregation got down on their knees. The women pulled their shawls over their heads, and everyone began a murmuring, pleading, chanting Maya prayer.

Jan listened for a while and then whispered, "The minister is using a Tzotzil style of prayer. He's praying in couplets. He's asking for God's mercy. He's saying that even though they've driven us out of our *parajes,* we still need to hear the word of God."

Jan paused, listened for a while again, and then continued, "The word he's using for God is *K'ajval,* literally, 'Our Lord.' It's the same word as *ahau* in Yucatec and it also means 'king' or 'boss.' It's the word the Classic Maya used to refer to their kings and nobility."

When the service was over, Jan and I went up to return the minister's Bible. Jan asked him where he was from.

"Milpoleto," the minister answered, referring to one of the east-end Chamula *parajes.* "And you," the minister asked Jan, "what religion are you?"

"I'm just a *haragan,*" answered Jan, using a Spanish word meaning a lazy, idle man.

"That's what I was once," said the minister, "but someday, like me, you'll find Jesus in your heart."

* * *

Afterward, Jan and I crossed the highway and walked up another dirt lane toward the other church. As we approached, the service ended and people began pouring out. The congregation was much bigger than that of the new church and we were soon engulfed by a curious crowd. One of the women, bolder than the rest and the only one not in traditional Chamula clothing, struck up a spirited conversation with Jan. Amid the Tzotzil, I heard the English words "hamburger" and "Los Angeles," and made out the name of the Summer Institute of Linguistics missionary whose converts had been the first expelled from Chamula. When Jan and the woman were done talking, she turned to me, said "Good-bye" in English, and walked away.

I asked Jan who she was.

"Her family was one of the first Summer Institute of Linguistics evangelical families," he said, "and most of them were killed during the first expulsions. There's a book about the first evangelicals with a section about her family. They came from a *paraje* called Niotic; as I recall, the caciques' men set fire to her house and then attacked the family with machetes as they ran out. Only she and her younger brother survived."

"Why was she talking about Los Angeles?" I asked.

"After her family had been killed, the SIL minister took her to the United States to testify about the atrocities that were being committed against the evangelicals. She was telling me that before she went to the United States, the SIL minister had warned her that she wouldn't be able to get the kind of tortillas she was accustomed to in the United States, so she'd better bring some corn flour. She didn't bring enough, however, and she was complaining to me that she'd had to eat white bread and hamburgers, both of which made her sick. You see, corn for the Maya is central to the idea of eating. In Tzotzil, the word for tortilla is *vaj.* The root verb for eating, which is related, is *ve,* and the word for food generally is *ve'lil,* which literally means "corn stuff.""

I asked Jan about the violence that had been inflicted on the woman's family.

"I'm not excusing it, but you have to put it in the context of the time. It was the tail end of the *pox* wars. Violence had become a part of daily life. Some of the evangelicals, moreover, were attacking the saints. They were saying things like 'They're just pieces of wood. Better to throw them in the fire and use them to cook tortillas.'"

As we headed back toward the car, I started thinking about Jan's argument that the most recent expulsions from Chamula had more of an economic than a religious rationale. I asked how many of the recently expelled were nonevangelical.

"I would guess about half."

"And how are they accepted in the evangelical communities?"

"Provided they observe certain norms of conduct, there's no problem. My *compadre,* for instance, is not Protestant, but lives on Gethsemane Street in Hormiga, a Protestant community on the edges of San Cristóbal. A while ago, I was visiting him when he dedicated his new house. In Chamula, a traditional house dedication ceremony involves sacrificing a chicken and censing the four corners with copal. My *compadre* conducted the ceremony, but before he did, he sealed off all the cracks and stuffed a rag under the door. He didn't want any of the evangelicals to know what he was doing. It reminded me of the way people used to smoke marijuana in college."

I asked Jan if he worried that the evangelicals would lose their Maya-ness.

"Most of the Chamula evangelicals are Presbyterians," he said, "and Presbyterians are essentially Calvinists. Five or six years ago I was very gloomy about the evangelicals. I was certain that the Calvinist idea of a divinely ordained civil order would mean the evangelicals would become subservient and politically conservative. But the opposite has happened. The evangelicals have been aggressive in asserting their rights. Recently the evangelical religious councils informed the gringo ministers that although they were welcome to sit in on the council meetings, they weren't to speak unless they were invited to do so. It isn't that they're hostile, it's just that they're confident that they can run their own communities. Chamula isn't falling apart, it's just metamorphosing, adapting to a world that lets Chamulas move in and out more easily than it used to."

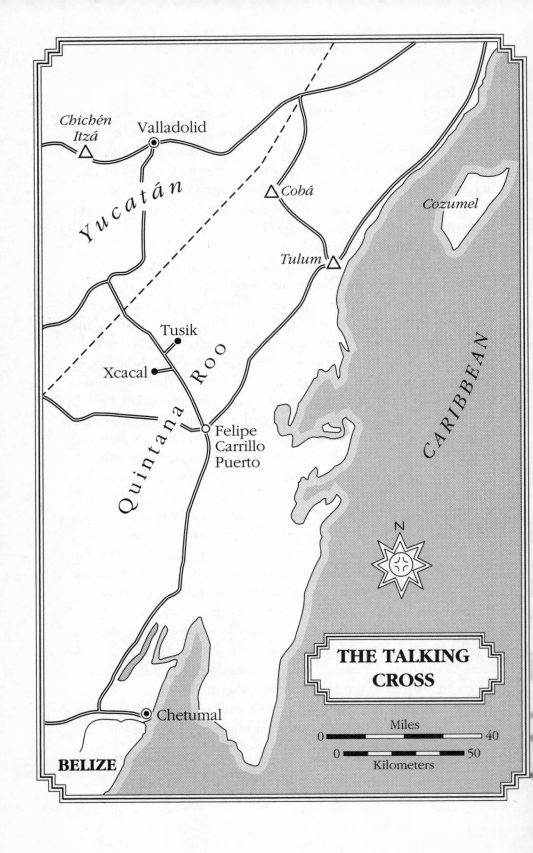

Chichén
Itzá

Valladolid

Yucatán

Cobá

Cozumel

Tulum

Tusik

Quintana Roo

Xcacal

CARIBBEAN

Felipe
Carrillo
Puerto

N

THE TALKING
CROSS

Chetumal

BELIZE

Miles

0 ▬▬▬▬ 40

0 ▬▬▬▬ 50

Kilometers

CHAPTER 11

The Talking Cross

YUCATÁN is where the Spanish first encountered the Maya, and the very name is a monument to the gulf that existed between the two cultures. The Maya called the peninsula *u luum ceh yetel cutz*, "the land of the deer and the currasow"; but when the Spanish asked where they had landed, the Maya are said to have responded, *"Ma c'ubah than,"* "We don't understand your language"—which became "Yucatán."

The Yucatán peninsula is a vast, raised ancient limestone seabed covered with only a few inches of soil. Save for the Puuc, a line of three-hundred-foot hills running partway across the peninsula's middle, it is perfectly flat. Water, or the lack of it, is perhaps the region's most distinctive feature. South of the Puuc, occasional streams and lakes break the stony surface, but north of them, in Yucatán proper, there is no surface water at all. What water there is lies fifty to a hundred feet below ground in caves or in the water-filled cenotes.

Vast and flat though the Yucatán may be, neither the weather nor the flora are uniform. In the north and west where little rain falls, dry brush grows to a height of thirty feet. As you travel south and east, however, rainfall increases and the trees get taller, until you arrive at a forty-mile-wide band of scrub rain forest—in many ways an extension of the Petén—running along the Caribbean coast.

To a large degree, the post-Conquest settlement of Yucatán divided along these climatic lines. The Spanish gravitated to the drier country in the northwest, especially to the cities of Mérida and Campeche, while over the years the eastern forest was gradually abandoned to the Maya. In the early 1940's, the anthropologist Robert Redfield observed that "since the Conquest the forests to the south [and east] have constituted a hiding place and a base of operations for Indians unreconciled to the Spanish and Mexican governments." More recently, the anthropologist Paul Sullivan has referred to the difference between the eastern and western halves of the peninsula as a "fault line ... a seam in the social, cultural, economic, and political fabric of the Western Hemisphere."

I was interested in this bipolar outlook on Yucatán, since it was along these lines that the sides in the Yucatán Caste War lined up. The Caste War, or "the revolution," as it is referred to by the descendants of those Maya who took part in it, was the most effective Maya rebellion ever. At its height, in 1849, the Maya came within a hair of driving all Ladino authority off the peninsula; as it was, they succeeded in creating an independent Maya state that endured until the turn of the century in the forests of what is now Quintana Roo.

The Caste War, well described in Nelson Reed's book, *The Caste War of Yucatán,* began in 1846 as a response to the aggressive usurpation of traditional Maya land after Mexican independence from Spain. The fighting started along the eastern frontier, where the Maya, whom the English in British Honduras (now Belize) cheerfully supplied with arms and ammunition, began attacking outlying towns and ranches. The inhabitants took shelter in thick-walled churches, bolting the doors and transforming them into formidable fortifications, but the Maya persisted. Where there was not enough soil to dig trenches, they advanced lying on their backs, pushing boulders with their feet. On one occasion, unable to storm a Ladino-held church, the Maya scaled the walls, cut the rafters, and collapsed the roof onto the defenders within.

In early 1848, as the Maya offensive gained momentum, a group of Yucatec bishops wrote to the Maya leaders urging peace. According to Nelson Reed, this is how the Maya chiefs responded:

And now you remember that there is a True God. While you were
murdering us didn't you know that there was a True God? You were
always recommending the name of God to us and you never believed
in his name. … And now you are not prepared nor have you the
courage to accept the exchange for your blows. If we are killing now,
you first showed us the way.

Nothing seemed to work for the Ladino forces. Attacking units
were ambushed, cut off, and wiped out. A group of filibustering
Alabama mercenaries, veterans of the Mexican War, suffered heavy
enough casualties during their first week of fighting that most of
them turned around and went home. By the spring of 1849, the
Ladino armies were preparing to make a last stand outside Mérida
while preparing to evacuate the peninsula by sea. To cover the
retreat of Mérida's civilians, the Ladino generals sent out several
harassing units to stall the enemy advance. To their surprise, these
units were unable to locate the Maya. Although it will never be
clear what happened, Nelson Reed cites the explanation given by
Leandro Poot, son of the rebel Maya leader, Crecencio Poot, to
Edward H. Thompson, an archaeologist and the turn-of-the-century
American consul in Mérida. Recalling the evaporation of the Maya
forces before *T-ho* ("the fifth point"), the Maya name for Mérida,
Poot told Thompson:

> The day was warm and sultry. All at once the *sh'mataneheeles*
> [winged ants—harbingers of the rainy season] appeared in great
> clouds to the north, to the south, to the east and to the west, all over
> the world. When my father's people saw this they said to themselves
> and their brothers, "Ehen! The time has come for us to make our
> planting, for if we do not we shall have no Grace of God [*gracia,*
> "corn"] to fill the bellies of our children."
>
> In this way they talked among themselves and argued, thinking
> deeply, and then when morning came, my father's people said, each to
> his *batab* [war captain], "*Shickanic,*" "I am going," and in spite of the
> supplications and threats of the chiefs, each man rolled up his blanket
> and put it in his food pouch, tightened the thongs of his sandals, and
> started for his home and his cornfield.

The withdrawal of the Maya forces before Mérida marked the end of the first phase of the Caste War. The Ladinos took heart and, within a year, drove a hundred thousand rebel Maya back across the peninsula and into the eastern forests. There, harassed by Ladino units, unable to plant their milpas, the Maya began to despair. Just as they did so, however, a second phase of the Caste War began.

In the bottom of a remote glade deep in the forests of the eastern side of the peninsula lay a water-filled grotto. Next to it grew a mahogany tree. Carved into the mahogany trunk, the Maya rebels found a cross, the *chan Santa Cruz*—"the little Holy Cross." It's not clear how the cross got there, but it is clear that the cross satisfied all the criteria of Maya spiritual space. The water in the wilderness grotto would have been *zuhuy*, "virgin": that which belongs to God, not man. The mahogany tree with the cross cut into it would have been not just any tree, but the World Tree growing from the watery surface of the underworld and recapitulating the creation of the universe. The cross began to speak to the Maya, giving them heart, rallying them again against the Ladinos. Adherents began to refer to themselves as *cruzob*, followers of the cross. Within no time a sizable *cruzob* settlement grew up around the little grotto. In 1851, though, a Ladino guerrilla unit heard of the site, raided it, and chopped down the mahogany tree. Concealed inside the grotto the Ladinos found a ventriloquist, a Maya by the name of Manuel Nahuat, who had been supplying the voice of the god. The Ladinos killed Nahuat, and no doubt concluded that, the hoax being exposed, the Maya would disperse.

This was not what happened. After the Ladinos departed, the Maya carved three "daughter crosses" out of the wood of the fallen "mother cross," the mahogany tree. Because of the desecration of the original site, the daughter crosses refused to speak, but they did issue written instructions to certain priests, and continued to rally the Maya. At first the daughter crosses were housed in a thatched hut, behind a screen that concealed them from the faithful, but as the *cruzob* cause prospered again and the Ladinos were driven back out of the forests, the Maya decided something grander would be appropriate. A massive stone church—the Santa Cruz Balam Na, the

"Holy Cross Jaguar House"—was erected to house the three Talking Crosses. A hundred feet long by sixty feet wide, the Balam Na had a high, vaulted ceiling and five massive buttresses along each wall. Around it grew a Maya city, Noh Cah Santa Cruz Balam Na, or "Great Town of the Holy Cross Jaguar House." In the town, Ladino captives toiled as slaves and a Ladino military band, captured intact in a victorious Maya engagement, taught music.

For the remainder of the nineteenth century, life continued thus on the Yucatán peninsula: the Ladinos on one side, the Maya in their capital on the other. Periodically the Maya would sally forth out of the jungle and massacre the inhabitants of some unfortunate Ladino outpost. Usually the Ladinos would retaliate. A no-man's-land grew up between the last of the Ladino settlements and the forests of the Talking Cross; as late as the 1930's it took two or three days to ride across it.

The end of Talking Cross independence came in 1900, when the Mexican federal government sent in troops under the command of General Ignacio Bravo. Using machine guns and repeating rifles against the Maya muzzle loaders, General Bravo landed on the Caribbean coast and marched Sherman style into the interior, devastating everything in his path. He not only captured Noh Cah Santa Cruz Balam Na, but renamed it Santa Cruz de Bravo and then connected it to the coast with a railroad line.

Why all this effort? General Bravo was less interested in the *cruzob* Maya than in the natural resources of the eastern side of the peninsula, and the price he charged the Yucatán government for his services was high. Despite ardent protests from Mérida, he broke off Yucatán's eastern forests and reconstituted them as the federally administered territory of Quintana Roo. Quintana Roo became a penal colony, and criminals were sent to work at logging camps set up throughout the territory's forests.

After their defeat by General Bravo, the Talking Cross Maya scattered. Some died as the result of epidemics introduced by General Bravo's men. Others chose to assimilate, but the most conservative, known as *los separados* for their refusal to associate with non-*cruzob* outsiders, withdrew to a remote area of jungle around a place called Xcacal. In 1929, several of their number sneaked into the Balam Na—since made over into a conventional Catholic church—and stole the daughter crosses, which they then installed in a Talking Cross church in Xcacal under permanent *separado* guard. The *cruzob* fanned out from Xcacal and founded several other *separado* towns, each with its own crosses.

In Mérida someone pointed out to me a small article in the back pages of a local paper mentioning that a new Talking Cross church had recently been dedicated in the town of Tusik in the middle of Quintana Roo. Tusik is a *separado* town adjacent to Xcacal. In the thirties it had been studied by a well-known Mexican anthropologist, Alfonso Villa Rojas. I asked around to find out what anyone knew about Tusik. People told me that the Tusik Maya were *"muy bravo,"* that they didn't like outsiders much, and that they periodically traveled to Valladolid to "bust up windows." I also discovered that the former Maya capital of Noh Cah Santa Cruz Balam Na had become a Ladino town named Felipé Carrillo Puerto, after a martyred Yucatec socialist of the twenties. That was it. No one else seemed to know anything. So I boarded a bus in Mérida and headed east toward Tusik and the land of the Talking Cross Maya.

The first thing that confronted me, as I stepped off the bus in Felipé Carrillo Puerto, was the massive hulk of the Balam Na. The bus had pulled up on one side of the town square. The Balam Na loomed on the other side. I crossed and entered the church. Its interior had been refurbished in standard Catholic, and so intent was I on trying to uncover some vestige of the building's past that I inadvertently stumbled upon its custodian stretched out on a pew, sleeping off the afternoon heat. I asked him if this was indeed the church that had been built by the Talking Cross Maya years ago.

"This is a Catholic church," he said, looking at me at first condescendingly, then pityingly. "The ancient Maya built tiny thatched temples on top of mountains of stone. Those were the *only* churches the Maya ever built."

I checked my bag into a hotel and wondered how to approach the town of Tusik. Months before, a well-connected Mexican friend had given me the name of the mayor of Carrillo Puerto. For lack of a better plan, I decided to look him up. I marched down to the modern, two-story *palacio federale*. The mayor was out, but his assistant suggested I speak to the municipal secretary, a man whom she referred to as *"el professor Roberto."* Professor Bob, as I came to call him, was a harried-looking man with bags under his eyes. His office was crowded with supplicants, but eventually I was given my fifteen seconds. I told Professor Bob that I planned to visit the new Talking Cross church in Tusik but wanted to ask him first for suggestions on how best to enter the community.

El professor looked at me wearily, as if he'd had a lifetime of trouble with Talking Crosses.

"There's only one Talking Cross," he said, "and it's in a chapel three blocks from here. You can walk down and see it any time you want to."

I knew which Talking Cross he was speaking of. It was the original grotto, now on the outskirts of town.

"As for all the other Talking Crosses," he continued, "they don't mean a thing, and you wouldn't be able to visit them anyway."

I persisted and Professor Bob suddenly hesitated, as if a thought had occurred to him.

"The man you need to speak to is the *comisario* of Tusik. His name is Justino Ake. He was just here. If you want to find him, he's eating just around the corner at the *Lonchería* Judith Raquel."

I went out into the witheringly bright sun, rounded the corner, and found Justino Ake just as Professor Bob had said I would, leaning on a wall outside the Judith Raquel. He was a powerfully built man with a pronounced Maya nose and deep, rich, copper-colored skin. The Ladino clothes he was wearing didn't seem to belong on him.

He was visibly startled when I approached and explained my interest in visiting Tusik. I told him I had read about the new church in the Mérida papers and wanted to see it, even if I didn't get to see the sacred cross that was inside. I was interested in the *cruzob* and how they were living in the modern period. As I spoke, I became aware that the *comisario* was staring at me with what I took for profound contempt. Everything I said started to sound like blather. Eventually I ceased speaking.

After a long silence, Justino said, "You will make a gift to *el santo*."

"I'd be happy to," I responded, much too cheerfully.

"Five hundred thousand pesos," he said.

This was two hundred dollars.

"Fifty thousand pesos," I countered—still more than I'd ever given any church.

"Give it to me now," Justino said. He explained that he had to give it to the *jefe de la iglesia*, the "head of the church."

I asked him who the *jefe de la iglesia* was, but Justino wouldn't tell me. I told him I'd bring the money to Tusik tomorrow and would give it to the *jefe* myself.

I watched Justino walk off. He walked slowly, arrogantly, as if he felt nothing but contempt for the white man's world— myself and all of Felipé Carrillo Puerto included. It was as if he were saying, "We don't need you. We don't feel any obligation to you. You're trespassers. If you want to come and see *el santo,* you'll come on our terms."

After Justino left, I followed Professor Bob's directions to the site of the original Talking Cross. It was located in a neat little park in a grove of trees a few blocks from the center of town. The park was named for, of all people, Manuel Nahuat, the ventriloquist. It featured a little museum, the general theme of which seemed to be that the Maya revolt had been justified, but now that the area was under federal control, "We must never allow this terrible tragedy to happen again." This was the Mexican government for you: masterful, and in many ways admirable, in its ability to murder and then enshrine its opponents.

As I left the museum, a caretaker asked me to sign the guest book. The name before mine was "Leandro Poot Poot" from Tusik.

The caretaker took me down to see the grotto, where a very small stream flowed under some rocks. The stream banks were littered with trash. Three wooden crosses, replicas of the daughter crosses, were set in the ground on a rise above the grotto. The caretaker was apologetic. The grotto had previously been deeper and there had been tunnels leading off the entrance—tunnels into which

Manuel Nahuat had once crawled. But when they'd built the houses around the park, the grotto had silted in.

I left the park and wandered back toward town, thinking about the wonderful congruence of the Maya and Christian crosses. Had the Maya sat down after the Conquest and asked themselves how they could best conceal their pre-Columbian beliefs in Christian clothing? Probably not. Non-Maya are always trying to divide Maya behavior into what is Maya and what is European. Barbara Tedlock, an anthropologist who works in the Guatemalan highlands, calls this tendency "European oppositional dualism," and contrasts it to the Maya tendency to be philosophically flexible, to absorb what is useful into their own worldview without abandoning their fundamental values.

"The Maya built pyramids over pyramids over pyramids," said Bill Hanks, a University of Chicago linguist with whom I'd spoken in Mérida. "There were lots of overlaps and only small differences. The Maya idea is that you don't destroy the past, you build upon it."

I passed a white concrete box of a house. Music was blaring out of its darkened doorway. It was Bob Marley's "Zion Train":

> "Two thousand years of history
> could not be wiped away so easily."

My hair stood on end.

The next day, when I asked the bus driver to drop me off on the highway next to a sign that said TUZIK, 3 KMS., he shrugged as if to say "It's your life," stopped the bus, and let me down. After he'd disappeared over the horizon, I was left in silence. A fly flew by, making a nice demonstration of the Doppler effect. I looked around at the flat landscape. Not another sign of human habitation. A lizard scurried across the baking pavement. A collared aracari—a toucan— winged purposefully overhead. I remembered reading that certain birds acted as scouts for the *balambob,* the lords, the jaguar spirits of the forest, and wondered what *separado* gods were monitoring my approach.

The Tusik road, rutted and potholed, ran off into a landscape of milpa and second-growth jungle. The road sides were heavy with blue and red flowers and the air was filled with the drone of honeybees. As I shouldered my bag and began to hike, I thought of the Maya bee god, Noh Yum Cab, "Great Lord Bee," who lived in the inaccessible jungles of the east, east being the place where the sun rose, the red place, the most powerful of the four cardinal directions. When Alfonso Villa Rojas first entered the *separado* villages in the early thirties, the Maya were keeping their bees in hollow logs stopped with clay. Bees were held in great esteem because bees supplied the wax for candles at saints' ceremonies and because their honey was used in making *balche*. Villa Rojas noted that if a bee was accidentally killed during the process of taking honey from a hive, the Maya carefully wrapped it in a leaf and buried it.

Villa Rojas' entry into the *separado* area was facilitated by a curious association of bees, eastness, redness, and Americans. During the thirties, the *separado cruzob* and the Mexican government were still skirmishing. The Mexican government was trying to impose primary school teachers on the *cruzob*. The *cruzob* considered the teachers spies and tried to prevent them from entering the villages by force of arms. Villa Rojas, who had been a schoolteacher before becoming an anthropologist, was forced to make his initial visits to the *separado* area disguised as an itinerant merchant. Even then, the *cruzob* wouldn't permit him to stay.

However, the Carnegie Institution archaeologist Sylvanus Morley, then engaged in a major restoration project at Chichén Itzá, happened to be a colleague of Villa Rojas'. The *cruzob* were curious about Morley, whose work they had heard about through spies. *The cruzob* knew that Morley was American, and they associated Americans with the British, who had supplied them with arms during the Caste War. More important, however, prophecy had it that *cak winkob*— "red people"—would someday come from the east as allies of a long-dead king of the ancient Maya, who, the *cruzob* believed, still lived underground. These *cak winkob* would be very tall, would have eyes like bees, and would be able to read hieroglyphics. Because the first Americans that the *separado cruzob* had encountered were archaeologists looking at hieroglyphic inscriptions at Tulum, and because

Tulum was the easternmost of the Maya ruins, the Maya already referred to Americans as *cacakmaak*, "very red men." Were the Americans the prophesized *cak winkob?* The debate raged through the *separado* councils. Late in 1935, the Maya decided to send emissaries to Chichén Itzá to find out. Among the emissaries were two trusted *cruzob* officers, Captain Concepción Cituk and Lieutenant Evaristo Zuluub, who had helped steal the daughter crosses from the Balam Na six years earlier.

In his book *Unfinished Conversations: Maya and Foreigners Between Two Wars,* Yale anthropologist Paul Sullivan describes the *cruzob* visit to Chichén Itzá. Morley knew that Villa Rojas wanted to do anthropological work in the *separado* area but that the *cruzob* would not admit him. Morley therefore made a point of having Villa Rojas with him when he showed the visiting *cruzob* around the site. The *separado* Maya had never seen Chichén Itzá before and they were fascinated—particularly by the ball court. They took its famous echoes as evidence of the presence of the *cilankabob,* their ancient predecessors. When Morley pointed out the temple that presides over one end of the court, the Maya visitors decided it was the office of one of the ancient kings. Sullivan recounts a conversation that ensued between Captain Cituk, the head of the Maya delegation, and the invisible king. Captain Cituk began:

> "Well hello. Well, I, I came to visit you, Mr. King, here in the town of Chichén Itzá. Because since long ago when the world was settled we have known that you are here, Your Majesty. We came to visit you. We came to greet you. We came to do our duty, here in the town of Chichén, here where your office is. Here we are conversing thus. God made you lord. We have come to visit you."

Another Maya, Sergeant Chaac, took the part of the king and responded:

> "Good. You, Don Concepción Cituk, if it is you, I am happy. Come and visit me in the heart of my town, here in the town of Chichén Itzá. I am very happy with all that is said [about] how it happened that the Revolution happened here in the town of Chichén."

The visit to Chichén Itzá was a success, and as a result, Villa Rojas was permitted to do his research among the *separado* Maya. Morley's relationship to the *cruzob,* however, became problematic. As Paul Sullivan points out, despite years of disavowal, Morley was never entirely able to shake the *cruzob* hope that he was going to lead a combined *cruzob-cilankabob* army in a war of annihilation against the Mexicans.

After walking for the better part of a mile up the Tusik road, I came across two piles of rocks. Two wooden crosses were protruding from each pile. I knew I was now entering the precincts of Tusik. This double pair of crosses marked one of the five sacred directions. There would be three other such markers at the three other cardinal points. The fifth sacred direction, the center, would be the middle of Tusik. I knew from reading Paul Sullivan's book that the town was built over an underground water-filled cave, and the Talking Cross church sat directly over the cave's roof. The fifth direction therefore recapitulated the World Tree cross-growing-out-of-the-underworld logic of Manuel Nahuat's grotto.

Not long after I'd passed the crosses, a man and a boy approached me from the direction of town. The man was carrying a plastic mesh bag. The son held a deer antler for shucking corn. Their eyes grew wide with fear when they saw me, and the son nervously clutched his father's sleeve.

"Where are you going?" the man asked.

"To Tusik," I responded, "to see how the *cruzob* are living. And you?"

"To the milpa," the man responded, scurrying fearfully away.

I walked on. Soon I heard the sounds of the village: dogs barking, turkeys gobbling, children playing. I smelled cook fires in the breeze. The road turned into a street sunken below lines of rough white limestone walls. The walls set off gardens, and in the middle of one of the gardens I could see a *choza,* the traditional house of the Yucatec Maya, with rounded ends, high, thatched roofs, and walls of vertical or basket-weave poles standing on low stone foundations. From the doorway, a Maya woman stared, wordless, her white *huipil* embroidered with flowers, her white Yucatec *pic,* or "skirt," extending below.

I smiled and waved like a politician in a parade, trying to cover up the fact that I wasn't at all sure of what I was doing. It came as a considerable surprise, therefore, when the road curved suddenly and led into the town plaza, when I was confronted with an enormous satellite dish surrounded by a chain-link fence.

I spotted a small store and sat down with a Coke on the sidewalk to contemplate this phenomenon. A Ladino-ized twenty-one-year-old came out of the store and sat down next to me. He told me that the *comisario,* Justino Ake, was in his milpa and wouldn't be back until four in the afternoon. I looked at my watch. Just past noon. I had time to kill. I asked about the satellite dish.

It was part of the Mexican government's Telesecundaria program, my companion explained, a program that beams secondary education programs to areas without schools. However, some of the *gente,* people, had discovered that by making a few adjustments, they could tune into channels not just from all over Mexico but from the United States as well.

I asked if this meant that the *gente* of Tusik had televisions.

"It does," he answered. "Many of the *gente* have gone to work in Cancún and have earned the money to buy television sets. Almost everyone has one."

I looked out over the Tusik plaza, an irregular piece of wasteland. On the far side I could see what I assumed was the new church, a white building with a red corrugated-metal roof. I asked my companion what had happened to the old church.

The old church had just been taken down, he explained. Its thatched roof had leaked beyond repair.

I asked if the cross still spoke.

"It doesn't," he answered. "It only gives signals. A man named Herman receives them through a set of crystals. Of course if you or I were to try to use the crystals, nothing would happen. Only Herman can use them."

Herman, I later discovered from Paul Sullivan, was a shaman, an *h-men,* "one who knows."

My presence, meanwhile, had attracted a crowd of curious children, and as the afternoon sun worked its way slowly across the sky, I learned the Yucatec Maya words for male and female turkey, male and female pig, dog, rabbit, iguana, and hat. I learned that African bees had made beekeeping dangerous, that there were jaguars in the *monte,* as well as peccaries and lots of deer, but neither pumas nor tapirs. A young man told me that the "new word" in Tusik was "Batman," and asked me what it really meant. I translated literally for him: "*Murciélago hombre.*" He walked away shaking his head, as if he were sorry he'd asked. When another young man asked me if I'd heard of the singing group Menudo, I decided it was time to go look for Justino.

Justino lived on a side street in a *choza* just like everyone else's. His wife, Maria, let me into the garden and called to Justino. Reluctantly, it seemed, Justino came out and invited me into the house. A television was tuned to a Mexican news channel. Justino's chair was pulled up in front of it. Somewhat sourly he produced another chair and invited me to sit. A dog raced into the room barking.

"*Pek!*" I shouted, using the word for dog that I had just learned in the plaza. The dog obligingly wagged its tail and put its head in my lap.

Justino's jaw dropped.

How was it, he asked after a moment of silence, that I'd known who he was the other day?

I explained the Professor Bob connection, which seemed to take a load off his mind. Suddenly he seemed almost pleased to see me.

He pointed to a picture of George Bush on the television screen and hesitatingly pronounced his name.

"George Bush," he said. "We see him often. He talks about Colombia and drugs. Colombia is a part of the United States?"

I laughed at Justino's astute sense of political geography.

"And Panama?" Justino asked. "Is this an example of a large country invading a small one?"

I resisted a political discussion with the *comisario* and steered the conversation instead to what seemed most immediately pertinent: where I was going to stay that night.

Justino, who had perhaps noticed that I was beginning to eye his house for hammock space, decided that I should go to a house near the church belonging to the brother of the *jefe de la iglesia.* Previous foreigners had stayed there. Justino didn't offer to take me to the house, he just told me how to find it.

Victoriano, as I'll call the brother of the *jefe de la iglesia,* had two houses: a concrete box along the street that was his sleeping quarters, and a traditional *choza* in the garden behind. Even though Victoriano's family had never laid eyes on me, never heard my name before, they made it seem perfectly natural that I should walk into their *choza* at dinnertime. Victoriano's wife, whom I'll call Basilia, and a daughter, Rosaria, were sitting on low wooden stools removing the kernels of corn from a pile of newly harvested ears. Their long, Yucatec-style *huipiles* were hitched up around their thighs. Behind them, a pot supported on three large rocks was simmering over an open fire. Overhead, vine-lashed poles supported a blackened thatch roof. In the middle of the room, two other daughters and a young son were at work weaving four hammocks stretched out on eight vertical poles.

Basilia indicated that I could sit by the door in a low hammock. "*Gracias,*" I said as I sat down.

One of Victoriano and Basilia's teenaged daughters, beautiful in a sparkling white *huipil,* put down her hammock weaving, walked over to me, leaned her face close to mine, and waved a finger.

"*Dios bo'otik,*" she scolded. "*Así se dice gracias*"—"That's how you say thank you."

The daughter, Bertha, instructed me to pull out a piece of paper and write down the Maya words. I followed her instructions carefully. It soon became apparent that Bertha and the son, Pedro, were the only ones in the house who spoke Spanish. Otherwise, it was Maya. Victoriano, a grizzled old man with thick eyebrows, several days' growth of beard, and heavily patched clothes, had collapsed into another hammock near mine; his shotgun dangled from the wall behind him. Periodically he would turn and address me in Maya. It was like the Englishman's approach to foreign language: if you speak your own language loudly and clearly enough, they're bound to understand. I shrugged helplessly.

Basilia summoned us to dinner in groups. Victoriano and I went together. We received bowls of chicken and rice in broth. Basilia and Bertha were patting out tortillas on a small table, toasting them on a *comal,* and then tossing them onto the coals until they puffed up like balloons. As they removed the tortillas from the heat and handed them to us, they gradually deflated.

I took my tortilla and bowl of stew over to a low stool and began to sit.

"No!" everyone shouted at once, breaking into giggles. It was the tortilla-making table.

Nine hammocks hung in the two rooms of Victoriano's sleeping house. After dinner I sat in mine receiving Maya lessons from Victoriano and Basilia's vociferous seven-year-old daughter. The older girls were preparing to go to a party in Xcacal. They changed their sparkling white *huipiles* for blindingly white ones. They put on gold necklaces and earrings and fixed sequined barrettes in their hair. When they walked by, they left a subtle trail of perfume. I was reminded that in Villa Rojas' day, Maya women scented their clothes with vanilla beans.

A truck filled with young Maya drove up. A ramp went down. The girls climbed up and the truck drove off. I felt abandoned.

Shortly afterward a summons arrived. A group of eight men, their faces in shadow, wanted me out on the street. They all knew my name. The two who knew Spanish spoke for the others. They wanted to know why I was in Tusik.

I told them about the fame of the Talking Cross, about the article on their new church, about how I'd met Justino, and about how he'd sent me to Victoriano's.

Where was I from? they wanted to know.

"New York," I answered.

They were not sure if New York was a city or a country, but they had heard of it.

"Is it true the buildings are twenty stories tall?" one asked.

"A hundred," I answered.

"And how do you get up and down?"

I explained the concept of elevator: "You want to get to the hundredth floor? You push a button."

The translation was followed by gasps.

I told them I was living in Chiapas in an area where there were different Maya languages than their own. They didn't believe me. One of them explained condescendingly that it was only here, in the center of Quintana Roo, that you found the real Maya.

To bolster their sense of solidarity, I told them about the war in Guatemala, about how the Guatemalan army had napalmed Maya villages and machine-gunned the *gente* from helicopters. As I did so, I thought of Villa Rojas' having warned the *cruzob* of the thirties of the Ladino engines of war, and of the *cruzob* lieutenant who said he was sure he could bring down the Ladino airplanes with a volley from twenty-five soldiers. They had been practicing, it turned out. They were already able to bring down *zopilotes,* buzzards, from quite high up.

"It's impossible for us to buy guns," one of the Tusik men complained to me. "The customs people stop us at Santa Elena."

Santa Elena was a town on the Belize border.

Had I been to Valladolid? a man asked.

I had. Valladolid, Ciudad Heroica and "Sultaness of the East"— as the tourist brochures put it—was historically the easternmost Ladino city in Yucatán; I'd spent the night there on my way to Tusik from Mérida.

"Do you know the church on the central plaza?"

I did. He was referring to San Gervasio, a beautiful seventeenth-century church that I had walked through just a few days before.

"The clock on the church tower," the man said, "there's no electricity to it. How do you think it runs?"

"I don't know," I responded.

"It's because it was made by *los Mayas antiguos!*" he told me triumphantly.

When I returned to Victoriano's, everyone had gone to bed. I lay down in my hammock and thought about the *cruzob* conception of history. I knew that the present-day *cruzob* believed that the ancient Maya cities had been built in another era, in the ancient "good" times by a people with magical powers called the Itzá. Nature had done the Itzá's bidding. When the Itzá whistled, stones moved. Brush burned without being felled, and corn cooked itself. But then the Itzá did something to offend the gods and were banished into the maze of underground caves and rivers beneath the peninsula. Under the ruins of the ancient cities—Chichén Itzá, Cobá, and Tulum—you could sometimes hear the conch-shell trumpets and hollowed-log drums of the Itzá.

Just as the Itzá had somehow offended the gods, so had the present-day *cruzob,* although perhaps not yet to the same degree. This was because the *cruzob* had allowed the Mexican government to intrude into Maya areas. Eventually the gods would have had enough (the satellite dish alone seemed sufficent cause), and an apocalypse like the one that had ended the Itzá era would bring an end to the present era. In *Unfinished Conversations,* Paul Sullivan expresses the *cruzob* view: "Maya will shed the blood of foreigners and allow their own to be shed, until the blood of all nationalities and races mingles in ankle-deep lagoons covering the central plazas of ... towns and cities." How well the Maya survive this apocalypse depends on how mindful they are of their gods during the waning years of the present era. If they have been properly hostile to foreigners and ceased their complicity in helping the outside economy conquer the Maya economy, some Maya would live on "as seeds for the new beginning." If not, Paul Sullivan writes, "True God will take it on himself to destroy us all, renew the face of the earth, and people it with creatures of another, improved design."

When I later asked Paul Sullivan about the Tusik man's San Gervasio clocktower comment, he explained that the clock tower's ceasing to function would be one of the signs of the impending apocalypse. Another would be the collapse of the famous sixteenth-century Franciscan Sisal Church in Valladolid into the cenote over which it is built. A third would be the reappearance, from underground, of an old lady who feeds children to huge subterranean serpents. Finally, at Chichén Itzá, a petrified feathered serpent would come to life and "wreak havoc on the creatures of this creation."

"When did the *cruzob* anticipate this apocalypse?" I asked Paul.

"The year two thousand and a little," he said.

After I had been lying in my hammock for a while, I heard Victoriano's son, Pedro. A young man in his early twenties, Pedro seemed an example of the sort of Maya on whom the gods would not look kindly during the Final Days. He had already told me about his work in the kitchen of a Cancún hotel, and he was perfectly obsessed with the world of foreigners.

"When I learn to speak English," he'd told me complicitally—as if he and I were the only sophisticates in this village otherwise populated by rubes—"I'll never be lost in the city. Someday, I'll go to the United States!"

Tonight, however, Pedro was drunk. I could smell it on his breath. I pretended I was asleep. Sleep, however, was not on the agenda because Pedro had brought a television set with him. Fumbling, he plugged the television into a wall socket, placed it on the floor just below my head, and, perhaps because he didn't want me to think Tusik a technologically backward place, turned it on full volume. He then crawled into his hammock and went to sleep. Although everyone else must have woken, no one said, or did, a thing. I was a guest in the house—an uninvited guest. I waited for a decent interval, until I could hear Pedro's heavy breathing, and then got up and turned the television off.

In the morning after breakfast, I found Victoriano strapping a burlap-bag saddle onto a mule. Since he did not speak English, I asked Bertha where he was going.

"He's going to the forest to cut poles for a corn crib," she answered.

"May I go with him?" I asked.

She didn't say a word. She just motioned for me to follow.

Dressed in rags and carrying a machete and an ax, Victoriano led the way through a maze of irregular, rocky side streets, sprouting with weeds and littered with dried corncobs. When we reached the edge of town the road became a path, which passed a banana grove, cut through a cornfield, and entered the vine-draped forest. After we had walked a considerable distance, Victoriano tied up the mule and wandered off into the forest. Looking up dreamily, assessing each tree and sometimes stopping to pronounce their Maya names, he finally selected a tree about eight or ten inches in diameter that branched about eight feet up.

"*Ya'*," Victoriano said, giving me the tree's Maya name.

He picked up his ax, felled the tree, and cut the branches just above the crotch. Together we hauled the trunk back to the path. There, Victoriano handed me the machete and indicated that while he went to look for another tree, I was to strip the bark off this one.

It was messy work. *Ya'*, I soon discovered, was the Yucatec Maya word for the *chicozapote*, the sapodilla tree from which *chicleros* collect the sap that forms the basis of chewing gum. The sap, a sticky white latex, seemed to adhere to everything it touched. Within minutes I was covered with latex and pouring with sweat.

Suddenly I looked up and saw a dog in the path behind me, bug-eyed with terror. Behind, clutching a shotgun, stood its equally bug-eyed master. I stared back for a moment before I recognized the man whom I'd passed coming into town the day before. After a long silence, he spoke: "Don't you have *chicozapote* in your country?"

I ran mentally through all the tree guides I'd ever read, and answered truthfully that no, to the best of my knowledge there were no *chicozapotes* in my country.

"Are you going to build a house?" he asked, his voice rising with incipient panic.

The man didn't wait for the story of Victoriano and the corn crib before he nervously inched his way past me. The dog, however, was another story. Long after its master had disappeared into the forest, it was still whimpering and whining. It seemed reluctant to leave the path, but could not muster the courage to walk past this terrifying apparition. Finally the dog gave up on the path, and made a wide circuit through the underbrush, being careful not to let me out of its sight.

An hour or so later, Victoriano and I had cut and stripped five heavy poles. We strapped the butt ends to the mule's saddle and, leaving the tops to skid along the ground, headed back to the house. I spent the afternoon helping Victoriano set the poles in the ground and, after we'd gone out and cut another smaller set, tying the frame together with vines that grew on the garden wall.

As we worked, two grandchildren, Reynalda and Filiberto, and their dog, Mosquito, watched. Reynalda, a bright nine-year-old with copper-colored hair, scaled an orange tree and, sitting like a monkey in its upper branches, began flirtatiously throwing down sweet oranges. When I indicated that I couldn't carry any more, she shinnied down from the tree, took my hand, and walked me around the garden pointing out fruits whose Maya names I couldn't begin to record. Under this child's guidance, I began to see the ecological complexity of what had appeared to be random growth in Victoriano's garden. Layered like the rain forest, it consisted of an overstory of fruit trees and an understory of vines and shrubs. It was the wild world in microcosm. I suddenly understood that this continuum between domestic agriculture and its natural surroundings was close to the very heart of Maya culture and was something long gone from our own experience.

Pedro's television found its way into Victoriano's *choza* that evening. Dinner consisted of *camotes*—sweet potatoes baked in the coals. After dinner, everyone wove hammocks and watched a Mexican show about a hacienda wedding. The men were dressed like mariachis. The women pouted in their white ball gowns and stomped indignantly. Victoriano's family found it hysterically funny. I never really understood why. Maybe I'd watched too much television. Afterward a pop music variety show from Mexico City came on. Victoriano was lying in the patched hammock by the door, and as each glitzy star strode onto the set, Victoriano would repeat the name to himself. He was particularly taken by "Judith," a woman with a sequin blouse and long, platinum-blond hair. Long after her act was over he was still asking in plaintive tones when she'd be on again.

When Julio Iglesias came on for a croon-off finale with the Brazilian singer Roberto Carlos, I decided to take a break. I went outside. The moon had not yet risen and the blue-black sky was full of stars. I found the Pleiades, what the Yucatec Maya call *tzab,* the "rattlesnake's rattle." I found Gemini, known as *ac,* "the turtle." Across the middle of the sky ran the Milky Way, the *sac be,* the "white way," the term that the ancient Maya also used for the straight-as-an-arrow raised limestone highways that had once connected their cities.

Early the next morning, the morning I was planning to leave

Tusik, the men whom I'd spoken with on the street two nights before arrived to take me to the church. I was escorted across the plaza and into a building with a blue tile floor, newly whitewashed walls, and even, as the men proudly pointed out, ceiling fans. A low masonry curtain separated the altar from the rest of the interior. The middle of the curtain wall was broken by an arch, painted with the words IGLESIA SANTA CRUZ. Beyond the arch was an altar holding a bower of bent sticks covering eight or nine crosses, each with a mirror draped around its neck and each wearing a *huipil.*

I asked which of the crosses was the sacred Talking Cross and received an evasive answer.

I asked if the space beyond the wall was La Gloria—"heaven" in Yucatec Maya cosmology. One of the men assured me that it was.

La Gloria is the place where Yum K'in—"the owner of the sun"—lived. It was Yum K'in who spoke to the faithful through his son, Juan de la Cruz. In Villa Rojas' time, La Gloria would have been guarded by a sentinel with a musket, and although I knew that the residents of Tusik were still organized into a military guard, no such sentinel was in sight.

I thought of what the University of Chicago linguist Bill Hanks, who had spent years studying with a Yucatec shaman, had told me about what he called the "principle of verticality" among the Yucatec gods. Like all aspects of Maya life, he explained, the gods were organized in relation to the five sacred directions, the four cardinal points plus the center. The center was the sacred cross, the World Tree, the *axis mundi* along which the gods were ordered. Those gods located at the bottom—below the surface of the earth, were evil—the further down, the more evil. Gods above the surface of the earth were benevolent, the higher, the more benevolent.

The four cardinal directions were strongest on the surface of the earth. As you traveled up or down the central axis, they gradually fell away, until eventually, as you neared the top or bottom, direction disappeared altogether. For instance, as you descended toward *metnal,* the Yucatec word for the underworld, the first direction to go was east, the most benevolent and most powerful of the directions, the red direction, the direction of the rising sun. The last to go was west, the evil place, the black place, the place of the dying sun. But even west eventually disappeared until at the bottom of the universe you were left with no directionality, just pure evil. The opposite took place as you ascended. East was the last direction to persist until even it fell off, and you arrived at La Gloria, dwelling place *Yum K'in:* owner of the sun, pure good, pure center.

As I thought of this, I suddenly understood that standing as we were on the roof of a water-filled cavern in front of the sacred Talking Cross, we were in fact at the center, the green place, the World Tree, the point of regeneration of life. I looked around at my escorts. They were standing with happy smiles, like a bunch of stoned college kids.

The shared bliss was cut short, however, by the arrival of the *jefe de la iglesia.* An assured man of fifty or sixty, he was wearing a white T-shirt with CON SALINAS DE GORTARI in bold black letters across the front. This was Victoriano's brother, the *unohochil,* "the big one," the senior commander of the Tusik guard. He strolled up to me confidently, shook my hand, exchanged a few pleasantries with the assembled, and then walked out again.

As soon as he left, my guides began hinting that it was time for me to make my offering. I was ready for them. I reached into my pocket, produced fifty thousand pesos, and handed it to one of the men. The others craned their necks shamelessly to see what I'd given. They seemed pleased.

When I got back to the house, Victoriano was saddling his mule again.

"Petuch!" he called out, beckoning to me and using the Yucatec version of my name.

It broke my heart to see his disappointment when I told him I was leaving.

As I trudged out past the church I saw a group of men sitting on a stoop.

"How did you like our church?" one of them called out.

"It was beautiful," I answered.

"Yes," the man agreed. "It's like *el cuerpo,* the body."

The others nodded in grave assent.

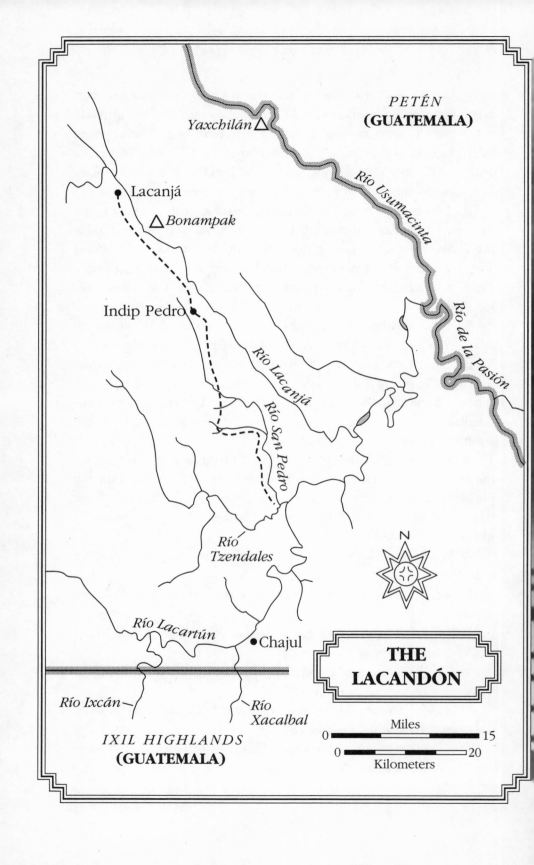

Yaxchilán △

PETÉN
(GUATEMALA)

Río Usumacinta

Lacanjá

△ *Bonampak*

Indip Pedro

Río Lacanjá

Río de la Pasión

Río San Pedro

Río Tzendales

N

Río Lacartún

Chajul

THE LACANDÓN

Río Ixcán

Río Xacalbal

IXIL HIGHLANDS
(GUATEMALA)

Miles
0 ▬▬▬▬ 15

0 ▬▬▬▬ 20
Kilometers

CHAPTER 12

The Lacandón

THE HEAT HIT ME LIKE A WALL as I stepped out of the cockpit of the Cessna 185 that had just flown me from the cool of the Chiapas highlands. The plane had landed on a rough, grassy airstrip in Chajul, a remote, jungle-bound colony on the southern bank of the Lacantún River just inside Mexico. Chajul's only connections to the outside world were the airstrip and the river. A mile or two to the south was the Guatemalan border, on the far side of which I could see forested, haze-shrouded hills rising toward the Ixil highlands.

My attention, however, was focused not on Guatemala, but in the other direction. Across the Lacantún River, north of Chajul, stretched more than twelve hundred square miles of unexplored rain forest, the last undisturbed section of the Lacandón and probably the largest remaining tract of rain forest in Mexico. On paper this was the Montes Azules park, but on paper only. The park had no administration, no paths, no guards, and no boundaries except theoretical ones. In fact, no one knew what was in it, which was basically why I had arrived in Chajul. Two or three days earlier, in the thin air of the San Cristóbal highlands, I had attached myself to an expedition that planned to traverse the park on foot, from south to north. The expedition's purposes were both scientific and political. More needed to be known about the park in order to bring pressure to bear on the government to stop the colonists who were already burning and clearing along its western border. My own objectives were more personal. To me it was a chance to go back in ecological time, to see something ur-Maya, to see the land the way it was before the arrival of the Europeans—perhaps even before the arrival of the Maya.

With me in the plane was the expedition doctor, José Luis Patjane, thirty-nine, a Mexican surgeon and amateur naturalist of Lebanese descent. Behind us in a second plane were the three other expedition members: its organizer, thirty-four-year-old Ignacio "Nacho" March, a Spanish-born Mexican wildlife biologist; Archie Carr III, forty-four, of the New York Zoological Society; and Tom Ensign, a thirty-eight-year-old cameraman from Bellingham, Washington, who was lugging a video camera with which he planned to record our adventures.

Until the evening before, we were to have been six. The sixth was to have been K'in Bor, a Lacandón Maya friend of Nacho's. K'in Bor was to have provided not just a general knowledge of the rain forest, but also his bow and arrow, a prospect that had intrigued me so enormously that it had overcome my last qualms about joining the trip. At the last minute, however, progress had caught up with K'in Bor. He lives in Lacanjá, a Lacandón Indian town that was to be the northern terminus of our hike. Shortly before he was to leave the jungle to join us in San Cristóbal, the electrical commission had appeared in Lacanjá and delivered an ultimatum. Electicity was arriving in the town. Before it did, though, the Lacandóns themselves had to dig the holes for the electrical poles. No holes, no electricity. The day before we were scheduled to leave, K'in Bor sent word that he wouldn't be able to come. The news was profoundly depressing for all of us, but there wasn't much we could do. Flying down over the jungle, looking beneath me at a terrifying landscape of impenetrable forests, tangled swamps, soaring limestone cliffs, and cascading blue rivers—unbroken by any sign of human habitation—I felt a deep chill and thought of what I had once overheard a guide saying to a group of English-speaking tourists standing in front of a large black-and-white photograph of a Lacandón Indian in the Museum of Anthropology in Mexico City: "These e-peoples are a-considered a-kings of the a-jungle because these a-jungles are a very a-dangerous. There are e-scorpions, e-snakes, e-spiders, e-scrocodiles. So, if you a-want to go a-into the jungles, you must a-have a man a-like a-this as a guide."

As José Luis and I struggled to haul our equipment to the side of the airfield, I marveled that such a mountain of gear proffered such meager fare. Our packs weighed about fifty-five pounds each. We hoped to be able to make the crossing in ten or twelve days, but we each had minimal food for fifteen days: fifteen little packets of a Wheatena-like substance mixed with powdered milk for breakfast; twelve lunches of either a granola bar or a pepperoni stick; and fifteen freeze-dried dinners that Archie had brought from Florida. For sleeping, we each carried a sleeping bag, a hammock, a mosquito net, and a sheet of plastic to drape over the assemblage. At the last minute, in an effort to save weight, Archie had cut out his bird book, binoculars, and a little radio with which he had hoped to be able to contact a meteorological station along the border in case we got into trouble.

Our plan for that first night was to stay at a biological research station a mile or so upriver from Chajul, where an ornithologist colleague of Nacho's, Eduardo Iñigo, was working. Nacho had radioed Eduardo and told him about K'in Bor's not being able to come. Through Eduardo we hoped to recruit a local person to take his place.

After the second plane landed, the five of us ferried our gear down to the river's edge, where we had arranged for Eduardo to pick us up in a launch. A small crowd of Chajul residents followed us, but didn't offer to help. As we waited for Eduardo to appear, I tried to make conversation with the *chajuleros* but found them, as a group, remarkably unfriendly. I managed to coax out of one of them that they had come from the state of Guerrero, where Acapulco is located, seventeen years before.

"Why did you come to the jungle?" I asked.

"The government sent us here," the man said. "The army was killing peasants in Guerrero then."

"Why?" I asked.

"For nothing," he said bitterly.

I subtracted seventeen years and arrived at 1972, the year that Lucio Cabañas, the Robin-Hood-like grandson of one of Emiliano Zapata's peasant generals, had taken on the bulk of the Mexican Army in the mountains of Guerrero. These, no doubt, were Cabañas sympathizers, exiled to the jungle for insurrectionary tendencies.

Eduardo showed up late, full of apologies. He had been upriver picking up one of his students, when he'd come across a group of surveyors from the Chiapas agrarian reform office laying out parcels of parkland prefatory to granting them to peasants from the south side of the river. Eduardo had had to stop and radio Mexico City to try to bring a halt to the situation.

The biological research station proved to be a ruin. Built at enormous expense in the early eighties, Eduardo told us that it had no sooner been completed than abandoned. The generator had long ceased functioning. The buildings were surrounded by ten-foot-tall scrub. Everywhere vines were snaking under the walls. Eduardo was doing a study of raptors for his master's degree in ornithology from the University of Florida and had two students working with him. The three of them had salvaged enough screens from what had been a complex of metal dormitories to make one dormitory habitable, but even so, at the far end a branch had crashed through the roof, opening two rooms to the sky.

After dinner, one of Eduardo's students entertained us with an account of his afternoon's work. He'd been seated in a clearing, trying to attract raptors by playing a tape recording of a wounded bird, when an ocelot had leapt out of the forest, pounced on the machine, realized its mistake, clawed the student, and fled.

We were examining the claw wounds when we were startled by a flash of light, a deep explosion, and then an earth-shattering blast.

Startled, I looked at Eduardo.

"Howitzers," he said. "From inside Guatemala. We hear them every night."

"The army fighting the guerrillas?" I asked.

"I don't think so," Eduardo responded. "From what I can tell, it's the Guatemalan army shooting at refugees both inside Guatemala and over the border in Mexico."

"Are the refugees guerrilla supporters?" I asked.

"The ones we see look more like poor Indians," Eduardo answered. "Most of them don't even speak Spanish."

Another shell landed on the other side of the river, shattering the evening quiet.

"A lot of the shells land in Mexico," Eduardo said. "One landed in my *lanchero*'s, boatman's, father's milpa. It dug a huge crater and almost buried him in mud. Another time, one of my students was out in the park with a pair of binoculars looking at birds, when a Guatemalan helicopter flew over and threw two hand grenades at him. When I'd left him that morning he'd been cheerful and enthusiastic, but when I came back that night he was huddled in a corner, crying, and saying that he never wanted to do fieldwork again."

The next morning, Eduardo's *lanchero* showed up with two recruits for our expedition. They were Elías Vásquez, twenty-two, and his cousin, José Francisco "Pancho" Domínguez, a year younger. They came from an *ejido* upriver from Chajul named Loma Bonita, "beautiful hill."

I asked Elías and Pancho about the previous night's bombardment. Elías told me that one of the shells had landed two hundred meters from his house.

"Are they shooting at guerrillas?"

"We see the guerrillas sometimes," Elías said, "but they're mostly deeper inside Guatemala. What the bombardment is about is to try to convince the Guatemalans who have fled to Mexico not to come back."

"What do the people of Loma Bonita think of the happenings in Guatemala?"

"We are taking note of the way their government treats its people," Elías responded, "and we're thinking."

We had revised our plans overnight. Originally, Eduardo was to have taken us downriver to a point at which we would climb over a mountain shoulder and then descend to the Tzendales River. This would put us in the vicinity of a long-abandoned logging camp that had been the setting for B. Traven's novel *Rebellion of the Damned*. From the Tzendales we would cut northeast to the San Pedro River, which we would then follow northwest to its headwaters. Somewhere in the San Pedro headwaters was Indio Pedro, the only settlement in the entire region. A tiny clearing in an ocean of forest, Indio Pedro was a former logging camp whose residents had stayed on. If we were lucky enough to find it, we planned to use it as a navigational reference point. Our maps showed a footpath leading north from Indio Pedro, across the Lacanjá River, to the ruins at Bonampak. If we made good time, and if the path still existed, we would make a side excursion to Bonampak and then walk from there to K'in Bor's village of Lacanjá. If we weren't making good time, we would head directly from Indio Pedro to Lacanjá.

However, the aerial view of our route had had a sobering effect. Instead of hiking overland to the Tzendales, we decided to take the launch farther downriver to the confluence of the Tzendales and the Lacantún, and then follow the Tzendales back upriver toward a line of waterfalls we had seen from the air. From there, we would cut overland to the San Pedro. This adjustment, we hoped, would shorten the trip by two or three days.

It was a brilliant morning, and as we loaded the launch and set off downriver, the Lacantún looked beautiful. It was the end of rainy season and the river was wide and riffled with fast water. Sand and gravel banks covered with aromatic white lilies marked the shallows. Two scarlet macaws winged their way overhead. In the top of a high tree Eduardo pointed out a rare king vulture, its huge white body and multicolored head standing out clearly against the blue of the morning sky.

As we traveled down the river, I asked Eduardo about his research.

"I'm studying the effects of forest fragmentation on raptor population," he explained. "There're at least forty-one, and probably forty-two, birds of prey in the Lacandón—that's more than in all of the United States and Canada put together—and by comparing the populations of the southern bank, which has been largely cleared, with those of the north, which is still wild, I hope to measure the effects of forest destruction."

Archie interrupted us and pointed to a three-foot-long crocodile gliding off a mudbank into the water.

"*Crocodylus acutus,*" he said. "The American crocodile. This is an ideal river for them. They're carrion feeders. Left alone they grow to twenty-five feet, although all the big ones have long since been hunted out."

I asked Archie if there were crocodiles in the forest interior.

"Those're caimans," he answered. "They're nocturnal and only grow to six feet."

After an hour or two on the Lacantún, we reached the Tzendales. We eased our way over a shallow gravel bank and followed the river in a northwest direction. At its mouth, the Tzendales was twisting and high-banked, narrower than I'd expected, and filled with fallen trees. After snaking our way upriver for half a mile, we reached the confluence of the San Pedro, the river we hoped to pick up later in our hike. The complexions of the two rivers were startlingly different. The San Pedro was brown. The Tzendales, as the result of some unseen mineral deposit, was blue.

We continued up the Tzendales, but not for long. Within a hundred yards it became completely clogged with fallen trees. We turned around, retraced our course to the San Pedro, and, without hesitation, followed it upstream. The San Pedro was not the most prepossessing of rivers. The banks were high and muddy, fringed with wicked-looking grasses and reeds, but at least we knew that as long as we stuck with the river, we'd be going in the right direction.

But the launch didn't get far on the San Pedro either. Within another half mile a low waterfall brought an end to the launch-borne phase of our expedition. To land our gear, we had to pull out our machetes and hack a space out of the sharp-edged reeds along the bank. Once we'd unloaded the boat, Eduardo wished us luck, turned the launch around, and headed back downriver.

Although the again-revised plan was to follow the San Pedro valley all the way to Indio Pedro, we could already tell that it wasn't going to be simple. The riverbanks were lined with what Nacho and José Luis referred to as *jimbale,* dense stands of thorn-bearing reeds, and it was clear that if we were going to get anywhere we would have to leave the river itself to find higher, and presumably more open, ground. The river looped its way up a valley that ran approximately 350 degrees north-northwest. We decided to walk west until we hit rising ground, and then to follow a 350-degree compass course until we were ready to return to the river in the evening.

This was the plan, but it rapidly became apparent that setting a compass course and following it were two different things. We were soon hacking our way around swamps, bogs, and interminable patches of *jimbale.* As we got farther and farther from the river without finding the rising ground we were looking for, we began—almost unconsciously—to bend around to the northwest. As we did so, I was struck by the realization that in the forest there were no reference points, nothing to hold on to, nothing to tell us how far we'd come or how far we still had to go. I stopped and looked around. The light was murky, the humidity oppressive, and what tall trees there were were buried in vines or in strangler figs. I looked over at Nacho, who, wielding his machete, had been leading the way. He was pouring with sweat.

"*Llano inundable,*" he pronounced, "seasonal flood plain. But, at last we're in the jungle, and our backpacks will only get lighter from here!"

Archie laughed.

"You have to understand," he said, "that both Nacho's parents come from Spain. He's conquistador, pure conquistador. He's Hernan Cortés driving his exhausted troops across the Petén."

Nacho looked pleased. He did have the face of an ascetic, a face that might have been painted by El Greco—gaunt cheeks, high cheekbones. He was the driving force behind the trip. I wondered what I was in for.

After several hours of walking, Archie's legs began to cramp and we ground to a halt in the middle of the interminable swamp. We gave up on returning to the river, cleared a campsite out of the tangled vines, slung the hammocks, and started a fire with the least-damp wood we could locate. Pancho and Elías filled our various pots and canteens with swamp water the color of apple juice. We were all severely dehydrated, so we purified the water with a silver nitrate solution, added some Gatorade that Archie had brought, and drank the foul combination.

As we sat around eating a supper of freeze-dried chili, Pancho asked Tom if he would tape them, as Pancho put it, "eating American food." Tom got out his camera and obligingly taped Pancho and Elías standing stiffly, their spoons poised over steaming packages of plastic.

I asked Tom what kind of work he did when he was at home.

"I make a lot of MTV-style videos," he told me. "I do work for a Seattle punk band called Nasty Mix."

Twilight arrived around five o'clock, and soon thereafter the birds and insects began their crepuscular rounds. Overhead an oropendola, a huge oriolelike bird, began to sing, its trill sounding like water dripping into a pool from a great height. Archie slapped a mosquito, examined it, and announced that it was from the genus *Anopheles,* which carries malaria.

A light rain began to fall. I pulled the plastic over my mosquito net and, exhausted, got into my hammock. I dozed off while listening to the popping sound made by huge drops of water falling onto the jungle leaves. An hour or two later, however, I suddenly awoke to the sound of a large animal prowling in the underbrush. It was closest to Pancho and Elías who, having refused hammocks, had built themselves a bed of palm fronds and draped their sheet of plastic over it. I heard them talking nervously among themselves. Suddenly, they switched on their flashlight. The animal, whatever it was, froze.

"Nacho," Elías called out in a nervous voice, *"aquí los tigres no comen la gente, verdad?"* The jaguars around here don't eat people, right?"

Nacho got out of his hammock and swept the forest edge with his flashlight. Nothing. Five minutes later, after we were all back in our hammocks, the creature got up, a mere ten or fifteen yards away, and ambled off into the forest.

From the size of the animal and the way it moved, the consensus was that it had been a jaguar. I lay back in my hammock and thought about these large cats. Once found from Argentina to Arizona, jaguars are the largest cats in the world after lions and tigers. Although in the Lacandón they seldom exceed 120 pounds, in parts of the Amazon they grow to 300 pounds and almost six feet in length. Their curiosity is legendary and they are said frequently to follow people in the jungle without the humans' knowing it. In his book *Los Mamíferos de Chiapas (The Mammals of Chiapas)*, Miguel Álvarez del Toro, the dean of Chiapas mammologists, describes being awakened in his hammock one night by the sensation of hot air blowing across his face. He opened his eyes to see a jaguar peering at him through his mosquito net. With this strange image in mind, I fell back to sleep.

The next morning we set out east in search of the elusive San Pedro. After we'd walked for an hour or two, Nacho stopped and examined some hoofed tracks.

"Collared peccaries," he said, referring to a species of native American wild pig.

I knew that Nacho was doing his master's research on peccaries, and I asked if these were the pigs he was studying.

"No, they're not," he answered. "There're two kinds of peccaries in the Lacandón: collared and white-lipped. I'm studying the white-lipped."

"How are they different?"

"The collared peccary is a small, adaptive animal that lives in a wide variety of habitats from Arizona all the way down through South America. The white-lipped is something else. The white-lipped grow to as much as a hundred pounds and have sharp tusks. They travel in herds of up to several hundred and only live in the deep forest. It's rare to see a herd, but they can be extremely dangerous. If we come across one, make for the nearest tree."

"Both collared and white-lipped peccaries are members of the family Tayassuidae," Archie added. "They split off from the Old World pigs some twenty million years ago, after one of their ancestors trotted across the Bering Strait. It's an interesting case of parallel evolution. Up until the Pleistocene, the period of the ice ages, there were a half dozen peccary species knocking around the New World, including a long-legged peccary. But the Pleistocene was a tumultuous period during which a large number of North American mammals—including the New World elephants, New World horses, and the saber-toothed tiger—became extinct. The Pleistocene winnowed out the peccaries until only the present species survived."

"What are the differences between the Old World pigs and the peccaries?" I wondered.

"There are morphological differences," Archie said, "such as scent glands and the ridge of coarse hair that bristles off peccaries' backs, but there are also behavioral differences, most notably, in the case of the white-lippeds, herding behavior."

Was the white-lipped peccary the so-called *jabalí*, the wild boar of Central American forests?

"*Jabalí* is the term used in Spain for the Old World wild boar," Nacho answered. "People use the word *jabalí* for white-lipped peccaries for the same reason that they use the Spanish words *tigre* for jaguar and *león* for puma. The Spanish saw everything in terms of their own experience. I prefer the word *peccary* to the word *jabalí*. The word *peccary* is derived from a Carib Indian word."

Nacho's point made me think of how jarring to the Spanish was the intellectual shock caused by the flora and fauna of the New World. The Bible was the source of most European knowledge of the natural world in the fifteenth and sixteenth centuries. In *The Columbian Exchange,* Alfred Crosby observes that the Bible explained "the heavens, earth, angels, plants, animals, and men." Most particularly, the Bible told the story of the Flood and of Noah's Ark, on which, Europeans believed, the breeding stock for all animal life had been preserved. That was fine for Europe and for the limited parts of Asia and Africa known to Europeans. They contained a limited number of species. But how to explain the myriad creatures of the New World? How to explain iguanas, anteaters, jaguars, tapirs, and tree sloths—creatures that, says Crosby, by their very existence "called into question the entire Christian cosmogony"?

On a practical level, the Spanish got around this problem by simply treating the New World as a religious renegade. The Spanish crown equipped the conquistadors with a document that they were legally obliged to read to the Indians before engaging them in battle. The document, the *requerimento,* reiterated the Bible-based view of creation and erected on it a legal and logical superstructure that essentially glossed over the huge differences between the Old and New Worlds. It began (as translated by William Gates in his 1937 editon of Landa's *Relación de las Cosas de Yucatán*):

> God, our Lord, One and Eternal, created heaven and earth, and a man and a woman, from whom you and I, and all the people of the world, were and are descendants. But because of the multitude thus begotten out of them in the past five thousand and more years since the world was created, it was necessary that some should go to one place and others to another, and divide into many kingdoms and provinces, since in one alone they could not sustain themselves. ...

The *requerimento* reminded the Indians that God had made Saint Peter "lord and superior of all the people in the world," and threatened to destroy them if they did not submit to the "Catholic kings of Castile." The point of this document, which was addressed to Indians but might as well have been addressed to the whole of New World life, was a stated refusal to understand, a public reiteration of the biblical explanation of creation in the face of a teeming strangeness that it could not explain. On some functional, administrative level the *requerimento* must have proved satisfactory. It is always easier to deny than to understand. But on a more profound level, it did no more than paper over the gaping hole that the discovery of the New World had torn in the European worldview. Unable to reconcile the fauna of the New World with the biblical stories of Noah's preservation of all life, subsequent European theologians were forced to postulate all sorts of heretical theories of multiple creations, which, as Crosby points out, were not fully ironed out until Darwin's time.

* * *

Around midday we reached the river again. It was now about fifteen yards wide and a beautiful, clear shade of green. Fish two feet long were cruising its submerged sandbars.

"At least here we have fishes and water," said Nacho in charmingly fractured English. "We won't die, and that is important."

That night we camped on a bluff above the river. While we were sitting around after dinner, Elías suddenly asked if there were *duendes* in the United States.

"Of course there aren't," answered Nacho impatiently.

"A friend of mine saw one on a sandbank along the Lacantún," Elías observed.

Pancho nodded in grave agreement.

I asked what a *duende* was.

"The *duende* is something you hear about throughout Mesoamerica," Archie answered. "He's a little bearded man with his feet on backward who travels with peccary herds. What happens is that someone goes out hunting peccaries and doesn't come back. His friends go out looking for him and find him wandering aimlessly in the forest. He's been enchanted by a *duende*. He's lost all sense of time and space."

I thought about *duendes* and this association with peccaries. Nacho had already told me that white-lipped peccaries only live in large unbroken tracts of tropical forest; and to me this made the white-lipped peccaries seem like something the Germans might call a *Waldgeist,* a "forest spirit." Álvarez del Toro claims that when peccary herds accidentally stumble out of the forest—into a ranch, for instance—they become disoriented and confused. Inside the forest, by contrast, white-lippeds have a system of trails that connect their favorite eating grounds and a strict order of travel: young and middle-aged pigs in front, females with sucklings in the middle, the biggest males and females next, and finally the oldest pigs. The peccaries even use mudbaths in hierarchical sequence, and there are persistent, although probably apocryphal, stories of a reddish-colored peccary leader. There was something beguiling in all this, the hint of a seductive, parallel, *duende*-ruled world that might tempt you to forget your own.

I looked over at Pancho and Elías. Their fears hadn't been eased by Nacho's scoffing. For the first time I noticed that they were more nervous about our situation than we were.

The next day, afraid to stray too far from the river, we hacked our way through reeds, vines, and what looked like lush walls of house plants. By the end of the day, exhausted, we stumbled to a halt under a huge straight-as-an-arrow mahogany rising directly from the riverbank. As we were making camp, the sky darkened and thunder began to roll. No sooner had we tied down our plastics than the wind gusted violently. Suddenly we heard a loud ripping of branches and tearing of vines, and then an earth-shaking crash as a tree hit the earth on the other side of the ridge we had just crossed. A moment later, another tree smashed to the ground just out of sight across the river.

I looked apprehensively at the mahogany above us, but there really wasn't anywhere to go.

"It's going to be a long night," I said.

"Why?" Nacho said. "This is nothing."

Just then the wind gusted and there was a loud crack overhead. I jumped under a small tree, my hands over my head. Nacho landed on top of me. A log-sized branch fell just where we'd been sitting.

"I'm going to get rid of that guy up there," Nacho said. "I told him to drop it directly on the fire."

We took the next day off. In the morning I lay listening to the roaring of a group of howler monkeys in some nearby trees and thinking of how strange it was to be in the middle of the rain forest. Although we kept ourselves busy, we could all feel the looming presence of the forest around us. It was not entirely comforting. Two days of slashing through thorns and vines had left me with the sensation that the forest was resisting our entry. We were bulling our way in, and already the forest had exacted a price. We'd lost our sense of distance. End-of-the-day debates over how far we'd traveled elicited wildly varying estimates. Although we knew we were still on the San Pedro, only two days out we no longer knew where.

As the howlers swung off through the treetops, two scarlet macaws took over, squabbling raucously overhead while an invisible toucan croaked away across the river. When a large and very noisy crested currasow flew to a branch over the water and began to cluck incessantly, I decided it was time to get up.

José Luis was already in the river taking his morning bath. Suddenly, he let out a shout. He was surrounded by a school of minnows and one of them had bit him on what the Mexicans call the *huevos*. Archie, who has a doctorate in tropical aquatic ecology, ambled to the riverside, peered at the little fish, and pronounced them tiny relatives of the piranha.

"In Costa Rica they get big enough to eat the ticks off cattle. Ranchers drive their herds into the streams so that the fish will clean them off," he said.

Archie spotted one of the larger fish that we had seen cruising the sandbars the day before.

"*Brycon guatemalensis*," he said, "commonly known as the *macabíl*. It's a fish that subsists on the fruit and flowers that fall from the trees."

We decided to go fishing. We had hooks and line and, after breakfast, scattered into the forest in search of reed poles. When Nacho returned, however, he was carrying not a pole but a basketball-sized termite nest.

"This is the way the Lacandóns fish," he said. "They break up termite nests and throw pieces into the river. It whets the fishes' appetites."

But since the *macabiles* seemed to be the largest fish in the river, we took Archie's suggestion and baited our hooks with dried fruit. I began with a dried apple. It attracted no interest. I switched to an apricot, which attracted only slightly more. However, the prunes worked like a charm, and soon we had a string of a dozen fish, the largest of which we made into a soup. As I sat eating, a *macabíl* head loomed up out of my bowl. Archie noted its heavy rounded teeth, which he said were designed to crack open seeds and nuts. Taking my cue from the New England taste for cod tongues and cheeks, I pried off its powerful jaw muscles and ate them. They were delicious.

* * *

The land finally began to rise after we left camp the next day, our fourth under way, and despite the constant recurrence of vines and *jimbales,* we began to get patches of respectable high jungle. Tracks ran everywhere, including the three-toed, dessert-plate-sized tracks of the tapir. We hadn't seen much wildlife, however—not many mammals anyway, a scarcity that Nacho attributed to the fact that in the rain forest ninety percent of mammals are nocturnal.

Still fascinated by white-lipped peccaries, I asked Nacho if they, too, were nocturnal.

"They're both diurnal and nocturnal," he responded. "They follow their own schedule."

White-lipped peccaries have few enemies beyond jaguars and man—and because a peccary herd is so dangerous, even jaguars are leery of them. Álvarez del Toro reports that a jaguar takes a peccary by shadowing the herd until it can pick off a straggler. It then leaps into a tree with its prey. The peccaries respond by going into a frenzy, surrounding the tree and attacking and destroying anything they can find, including, sometimes, each other. The jaguar typically waits them out in the tree, although this can take a day or longer.

Nacho suddenly froze at the bottom of a muddy *brook.* The ground was covered with fresh peccary tracks.

"I smell peccaries," he said.

I didn't smell a thing. I assumed that Nacho was putting me on. But as I listened, I began to hear a peculiar scuffling and snapping in the distance. We put down our packs and crept to the top of a ridge in front of us. From the ridge top the scuffling mixed with a low grunting and a knocking that sounded like the wooden percussion blocks in an orchestra.

"Those're their tusks clacking against their molars," Nacho said. "It's a big herd, white-lippeds, and they're headed our way."

Thanks to the thick underbrush, the peccary herd was still invisible, but the sounds emanated from a wide arc of jungle directly in front of us. We decided to split up and approach the herd from its two flanks. Archie, José Luis, and Elías went one way, Nacho, Pancho, and I, the other. So eager were we to see the pigs that we abandoned Tom, fumbling, trying to get his video camera unsheathed.

As we split up, Nacho reminded us to keep a tree in mind in case the pigs charged.

We crept forward until we could make out a few of the peccaries rooting around on the forest floor. They were broad-shouldered, torpedo-shaped creatures. Their snouts were pink, their noses white, and the rest of their bodies black. A line of spiny bristles stood in a ridge along their backs. No sooner did we catch sight of the peccaries, however, than the peccaries caught sight of us. Pancho, Nacho, and I scrambled into the lower branches of our chosen trees, but when the pigs edged nervously away, we climbed down and followed. Just then the peccaries noticed Archie and his group, did a mass about-face, and stampeded back toward us. The forest reverberated with hoofbeats and tearing shrubbery. I looked around. The tree I had just descended was ten yards behind me. The next one I'd been aiming at was at least five yards ahead—in the direction of the charging peccaries. Out of the corner of my eye I spotted a closer tree, its trunk about a foot in diameter at the butt. It was wound with a thick vine, and its top was obscured by the foliage above. Not a very big tree, but not having a lot of choice or time, I leapt for it anyway. No sooner had I gotten a few feet off the ground than the whole tree crumbled. I collapsed in a heap on the forest floor, dead branches showering all around me. Fortunately for me, the noise was tremendous. In the end, the peccaries may have been more frightened than I was. They'd surely seen a lot of strange creatures in their lives—jaguars, snakes, caimans, God-knows-what-else—but I doubt they'd ever seen a gringo journalist fall out of a rotten tree. For a moment longer the forest was filled with a confused thrashing and crashing. Then they were gone.

I picked myself up off the ground. Nacho came over, eyes glowing.

"That's an orgasm for me," he said.

"How many do you think there were?" I asked.

"At least eighty."

"Have you seen a herd like it before?"

"To see a herd of white-lipped peccaries is a very rare occurrence," he said, still beaming. "I've seen only one other herd in my life, near Bonampak, and it was only half the size of this one."

The pigs left a powerful musty odor behind them, like too many people locked in a small room. Nacho offered a granola bar—a considerable bribe, given our stores of food—to anyone who could find peccary scat for his studies. The only thing we turned up, though, was a freshly killed, scoured-out armadillo carcass.

"A jaguar or a puma probably got it last night," Nacho said.

When we turned to pick up our packs, I realized that in the process of pursuing the peccaries, I had completely lost my sense of direction. I clutched instinctively at the compass around my neck, but quickly realized that it was useless. The compass could tell me which way was north, but not how to get back to the gear. I was seized with an irrational panic. The forest had already robbed us of our ability to gauge distance. Now it was threatening our sense of direction as well. I looked at the wall of uniform green around me and thought of the twin components of our navigation—the compass and the river valley—realizing what a flimsy construct they were. As I did so, I had a vision of a *duende,* his feet on backward, galloping away.

The river had remained our touchstone. Every day we cut away in search of high ground and every night we returned to it. As long as it was there, we knew we were headed in the right direction. Two nights after we saw the peccaries, we returned to the river only to find that it had fragmented into a half dozen streams of similar size wandering in a westerly direction across a swampy plain. Our maps were no help. They showed the San Pedro as a single channel all the way to its source near Indio Pedro. We had a choice of either following our compasses in the northwesterly direction we knew we wanted to follow, or staying with what we hoped was the main channel of the river. Since we did not really know where we were on the map, a compass course seemed the riskier of the two choices. We chose the river.

But following the now-braided river valley meant contending with more swamp, so we decided, at Archie's suggestion, to speed our progress by dividing into two leapfrogging groups of three machetes each. Tom was granted dispensation in order to continue taping. While one group cut, the other rested, then carried their packs to the trailhead and took over the cutting.

I worked with Archie and Elías. Our machetes rang, each with its own tone, and as Archie cut he sang the song of the Jabberwock:

> 'Twas brillig, and the slithy toves
>   Did gyre and gimble in the wabe;
> All mimsy were the borogoves,
>   And the mome raths outgrabe.

> "Beware the Jabberwock, my son!
>   The jaws that bite, the claws that catch!
> Beware the Jubjub bird, and shun
>   The frumious Bandersnatch!"

Elías listened, uncomprehending, to the extraordinary cadences. When Archie had completed the rest of the poem, Elías paused for a minute and then said, "*Archie está alegre. Alegre en su corazón.* Archie is happy. Happy in his heart."

The swamp seemed to guide us backward into the heart of the forest. Woven spiders' nests spiraled irresistibly inward to the dark undersides of rotting logs. A group of angry red army ants were looting the larvae out of a wasp's nest. A humming that sounded like an electrical generating plant in the distance originated from a bees' nest. Around midday we came upon a troop of spider monkeys in the top of a huge tree supported by dinosaur-fin buttresses. A group of four adults, two carrying babies, and one adolescent, they chattered and screamed, shook branches, and threw sticks.

"*Oh, estan muy bravos, muy enojados,*" Elías said. "They're very brave, very angry."

New World monkeys are considered remarkable for their uniformity, at least when compared to the monkeys of Africa, motherland of primates. Primatologists think that all New World monkeys are probably descended from a small population of African monkeys who migrated to South America during the Eocene, forty or fifty million years ago, perhaps on a floating island. They believe this to be the case both because the fossil ancestors of South American monkeys are strikingly similar to then contemporary African species, and because South America, which originally calved off from Africa, was then much closer to Africa than to North America. If African monkeys did cross into a monkeyless New World during the Eocene, it might have been their last chance to get aboard. The two continents continued to drift apart for tens of millions of years thereafter, until South America finally arrived at its present proximity to North America. During all this period, South America developed on its own, in biological isolation from the rest of the world, including North America. Such creatures as tree sloths, armadillos, and the true anteaters existed in South America and nowhere else.

Although made and broken several times earlier, the present land bridge between North and South America was made some three million years ago, and an exchange of species began that continues to the present day. Not only the monkeys but many other animals as well worked their way northward into the unbroken belt of tropical forest that once covered the Lacandón, the Petén, and the southern Yucatán peninsula. Among the most successful of the northward-bound South American migrants was the porcupine, which made it all the way to the Arctic.

A short while after we left the spider monkeys, Archie came across some fresh tapir tracks and, next to them, a pile of dung that looked just as if it had come off the stable floor. I remarked on the similarity to horse manure.

"That's because the horse and the tapir are closely related," Archie said. "In the fossil record, the horse was a tiny three-toed creature that browsed, like the tapir, on leaves. As it evolved, two of its toes shrank and the third enlarged into the hoof."

Of all the animals we might have come across in the forest, I most wanted to see a tapir, although I knew it was unlikely because the tapir is notoriously shy. A tailless, thick-skinned animal that grows to six hundred pounds, the tapir—at least Baird's tapir of Central and South America—is nearly amphibious. When threatened, it makes directly for water. Álvarez del Toro says it sometimes sleeps there, with only its long nose visible above the surface. Up until the period of Pleistocene extinctions, the tapir was widely distributed in the tropics, but now only three species survive, three in Central and South America and one in Malaysia. Because its habitat is disappearing so quickly, Baird's tapir is an endangered species.

When we caught up with Nacho and his crew, he told us that they were sure they had heard a tapir crashing off into the underbrush, although they hadn't actually seen it.

"The Lacandóns call the tapir *caxir tzimin,*" Nacho said, "which means jungle horse. They believe that tapirs were the horses of the ancient Maya and that the ancient Maya kept them tethered by their tails. The ancient world came to an end when Kisin, the Earthlord, created a terrible earthquake. The tapirs were so frightened that they ran off without their tails."

Struck by all the strange creatures we were now encountering, I asked Nacho what he felt was distinctive about the fauna of the Lacandón.

"We don't know enough about it to say," he answered. "But it seems clear that the Lacandón is a place of Pleistocene refuge."

"Pleistocene refuge?"

"During the lowering of global temperatures that accompanied the ice ages, the tropical flora and fauna that until then had been found across wide sections of the globe survived in only relatively small pockets. This means that in places such as the Lacandón ancient species have survived that are extinct elsewhere."

As I picked up my machete and prepared to cut off into the swamp, I tried to imagine what this meant in terms of the forest we were traveling through. For one thing, I knew it meant that the process of evolution, broken in the temperate latitudes by the ice ages, had continued unabated in rain forests. In that sense places like the Lacandón serve as repositories of the accumulated possibilities of life on earth. Since climate change—perhaps even radical climate change—is a given in the future, the ability of the earth to make the necessary adjustments might well depend on the degree of preservation of its biological heritage. It struck me that the ignorance which has allowed the destruction of the forests is not significantly different from the ignorance epitomized in the Spanish *requerimento.* Just as the Spanish confused their own cosmogony with truth, so have we confused the needs of our industrial society with the needs of the earth itself.

For three days we wandered across the swamp, until the river channel we were following had shrunk to a small, meandering stream. At that point we gave up on it and decided to cut north across the braided river system until we hit either the main river or the rising ground that would indicate the eastern edge of the valley that held Indio Pedro. At the end of the day we finally located high ground consistent with the valley edge we'd been looking for. Although we weren't sure how we would find Indio Pedro, we hoped that in the next day or two we'd come across some sign of human habitation that would lead us there.

That night, exhausted, we camped between the swamp and the unexplored ridge above us, right on top of what looked like a game trail. Nacho had some sections of vine strapped to the back of his pack. He chopped them up and brewed them in water to make cups of reddish, slightly sweet tea. After dinner, owls hooted and whistled. José Luis recognized one that he said subsisted on fruit bats. Just after darkness had fallen, and we got into our hammocks, it rained briefly and thereafter the forest was filled with the popping of raindrops and a mysterious snapping of twigs.

Around nine, Archie was up pointing his flashlight into a tree. Some creatures were making what sounded like loud Bronx cheers. Archie couldn't see them, but decided they were kinkajous. No sooner had he gotten back into his hammock than three or four coatimundis decided to raid the camp. Long-nosed, long-tailed members also of the raccoon family, they squealed and snarled for an hour, vociferous in their indignation at finding us blocking their path. After they finally left, I heard the low grunting of a herd of white-lipped peccaries passing in the distance.

At three I woke to the sense of a very large creature passing fifteen yards from my hammock. It was moving like a tank, brushing aside large branches and snapping small logs underfoot. Inside my hammock, inside my mummy bag, I felt like a trussed chicken in a rotisserie. My mouth went dry and my palms grew wet. Reason flew out the window. If this was a jaguar, I was cooked. I grabbed my flashlight, groped for the edge of my plastic canopy, and pointed the beam in the direction of the noise. The light from the flashlight's little AA batteries barely dented the night, nor did it frighten off whatever beast it was, which continued on its cumbersome way. I saw Elías and Pancho's light go on. It was some consolation to know that no matter how spooked I was, they were spooked a hundred times over. I called out, asking if they'd heard the animal. Pancho answered that they had.

Pancho's English had been coming along nicely. He had begun to speak in memorized sentences rendered in cadences not unlike those used by automated directory assistance telephone operators.

"Peter," he called out.

"What?" I answered.

"Be careful," he warned.

The rising ground put us in good spirits, and we spent the next day in relatively open terrain, alert for signs of Indio Pedro. On our second day, however, the drainage of the irregular ridge we were following suddenly reversed. Instead of running west toward where we imagined Indio Pedro to be, the streams we passed were running east. The answer to this puzzle became apparent toward the end of the day, when we came down off the ridge, traversed a dense swamp, and emerged, blinking like pupfish, on the banks of a wide river. The water was clear and quiet, the banks lush and draped with heavy fruit-bearing foliage. Parrots whistled and squawked from high trees. We made camp, set aside thoughts of caimans, and swam. Afterward we worked on a theory to explain the anomalous river. We decided we'd overshot Indio Pedro and had traveled both farther north and farther east than we'd imagined. This was the Lacanjá, the next river east of the San Pedro. There was nothing else of its size. It flowed down from the Lacandón village of the same name. Lacanjá, Nacho told us, meant "serpent water" in Lacandón Maya.

After the initial elation, however, I began to wonder. The river was so wide and so beautiful that it seemed as if there should have been someone on it. I half expected to see a dugout canoe filled with happy Lacandóns come around the bend and lead us out of the jungle. Having formulated the thought, I realized that what was really bothering me was the feeling that we had all agreed too readily on our location. Perhaps it was easier to do that than to admit that we didn't really know where we were. I took stock of our situation. We were now ten days out, and although we were getting low on staples ranging from sugar to cigarettes, we still had five days of food left. Pancho and Elías were a problem, however. They'd not only become convinced that we didn't know where we were going (a not unreasonable conclusion), but they'd eaten their twelve days of lunches within the first week. When I'd asked them why, Elías had answered that they'd been dying of hunger.

"With you gringos it's different," he'd said. "You're used to not eating. But we're accustomed to three good meals a day."

I had to laugh at this formulation. But we'd been breaking off bits of our diminishing stock of granola bars ever since to share with them at lunch.

I spent a tormented night. Sand flies small enough to get through the mesh of my mosquito net feasted on me until dawn. When I got up, complaining, Nacho looked up from his cup of coffee and blandly told me that sand flies were the carriers of leishmaniasis, "chiclero's disease," a protozoan infection that caused persistent face ulcers and, left untreated, could lead to death through secondary infection.

Nacho was studying the map, revising our route. Directly across the Lacanjá the map showed a long ridge, the Sierra Cojolita, which paralleled the river and eventually passed directly behind Bonampak. It seemed clear that if we could stay in the narrow corridor between the ridge and the river, it would be impossible to get lost. Bonampak, moreover, was not far—although how far was a question, since we didn't know where we were on the Lacanjá.

After breakfast we walked upstream until we came to a large tree that had fallen most of the sixty or seventy feet across the river. We covered the last six feet with a pole-and-rope bridge and then gingerly, with our packs unbuckled in case we fell, traversed the river.

The far bank was covered with a mangrovelike swamp, which we cut through until the ground began to rise toward a ridge. Praying silently that this was, in fact, the Sierra Cojolita, we turned northwest.

The ridge was a welcome change. Not only were its slopes open, but the summit consisted of a remarkable uplifted band of stone that ran 320 degrees northwest—our revised direction of travel—in a line straight enough to have come off an engineer's board. Five or six yards wide, this stone band arched over hilltops, dove under streams, and always reappeared on the other side. The most extraordinary thing about this ridge, however, was that it wasn't entirely natural. Although covered with leaf mold and broken by trees, we could easily see that it had been built up and that its edges had been squared off with cut stone. My sense that we'd arrived in an area that should have been populated hadn't been entirely misplaced. It had been populated—a thousand years ago. Somehow, we'd stumbled onto a *sacbe*, an ancient Maya road.

Discovering this road gave rise to conflicting emotions. On the one hand, we knew that we were in a sector of the jungle that had once been considered habitable, and that the road presumably led somewhere. On the other hand, where did it lead? To Bonampak? Or to the ruins of some undiscovered city where we would all starve to death among crumbling temples and broken stelae? Ultimately, as long as the road took us in the direction we thought we should be traveling, it didn't seem to matter. Like the trip itself, it was a gamble.

As we proceeded along the ridge, the contrast between the road and the surrounding wilderness made me think of the supposed incongruity of the Classic-era Maya having raised a civilization out of the rain forest. In Western European thought, civilizations are supposed to arise in the dry lands, preferably those of southwest Asia. According to the formula, rain forests are only suited to the crudest slash-and-burn agriculture. The academic logic has therefore been that milpa agriculture, the basis of the Maya civilization, is too simple a productive unit to have supported a superstructure of any sophistication.

Even setting aside the question of raised-field agriculture, it was clear to me that the idea of milpa agriculture as unsophisticated was based on ignorance. In his doctoral study of traditional Lacandón agriculture, the ecologist James Nations discovered that instead of simply burning a patch of jungle, planting corn for a few years, and then moving on—the cliché view of jungle farming—the Lacandóns took a much more complicated approach that both mimicked the ecological complexities of the surrounding forest and took advantage of the peculiar dynamics of forest disturbance. Immediately after burning, the Lacandóns protected the soil by planting root crops and fast-growing trees. Then they planted their corn. Rather than stopping with the corn, however, the Lacandóns proceeded to plant more than eighty different food and fiber crops in a sequence dictated by the flowering of natural species in the forest. In order to reduce the possibility of the spread of plant-specific diseases, these crops, which included beans, sweet potatoes, onions, pineapple, chili peppers, bananas, cotton, and tobacco, were grown in isolated bunches. They were also grown in layers, with plants at different levels above the soil and roots at different levels in the soil, thus creating ecological niches to which each plant was best suited. By the time the field was exhausted, the trees had grown high enough to form what the Lacandóns call a *pak che kol,* a "planted tree garden," containing cacao, citrus, rubber and other trees, and shrubs; it would not only serve as an orchard but would also attract wild animals, thus making the recuperating milpa a source of game until it was ready for cutting and burning again.

Was there any connection between present-day Lacandón agricultural techniques as described by Nations and the agricultural techniques of the ancient Maya? It seems likely, if only judging from comments of Colonial-era Spanish chroniclers who ventured among the independent Maya of the Lacandón and marveled at how much better fed they were than their highland counterparts.

But that opens the whole question of who the present-day Lacandóns are. Until recently people assumed that they were the direct descendants of the Classic Maya, but subsequent research has proved that this is only half true. Cholti-speaking descendants of the Classic

Maya did survive in the Lacandón for almost two hundred years after the Conquest. They had a fortress capital in the middle of Lake Miramar, less than twenty miles from where we were hiking, that had stone houses, plazas, and pyramids. But as part of the same 1695 campaign that defeated the Itzá city of Tayasal in Lake Petén Itzá, the Spanish finally subdued the Lacandón Cholti and removed them to the highlands. Among their possessions, the Spanish found a missal and a breviary belonging to Domingo de Vico, Las Casas' disciple, whose murder had brought a close to the Verapaz experiment a hundred and fifty years earlier.

It was just at the time of the conquest of the Cholti Lacandóns in the southern end of the forest that the descendants of the modern Lacandóns began arriving in the north. Migrants from across the Usumacinta, these people were part of a gradual migration of northern Yucatec-speaking Maya into abandoned areas of the south. Gradually, the Yucatec Lacandóns spread over what had been Cholti territory, but on a lower level of economic development. The Cholti had had cities. The Yucatec Lacandóns lived in isolated family compounds deep in the forest, avoiding contact with outsiders. It wasn't until the 1940's that these Lacandóns, in response to growing migration into the jungle, began to coalesce into the two principal towns in which they now live: Nahá, in the north, and Lacanjá, our destination, in the south.

Lacanjá and Nahá are sufficiently different to raise some interesting questions. Nahá, under the spiritual leadership of a ninety-year-old elder named Chan K'in Viejo, has retained its traditional non-Christian beliefs and in many ways seems both a town and a community. Lacanjá, on the other hand, lost its spiritual heritage when its religious leader died in the 1940's and an itinerant Catholic priest told the Lacandóns that his death resulted from their worshiping false gods. Thereafter the group was spiritually adrift until the late fifties, when a Summer Institute of Linguistics medical missionary named Phillip Baer convinced them of the wonders of becoming Baptists.

Baer and a fellow SIL researcher, William Merrifield, wrote a book about the Lacanjá Lacandóns. The book consists largely of a necrology stretching from the mid-nineteenth century to shortly before the book's publication in 1971. Baer's purpose was to contrast the violence of Lacandón life before his arrival with its relative peacefulness afterward. Life was indeed violent beforehand. Having compiled the vital statistics of 263 Lacandóns, Baer and Merrifield discovered that the average life span of the male Lacandón before their arrival was thirty-three years and that of the average Lacandón woman only slightly longer. They also noted that the largest single cause of death was homicide, and that seventy-five percent of these homicides were the result of feuds over women (the Lacandóns were, and still are, polygamists).

In many ways the most interesting statistic of all, however, is that fully ninety-five percent of the homicides in Baer's surveys took place among the Lacanjá Lacandóns. The northern Lacandóns of Nahá, who successfully resisted years of Baer's efforts to convert them, were, and still are, a much less violent people.

What accounts for the differences between the southern and northern Lacandóns? There is no clear answer to the question, but it is difficult to discount the possibility that, despite their speaking the same Yucatec-based language as the northerners, the southern Lacandóns are at least partly descended from the earlier Cholti-speaking inhabitants of the forest. Geography alone argues for this. The last independent Cholti lived in a region of the southern forest that had been home to a number of the southern Lacandóns before they moved to Lacanjá in the 1960's. For at least fifteen years after their surrender to the Spanish in 1695, the Cholti continued living in this same region under the supervision of friars. Throughout this period the friars busied themselves trying to round up hold-outs and recidivists. That their task was a difficult one is evident from a despairing letter sent by one of the friars (quoted in Victoria Bricker's *The Indian Christ, the Indian King*):

> Nor when we tell them to come together, nor when the captain tells them, nor when we say they must stop painting themselves and come to Mass, and to the women that they must leave off all their wicked ceremonies, the rubbish and painting of their heathendom, telling them this with all love and smiling faces, they do not heed us and if we show anger and tell them that God will punish them and they

will go to hell, they laugh and say they are Lacandóns, and that is their custom, and they laugh at us.

Given this recalcitrance, it is hard not to imagine that some of the Cholti eluded the Spanish dragnet and eventually intermarried with the northern newcomers, losing their language but not their bellicose character.

The forest through which we were walking was at last the beautiful high jungle we'd been hoping for. On the second night after crossing the river, we camped next to a small stream that splashed down over a series of descending rim pools. Huge mahogany trees soared overhead, giving the jungle an open, airy quality. Along the stream banks we found two cacao trees, their yellow-green, grapefruit-sized fruit growing directly out of the trunk.

"*Cacao silvestre,* wild cacao," Nacho noted, "although it's not clear whether the cacao found in the Lacandón is native or introduced by the ancient Maya."

I watched as Pancho and Elías ate the pulp of a fallen pod, carefully spitting out the seeds, which contain the stimulant theobromine.

In the morning, after we left camp, we ran into another troop of spider monkeys. Again, they shrieked and threw branches at us, one of which narrowly missed Tom and his camera.

This raucous demonstration is the same that spider monkeys use to repel jaguars, their primary predators. But this behavior stands in stark contrast to the way the monkeys behave in the face of the still-more-menacing harpy eagle, the world's largest eagle. The harpy eagle is a canopy dweller that drops down on its prey from above. When the monkeys detect its presence they go stony silent, and their silence is understandable. With its double-crested head, huge hooked beak, and seven-and-a-half-foot wingspan, the harpy eagle is a primeval bird, a throwback to another era. The female is larger than the male, grows to twenty pounds, and can handle prey the size of small deer.

Later that day, Archie, Elías, Tom, and I were resting at the trailhead when Pancho arrived and told us that Nacho and José Luis had unknowingly stepped over a fer-de-lance. The snake had been a small one, about fourteen inches, coiled on the trail. This was unwelcome news, since we had to go back over the same section of the trail to retrieve our packs. Eyes glued to the ground, we walked until we reached the packs, then turned and started forward again. Archie lagged behind, however, and after we'd been walking for a few minutes, he stopped and yelled out that a fer-de-lance a foot long was in the trail right in front of him. Either we, too, had walked directly over the snake or it had been lurking by the trailside. As we walked on, a third possibility occurred to me. A six-foot female fer-de-lance gives birth to as many as sixty or seventy foot-long young. The young are potentially as toxic as the adults; if we had threaded our way through the aftermath of such a birthing, we'd been lucky. The action of a fer-de-lance's toxin is hemolytic, which means that it destroys red blood cells and breaks down the walls of the blood vessels. Victims die from massive internal bleeding. Although José Luis had serum in his kit, we couldn't count on its effectiveness.

That afternoon we camped by the side of a winding, fish-filled river. After we'd strung the hammocks, we sat down to discuss our situation. Our lunches were long gone, and after the next morning's breakfast, only one dinner and one breakfast would remain. In an attempt to explain our nonarrival at Bonampak, we'd been recalculating backward the point at which we'd crossed the Lacanjá. It was clear that this no longer made sense and although no one believed our navigational theories any longer, no one had better ideas to propose. Our maps were useless except for the increasingly futile exercise of trying to force the unruly landscape to correspond to map features. Basically, we were lost. Our only consolation was that we knew we'd been traveling in a consistent direction, a direction that we knew would eventually bring us out. When and where was another question. The jungle that had resisted our entry now seemed to be resisting our exit.

We discussed ways of surviving after the food ran out. Fishing seemed the best possibility, but we'd run out of dried fruit, and over the course of the preceding two weeks Pancho and Elías had lost seventeen of our twenty fish hooks. Someone had the idea of converting a hammock to a fish net and Nacho pointed out an evil-looking plant with a swollen root bulb and thorny vines that he said was *barbasco,* a plant used by the Lacandóns, and indeed by indigenous peoples throughout South America, to poison fish. Archie said that *barbasco* contained the same compound as rotenone, a commercial fish poison.

After our discussion ended, I lay back in my hammock. The afternoon was achingly beautiful. A tinamou whistled plaintively in the distance. A ray of light shone through a filigree of palm fronds over the camp and pierced the smoke of our fire before exploding in a pool of burning jade in a corner of the river. The uncanny beauty enhanced my perception of how much more dangerous the forest suddenly seemed. Earlier in the trip, when we thought we knew where we were, when we'd had plenty of food and plenty of time, the forest had been a strange and menacing presence, but still something on the periphery, something on the edge of our consciousness. Now it seemed both more powerful and more animate. I thought of the linguist Bill Hanks's "principle of verticality." The Maya, he said, didn't speak of walking "in" the forest, they spoke of walking "under" the forest. This was because they viewed the forest as a dangerous place, equivalent to being in the underworld. The sacred directions didn't exist in the forest. Therefore things weren't ordered, didn't have their place. As a result, humans were at the mercy of everything from snakebites to the ubiquitous and dangerous *balam* spirits. We were going to have to become a lot more observant, experience the forest on a different level, acknowledge its power. We'd be lucky if it let us go.

That night I slept as if I'd been drugged. I had a recurring dream that I was borne aloft in a bower of vines. It was supremely comfortable. All night long I felt myself falling backward into darkness.

After we set out in the morning, we found a mamey tree. We gathered and ate its sweet, coral-colored fruit, then discarded the pits, although I'd read that they were famine food for the Lacandóns. The Lacandóns pound the pits into a paste, rinse it to get rid of its bitterness, and make the resulting dough into an oily tortilla.

We were still following the *sacbe,* as we had been for the last four or five days. It continued its northwesterly course, rising and falling with the terrain, until, late in the morning, it arrived at a small temple, fifteen feet square. The temple's sharp corners protruded from under a thin layer of leaves and soil. Everywhere, worked stone erupted from the jungle floor. Just where the temple appeared, however, the ridge ended, as did the *sacbe.*

In front of us rose a steep mountain, the largest we'd seen by far. For the first time on the trip, cicadas were singing. This mountain was definitely not on the map—at least not where we had located ourselves. We decided to climb it and see if we could get a view. If the river was still to our west, we might be able to get a glimpse of it. If there were more mountains to the west, we were lost.

It took an hour and a half of hard work to reach the summit. On the top, looking for a ridge from which we'd be able to see the surrounding land, I found a piece of snakeskin lying on a rock ledge. It was five feet long and clearly only a fraction of the snake that had shed it. Archie thought the skin was from a boa. I hoped it wasn't from a bushmaster, a snake that grows to twelve feet, the largest poisonous snake in the Americas.

The view, when we found it, was not encouraging. We were surrounded by mountains—although to our west, over a ridge or two, we thought we could make out a valley. Dissension, building for days, broke out. José Luis, normally taciturn, wanted to bolt north through the mountains in the hopes of reaching a road that we knew was somewhere in that direction. Pancho declared that although he trusted our compasses, he had no faith at all in our maps. He and Elías suggested that it was time for us to split up, for each to go on his own. Archie assured them that if they did this, they'd die. Eventually Nacho brought us around to his position: despite the intervening mountains, we should change our course from northwest to due west and try to reach the valley that we thought we could see in that direction.

It was Elías who spotted the cut sapling. Graying with age, its top had been sliced off with a machete. One cut sapling led to another, two cuts into three, and three into the faintest signs of a trail—the first we'd seen in fourteen days. Over the next ridge the trail became more distinct. Like a torrent gaining force, it pulled us down the mountain. Elías was in the lead. After twenty minutes he stopped and pointed to a young tree that had been cut off six feet above the ground.

"Now I know we're getting close to a settlement," he said. "These are the poles we use to make our roofs."

The path became wider, its shoulders sprouting with yellow flowers. We crossed a newly planted coffee grove, passed a banana tree, and finally arrived at a recently burned-over milpa. A child's dress hung forlornly from a scarecrow frame.

Elías reached down and picked up a piece of sugarcane. He chopped it with his machete and handed me a section. I peeled and began to chew. My mouth gradually filled with the fermented taste of raw cane sugar. It was delicious beyond anything I could imagine. I was struck with the mastery over plants that this farmer had demonstrated and felt something of the awe that hunting people throughout history must have felt for the powers of agriculturalists.

The path led us across a maze of streams bridged by fallen logs, and finally to the edge of a wide green pasture in which a dozen skinny horses were grazing. Two hundred yards away, a line of thatched huts crowned a ridge. Indian women in bright clothing emerged and stared, their hands nervously stroking their jaws. Beyond, a rooster crowed. We all sat down on the edge of the pasture, while Nacho went ahead to negotiate. I leaned back on my pack, felt the soft afternoon breezes waft over me, and marveled at a fat half moon hanging low in the open blue sky.

From our vantage point we watched Nacho introduce himself to the settlement's inhabitants. After a few minutes, we saw him put down his pack and walk up the ridge to a round house with vertical-pole walls and a wide thatched roof. When he reappeared, he waved for us to come join him. We picked up our packs and hiked toward the ridge. Nacho met us by the first of the houses.

"Welcome to Indio Pedro," he said.

Let's just say our surprise was extreme. This meant that we'd been off course ever since we'd left the San Pedro ten days before, that the big river hadn't been the Lacanjá at all. But this only occurred to us slowly. We just stammered and blinked confusedly—newly rescued *duende* victims.

Nacho led us to the round building, where Indio Pedro himself came out to greet us. A Tzeltal Indian of about fifty, he told us that his father had lived on the site before him, and that his grandfather had been a logger who'd died on the banks of the Tzendales.

"Now," he explained, "God is my landlord."

The settlement of Indio Pedro did, in fact, have a certain Robinson Crusoe quality. Next to the house, Don Pedro, as Nacho called him, showed us the horse-powered *panela* mill with which he made his own sugar. Behind the sugar mill was an enormous pile of freshwater snail shells from which he said he extracted the lime for his tortillas. He indicated the horses in the field below and said that he used them to transport his coffee to sell in Lacanjá.

Indio Pedro took us to an open-sided hut in which he said we could hang our hammocks. He pointed across a field toward a bathing pool that he'd dug at the end of a long irrigation ditch. As we walked out over the fields, we felt the afternoon sun warming our backs. I listened to the faint roaring of howler monkeys in the distance. It made me think of foghorns wailing over the ocean.

"Imagine," José Luis said, while sitting in Indio Pedro's bathing pool, "just a few hours ago I was wondering if I'd ever see my wife and children again."

We hired Indio Pedro and one of his horses to take us to Lacanjá, which he said was a full day's walk. When he brought the horse in from the pasture in the morning, its neck was dripping blood from two puncture wounds. Archie said they were the result of a vampire bat bite.

As we set off for Lacanjá, I happened to see Nacho absentmindedly check his watch. Indio Pedro saw him also.

"How many hours are there in your day?" he asked.

The hike to Lacanjá took eight hours. We walked at a breakneck pace, following a pack trail ankle-deep with mud that sucked at our boots every step of the way. Over the course of the day we became strung out along the trail, and in the end, Tom, Elías, and I were the first to arrive. We sat down on the grass in front of a wooden shack that served as the Lacanjá store and began eating potato chips and drinking soda.

A group of Lacandóns gathered around us. These were not the long-haired white-tunicked Lacandóns of lore. These were wiseguy Lacandóns with reflector sunglasses, pointed shoes, and tight trousers. One of them asked Tom where he was from. Tom answered that he was from the state of Washington. Confusing Washington state and the District of Columbia, the wiseguy Lacandón cackled knowingly.

"They smoke pure marijuana in Washington, right?"

This unexpected reception brought to mind the recent history of the Lacandóns. Only four hundred in number, they'd been granted a huge forest reserve in 1971. Ostensibly designed to help preserve the traditional Lacandón way of life, the grant also happened to stream-line the title search process for logging companies who wanted to cut in the jungle. Flattered, showered with trinkets, the Lacandóns began to refer to government representatives as *winik ku sihik t'a k'in*, "the men who give away money." (*T'a k'in*, the Lacandón word for money, literally means "the shit of God"). Many Lacandóns began to hire other Indians to tend their milpas. James Nations estimates that in the mid-seventies, at the time he made his study, only fifteen percent of the Lacandóns still made the traditional milpas.

After Nacho and the others arrived, we set off for a house a mile away that Nacho used as a base for his peccary studies. We planned to spend the night there.

"It took me years to discover that Lacanjá is not a community at all," Nacho told me as we walked. "It's a group of clans accustomed to living separately in the jungle, but thrown together by demo-graphic pressures. The Lacanjá Lacandóns have little sense of com-mon interest. Some, like K'in Bor, are traditional. Some, like the ones down by the store, are not. In general, different clans keep apart."

Lacandóns must be among the most filmed people in the world, and when we got to Nacho's house, we discovered that it was already occupied by a film crew from Seattle come to film an encounter between the Lacandóns and a delegation of tribal leaders from the northwestern United States.

The filmmakers, who had apparently met an indifferent-to-hostile reception when they arrived earlier in the day, were trying to plan their next day's work. They talked about "feelings," and "sensitivity," and "peoples' needs." We were more concerned with such concepts as "dinner," and "hammock," and "sleep."

We fed the film crew that night by adding extra water and making a soup out of the last of our freeze-dried dinners. After we had eaten we sat outside in the twilight while José Luis removed a botfly larva from my arm. Nacho pointed out that the scientific name for this hideous little creature is *Dermatobia hominus,* which he translated as "living below the skin, man-eating." The botfly lays its eggs on a mosquito that introduces the botfly egg under the skin in the process of biting a mammal—in this case myself. There the egg develops into a two-inch larva before emerging to pupate into a fly. I was glad to evict my larva before it got that far. White, about a quarter of an inch long, it came sailing out of my arm and landed on the flap of my front shirt pocket.

While we were seated outside, K'in Obregón, the septuagenarian head of the clan group in which Nacho's house is located, came by for a visit. White-tunicked and barefoot, with a barrel chest, gray hair hanging below his shoulders, and an oriental-looking mustache, I already knew K'in Obregón as one of Phillip Baer's favorite reprobates. Baer claims that Obregón was responsible for three murders, the first committed at age twenty-two when he shot an arrow through the chest of another Lacandón who'd come to steal Obregón's clan's women. In this case, however, Obregón came peacefully, preceded by white-tunicked grandchildren who frolicked in the twilight like wind-born milkweed seeds.

Obregón asked Nacho about our trip. When Nacho told him about all the animals we'd encountered—the *jabalí,* the *coatimundi,* the *faisans* (large turkey-sized birds), and the *macabiles*—K'in Obregón repeated each word with a hushed, exaggerated excitement, as if each creature we'd seen somehow was a sign of great portent. I had the feeling, however, that K'in Obregón's attention was else-where. He kept peering in at the filmmakers, who in the face of our boisterous invasion had retreated to their hammocks. The next day, I gathered, he extorted a watch from them. Someone saw him with it later in the day, proudly strapped upside-down to his wrist.

Later, back in San Cristóbal, I spoke with a member of the delega-tion of Northwest Indians that had been visiting Lacanjá. The man, a six-foot-five-inch, 250-pound Lummi Indian from Washington State named Cha-das-skidum, or Ken Cooper in English, was con-cerned that the Lacandóns were losing their forest and that this would affect their spiritual well-being.

"When they're young," he said, "all indigenous people go into the forest and stay there until the forest speaks to them, until they become part of it. When that happens, the forest shows them how to get out. It's like you guys. You didn't get out of the forest because you were tough or smart. You got out because the forest was ready to let you go."

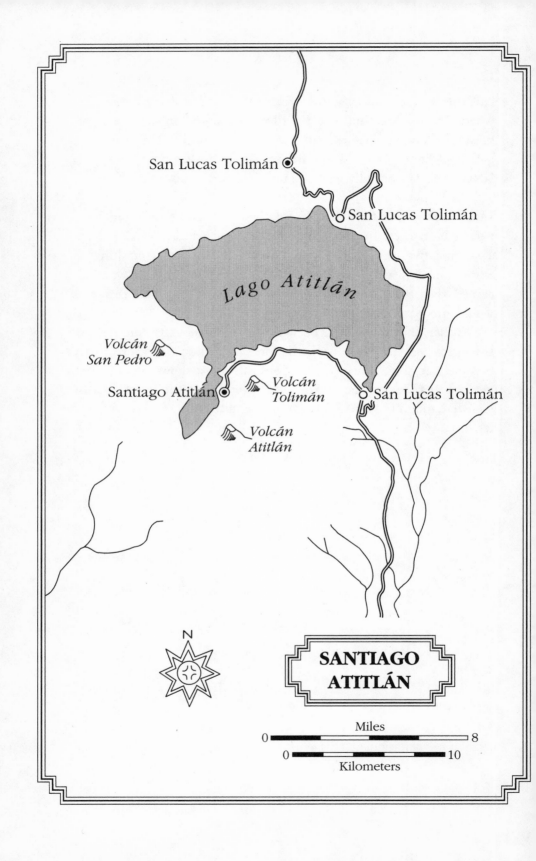

San Lucas Tolimán

San Lucas Tolimán

Lago Atitlán

Volcán San Pedro

Santiago Atitlán

Volcán Tolimán

San Lucas Tolimán

Volcán Atitlán

N

SANTIAGO ATITLÁN

Miles

0 _____ 8

0 _____ 10

Kilometers

CHAPTER 13

Maximón

T HE LIGHT WAS FADING as we passed along the ancient stone
streets of Santiago Atitlán, a Tzutujil Maya town of some
twenty thousand inhabitants situated on an inlet of Lake Atitlán, a
huge, volcano-ringed body of water five thousand feet up in the
western Guatemalan highlands. Santiago Atitlán is a profoundly
Maya town with a reputation for having retained a great deal of its
pre-Columbian heritage. But it is also one of the towns most affected
by Guatemala's violence. After the town sided with the guerrillas,
the army moved in, followed by army-sponsored death squads.
Uncounted *atitecos,* as the residents are called, were assassinated.
Ultimately, the town was left fearful, violence-prone, and divided. I
had come to see how the town's pre-Columbian traditions had survived this holocaust.

It was Tuesday of *Semana Santa*—"Holy Week"—and with me was
Robert Carlsen, a Tzutujil-speaking anthropologist from Colorado
who has worked in Santiago Atitlán for a number of years. Robert was
taking me to an *atiteco cofradía,* the Guatemalan equivalent of a Chiapas *cargo,* to witness the veneration of Maximón, a Maya god whose
name is a conflation of that of the ancient Maya Earthlord, Maam
("grandfather") and the Christian Saint Simón (Simon Peter, the first
apostle). Maximón is represented in Santiago Atitlán by a small,

wooden-masked figure kept hidden in the rafters of a *cofradía* house and traditionally brought down twice a year under highly ritualized circumstances. One of his two appearances takes place during Holy Week, when Maximón participates in Maya ceremonies leading up to Good Friday. Like so many other ceremonies in the Maya region, however, Holy Week serves as a cover for an important pre-Columbian festival. March is the month of the vernal equinox, the point at which the sun is reborn, the rains are about to start—and, the *atitecos* believe, when the world is about to be transformed from female to male. I had come full circle. It was the five lost days again.

Robert paused where we could see both the lake below us and the three towering ten-thousand-foot volcanoes that encircle the town. Waves rippling across the water's surface reflected both the deep purple of sunset and the inky blue-black of approaching night. The tops of the volcanoes glowed a faint rose, while their bases were already enveloped by grays and umbers. Robert explained the town's history to me by peeling back linguistic layers.

Across the inlet he pointed out San Pedro volcano which, he said, was known in Tzutujil as Chichuk, "the elbow," reflecting "the Maya idea of the world as a human body."

Robert then indicated the two huge volcanoes behind the town, Tolimán and Atitlán. "Locally they're called Ltib, 'Grandmother,' and Pral, 'at her children.' The names come from a version of the Popul Vuh still told among the *atitecos*. The *atiteco* Popul Vuh is known as the R'xin Tuj, 'the sweat lodge story.'"

"How similar is the *atiteco* Popul Vuh to the Quiché version?" I asked.

"It's very similar," Robert told me, "but it excludes the underworld incidents. The *atiteco* story contains the concept of Xibalba, but it's very secretive and very taboo."

"Who tells the R'xin Tuj?"

"*Cofradía* members referred to as *escribanos,* scribes, who're often members of storyteller lineages."

"And why is it the 'sweat lodge story'?"

"Sweat lodges are associated with femaleness, with the moon, with birthing, cleansing, and fertility."

Below Chichuk volcano, Robert pointed out the ruins of the pre-

Columbian capital of Chi-ya, "by the water." Before the arrival of the Spanish in 1524, its residents referred to themselves as the Tzinquinaha, the "birdhouse people." Afterward they became *atitecos,* from "Atitlán," meaning the same as Chi-ya but in Nahuatl, the language of the Spanish auxiliary. The present town of Santiago Atitlán was founded in 1575, when Franciscan friars built a massive, stone church and moved the "birdhouse people" across the lake.

"As far as I can tell," Robert added, "after the initial burst of sixteenth-century missionary zeal there were no permanent priests in Santiago Atitlán. The only priests that ever came made occasional visits from the departmental capital of Sololá, across the lake. That's why there's such a strong pre-Columbian element in ceremonies like Maximón's."

We continued our way into town and, not long afterward, came upon a large green building, ballooning incongruously out of the narrow stone streets. Loudspeakers fastened to its upper stories rained down loud hymns. From the door we could see *atitecos* dancing, singing, clapping, and rolling their eyes.

"It's the Elim Church," Robert said, "the largest of the nineteen Protestant evangelical churches that have sprung up in Santiago Atitlán in the aftermath of the violence. The Elim Church is completely Indian. The members have no sense of Protestantism as a world force. In fact, they have no relations with the other churches in town and are very remote from the parent church in Guatemala City. Elim services are like the nineteenth-century ghost dances. They're completely apocalyptic. The members believe that these are the last days, that Christ will return soon, and that the *atitecos* will all die together."

Night had fallen by the time we reached the central market. The vending areas were illuminated by candlelight, and *atiteca* women were sitting cross-legged behind piles of lake fish, the flickering candlelight gleaming in the fishes' eyes and picking out the silver-foil thread in the women's *huipiles.* Above the market we crossed the darkened plaza in front of Santiago Atitlán's cavernous Roman Catholic church. Set high on a wall, the church had a wide arc of steps descending to the plaza.

"The church had fallen into ruins by the mid-nineteen-sixties,"

Robert said. "However, in 1965 it was loaned to the diocese of Oklahoma City, Oklahoma. Since then there've been North American priests in Santiago Atitlán. The most famous, of course, was Stanley Rother, who was killed here in 1982."

I asked what had happened to Stanley Rother.

"It was before I came, but people say that at the height of the violence Rother went on vacation to Oklahoma. He wasn't an activist priest, but while he was in the United States, he spoke to a number of church groups and urged people to write their congressmen concerning the situation in Guatemala. An American parishioner wrote the Guatemalan government that Rother was meddling in politics. The death squads came for Father Rother as soon as he returned. They broke into the parish house at night and killed him with machetes. He seems to have put up a struggle. He was probably smart to do so. If they'd taken him away, they would have tortured him."

The Maximón *cofradía* house was a cinder-block-and-tile structure located above the street at the top of an unmarked flight of stairs. A porch looked out over the lake far below. Robert pushed open the door and we entered a single room twenty by twenty-five feet. Benches lined the walls. Woven straw mats covered the tile floor. From the ceiling hung bananas, mandarins, bromeliad sprays, mahogany-colored squash, and long strands of an orange-fruiting vine. Traditionally, this fruit would have been brought from the coast by a delegation of young, newly married *atiteco* men who made a special trip over the mountains for it. Having abstained from sex for the length of time of this excursion, they and their wives were supposed to have an orgy of it upon their return. The young men's sexual powers came from Maximón.

Although we had arrived at the *cofradía* house early, the room was already crowded. Robert knows the *cofradía* members and, upon our entry, one of the officers rose to greet him. A dignified elderly man, the officer was dressed in a traditional *atiteco* outfit. A red sash cinched a pair of knee-length, red-and-white-striped trousers. Birds, the *Tzinquinaha* totem, were embroidered into a latticework pattern around the trouser hems. On his head, the man wore a tasseled, striped cloth. In Tzutujil, this was known as the *x'cajcoj zut*. "*Zut*" referred to the rectangular shape of the cloth; "*x'cajcoj*" to the toasted-cacao color of the natural brown cotton from which the cloth was once woven.

In a paper that he coauthored with Martin Prechtel, an American artist who once lived in Santiago Atitlán, Robert described the symbolism of the *x'cajcoj zut* as representative of the duties of *atiteco cofradía* members. The *cofradía* members refer to themselves as *ajsamalaj acha,* meaning "working men," and see their primary duty as carrying the sun on its annual round.

The women *cofradía* members were gathered on the opposite side of the room. Their *huipiles* were decorated with the same latticework pattern and embroidered with the same birds as the hems of the men's trousers. Around the blouses' necklines were woven the shapes of the volcanoes surrounding the town. The opening through which the women placed their heads therefore represented the lake itself. Their heads were tightly bound with thin bands of cloth coiled around and around until they formed a disklike brim that seemed to orbit their heads like the rings of Saturn.

"The headbands are called *xk'ap,*" Robert said. "Anything wound in like that is considered female, and is symbolic of the underworld, the fallow, the uterine. You see, the core paradigm of Maya religion is that everything evolves into its opposite. The *atitecos* divide the year into halves: a female half that has to do with gestation, dryness, and death and a male half that has to do with rebirth. The transition between the two is now, at the equinox, just before the rains start, when the world is half male and half female. That's Maximón's power. He's the attraction of opposites: day to night, wet to dry, male to female."

We had taken seats on a bench along a wall, but by ten o'clock it had become so crowded that we were forced to climb up on the bench and stand. A band trooped in, seven young men carrying two guitars, a mandolin, an accordion, a reed pipe, and two drums. Although they wore sashes and traditional *atiteco* trousers, their choice of shirts and hats was more variable. One had on a Mets T-shirt. Another T-shirt read ATLANTIC CITY. A third wore a blue plastic batting helmet ringed with Batman stickers.

The band set up in front of our bench. One of the drums, the *tun,* was a slit log laid horizontally on the ground. The other was a hollowed-out cross section of a tree trunk known as a *k'joum.* When he saw me staring at the instruments, one of the drummers reached into his pocket, produced a cassette, and sold it to me for fifteen quetzales—$3.50. The cassette identified the group as AjTzu'utjila, "The Tzutujils." The title song was *"Bis Kxin Principali,"* "The Lament of the *Principales."* According to the liner notes, the song touched "deep in the hearts of the *principales* of any of the *cofradías,"* and had to do with the sadness that they felt when their year of long service was over.

Another song was *"Mam Ala',"* "The Grandfather Child." "After the invasion and the Spanish domination," the liner notes read, "Tzutujil culture suffered greatly as the result of the imposition of the new religion and the new laws. One of the *naguales* of the time [men of the spirit world] cried bitterly for what was happening to his town:

> "So that you don't forget our culture,
> so that you don't forget our God [*Rilaj Maam*],
> so that you don't forget what is ours,
> this is how we will remember."

Several of the *cofradía* officers began lighting candles and, when they were done, someone extinguished the electric lights. The members of the band commenced singing in high nasal voices while accompanying themselves with trancelike string music. The *k'joum* throbbed underneath. Someone closed the door and the room temperature began to rise rapidly. Beads of moisture were forming on the wall behind me. A small boy fainted.

"They're about to bring down Maximón," Robert said. "They're closing the door because Maximón's sexual power can't be allowed to escape."

An elderly man wearing *cofradía* clothing climbed stiffly onto a tabletop and reached into the rafters.

"That's the *telinel,"* Robert said. "His title derives from the Tzutujil word *telek,* which means "shoulder." He's referred to as 'Maximón's horse' and he's the only one allowed to carry Maximón."

The *telinel* seemed to move painfully.

"A few months ago," Robert explained, "three men approached the *telinel* in the street and fired at him from point-blank range. One bullet passed right through him. The others somehow missed. People say a veil descended from heaven and deflected the other bullets. The people consider it a miracle."

"Who shot him?" I asked.

"The *telinel* knows. He's seen his attackers in his dreams. But he won't identify them."

"In his dreams?"

"He's an *ajkun,* a 'day keeper,' a shaman, a son of Maximón. The shamans generally function outside the *cofradía* system, but since Maximón is their patron, they're included in this case."

The *cofradía* elders cleared a space on the floor and rolled out a woven reed mat. Several held up sheets, screening the area from onlookers. Slowly, deliberately, the *telinel* began to pass things from the rafters. The light was bad. It was hard to see what they were. People craned their necks, stood on tiptoes.

When the *telinel* was finished, he climbed into the shrouded enclosure. For five minutes he stayed there, pushing, moving, arranging, then suddenly the lights switched on, the door opened, the sheet dropped, and there stood a curious figure three or four feet high wearing billowing *atiteco* knickers, a giant pair of boots, and two wide-brimmed felt hats. It was Maximón. He had a large wooden head, and a cigar protruded from his mouth. Draped across his back were bright scarves, the outermost bearing an image of the Virgin of Guadalupe.

The sight of Maximón reminded me of an incident I'd read about involving Maximón and a Catholic priest: Perhaps because of his un-Christian heritage, Maximón has a number of unflattering Christian aspects, including Judas Iscariot and Pedro de Alvarado, the conqueror of Guatemala. It was Maximón's Judas aspect that, in 1950, made him run afoul of the Catholic church.

A visiting Dominican named Padre Godofriedo Recinos, angered by what he perceived as the *atitecos'* worship of the betrayer of Christ, decided to forbid the Maximón cult. *Cofradía* members say that Padre Godofriedo threatened them with a gun. The *cofradía* members tried to explain to Padre Godofriedo that if they were to follow his orders, Maximón would strike him mad, which perhaps he already was.

The *cofradía* members refused to back down, and in the end Padre Godofriedo departed in frustration. But six weeks later he and another priest took a launch back across the lake, sneaked into the *cofradía,* and stole the Maximón mask. What happened to the mask thereafter is not clear, but somehow it ended up in Paris, in the collection of the Musée de l'Homme. The *atitecos,* who did not know where Padre Godofriedo had taken Maximón, explained his absence by saying that Maximón's fame had reached Rome: The Pope had sent for Maximón so that he could adore him.

This story is related in an article written by E. Michael Mendelson, an anthropologist who did seminal work in Santiago Atitlán in the mid-1950's. It was Mendelson, an Englishman who later changed his name to Nathaniel Tarn and had a distinguished career as a poetry and literature professor at Rutgers University, who arranged to have Maximón brought back in 1978. I asked Robert how it happened.

"It was Nathaniel Tarn who traced the mask to the Musée de l'Homme," Robert told me. "He and my friend Martin Prechtel, who lived here until he was chased out by death squads, persuaded the French to return the mask to its rightful place. The French ambassador decided to return it in person. He put Maximón in a suitcase, rented a launch, and brought him across the lake chained to the wrist of a French woman diplomat in a business suit."

"Chained to the wrist of a French woman diplomat in a business suit?"

"The French flair for the dramatic," Robert said.

The *cofradía* members knelt down before the little figure and began to pray. As the music played, they made the sign of the cross, implored, gesticulated. They leaned their faces into Maximón's and, tears pouring down their cheeks, pleaded for personal favors. Maximón stood throughout his audiences, but after a while the *telinel* determined that he had tired, and tenderly laid him down. The *cofradía* members then censed him with copal and began placing offerings on his chest. Someone presented two bananas, someone else a pack of cigarettes, someone else a bundle of candles.

Big cloudy bottles of booze began to circulate. Robert described the booze as a specially fermented concoction referred to as *tzihuan ya*, "canyon water," made with the fruit brought by the young men from the coast. I would not have been at all surprised to learn that its water component had been made with some *atiteco* version of *zuhuy ha*, the "virgin water" of Yucatec rituals, and when a *cofradía* member summoned Robert to pay his respects to Maximón I began to ponder the question of Maximón's larger identity.

In Santiago Atitlán, Maximón is the god of destructive nature, of floods, earthquakes, and storms. A traveler and walker, he is associated with snakebites, is the inflicter of madness, and is worshiped at the mouths of caves. Michael Coe associates Maam (Maximón) with the Yucatec god Pauhatun, also known as God N, one of the most powerful underworld gods. In fact, Pauhatun is the quadripartite god taking part in the hallucinogenic-enema ritual depicted on the funerary vase in Michael Coe's *Lords of the Underworld*. Eric Thompson, in his book *Maya History and Religion,* says that Maam was the god of the five lost days in pre-Hispanic Yucatán, and that among the Kekchi of the Alta Verapaz section of Guatemala, people were afraid to mention his name lest he carry them off. It was strange, therefore, to see *atitecos* treating Maximón with such tender reverence, but I knew that this merely reflected the different concepts of evil held by ourselves and the Maya. To us, evil is something absolute, something to be resisted at all costs. To the Maya, evil is the principle of death and decay in nature and therefore an integral part of life. Gods like Maximón are terrifying, but they're also part of the earth's fertility. Thompson notes that "there is a widespread Maya belief that darkness and the underworld are evil, but as [the underworld] reaches up to immediately below the surface of the earth, it also produces crops." And, indeed, Robert Carlsen and his colleague Martin Prechtel have argued that an agricultural metaphor, referred to as *jaloj k'exoj,* governs the relationship of the living and dead worlds in Santiago Atitlán. *Jal* is the change manifested by a thing as it proceeds through its individual life cycle, from birth through youth, old age, and finally death. *K'ex* is the transfer of life between generations, the transfer of life from one to many. In Tzutujil, *jal* is the word for a dried ear of corn with the kernels still attached. Once the kernels have been removed, however, the ear is considered to have died and its seeds become its *k'exel,* its "replacements." *Atitecos* consider their grandchildren their replacements and frequently give grandparents and grandchildren the same name.

While Roberto knelt and prayed to Maximón, I was handed a shot glass full of *tzihuan ya.* It was sweet and potent, and made the music seem even more ethereal. Several shots of canyon water later, I found myself talking to a young *atiteco* about good and evil, tradition and the future—things I would never have discussed sober—when the man suddenly stopped me as if he needed to unburden himself of a secret.

"I live in Mexico," he said.

"In Mexico?"

"Yes," he said. "The death squads were after me. Someone tipped me off. It's my first time back in eight years."

At four in the morning, I left the *cofradía* house to get some sleep in a hotel room that Robert had rented in town. I left Robert slumped over a table dozing next to some *cofradía* officers. I woke him and told him I was going. He said that Maximón would be marched through town the next morning to a little chapel on the side of the church plaza. There he would be hung on a post representing the tree of life, the World Tree that the *atitecos,* along with the ancient Maya, believe to be at the center of the universe.

I reappeared at the *cofradía* house at ten the next morning and found Robert sitting bleary-eyed on the porch. A large crowd of *atitecos* had gathered. Inside, I found the *cofradía* officers clutching their silver-tipped canes in preparation for the march into town. The *telinel* picked up Maximón. Robert had told me that the *cofradía* officers were worried about whether the *telinel* would be physically up to the task of carrying Maximón and they seemed relieved when he was able to handle the load. As Maximón and his horse stepped out through the *cofradía* door, a group of boys began rotating noisemakers—wooden flaps mounted on the tops of long poles.

"*C'ar c'ar*," Robert explained. "The noise they make is supposed to sound like that of the *xaar*—the blue jay—another of Maximón's identities."

A huge throng followed Maximón through the streets. The procession first stopped at the municipal building, recently rebuilt after having been blown up by the guerrillas. There, Maximón lay for an hour or two in repose on a bed of fruit. When he emerged again, the *cofradía* officers accompanying him were now carrying a ladder and a rope. The group marched up to the plaza. There, in a small chapel at the end of an arcade, Maximón was hung from a wooden beam.

I stood for a while with the *cofradía* officers keeping vigil around their god, but eventually I wandered off to see the interior of the Catholic church. Statues of saints lined the walls. Small groups of *atitecos* were making obeisance, the murmur of their prayers rising upward toward the roof high above. Along one wall I found a monument to Stanley Rother. PRIEST MARTYR—BORN OKARCHE, OKLAHOMA, MARCH 27, 1935. ASSASSINATED JULY 28, 1981. THIRTEEN YEARS IN THE PARISH.

Robert had told me that after Father Rother was killed, his family wanted to bring his body back to Oklahoma. But Father Rother had been popular, and the *atitecos* refused to let his body go. A compromise was worked out. Father Rother's body was sent back to Oklahoma, but without his heart, which was buried in the Santiago Atitlán church. I thought of a priest I'd met in eastern Guatemala who'd heard this story and had related it to me with the wide-eyed reverence usually reserved for Christians fed to lions. Like the *telinel*, Father Rother had passed into the realm of *atiteco* legend.

The apse was dominated by a beautifully carved altarpiece that culminated high above the altar in a mountain peak with human figures, clutching staffs, on either side. While I was admiring it, Robert caught up with me.

"The altarpiece was carved when Santiago Atitlán was under

cofradía control," he said. "If you look on the very top of the mountain you can see a cross sprouting corn ears. The *atitecos* call the sprouting cross Kotsej Juyu Ruchiliew, 'flowering mountain earth.' It refers to the World Tree. The *atitecos* think that the original World Tree was at the center of the earth and was the source of all life. It sprouted not only things like rocks, corn, and deer, but also individual segments of time."

I was startled by the conceptual similarity to the representation of the Foliated Cross at Palenque.

"The idea of a tree as the central support of life is an idea that's recapitulated throughout *atiteco* life," he told me. "Old men are *nim chie nim kam*—'old tree, old vine.' Children are leaves, and grandchildren are *tzej jutae,* or 'sprouts,' that is, future trees. The same idea operates in the organization of the town. The *principales,* the veterans of the various *cofradías,* are the trunk; the *cofradías* are the branches; and each individual *cofradía* is a 'dawn house,' which, through feeding the tree, gives birth to time. That's what *costumbre* is all about— nourishing the tree of life."

Costumbre, "custom," is the word used in Guatemala to refer to the religion of the traditional *cofradía* Maya. Up until the reform governments of the nineteen-forties and fifties, the *cofradías* were not only the religious, but also the political authorities in Guatemalan Maya towns. They had in effect negotiated a deal with the non-Maya world in which they were granted cultural autonomy in exchange for cooperation with certain outside demands. But after the 1954 coup the exploitation of the Indian worsened and Catholic Action, with its social programs and emphasis on self-improvement, began to grow at the expense of the *cofradías.* As we walked out of the church I asked Robert about the relationship between *atiteco cofradías*, Catholics, and evangelicals.

"People think that the evangelical religions are the only ones that have grown in Maya communities," he responded. "But if you look at the last twenty-five years, the Catholic church has grown much faster than the evangelicals. The reason people don't understand this is that they've always thought of the *cofradía* members as Catholics. In my opinion, that's a misconception. In the mid-sixties, the

Catholics did a survey of Santiago Atitlán which concluded that only seven percent of the town was Catholic. The rest were what they called *costumbristas*. In the twenty-five years since that study, the *costumbristas*, and not the Catholic church, have been the big losers. According to my surveys, *costumbristas* now account for only ten percent of the town."

Did the Catholics and the evangelicals specifically reject the pre-Columbian traditions of the *cofradías?*

"Both the Catholics and the evangelicals continue to consult shamans. Many of them keep Maya deities in their houses. As you saw when we passed the Elim church, the evangelicals often schedule their services on important *cofradía* days, which is an acknowledgment of the importance of those days. However, what's really being lost is a systematic knowledge of the ancient religion."

That night we caught up on sleep at a house Robert rents outside town. But the next morning, after a swim in the deep-blue waters of the lake, we returned to visit another *cofradía*, one responsible for the care of what Robert called the "San Martín bundle." To the *atitecos*, the various forces of nature are controlled by *dueños*, or "owners," often represented by Catholic saints. The head *dueño* is San Martín, the king of undomesticated nature. Jesus Christ is one of his servants. His bundle, the contents of which are secret, is a box containing objects symbolizing the forces of nature from the time of the mother-father of everything—the time before the world was differentiated into the opposites that create its motion today. The *atitecos* consider the management of the forces in the San Martín bundle to be fraught with danger and feel that it requires a collaborative effort between humans and gods.

We arrived at the San Juan *cofradía* house at nine in the morning and sat down with the *cofradía* officers for a breakfast of turkey, chili, and tomato stewed in corn broth. When we had finished eating, we crossed the courtyard to the San Juan dawn house, a room slightly smaller than the Maximón equivalent of two nights before. The floor was strewn with pine needles, and the air filled with a thick, waxy floral scent. When my eyes adjusted to the dim light, I could see that the ceiling was hung with sprays of cohune palm permeating the air with their scent and dropping their tiny white sweet-smelling blossoms onto the *cofradía* floor. As I fingered one of the sprays, I was startled to find myself looking into the the face of a squirrel peering down from the rafters. It took me a moment to realize that it was stuffed and dessicated and that the rafters were full of dried animals.

Robert and I went over to greet the *alcalde,* the head of the *cofradía.* A heavy-set man with a gentle face, he was sitting in an Adirondack chair but rose as we approached, exposing a picture of the Virgin Mary taped off-center to the chair back. Behind him on the wall hung a drawing of the Foliated Cross at Palenque. I wondered how it came to be there.

"They're into that kind of thing," Robert said distractedly.

When Robert introduced me as Pedro, the *alcalde* laughed. "Ah, Simón!"

Robert smiled. "Whenever they talk about Pedro they mean Maximón."

A band had set up at the far end of the room in front of a pile of moth-eaten deerskins. Like the Maximón band, this one consisted of string instruments, a pipe, a *tun,* and a *k'joum,* but instead of an accordion, the group had castanets and a violin. Carved on the *tun* was the group's name—Xiim Acha, "Men of Corn." Robert indicated a dignified man holding a guitar and said that he was the group's leader.

"He and Martin Prechtel are the only survivors of an earlier group called Ju'luuj Tijaax, an *atiteca* calandar name. Six others were assassinated by the army. Martin, who is married to an *atiteca* woman, only escaped because he was tipped off. Even so, the day afterward they machine-gunned his house."

I started to sit on the ground, but one of the *cofradía* members stopped me and insisted that I sit on a bench behind a table covered with a large deerskin with head and antlers still attached. The antlers were wrapped in pink, yellow, and blue ribbons.

When the band began to play, one of the *cofradía* members got up to dance. Like the other *cofradía* officers, he wore striped Tzutujil trousers and a *x'cajcoj zut* around his head, but he also also sported a blue T-shirt that read DOMAINE CHANDON, NAPA VALLEY, CALIFORNIA. The music seemed to possess the man. As he danced, he began to twitch, to laugh, to sing.

"That's the *nabeysil*," Robert said. "He's the bundle priest, the one who handles the Martín bundle. And he really is a Maya priest. The other shamans in Santiago Atitlán are practicing shamans whom people hire for health problems, but the *nabeysil* is a super-shaman whose only role is religious. People say that he's not a *nagual*, a reincarnation of one of the original thirteen rain-god spirits from whom all *atitecos* are descended, but the next thing to it—a half-*nagual*. He's the adopted son of Baltasar, E. Michael Mendelson's informant, a famous shaman who died ten years ago at the age of ninety."

While the *nabeysil* was dancing in front of our table, he cradled the ribbon-bedecked deer head in his hands, talking to it, reasoning with it. His face had a plastic quality and seemed to flash through different personalities. At one point, his eyes wrinkled up, his mouth widened, and I could have sworn he became a jaguar.

"He's a wild man," Robert said. "My daughter calls him 'earthquake man,' or 'the table dancer.' She came in here one afternoon, and found him up dancing on the table."

The music stopped and a bottle of *kuxa*, moonshine, began to make the rounds. After everyone had had a drink, an ancient toothless *cofradía* member went over to the pile of deerskins behind the band, pulled the top one off, and draped it over himself. Another *cofradía* member took the beribboned deerskin off our table and draped it over himself. A woman censed the two with copal smoke. The *alcalde* stood up with a can of aerosol deodorant and sprayed them. Then he made his way around the room, spraying everyone's hair, including mine.

"A recent innovation," Robert said. "Other *cofradías* do it. It's considered very holy."

The man in the deerskin with the ribbon-wrapped antlers knelt and prayed to each of the four sacred directions. The band member started beating the *tun*. The *xul*, a reed pipe, joined in, followed by the guitars and then the *k'joum*.

"These are the songs of Maximón," Robert said. "They're very old, maybe pre-Columbian."

The man began to shuffle back and forth in time to the music. The other man, clutching his deerskin with one hand and brandishing a dead squirrel in the other, followed behind, dancing in pursuit, making whistles and high-pitched sighs as he went.

"This is the story of the jaguar and the deer," Robert said. "The man behind is the wind jaguar, who is associated with death and dryness. The man in front is a *nagual* masquerading as a deer, a creature which the *atitecos* associate with sacrifice. It's the *atiteco* creation story. The idea is that at the beginning of time, the world belonged to the wind jaguar. The sun was frozen in the sky and could not move. It wanted to move, however. It wanted the world to proceed, so it created the deer, which was also one of the original thirteen *naguals*. The wind jaguar went in pursuit of the deer, and as the chase began, the jaguar requested the assistance of the mountains and all the animals, calling out to them and thus giving them their names for the first time. That's what the man behind is doing now. He's calling out the names of the landscape. The squirrel he is carrying is one of the animals he has enlisted to chase the deer."

The band played on, the deer and the jaguar dancing through clouds of incense.

"When the jaguar corners the deer, he pounces, but he misses and impales himself on a cedar tree. The death of the jaguar allows the sun to move, time to proceed. It also means that the *nagual* survives and because the *nagual* survives, the first man survives also. Humans are thus allowed on earth because of the willingness of the original deer to be sacrificed. Because of its willingness to be sacrificed, the world was put in motion."

When the dance was over, the *nabeysil* came around with a bottle and a shot glass. "*Guatemala número uno!*" he shouted, his eyes delirious with joy, "Vinicio Cerezo!" Cerezo was the president of Guatemala.

When he had poured *kuxa* for the whole room, the *nabeysil* went over and began to pray in front of a box hanging over an altar along one side of the room. Suspended from the ceiling with ropes, the box was carved with the figure of a prancing deer and a large peccary.

Someone closed the door, cut the lights, and passed out candles. The *nabeysil* opened the box and lifted out a cloth-covered bundle. In the corner, a woman began to beat another *tun*. The *nabeysil* walked the bundle to the middle of the floor. The *alcalde* sprayed it with deodorant. The *nabeysil* genuflected to the four sacred directions. The band began to play.

"This is the song of San Martín," Robert said. "But in their songs, the *atitecos* use Maya, not Christian categories. So it's not 'San Martín,' but '*Nagual* Martín.'"

The *nabeysil* began to dance. The *alcalde* got up and joined him. In his arms the *alcalde* cradled the wooden figure of a recumbent lamb. After a while, the two of them lined up in front of the table at which we were sitting. People began to pass in front of them, bowing their heads and kissing first the *nabeysil*'s bundle, and then the *alcalde*'s lamb. I noticed the *alcalde* talking to the lamb, holding up a shot glass full of alcohol to its lips.

"He's commenting on how hot it is in here," Robert said. "He's saying that the lamb is making a big sacrifice. From the Western point of view, one day flops down in front of the next. We're insignificant in the process. But the *cofradía* members are up there moving the sun across the sky right now. During sacred times of the year, some go without sleep for ten days in a row. They don't always enjoy it, and they don't always enjoy the drinking, but without sacrifice, there's nothing. That's the Maya notion: *Hay que cumplir*, 'You have to carry it out.'"

I got in the line to pay my respects to the sacred objects. When my turn came to kiss the Martín bundle hem, the *nabeysil* laughed and shouted, "*Siete número!*"—or something that sounded like that— then looked at me expectantly. I looked back at him with helpless incomprehension. "*Siete número!*" he said again. I turned to the *alcalde*. The *alcalde* averted his eyes. I shrugged and passed on.

After everyone had been through the line, the *nabeysil* danced the Martín bundle over to the altar, laid it down, and carefully sprinkled it with flower petals. Another bundle was danced out. This was the María bundle, Robert explained, a female *nagual*, a moon or a rain goddess or both—I never quite got it straight. When it was danced back to its place on the altar, the doors were thrown open. As if from some alien planet, light streamed in through the clouds of incense. Little *atiteca* girls stood on the threshold peering curiously into the murk, their barefeet curled shyly around each other, the ends of their ponytails in their mouths. It became clear that the room was low on booze. The outdoors had an irresistible attraction to me, so I volunteered to get some, and was given directions to a little *tienda* around the corner.

O, how fresh the world looked when I stepped into the courtyard: the pounded red earth; the adobe houses; weathered, silver-checked pine pillars; the high pile of the stone walls. It all seemed to glow, to be possessed of a timeless, hard-edged beauty. It was as if I'd never seen it before.

I looked up. Chichuk volcano floated like a cloud over the town, patchwork milpas soaring toward its tangled cloud-forest summit.

I wove my way unsteadily to the *tienda,* braved the stares of the proprietor—no doubt a sober evangelical—and bought a half-dozen flasks of Quetzalteca-brand *aguardiente,* a cheap, clear sugarcane rum that Guatemalans sometimes refer to as Inditas because each flask carries the image of a cheerful, Chiquita-Banana-like *quetzalteca* Indian. My arms full, I wove my way back to the *cofradía* again.

The band had resumed playing and people were again dancing—males with males, females with females. One of the deer-jaguar performers invited me onto the floor. Back and forth we shuffled, back and forth. When we were done, he laughed, slapped me on the back, and sat down to light his pipe.

Next, I danced with the *nabeysil.* He was still flying.

"*Naturaleza!* Nature!" he cried, his eyes bugged wide, "*Que viva naturaleza!*"

I was about to chalk this up to free association when I remembered that Bill Hanks had told me that for Yucatec shamans the word *naturaleza* was a collective noun used to refer to the guardian spirits of the five sacred directions. Yucatán was a long way from Santiago Atitlán, but who could say?

When I danced with the *alcalde,* he asked me how far away the United States was. I told him.

"And how much does it cost to get there?" he asked.

I told him what the airplane fare was to New York.

He winced.

"Does the United States have *santos?*" he asked.

"Yes," I answered. "In the churches."

"But *santos grandes* like here?"

"No."

Afterward the *alcalde* knelt in front of the altar and began to pray. He prayed mostly in Tzutujil, but occasionally in Spanish. We had made a donation to the costs of the *cofradía,* and I heard the words *"gringo," "extranjero"* (foreigner), and *"gracias."* He seemed saddened. "Here we are *tranquilo, alegre,*" he said. "Next year, we don't know."

It was late afternoon when we left the *cofradía.* That evening I ate roast lamb in the parish house with the American priest, Tom McSherry, four nuns—three Guatemalans and a Salvadoran—and Paul Goepfert, a novelist friend of Robert's who lives in nearby San Lucas Tolimán. The room was large and wood-paneled, just upstairs from where Father Stan had been hacked up. I spent considerable time trying to get Tom McSherry to tell me at what point he considered *costumbre* incompatible with Roman Catholicism, but I didn't get many answers. To be sure, my inquiries were *aguardiente*-fueled and therefore not as subtly posed as they might otherwise have been—but carelessly expressed opinions, in Santiago Atitlán, are dangerous. After we left, Paul explained that Tom McSherry had attended the Maximón ceremony the year before and that his parishoners still had not forgiven him. Essentially, he'd been a captive of Catholic Action ever since.

We returned to the *cofradía* and drank and danced, even though the music had ceased. Around eleven in the evening, Robert herded us back to the plaza where San Juan Carajo, "Saint John the Prick," would be paraded around town in pursuit of María Andalur. Associated with a Maya moon goddess, María Andalur was the patroness of weaving and childbirth. San Juan represented some fertility principle and was perhaps related to Maximón. Robert wasn't entirely sure. Out of their union, however, the New Year would be created.

The streets were jammed by the time we arrived in the vicinity of the plaza, and the atmosphere was charged. The two life-sized saints, carried on biers by four men each, raced back and forth charging each other, fleeing, and sending *atitecos* flying in all directions. Taking place in darkness (the town doesn't have street lights), the event had a hallucinatory quality. At one point I stumbled, and San Juan raced by. He was decked out in a blue robe, with a pink scarf wrapped around his neck. His head was crowned with a skullcap, made of reeds that rose to a point topped with a long reed resembling a bird feather. A hand was raised chest high and a finger pointed pedantically skyward, like a university professor delivering a lecture.

I tried to pursue the saints, but my limbs were refusing orders. Just when the sidewalks began to look like featherbeds, Paul Goepfert found me and tactfully escorted me to his car.

The next day, Good Friday, happened also to be Friday the thirteenth. When we'd been in the church several days before, Robert had shown me a small hole in the middle of the floor which, he said, was the *r'kux,* the umbilicus, the center of the world.

"On Good Friday they raise a crucified Christ from the *r'kux.* To the *atitecos,* the cross represents the World Tree. Christ is wearing a cloak and the cross is raised in such a way that the cloak falls open, revealing fruit and small animals inside."

My plan had been to be at the church in time to see the World Tree cross lifted out of the umbilicus of the world. But by the time I arrived the cross had been raised, lowered, and set aside and what, up until now, had been a Maya ceremony had suddenly turned Spanish Catholic. Christ himself had been taken down and placed in a flower-covered glass casket illuminated by strings of multicolored Christmas lights. The casket was attended by a dozen penitents clad in purple. Behind, on a miniature bier of its own, was a Yamaha ET500 generator borne by four more penitents. Around them a procession was forming. Hundreds of Catholic *atitecos* stood around clutching white candles. I saw María Andalur and San Juan Carajo looking innocent of their previous night's antics. The only hint of Maya belief came from four *atiteco* boys on their hands and knees peering nervously into the *r'kux* as if afraid they might fall into the center of the earth.

I was not feeling particularly perky, so I left the church by a side door and collapsed along a sunny wall of the cloister with some giggling Maya kids and their old dog. After a while I mustered enough energy to slink through some side streets toward the plaza. On the way I passed a sleazy-looking building with a sign over it that said VIDEO CLUB. Underneath were advertisements for the day's offering: *Robot Bampiro (Robot Vampire), La Fuerza Bruta Acción (Brute Force Action)*.

I found Robert standing with the Maximón *cofrades,* who were solemnly clutching flower-encrusted crosses under the plaza arcade. Still suspended from his tree, Maximón had been moved to a porch outside the chapel. Beneath him sat the *cofrade* women in their Saturn-ring helmets, feet drawn underneath them, burning candles cradled in their laps.

I asked Robert what was going to happen. He explained that when Christ descended from the church to the plaza below, the *telinel* would carry Maximón out for a symbolic confrontation. During the confrontation Maximón would inseminate Christ, thereby preparing the way for the rebirth of the New Year. This, at least, was how the *cofradía* members saw it. The Catholics no doubt interpreted the confrontation differently. In any case, after the encounter Maximón would retire to his dawn-house rafters.

Christ's procession moved slowly out of the church and began to make its lugubrious way down the church steps. A bass drum beat morbidly. A brass band blared out a tune so funereal that I wanted to wrench out my hair. The Yamaha generator hummed. The purple penitents rocked their biers back and forth, one step forward, one step back. It took the procession forty-five minutes to get even halfway down the steps to the plaza. The whole thing seemed interminable. Robert fulminated.

"It's pure power politics," he said. "Catholic Action showing they're in charge. It used to be that when Maximón was ready, Christ would come out."

I glanced at Maximón. Hanging from the gallows, his work nearly done for another year, he seemed unperturbed.

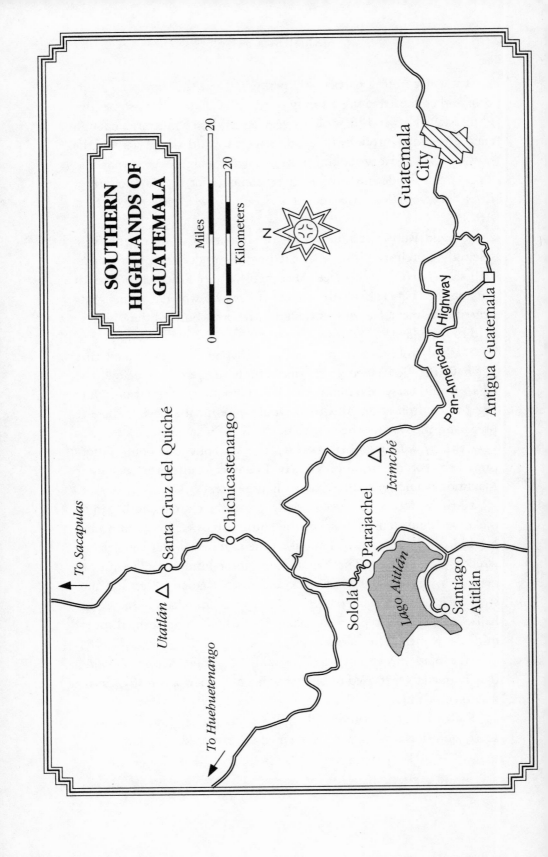

SOUTHERN HIGHLANDS OF GUATEMALA

Miles

0 _____ 20

Kilometers

0 _____ 20

N

To Sacapulas

Utatlán △   Santa Cruz del Quiché

To Huehuetenango

Chichicastenango

Iximché △

Sololá   Parajachel

Lago Atitlán

Santiago Atitlán

Pan-American Highway

Guatemala City

Antigua Guatemala

CHAPTER 14

Domitila

THE MOST SIGNIFICANT CHANGE that Catholic Action brought about in Guatemalan life during the sixties and seventies was the establishment of a group of educated, Spanish-speaking Maya, many of whom came to positions of power in their villages without having worked their way up through the traditional *cofradía* hierarchies. These educated Maya—cooperativists, catechists, health promoters, trade unionists, and literacy teachers—became leaders of a broad and powerful movement to improve the standing of the Maya in Guatemalan society. Once the violence began, these Maya were the ones whom the army systematically targeted for assassination.

The purpose of the army's terror campaign was to traumatize the Maya. If you look at Guatemala today, however, the army's campaign clearly failed. The Maya population of Guatemala is in ferment as never before. And as a result of the violence they experienced, ordinary Maya who had previously thought of themselves as Quichés, Ixils, Tzutujils, or Cakchiquels now refer to each other as Qawinaq, a generalized Quiché word meaning "our people." The word *winaq* is the Quiché Maya version of the proto-Maya word *uinic*, or "twenty," the Maya definition of the essential element of humanity.

A number of Catholic Action leaders who were lucky enough to survive the violence have also redefined themselves, starting a pan-

Maya movement whose purpose is to take another look at their Maya heritage. Members of the movement, many of whom had previously considered themselves Catholic, now argue that Catholicism is a colonial doctrine. They speak of belonging to the "Fourth World," of their relationship to the non-Maya world being defined by a "dialectic of conquest."

On a practical level, the efforts of this movement have centered around the Academia de Lenguas Mayas, the Academy of Maya Languages. The Academia's initial ambition is to codify the grammars and alphabets of the various Guatemalan Maya languages and from there to build toward some kind of cultural, and ultimately political, autonomy. This doesn't sound particularly inflammatory, but in Guatemala even alphabets are controversial. The Summer Institute of Linguistics, for one, has bitterly opposed the Academia's efforts because of the degree to which the new alphabets would supplant the Institute's own, which they have used to publish dozens of Bibles and uncounted religious tracts.

Just prior to my visit to Santiago Atitlán, I listened to a speech at the Alliance Française in Guatemala City given by Demetrio Cojtí, a Cakchiquel Maya at the center of the Academia movement. Demetrio is perhaps thirty-five, with stylishly cut hair and aviator glasses. He was educated at the Instituto Santiago, the most famous of the half-dozen or so Catholic-run Indian boarding schools that constitute the principal source of Indian education beyond the village level in Guatemala. People told me that Demetrio had been expelled from the Instituto for rebelliousness and had gone to work as a laborer, but that a friendly priest had found him and arranged for him to study in Belgium. There Demetrio earned a doctorate in communications, which made him the only Maya Ph.D. in Guatemala, a fact widely commented on. The day I heard him speak, it was clear that the several hundred Maya in the audience were extremely proud of him.

When Demetrio took the microphone and began talking, the room crackled with excitement. His delivery was clear, confident, rapid-fire, and sarcastic. I might have been listening to Malcolm X in the early sixties. He opened his speech by comparing the relationship between the Ladinos and the Maya in Guatemala to that between the European countries and their colonies in Africa.

"We're the owners of this land," Demetrio said. "How was it taken from us? By invasion and conquest. Now we live in a typical colonial situation. The pattern is to assimilate, to destroy the Maya languages. We're losing our culture at an incredible velocity. The Maya languages have been relegated to the markets, to the servants' quarters, to the mountains, and the ravines. Who speaks Maya in the Congress? No one. On television? No one except the evangelicals. Who teaches it in the schools? No one. In thirty or forty years only the old people will speak it."

Demetrio went on to describe the efforts of the Academia to promote Maya languages. "We Maya have always resisted our colonial situation. It used to be that we would say yes and then do the other thing, but this is the beginning of a new stage of articulated, conscious resistance. Language is the heart of it—the heart and soul of the people [*alma y corazón del pueblo*]. Cultural things can change, but language is eternal."

After the presentation I introduced myself to Demetrio and asked if I might talk with him further. He suggested we meet for breakfast the next morning. When I asked him where, he suggested a McDonald's on the edge of the capital.

I was staying in Antigua, forty-five minutes outside the city, so I got up at six the next morning and flagged down a rickety schoolbus bound for the capital. At the *periférico,* on the outskirts of town, I got off near the Calzada Roosevelt and trudged across a parking lot toward the all-too-familiar golden arches. I suspected that the locale of our meeting had been chosen for ironic effect—mass culture, the gringo's burden.

Inside, I found Demetrio reading a newspaper. We ordered pancakes and sausages from a waitress in a prim uniform, carried our plastic trays to a plastic table, and sat down on modular plastic seats. Mood music filled the air. All around us, upper-class Guatemalan teens with baggy surfing shorts and braces on their teeth were eating American-style breakfasts.

I asked Demetrio who belonged to the Academia de Lenguas Mayas movement.

"It's more a current of thought than a movement," he said.

"There're about five hundred activists. Almost all are the sons and daughters of campesinos (milpa farmers), but very few are campesinos themselves."

And what about educational backgrounds?

"Almost all went through the Catholic schools. In fact, the majority of educated Maya are from a Catholic-school background, not state school, and certainly not evangelical. The evangelicals act as if God were North American and Indian culture were satanic."

What did he feel about the value of Catholic education for the Maya?

"Its first stage is the destruction of Indian identity and Indian language. Next it becomes a process of Ladinoization. In some cases, this leads to *ladinoización triunfante*, but this depends on the Ladinoized Indian being accepted by other Ladinos. In other cases, where the Indian is not accepted, it leads to a counterreaction—what I call the *efecto boomerang*."

I had the distinct impression that Demetrio was describing his own experience.

"And what kind of education would you advocate?"

"We would separate the school system into the different languages and, to the degree to which it is appropriate, teach people in their own language."

I knew from Nora England, an American linguist active in the Academia movement, that Demetrio had argued that Guatemala was not a nation, but rather a state containing many nations, and I asked whether he ultimately envisioned some kind of political autonomy.

"Perhaps," he said, "but we're not at that point yet."

"How many Guatemalan Maya are now truly literate in their own languages?" I asked.

"Probably a hundred."

I told Demetrio that this seemed incredible to me, considering that the government claimed to be running bilingual programs in Indian schools.

"The purpose of the bilingual program as it's currently designed is assimilation. Ninety percent of the teachers, even when they're Maya, are cases of *ladinoización triunfante.* They use Maya languages merely as a tool for teaching Spanish. They're alienated from their own languages. At the Academia de Lenguas Mayas, we're training Maya to be able to teach their own languages for their own sakes."

I wanted to know why the Summer Institute of Linguistics had been so opposed to Academia's efforts.

"When we began our project to create a unified alphabet in 1986 and 1987, the Summer Institute of Linguistics was our first opponent. In order to have a common grammatical approach to all the Maya languages we were trying to choose between four different alphabets. We then planned to lobby the Congress to adopt the best of them as the standard alphabet for the Maya languages of Guatemala. The alphabet in which the Summer Institute of Linguistics had printed their Bibles was another one altogether, and was clearly inferior to the other four. It was as simple as that. They didn't think the Indians had the brains to organize their own linguistic movement. They'd always treated Indians like 'boys.' We were a negation of their whole approach."

I shifted gears and asked Demetrio what he felt about the guerrillas.

He glanced around almost imperceptibly. "The guerrillas used efficacious methods. They spoke to the Maya in their own languages. But their approach had one fundamental flaw. Their interest in the Maya derived from a theoretical conclusion that the Indians had a revolutionary potential that the guerrillas could use. They therefore wanted to proletarianize the Indians until they were no longer Indians. To them, it was all a question of the conflict of classes. They only talked about discrimination. They didn't talk about colonialism or ethnicity. They incorporated Indians into the movement, but only as far as the middle level. Because of this, many Indians felt that if the guerrillas had won, it would only have been a change of masters."

One focus of the Academia movement has been to revive interest in non-Christian Maya religion. Although there is a lingering suspicion between the *cofradías* and the former Catholics of the Academia, a number of Academia members have sought out shamans, attended pre-Columbian Maya rituals, and even used the Popul Vuh as a Bible. I asked Demetrio what he felt about the role of religion in the movement.

"I don't want to get into this area because it's divisive," he said, "and also because I'm weak in it." But then he paused and looked almost wistful. "You see, my father was a Catholic Action evangelist. At age seven he sent me away to school in Guatemala City. At age seven I went from the *horario del sol,* 'the schedule of the sun,' to the *horario del reloj,* 'the schedule of the clock.' At age seven, I went from hearing Mass once a week to hearing Mass every day, from *el mundo cakchiquel* to *el mundo castellano.*"

Maybe it was because Demetrio had been unable to answer my questions about religion that I found myself, a week or so after our breakfast, jumping down from a crowded pickup truck in the central plaza of a Maya town deep in the highlands, where I hoped to pursue the question. The town was in the middle of a dissected, or broken, plateau, at five or six thousand feet. The surrounding landscape reminded me of Chiapas. Dried cornfields awaiting the first rains lay interspersed with patches of pine forest. Adobe houses, their low tile roofs the color of the red earth, clung to the hollows. My instructions, once I'd arrived in the town plaza, were to ask for a woman I'll call Domitila Canek. "*Allá, yo soy conocida,*" she'd assured me, "There, I'm known."

I'd met Domitila in Chiapas when she and a group of other Maya involved in the Academia movement had come to attend a Mayanist conference in San Cristóbal. Domitila is a woman in her early thirties who dresses in traditional clothing and in most ways looks like a typical Maya villager, but she has an indescribable charisma that seems to draw people's attention. I'd gathered that many members of her family had been killed during the violence, that she'd fled to the United States, and that she'd returned to Guatemala after being summoned in a dream by one of her murdered brothers. The final day of the Mayanist conference had included a field trip to a nearby archaeological site. I'd spotted Domitila standing next to a stela, introduced myself, and asked if I might look her up when I was next in Guatemala. As we were talking she suddenly pulled a liquid-filled plastic vial from beneath her sash and proceeded to anoint, then pray at, the stela.

"If I don't, there'll be no rain," she explained.

* * *

My first inquiry about Domitila in her town drew a blank, although perhaps it was just the anomaly of a gringo suddenly appearing in a remote Indian area. My second attempt turned up a cousin named Lucio, who seemed alternately incredulous and protective. Several times he asked me if I was sure that it was his cousin, "*indígena,*" that I'd come to visit. When I assured him that it was, he agreed to lead me to her house but made it clear that if I caused any trouble, I'd be sorry.

Domitila's town had the atmosphere of overcrowded sullen cynicism that I'd come to associate with refugee-flooded, violence-hardened highland towns. I followed Lucio up a narrow street lined with low concrete walls. A few blocks from the plaza, he paused and led me into a storefront, the shelves of which bore a few cans of chili, some dried *frijoles,* some rice in plastic bags, and not much else. The rear of the store opened into a bright interior courtyard in which I could see coffee beans drying on a concrete slab, a stack of newly split wood airing under a line of clean laundry, and a chicken tethered to a hibiscus bush.

A tiny, gray-haired woman in a striped *corte* and a brightly colored *huipil* came out to greet us. She introduced herself as Katerina and said she was Domitila's mother. Did I know about Domitila's accident? On her way home a few days before she'd been hit by a car while crossing the street in the departmental capital. She was all right, thank God. Did I want to see her?

I followed Katerina into a room off the corner of the courtyard. Wrapped in a blue bathrobe, Domitila was stretched out on a double bed. Her face was swollen. Her head and ankles were wrapped in handkerchiefs. Friends and family members were gathered around. A radio was playing marimba music. On the wall opposite her, a portrait of Pocahontas hung next to a velveteen tapestry of a heroic-looking North American Plains Indian lancing a buffalo.

Although I'd told Domitila I was coming, she seemed surprised to see me. Someone produced a chair, and I sat. The majority of Domitila's visitors were young men and she introduced them generically as "*compañeros Mayas.*"

"It is our custom, when someone is sick, for friends to come and visit," she explained. "The marimba makes it *mas alegre*."

The conversation resumed. Or rather, Domitila, swathed in her scarves, propped up on a pillow, resumed talking, while the *compañeros,* leaning forward attentively, elbows on knees, resumed listening.

After a while Katerina came in and summoned me to the kitchen. There, she introduced me to Domitila's father, Francisco, a rail-thin man with a gentle smile. Francisco politely gestured for me to sit down at a table laid with a pile of thick, fresh tortillas and steaming bowls of squash points in broth. After a little while, Domitila hobbled in to join us.

Domitila asked where I'd come from. I told her about Santiago Atitlán, the Maximón *cofradía,* the *telinel* being shot, and the curtain that had descended from the sky to protect him.

Domitila and her parents listened intently.

"It's like my accident," Domitila said. "I was thrown in the air and landed on my head on a car hood. People who saw the accident were certain that I'd been killed. But I only have bruises and sprains. I wasn't meant to die."

Francisco asked who'd shot the *telinel.*

I told him what Robert had told me: that only the *telinel* knew because he'd seen his would-be assassins in his dreams. Francisco nodded sympathetically. The Maya attach great significance to dreams.

I alluded to having drunk too much at the *cofradía* ceremonies.

"You drink incorrectly," Domitila scolded. "You should drink not to get drunk, but to honor the earth. Alcohol is the blood of corn. It's meant to nourish the earth. The earth is living. It has to eat. You don't see that it's trying to embrace you."

After lunch, Domitila went back to her bed to lie down. Katerina showed me to my quarters, a room along one side of the courtyard containing a cot and a light bulb. After Katerina left, I put down my bag and began feeling uncomfortable. At lunch I'd discovered that through a misunderstanding, Domitila had been expecting me the weekend before. My original plan had been to try to travel with her to the ancient capital of her people, which was nearby, or at least to some local shrine, but following her accident this no longer seemed possible. With the stream of well-wishers, moreover, it seemed a bad time to impose my presence. I'd asked if I could spend the night, talk to Domitila some, and then head back to Chiapas the next day. This had been agreeable to Domitila.

I was sitting on a stoop in front of my room when Francisco came over. Dressed in the *traje* of his group, he began, unsolicited, to tell me about their lives.

He said that they'd originally lived in an *aldea* twelve miles from the town. But then the army had come and told them that there were armed evil people in the mountains.

"We didn't have arms, but they attacked us anyway, with helicopters and machine guns. It was the department commander who was responsible, a man who calls himself a Christian. The people who ran were killed where the army found them. The people who stayed were shot praying in their houses."

Francisco told me that he'd had a dream that had told him to leave the *aldea*. Had he not had the dream, he would have died also. Katerina didn't want to go. She'd argued that the *aldea* was where they had their land and their family. But I thought to myself, 'God hasn't called me yet,' and we moved to town. That's how we survived."

But the army killed Francisco's three sons. As a result, he felt sad all the time.

"I'm getting old," he told me. "I can't work the way I used to, and I have no more sons to help me. And it's not just me. There were widows with four or five children to raise. Now the children are sixteen or seventeen and they're angry. I'd move back to the *aldea*, but I'm afraid it will start all over again."

When Francisco finished this story, what struck me was not just what he said, but the way he said it. He clearly felt the injustice. I was from the outside world. He was offering me his experience to make sense of it. But beyond Francisco's sense of injustice, I was struck by his gentleness and lack of anger. I decided it was time to talk with Domitila.

When I knocked on the door of her room, she was dozing, but

opened her eyes and told me to come in. I said that I'd spoken with Francisco about their lives in the *aldea* and wanted to ask her what she remembered about it.

"We were very poor," Domitila said. "Our house was straw, and there were many things that we wanted that we could never have."

She explained that her father had grown up practicing "the religion of his ancestors," that in his youth "Catholicism hadn't yet arrived in the *aldea*." Her mother, however, had been a Catholic from town and had had a big influence on her father. He'd become a Catholic, a member of Catholic Action, a community leader. First he'd become a *regidor,* then an *alcalde,* and finally a *principal.* He'd been the president of the school committee and the road committee. He'd led the struggle for a system to supply potable water.

"But all that stopped when the first of my brothers was killed in June 1981. My brother and my parents were returning from church one night when they were jumped by seven men. The men took my brother. As they dragged him off he shouted to my parents not to worry about him because God would take care of him. It was the last time we ever saw him. After that my father quit politics. He blamed himself for my brother's death."

Domitila told me that she'd always been close to her father, that she'd followed him everywhere. He had taught her to read and write in their language. In 1967, when she was twelve, the government opened a three-year primary school in their *aldea* as part of an alphabetization program.

"I wanted to go to school," Domitila said. "But my father didn't want me to, because it wasn't the custom for girls. I went anyway and was the first girl in the *aldea* to graduate from primary school."

After that, again against her father's will, Domitila went on to a second three years of primary school in town. She lived with an aunt. However, the second three years of primary school were taught in Spanish. Domitila didn't speak Spanish and as a result, she "experienced much hardship and suffered much discrimination." But by working as a translator for the local health center, she picked up enough Spanish to graduate.

By then Domitila was seventeen, and she decided that she

wanted to become a teacher. She would have been the first Indian woman from the whole region to become a teacher, but people were beginning to speak against her.

"They couldn't understand why I didn't want to get married," Domitila explained.

Domitila and her father fought about it, but in the end he let her go. She attended a six-year program at the Instituto Indígena Nuestra Señora del Socorro in Antigua. A priest who was a friend of the family's helped pay the fees.

"The Instituto was a teacher's school for Indian women," Domitila told me, "the only one in the whole country. It was run by very conservative nuns. Because the students were all Indians, they fed us very badly. They gave us a few beans and two tortillas a day. Beyond that, there was only several-day-old bread."

Domitila graduated from the Instituto in 1979, but "because of the discrimination against Indians," she wasn't able to get a job. So she returned to her department and began working with a Catholic priest as a teacher in a string of *communidades de base,* Catholic communities influenced by liberation theology.

"For two years I traveled between *aldeas* teaching courses in Maya culture. It was a time when the violence against people doing the sort of thing I was doing was growing every day. Many of my friends were killed. Late in 1981, my second brother was kidnapped. We never saw him again. After that I told my father that I wanted to join the guerrillas. He started to cry and told me I'd only wind up being killed also, and that then he'd have no one left. I didn't know what to do. It was no longer safe for me to stay, but I had nowhere else to go. A priest with whom I'd been working took pity on me and gave me the air fare to California, so that's when I went to the United States."

Domitila didn't know a soul in the United States and didn't speak any English. A priest met her at the airport and found her a temporary place to stay.

"But after that," she said, "I never saw him again."

At this point in her story, Domitila paused, hoisted herself out of bed, and painfully lowered her feet to the floor. I could see scars on both her knees and scratches and bruises on her legs. She told me to follow her, and we walked together to a room at the back of the courtyard. Inside, she pulled a hanging off the front of a tall cupboard and swung open the doors. The cupboard was crammed with books, from top to bottom. There were books in English, Spanish, Maya, books of poetry, books on nature, on religion, and on North and South American Indians. I was astonished. It made me think of something the linguist Nora England had told me, that during the worst of the violence, the few Maya who had owned books had had to conceal them, or even burn them. For an Indian to have been found with books was a reason for being killed.

Domitila explained that this was her office, gestured for me to sit, pulled a few things out of the bookcase, and left the room. I looked at what she'd given me: books, magazines, pamphlets. One of the magazines was a California religious publication containing a brief article about her life. Another was a volume of her poetry. I read the article, then began the poetry, which appeared to date from when she had been in the United States. I was reading a poem about the blank, pale faces of North American men when Domitila reappeared, looking tired.

I sensed that my time was about up, so I returned the books and asked Domitila if she had the energy for a few more questions.

After she lay down again, I asked her about her time in the United States.

"I was undocumented," she said. "I was there illegally for five years. At first I worked in a rubber factory. My fellow workers were mostly Mexican women. The conditions were bad. We had no glasses, no gloves. The fumes gave us headaches and made us sick. So I organized the women and won some health improvements. Later I worked in an auto parts factory. There, I met some North American Indians—Arapahos, Hopis, and Navajos. They were part of a movement called the Native American Church. Through them, I started going to sweat lodges and to peyote ceremonies. The peyote opened my mind. It made me realize that my problem was that I had knowledge but I didn't have feeling. I realized that my Catholic training had given me the idea of hell; that when Catholics thought of the earth, they thought of hell. I realized how dependent we Maya are on the earth, how, for us, everything is conscious; how the air, the water, the animals, and the sun are all speaking to us. But I also realized another thing—how sick I was."

"From the rubber factory?" I asked.

Domitila looked at me impatiently. "I had heard from my parents that my youngest brother, Narciso, had also been murdered, and that our house in the *aldea* had been burned down. Narciso was only fourteen. They beat him up and left him to die in a milpa. I was sick in my heart because of what was happening to my family.

"At one of the peyote ceremonies I met a Hopi medicine man named Henry Tyler. He was in his eighties. His spirit was the eagle. I told him about my sickness and asked him what I could do about it. He taught me the spirituality of fire, water, and stone. I learned that the Hopi outlook was the same as the Maya. He told me that I should become a *sacerdote* Maya—a Maya priest."

I asked Domitila how she'd returned to Guatemala.

"My brother, Narciso, appeared to me in a dream and told me it was time. He told me that I had work to do in Guatemala and showed me how to get through the airport."

I looked over Domitila's bed and noticed a picture frame enclosing oval-shaped portraits of three young men.

"Those are my brothers," Domitila said. "Narciso is the one at the bottom."

The bottom portrait was of a young man, a boy, really, with an oversized starched white collar and a black tie that looked as if it was strangling him. His hair was brushed over his forehead but even the solemnity of his pose couldn't dampen what appeared to me to be an innate mirthfulness. It was hard for me to imagine Narciso either as a threat to the Guatemalan government or as a spirit guide through its formidable security apparatus.

"Didn't you have trouble with customs when you got to the airport?" I asked.

"My papers were more or less in order," she answered. "But people have been killed for worrying too much about those things. I had spiritual protection."

I asked Domitila if, upon her return, she had followed through on Henry Tyler's advice that she become a Maya priest.

"After I told the old people here what Henry Tyler had said, they said that I would die if I didn't become a shaman. I'm studying now."

"Where?" I asked.

"In the the neighboring department."

"What town?"

"I'm not crazy," she said. "I won't tell you."

I heard a sound at the door behind me. I glanced back and saw that several visitors had arrived.

"If you'll excuse me," she said. "I have some business with my *compañeros.*"

Several hours later, after supper, I was in my room lying on my cot and staring at the ceiling, when I heard Domitila outside.

"*Usted!* Hey you!" she called out, keeping me at a distance by using the formal form of address.

"*Yo,*" I answered, responding with what I thought was a passable Spanish–New York street-slang pun.

Domitila told me that she had a meeting to go to with her *compañeros,* but that her parents were going to take a sweat bath and that I should join them.

I hadn't noticed the sweat lodge, but there it was, a low adobe hovel, perhaps five feet high and six feet around, next to a pile of horse fodder.

I thought of the *pib na,* the underground sweat lodge on the Temple of the Cross at Palenque, the place from which Chan Bahlum had departed on his ritual journeys into the underworld. Robert Carlsen's obversation that sweat baths were associated with birthing, cleansing, and fertility came back to me. I realized that during not just my visits to the five-lost-day ceremonies at Chenalhó and Santiago Atitlán, but also my trips into the Belize cave, the Lacandón wilds, and the Ixil killing fields, I'd been treading in the Maya underworld. I knew that in Maya terms I needed to be purified. I would soon be leaving the Maya for my own world, and I hoped this one sweat bath would cover everything I'd been exposed to during more than a year of travel.

I took off my clothes, wrapped myself in a towel, and crossed the courtyard. I followed Francisco, who lifted a blanket, stooped, and entered the lodge interior. Inside, the smoke stung my eyes. The only light came from the reddish glow of a pile of coals against one wall. Francisco sat me down on a wooden board a few inches above the floor. After a while Katerina joined us. She was wearing only her *corte,* and as she crawled through the door, the light briefly caught her gentle, creased face.

Katerina pinned up the blanket behind her, picked up a dried gourd, and began to ladle water onto some rounded stones around the edge of the firepit. The stones hissed and popped. Scalding hot steam filled the lodge, searing its way into my lungs. Francisco told me to get closer to the floor if the steam became too hot for me. From out of the darkness, he handed me a swatch of palm fronds.

"*Así se llama el fuego.* This is how you call the fire."

He and Katerina began to flay themselves with their fronds. As he did so, I could hear Francisco muttering under his breath: "*Dios santo! Señor Jesucristo Maestro!*"

Sweat poured off my body. The fronds stung as they rasped across my skin. After a while Francisco told me it was time to scratch myself with my fingernails. When I didn't do it to his satisfaction, he said something in Maya that made Katerina laugh, leaned his bony arms over, and did it for me. I felt like a child. Afterward I poured hot water over myself. Days of anxiety washed away.

Back in my room, I was rolling out my sleeping bag to the amplified sounds of competing evangelical services blaring over the town, when I heard voices and noticed a light coming over the top of the wall. I hated to do it, but I couldn't resist. I climbed up on the bed and put my eye to a seam just below the ceiling. From my vantage point I had a partial view of a dimly lit, dirt-floored room with a fire smoldering next to a Maximón figure in one corner. I could see several of Domitila's mysterious *compañeros* and then Domitila herself holding a smoking, incense-filled censer.

I climbed down and stretched out on my bed. I thought about just how much of my experience of the Maya had been like this— brief glimpses over metaphorical walls. I consoled myself with the feeling I'd had in Chenalhó: that the Maya belonged to another world that I'd never really be part of. But even as the thought occurred to me, I realized how misguided it was. I was essentially reiterating the idea of multiple creations that European theologians had thrown up to protect themselves from the strangeness of the New World. Attitudes hadn't really changed that much. After five hundred years, we were still denying the legitimacy of an Indian point of view, still trying to relegate the Maya to a parallel universe that wouldn't interact with our own. I realized that if I'd learned anything at all from the Maya, it was that we all lived in the same universe. It was just that that universe was bigger and stranger than I'd previously imagined.

The next morning, after I'd packed my things, I asked Domitila if she had time for a few more questions.

She said that she did.

What did she think of the present situation of the guerrillas?

"The people are a little disorganized now," she responded. "They lack money. They have administrative problems, but they might reformulate themselves."

After saying this, however, Domitila paused as if she were dissatisfied with her answer.

"You have to understand something," she continued. "I'm fighting a war, but it's not a political or a military war. The war I'm fighting is the war against occidental thought. What my *compañeros* and I were doing in the room next to yours last night was a cleansing ceremony, which is what you need to do also. That's why I made you take a sweat bath last night."

Domitila watched me eagerly scribbling her words down in my notebook.

"Another thing," she said. "You can't always be writing.

There are things you can only learn from living with the people, things you can only learn in your heart."

A Note on Usage and Pronunciation

When referring to people, Mayanists prefer the word *Maya* to *Mayan*. Some sources use *Mayan* to describe languages and sometimes, by extension, art and culture. Because the correct usage of *Mayan* is not agreed upon, and for the sake of simplicity, I have used *Maya* for both the people and their languages throughout.

Also for simplicity, I have used only one pronunciation mark that applies specifically to Maya languages. The Maya use a glottal stop similar to the break between the two *t*'s in the Scottish pronunciation of the word *bottle*. In Maya words, the glottal stop is indicated by an apostrophe after the glottalized letter. *K'in*, for instance, is pronounced "kuh-een."

A few other rules are worth noting. Vowels follow Spanish conventions:

> *a* is like *a* in "father."
> *e* is like *ay* in "pray."
> *i* is like *ee* in "flee."
> *o* is like *o* in "hello."
> *u* is like *oo* in "boot."

Certain consonants also differ from English pronunciations:

> **c** is always hard, as in "cat."
> **j** is pronounced like an English *h*.
> **x** is pronounced "sh."

A Glossary of Spanish, Maya, and Other Terms

alcalde   Literally "mayor." Important position in various Maya religious fraternities.

aldea   Guatemalan term for an Indian hamlet.

cabecera   Literally "head" or "source." The ceremonial center of an Indian municipality.

cargo   "Weight" or "load." In the Maya region of Mexico a Maya religious office or religious fraternity.

cenote   A deep water-filled sinkhole. Especially in the Yucatán.

Classic   The period between roughly A.D. 200 and 800, when ancient Maya culture flourished in the rain forests of Belize, the Petén (Guatemala), and parts of lowland Chiapas.

cofradía   Term used in Guatemala for a Maya religious fraternity.

coleto(a)   Resident of the city of San Cristóbal de las Casas, Chiapas.

compadre, comadre   Godfather, godmother, close friend, or relative.

corte   Traditional Indian woman's full-length skirt.

ejido   Collective farm granted to landless peasants after the Mexican Revolution.

finca   Farm, plantation, estate. Frequently refers to a coffee plantation.

fray   Friar.

huipil Traditional woven and/or embroidered Indian woman's blouse. Worn with a *corte,* or traditional skirt.

Lacandón A region of rain forest between the Petén and the eastern slopes of the Chiapas highlands. Inhabited by Maya known as "Lacandóns."

Ladino A person of mixed Indian and non-Indian blood. Also used for Indians who have abandoned their cultural identity.

lanchero Operator of a motor launch.

milpa A plot of land used to grow corn, beans, squash, and other crops.

municipio A municipality. In Maya areas, a *municipio* is typically made up of a *cabecera* and its surrounding hamlets.

paraje Chiapas term for an Indian hamlet.

pasión Principal *cargo* holder during Chiapas Maya carnival ceremonies.

Petén The northern department of Guatemala. Covered largely by rain forest, it was the center of Classic Maya civilization until the collapse around the year A.D. 800, after which it was gradually abandoned.

Post-Classic The period between roughly A.D. 800 and 1300, when the centers of Maya civilization shifted to the Yucatán in the north and to the Guatemalan highlands in the south.

pox Chiapas moonshine. Pronounced "posh."

principal Maya elder who has served in important *cargo* or *cofradía* posts.

regidor Ceremonial policeman in Chiapas religious *cargos.*

traje Traditional Indian clothing.

Selected Bibliography

Álvarez del Toro, Miguel. *Los Mamíferos de Chiapas.* Tuxtla Gutiérrez, Chiapas, Mexico: Universidad Autonoma de Chiapas, 1977.

Andrews, E., Wyllys, V., and Sabloff, Jeremy A. eds. *Late Lowland Maya Civilization.* School of American Research Advanced Seminar Series. Albuquerque: University of New Mexico Press, 1986.

Baer, Phillip, and Merrifield, William R. *Two Studies of the Lacandóns of Mexico.* Publications in Linguistics and Related Field Series, No. 33. Norman, Okla.: Summer Institute of Linguistics, 1971.

Bancroft, Hubert Howe. *History of Central America. The Works of Hubert Howe Bancroft,* vols. 6–8. 38 vols. 1883–1890. Reprint (38 vols.), New York: McGraw Hill, Arno Press, 1967.

Berlin, Heinrich. "El Glífo Emblema en las Inscripciones Mayas." *Journal de la Société des Américanistes* 47 (1958): 111–119.

———. "Glífos Nominales en el Sarcophago de Palenque." *Humanidades* 2 (1959): 1–8.

Black, George. *Garrison Guatemala.* New York: Monthly Review Press, 1984.

Breedlove, Dennis E. *Introduction to the Flora of Chiapas.* San Francisco: California Academy of Sciences, 1981.

Bricker, Victoria. *The Indian Christ, the Indian King: The Historical Substrate of Maya Myth and Ritual.* Austin: University of Texas Press, 1981.

———. *Ritual Humor in Highland Chiapas.* Austin: University of Texas Press, 1973.

Brown, Leslie. *Eagles.* New York: Arco, 1970.

Cambranes, Julio Castellanos. *Coffee and Peasants in Guatemala: The Origins of the Modern Plantation Economy in Guatemala, 1853–1897.* Woodstock, Ver.: CIRMA/Plumstock Mesoamerican Studies, 1985.

Carlsen, Robert, and Prechtel, Martin. "The Flowering of the Dead: An Interpretation of Highland Maya Culture." *Man: The Journal of the Royal Anthropological Institute* 26 (1991): 23–42.

———. "Weaving and Cosmos Among the Tzutujil Maya of Guatemala." *Res* 15 (1988): 121–132.

Carmack, Robert, ed. *Harvest of Violence: The Maya Indians and the Guatemalan Crisis.* Norman, Okla.: University of Oklahoma Press, 1988.

Coe, Michael D. "The Hero Twins: Myth and Image." In *The Maya Vase Book: A Corpus of Rollout Photographs of Maya Vases,* vol. 1, by Justin Kerr. New York: Kerr Associates, 1989.

———. *Lords of the Underworld: Masterpieces of Classic Maya Ceramics.* Princeton: The Art Museum, 1978.

——— *The Maya Scribe and His World.* New York: Grolier Club, 1973.

Colby, Benjamin N., and van den Berghe, Pierre. *Ixil Country: A Plural Society in Highland Guatemala.* Berkeley: University of California Press, 1969.

Collier, George. *Fields of the Tzotzil: The Ecological Bases of Tradition in Highland Chiapas.* Austin: University of Texas Press, 1975.

———. "Peasant Politics and the Mexican State: Indigenous Compliance in Highland Chiapas." *Mexican Studies/Estudios Mexicanos* vol 3 (1987): 71–98.

Colón, Ferdinand. *The Life of the Admiral Christopher Columbus by his Son Ferdinand.* Translated and annotated by Benjamin Keel. London: Folio Society, 1960.

Crosby, Alfred W., Jr. *The Columbian Exchange: Biological and Cultural Consequences of 1492.* Westport, Conn.: Greenwood Press, 1972.

Crow, John Armstrong. *The Epic of Latin America.* 3d ed. Berkeley: University of California Press, 1980.

de Vos, Jan. *La Paz de Dios y del Rey: La Conquista de la Selva Lacandona por los españoles 1525–1821.* Tuxtla Gutiérrez, Chiapas, Mexico: Gobierno del Estado de Chiapas, Coleccion Ceiba, 1980.

———. *Oro Verde: La Conquista de la Selva Lacandona por los madereros tabasqueños 1822–1949.* Mexico City: Instituto Nacional de Arqueología y Historia, 1989.

Díaz del Castillo, Bernal. *The True History of the Conquest of Mexico.* Translated by Maurice Keatinge, Esq. New York: Robert M. McBride, 1927.

Ditmars, Raymond L. *Snakes of the World.* New York: Macmillan, 1931.

Farris, Nancy. *Maya Society Under Colonial Rule: The Collective Enterprise of Survival.* Princeton: Princeton University Press, 1984.

Forsyth, Adrian, and Miyata, Ken. *Tropical Nature: Life and Death in the Rain Forests of Central and South America.* New York: Charles Scribner's Sons, 1984.

Furst, Peter T., and Coe, Michael D. "Ritual Enemas." *Natural History,* March 1977, 88–91.

Gossen, Gary H. *Chamulas in the World of the Sun: Time and Space in a Maya Oral Tradition.* Prospect Heights, Ill.: Waveland Press, 1974.

Greene, Graham. *The Lawless Roads.* New York: Penguin, 1982.

Griffen, Gillett. "A Most Happy Mayanist." *Archaeology,* September/October 1991, 32–38.

Guatemalan Church in Exile. *Guatemala: Security, Development, and Democracy.* Washington, D.C.: Washington Office on Latin America, 1989.

Guiteras-Holmes, Calixta. *Perils of the Soul: The World View of a Tzotzil Indian.* New York: Crowell-Collier Publishing, The Free Press of Glencoe, 1961.

Hammond, Norman. *Ancient Maya Civilization.* New Brunswick, N. J.: Rutgers University Press, 1982.

Hanke, Lewis. *The Spanish Struggle for Justice in the Conquest of America.* Boston: Little, Brown and Co., 1965.

Hill, Robert M., and Monaghan, John. *Continuities in Highland Maya Social Organization.* Philadelphia: University of Pennsylvania Press, 1987.

Kavanagh, Michael. *A Complete Guide to Monkeys, Apes, and Other Primates.* New York: Viking, 1984.

Kerr, Justin. *The Maya Vase Book: A Corpus of Rollout Photographs of Maya Vases,* vol.1. New York: Kerr Associates, 1989.

King, Arden. *Cóban and the Verapaz: History and Cultural Process in Northern Guatemala.* Middle American Research Institute Publication No. 37. New Orleans: Tulane University Press, 1974.

Knorosov, Yuri. "The Problem of the Study of the Maya Hieroglyphic Writing." *American Antiquity,* vol. 23 (1958): 284–291.

Landa, Diego de. *Landa's Relación de las Cosas de Yucatán: A Translation.* Trans. and ed. Alfred M. Tozzer. Papers of the Peabody Museum of American Archaeology and Ethnology, Harvard University, vol. 18. Reprint. New York: Kraus Reprint Corporation, 1966.

———. *Yucatán Before and After the Conquest.* Trans. and ed. William Gates. New York: Dover, 1978.

Laughlin, Robert M., collected and trans. *The People of the Bat: Mayan Tales and Dreams from Zinacantán.* Edited by Carol Karasik. Washington, D.C.: Smithsonian Institution Press, 1988.

Lovell, W. George. *Conquest and Survival in Colonial Guatemala: A Historical Geography of the Cuchumatán Highlands, 1500–1821.* Kingston and Montreal: McGill–Queen's University Press, 1985.

————. "Surviving Conquest: The Maya of Guatemala in Historical Perspective." *Latin American Research Review* 23 (1988): 25–57.

MacLeod, Barbara. *Numen of the Night Sun: Further Chronicles of Xibalba.* Mood Publishing, Look Mom! Comics, 1983.

MacLeod, Barbara, and Puleston, Dennis. "Pathways into Darkness: The Search for the Road to Xibalba." In *Tercera Mesa Redonda de Palenque,* Vol. 4, edited by Merle Greene Robertson. Palenque: Pre-Columbian Art Research, and Monterey: Herald Printers, 1979.

MacLeod, Barbara, and Reents-Budet, Dorie. *The Archaeology of Petroglyph Cave.* Forthcoming.

MacLeod, Murdo J., *Spanish Central America: A Socioeconomic History, 1520–1820.* Berkeley: University of California Press, 1973.

MacLeod, Murdo J., and Wasserstrom, Robert, eds. *Spaniards and Indians in Southeastern Mesoamerica: Essays on the History of Ethnic Relations.* Lincoln: University of Nebraska Press, 1983.

Manz, Beatriz. *Refugees of a Hidden War: The Aftermath of Counterinsurgency in Guatemala.* Albany: State University of New York Press, 1988.

March, Ignacio J. "Los Lacandones de Mexico y su Relación con los Mamíferos Silvestre: Un Estudio Etnozoológico." *Biotica* (1987): 43–56.

Means, Philip Ainsworth. *History of the Spanish Conquest of the Yucatán and the Itzás.* Papers of the Peabody Museum of American Archaeology and Ethnology, Harvard University, vol. 7. Cambridge, Mass., Harvard University, 1917.

Menchu, Rigoberta. *I, Rigoberta Menchu: An Indian Woman in Guatemala,* edited by Elisabeth Burgos-Debray, translated by Ann Wright. London, New York: Verso, 1984.

Mendelson, E. Michael. *Los Escandolos de Maximón: Un Estudio Sobre la Religión y la Visión del Mundo en Santiago Atitlán.* Guatemala City: Tipografía Nacional, 1965.

————. "Maximón: An Iconographical Introduction." *Man: The Journal of the Royal Anthropological Institute,* vol. 59 (1959): 57–60.

————. "A Guatemalan Sacred Bundle. *Man: The Journal of the Royal Anthropological Institute* 58 (1958): 121–126.

Montejo, Victor. *Testimony: Death of a Guatemalan Village.* Translated by Victor Perera. Willimantic, Conn.: Curbstone Press, 1987.

Morley, Sylvanus G. *The Ancient Maya.* 3d ed., revised by George W. Brainerd. Stanford: Stanford University Press, 1956.

Morris, Walter F., Jr. *Living Maya.* New York: Harry N. Abrams, 1987.

Napier, J. R., and Napier, P. H. *The Natural History of the Primates.* Cambridge: MIT Press, 1985.

Nations, James D. *Population Ecology of the Lacandón Maya.* Unpublished Ph.D. dissertation in anthropology, Southern Methodist University, Dallas, Texas, April 1979.

———. "The Rain Forest Farmers." *Pacific Discovery,* January–February 1981, 1–9.

Payeras, Mario. *Days of the Jungle: The Testimony of a Guatemalan Guerrillero, 1972–1976.* Translated by Lita Paniagua. New York: Monthly Review Press, 1983.

Pearce, Kenneth. *The View From the Top of the Temple: Ancient Maya Civilization and Modern Maya Culture.* Albuquerque: University of New Mexico Press, 1984.

Prescott, William H. *History of the Conquest of Mexico and History of the Conquest of Peru.* New York: Random House, Modern Library, 1936.

Proskouriakoff, Tatiana. "Historical Implications of a Pattern of Dates at Piedras Negras, Guatemala." *American Antiquity* 25 (1960): 454–475.

Rabinowitz, Alan. *Jaguar.* New York: Arbor House, 1986.

Recinos, Adrián. *Popul Vuh: The Sacred Book of the Ancient Quiché Maya.* Translated by Delia Goetz and S. G. Morley. Norman, Okla.: University of Oklahoma Press, 1950.

Recinos Adrián, ed. "Titulos de la casa Ixquín-Nehaib, Señora del territorio de Otzoya." *Crónicas Indígenas de Guatemala,* pp. 71–94. Guatemala City: Editorial Universitaria, 1957.

Recinos, Adrián, and Goetz, Delia, trans. *The Annals of the Cakchiquels.* Norman, Okla.: University of Oklahoma Press, 1953.

Redfield, Robert. *The Folk Culture of Yucatán.* Chicago: University of Chicago Press, 1941.

Redfield, Robert, and Villa Rojas, Alfonso. *Chan Kom: A Mayan Village.* Carnegie Institution of Washington Publication No. 448. Washington, D.C.: Carnegie Institution of Washington, 1934.

Reed, Nelson. *The Caste War of Yucatán.* Stanford: Stanford University Press, 1964.

Roys, Ralph. "The Indian Background of Colonial Yucatán." Carnegie Institution of Washington, Publication No. 548. Washington, D.C.: Carnegie Institution of Washington, 1943.

Rus, Jan. "Whose Caste War? Indians, Ladinos, and the Chiapas 'Caste War' of 1869." In *Spaniards and Indians in Southeastern Mexico: Essays on the History of Ethnic Relations,* edited by Murdo MacLeod and

Robert Wasserstrom. Lincoln: University of Nebraska Press, 1983.

Schele, Linda, and Freidel, David. *A Forest of Kings: The Untold Story of the Ancient Maya.* New York: William Morrow and Co., 1990.

Schele, Linda, and Miller, Mary Ellen. *The Blood of Kings: Dynasty and Ritual in Maya Art.* Fort Worth: Kimbell Art Museum, 1986.

Simon, Jean-Marie. *Guatemala: Eternal Spring, Eternal Tyranny.* New York: W. W. Norton, 1987.

Simpson, George Gaylord. *Splendid Isolation: The Curious History of South American Mammals.* New Haven: Yale University Press, 1980.

Smith, Carol A. "Local History in Global Context: Social and Economic Transitions in Western Guatemala." *Comparative Studies in Society and History* 26 (1984): 193–228.

Stehli, Francis G., and Webb, S. David, eds. Topics in Geobiology Series, Vol. 4, *The Great American Biotic Interchange.* New York: Plenum Press, 1985.

Stephens, John L. *Incidents of Travel in Central America, Chiapas, and Yucatán,* 2 vols, 1841. New York: Dover Publications, 1969.

Stoll, David. "Evangelicals, Guerrillas, and the Army: The Ixil Triangle Under Rios Montt." *Harvest of Violence: The Maya Indians and the Guatemalan Crisis,* edited by Robert Carmack. Norman, Okla.: University of Oklahoma Press, 1988.

Stuart, David, and Houston, Stephen D. "Maya Writing." *Scientific American,* August 1989, 82–89.

Sullivan, Paul. *Unfinished Conversations: Maya and Foreigners Between Two Wars.* New York: Alfred A. Knopf, 1989.

Tedlock, Barbara. *Time and the Highland Maya.* Albuqerque: University of New Mexico Press, 1982.

Tedlock, Dennis, ed. *Popul Vuh: The Definitive Edition of the Mayan Book of the Dawn of Life and the Glories of God and Kings.* New York: Simon & Schuster, Touchstone, 1985.

Thompson, J. Eric S. Introduction to *The Hill-Caves of Yucatán: A Search for Evidence of Man's Antiquity in the Caverns of Central America,* by Henry Chapman Mercer. 1896. Reprint. Norman, Okla.: University of Oklahoma Press, 1975.

———. *Maya History and Religion.* Norman, Okla.: University of Oklahoma Press, 1970.

———. *The Rise and Fall of Maya Civilization.* Norman, Okla.: University of Oklahoma Press, 1954.

Todorov, Tzvetan. *The Conquest of the Americas: The Question of the Other.* Translated by Richard Howard. New York: Harper and Row, 1984.

Tozzer, Alfred M. *A Comparative Study of the Maya and the Lacandóns.* New York: Macmillan, 1907.

Turner, B. L., and Harrison, Peter D., eds. *Pre-Hispanic Maya Agriculture*. Albuquerque: University of New Mexico Press, 1978.

Villagutierre Soto-Mayor, Juan de. *History of the Conquest of the Province of the Itzá*. Translated by Brother Robert D. Wood, S.M. Culver City: Labyrinthos, 1983.

Villa Rojas, Alfonso. *The Maya of East Central Quintana Roo*. Carnegie Institution of Washington Publication No. 559. Washington, D.C.: Carnegie Institution of Washington, 1945.

Vogt, Evon Z. "Indian Crosses and Scepters: The Results of Circumscribed Spanish-Indian Interactions in Mesoamerica." Paper presented at Word and Deed: Interethnic Images and Responses in the New World, a conference held in Trujillo, Spain, December 12–16, 1988.

———. *Zinacantán: A Maya Community in the Highlands of Chiapas*. Cambridge: Harvard University Press, Belknap Press, 1969.

von Hagen, Victor Wolfgang. *Maya Explorer: John Lloyd Stephens and the Lost Cities of Central America and Yucatán*. 1947. Reprint. San Francisco: Chronicle Books, 1990.

Warren, Kay B. *The Symbolism of Subordination: Indian Identity in a Guatemalan Community*. Austin: University of Texas Press, 1978.

Wasserstrom, Robert. *Class and Society in Central Chiapas*. Berkeley: University of California Press, 1983.

White, Richard. *The Morass*. New York: Harper and Row, 1984.

Whitlock, Ralph. *Everyday Life of the Maya*. New York: Dorset Press, 1987.

Wilson, Edmund. *The Bit Between My Teeth: A Literary Chronicle 1950–1965*. New York: Farrar, Straus and Giroux, 1965.

Wright, Ronald. *Time Among the Maya: Travels in Belize, Guatemala, and Mexico*. New York: Weidenfeld and Nicolson, 1989.

Ximénez, Francisco. *Historia de la Provincia de San Vicente de Chiapa y Guatemala de la Orden de Nuestro Glorioso Padre Santo Domingo*. 3 vols. Guatemala City: Tipografía Nacional, 1929–1931.

Index